Readings and Study Guide

American Government

Brief Second Edition

Readings and Study Guide

*American Government
Freedom and Power*

Brief Second Edition

THEODORE J. LOWI

Cornell University

BENJAMIN GINSBERG

Johns Hopkins University

and

ALICE HEARST

Smith College

W.W. NORTON & COMPANY
NEW YORK   LONDON

The text of this book is composed in New Baskerville ITC with the display set in Optima.
Manufacturing by Haddon Craftsmen, Inc.

ISBN 0–393–96238–5

W.W. Norton & Company, Inc., 500 Fifth Avenue, New York, N.Y. 10110
W.W. Norton & Company Ltd., 10 Coptic Street, London WC1A 1PU

1 2 3 4 5 6 7 8 9 0

Contents

Study Guide

Preface

This volume is intended to be an American government study guide in the fullest sense of the term. It is designed both to guide students through *American Government: Freedom and Power*, Brief Second Edition, and to enrich students' understanding of American government. For this reason, in addition to the customary study guide materials, the first part of this volume contains a number of readings—articles, essays, and court cases—that illustrate the key concepts presented in the parallel chapter of the textbook. A headnote introducing each of these readings explains its significance *and* its precise relationship (including the page location) to the major concept presented in the core text. In this way, students will know what each case, "is a case of."

The readings include classic pieces such as selections from the major Federalist papers and de Tocqueville's *Democracy in America*, more contemporary essays from academic journals and important newspapers and magazines such as the *Washington Post* and the *New Republic*, excerpts from major Supreme Court cases, and selected statutes. By reprinting classic works in American government, we hope to acquaint students with some of the most profound thinking and writing on politics in the English language—thereby underlining and reinforcing the theoretical issues raised in our book. The more contemporary essays are designed to provide students with lively and current illustrations of the phenomena and institutions we discuss in the text. The court cases are selected for their importance in establishing the legal and institutional framework of American government. In every instance, we *strongly* urge students to read the headnote preceding the reading for a useful and concise statement of the significance of the reading and its relationship to the text.

The second part of this volume is a study guide designed to take students step by step through each chapter of the textbook. It includes chapter outlines, review questions, key terms, and annotated bibliographies. The study guide is designed to help a serious student focus on the most important issues and concepts addressed by the text. Used in conjunction with the text, it can be a very useful resource for exam and term paper preparation as well as for students who simply want to be certain that they have read and understood the book's major points.

We strongly encourage students to review and ponder the readings and cases in conjunction with the text, and to use the study guide as a learning tool. We are confident that these materials will help students to learn more about *American Government* and American government.

Theodore J. Lowi
Benjamin Ginsberg
Alice Hearst

November 1, 1991

Readings and Study Guide

American Government

Brief Second Edition

The Readings

CHAPTER 1

Freedom and Power: An Introduction to the Problem

GOVERNMENT AND CONTROL

See text pp. 4–5

As the text notes, all governments must have, at the very least, the power to enforce public order and the power to collect public revenues. In the debates preceding the adoption of the United States Constitution, the scope of these powers was very much at issue as the Federalists and Antifederalists battled over whether to create a strong central government or retain the confederated structure under which the country had operated since the Revolution. In the following Federalist papers, Alexander Hamilton argues in favor of creating a strong central government with power to provide for the public defense and the power to raise public revenues as necessary to carry out its essential public functions.

To understand the force of these arguments, it is important to remember that they were advanced against the backdrop of state sovereignty: under the Articles of Confederation, states created and maintained their own militias; states also controlled the means by which funds were generated for national purposes. Hamilton argued that these defects left the federal government "in a kind of tutelage to the State governments," sapped of the energy and creativity required to sustain a union.

Alexander Hamilton
The Federalist No. 23 *

The necessity of a Constitution, at least equally energetic with the one proposed, to the preservation of the Union is the point at the examination of which we are now arrived.

This inquiry will naturally divide itself into three branches—the objects to be provided for by a federal government, the quantity of power necessary to the accomplishment of those objects, the persons upon whom that power ought to operate. Its distribution and organization will more properly claim our attention under the succeeding head.

The principal purposes to be answered by union are these—the common defense of the members; the preservation of the public peace, as well against internal convulsions as external attacks; the regulation of commerce with other nations and between the States; the superintendence of our intercourse, political and commercial, with foreign countries.

*Alexander Hamilton, *The Federalist No. 23*, ed. Clinton Rossiter (New York: NAL, 1961).

The authorities essential to the common defense are these: to raise armies; to build and equip fleets; to prescribe rules for the government of both; to direct their operations; to provide for their support. These powers ought to exist without limitation, *because it is impossible to foresee or to define the extent and variety of national exigencies, and the correspondent extent and variety of the means which may be necessary to satisfy them.* The circumstances that endanger the safety of nations are infinite, and for this reason no constitutional shackles can wisely be imposed on the power to which the care of it is committed. This power ought to be coextensive with all the possible combinations of such circumstances; and ought to be under the direction of the same councils which are appointed to preside over the common defense. . . .

Whether there ought to be a federal government intrusted with the care of the common defense is a question in the first instance open to discussion; but the moment it is decided in the affirmative, it will follow that that government ought to be clothed with all the powers requisite to complete execution of its trust. And unless it can be shown that the circumstances which may affect the public safety are reducible within certain determinate limits; unless the contrary of this position can be fairly and rationally disputed, it must be admitted as a necessary consequence that there can be no limitation of that authority which is to provide for the defense and protection of the community in any matter essential to its efficacy—that is, in any matter essential to the *formation, direction,* or *support* of the NATIONAL FORCES.

Defective as the present Confederation has been proved to be, this principle appears to have been fully recognized by the framers of it; though they have not made proper or adequate provision for its exercise. Congress have an unlimited discretion to make requisitions of men and money; to govern the army and navy; to direct their operations. As their requisitions are made constitutionally binding upon the States, who are in fact under the most solemn obligations to furnish the supplies required of them, the intention evidently was that the United States should command whatever resources were by them judged requisite to the "common defense and general welfare." It was presumed that a sense of their true interests, and a regard to the dictates of good faith, would be found sufficient pledges for the punctual performance of the duty of the members to the federal head.

The experiment has, however, demonstrated that this expectation was ill-founded and illusory; and the observations made under the last head will, I imagine, have sufficed to convince the impartial and discerning that there is an absolute necessity for an entire change in the first principles of the system; that if we are in earnest about giving the Union energy and duration we must abandon the vain project of legislating upon the States in their collective capacities; we must extend the laws of the federal government to the individual citizens of America; we must discard the fallacious scheme of quotas and requisitions as equally impracticable and unjust. The result from all this is that the Union ought to be invested with full power to levy troops; to build and equip fleets; and to raise the revenues which will be required for the formation and support of an army and navy in the customary and ordinary modes practiced in other governments.

If the circumstances of our country are such as to demand a compound instead of a simple, a confederate instead of a sole, government, the essential point which will remain to be adjusted will be to discriminate the OBJECTS, as far as it can be done, which shall appertain to the different provinces or departments of power; allowing to each the most ample authority for fulfilling the objects committed to its charge. Shall the Union be constituted the guardian of the common safety? Are fleets and armies and revenues necessary to this purpose? The government of the Union must be empowered to pass all laws, and to make all regulations which have relation to them. The same must be the case in respect to commerce, and to every other matter to which its jurisdiction is permitted to extend. Is the administration of justice between the citizens of the same State the proper department of the local governments? These must possess all the authorities which are connected with this object, and with every other that may be allotted to their particular cognizance and direction. Not to confer in each case a degree of power commensurate to the end would be to violate the most obvious rules of prudence and propriety, and improvidently to trust the great interests of the nation to hands which are disabled from managing them with vigor and success.

Who so likely to make suitable provisions for the public defense as that body to which the guardianship of the public safety is confided; which, as the center of information, will best understand the extent and urgency of the dangers that threaten; as the representative of the WHOLE, will feel itself most deeply interested in the preservation of every part; which, from the responsibility implied in the duty assigned to it, will be most sensibly impressed with the necessity of proper exertions; and which, by the extension of its authority throughout the States, can alone establish uniformity and concert in the plans and measures by which the common safety is to be secured? Is there not a manifest inconsistency in devolving upon the federal government the care of the general defense and leaving in the State governments the *effective* powers by which it is to be provided for? Is not a want of co-operation the infallible consequence of such a system? And will not weakness, disorder, an undue distribution of the burdens and calamities of war, an unnecessary and intolerable increase of expense, be its natural and inevitable concomitants? Have we not had unequivocal experience of its effects in the course of the revolution which we have just achieved?

Every view we may take of the subject, as candid inquirers after truth, will serve to convince us that it is both unwise and dangerous to deny the federal government an unconfined authority in respect to all those objects which are intrusted to its management. It will indeed deserve the most vigilant and careful attention of the people to see that it be modeled in such a manner as to admit of its being safely vested with the requisite powers. If any plan which has been, or may be, offered to our consideration should not, upon a dispassionate inspection, be found to answer this description, it ought to be rejected. A government, the constitution of which renders it unfit to be trusted with all the powers which a free people *ought to delegate to any government,* would be an unsafe and improper depository of the NATIONAL INTERESTS. Wherever THESE can with propriety be confided, the coincident powers may safely accompany them. This is the true result of all just reasoning upon the subject. And the adversaries of the plan promulgated by the convention would have given a better impression of their candor if they had confined themselves to showing that the internal structure of the proposed government was such as to render it unworthy of the confidence of the people. They ought not to have wandered into inflammatory declamations and unmeaning cavils about the extent of the powers. The POWERS are not too extensive for the OBJECTS of federal administration, or, in other words, for the management of our NATIONAL INTERESTS; nor can any satisfactory argument be framed to show that they are chargeable with such an excess. If it be true, as has been insinuated by some of the writers on the other side, that the difficulty arises from the nature of the thing, and that the extent of the country will not permit us to form a government in which such ample powers can safely be reposed, it would prove that we ought to contract our views, and resort to the expedient of separate confederacies, which will move within more practicable spheres. For the absurdity must continually stare us in the face of confiding to a government the direction of the most essential national interests, without daring to trust to it the authorities which are indispensable to their proper and efficient management. Let us not attempt to reconcile contradictions, but firmly embrace a rational alternative. . . . I trust, however, that the impracticability of one general system cannot be shown. I am greatly mistaken if anything of weight has yet been advanced of this tendency; and I flatter myself that the observations which have been made in the course of these papers have served to place the reverse of that position in as clear a light as any matter still in the womb of time and experience is susceptible of. This, at all events, must be evident, that the very difficulty itself, drawn from the extent of the country, is the strongest argument in favor of an energetic government; for any other can certainly never preserve the Union of so large an empire. If we embrace the tenets of those who oppose the adoption of the proposed Constitution as the standard of our political creed we cannot fail to verify the gloomy doctrines which predict the impracticability of a national system pervading the entire limits of the present Confederacy.

PUBLIUS

See text p. 9

The year 1989 is now commonly credited as marking the end of the Cold War between the United States and the countries of Eastern Europe. Major democratic reforms were introduced in the Soviet Union, and East and West Germany moved toward reunification, leading some observers to remark that the United States had "won" the Cold War.

These comments are no doubt premature, since there is no certainty that the countries experimenting with new governmental systems will want to follow the constitutional model found in the United States. As political scientist James MacGregor Burns *remarked in a 1990* New York Times *editorial, the United States has as much to learn from the current reform movement as the nations embroiled in the reforms themselves. Burns suggests, for example, that the United States should consider adopting a parliamentary system instead of its cumbersome, tri-partite system ordained in the Constitution.*

In any event, Western countries, especially the United States, might do well to think carefully about what the advent of a new democratic era actually means. In the following article, Raymond Gastil argues that a truly democratic system embraces a concept of both political and civil rights, and that no revolution can be complete without reference to both.

Raymond D. Gastil
"What Kind of Democracy?"[*]

As we congratulate ourselves on a world becoming increasingly democratic, we should recall that several times before in the past century it seemed that democracy had won universal acceptance, but the acceptance was much less trustworthy than had been imagined. In 1900–1901 leading newspapers announced the good news that the twentieth century was to be the century of democracy; in 1920 a prominent authority on political systems could write that democracy no longer had any challengers.

A society is generally said to be a full democracy if it has a political system that guarantees both the civil and political liberties of its people. In other words, a democracy must not only allow its people to choose freely who will govern them but also guarantee the freedoms of expression and organization, which make possible effective oppositions that can compete for, and eventually attain, office. Unfortunately, in most historical treatments of the growth of democracy the emphasis tends to be on the existence of electoral or legislative mechanisms that allow for choice, with less attention paid to those civil liberties that make that choice effectively free.

It is easy, and probably fundamentally wrong, to assume that the most important characteristics of democracy are the political rights that the word "democracy" most clearly implies. Let me use personal experience to explain this. Annually from 1973 until last year I produced the Comparative Survey of Freedom, which placed countries on a continuum of freedom. I tried to balance aspects of democracy by using a rating system that included both political rights and civil liberties in the final score. During the first few years of the survey I considered that when the final scores of two countries tied, I would give the rating for political freedom—that is, for the extent to which there were free elections and those elected gained power—the greater weight. Perhaps I made this choice because it was much easier to get information on elections and legislators than on the state of civil liberties in a country. However, as time went on and experience accumulated, I dropped

[*]Raymond D. Gastil, "What Kind of Democracy?" in *The Atlantic Monthly* (June 1990). Reprinted with permission.

this largely theoretical distinction in weighting. In the past few years I have come to believe that if one thinks of freedom, or in this case democracy, in time periods longer than a year, civil liberties will be seen as the more important of the two kinds of democratic freedom. I came to realize that political rights without civil freedoms would offer few of the values that I cherish in democratic societies, while civil freedoms without political rights (insofar as this is conceivable) would offer the major values that I understand democracy to promote. The primacy of civil freedoms becomes even more apparent in societies whose governments appear to respond to the popular will as expressed by the communications media, demonstrations, and other informal channels with more alacrity than they do to the often indeterminate results at the polling station.

Democracy as we know it has two quite different roots. The first is the universal desire of people to manage their own affairs, or at least to have a say in who manages their affairs. In the primitive band all adults, or sometimes all heads of families, tended to have a say in the affairs of the band. This tribal or village democracy can be traced down through all of history. The democracy of ancient Athens is no doubt the most famous example of a community ruling itself—a community of relatively large scale. Of course, women, slaves, and other outsiders were excluded. But a substantial part of the population took an active role in the decisions of the society; when "the people," thus defined, changed their minds, society moved in the direction of the change. When we speak of the democracy of the medieval Swiss cantons, or of the units of the Iroquois confederacy, this is also the democracy we have in mind. The democracy of the New England towns of the seventeenth century and the democracy of the Swiss communities of Rousseau's day, including his native Geneva, were essentially successive expressions of the tribal or community democracy of primitive society. Though for limited purposes these might form together in larger "leagues," they were little more than alliances among independent units whose interrelationships might be no more democratic than those in nondemocratic leagues.

The second root of modern democracy is liberalism, defined as that set of social and political beliefs, attitudes, and values which assumes the universal and equal application of the law and the existence of basic human rights superior to those of state or community. As used here, the term "liberal" is not meant to suggest any particular economic doctrine, or doctrine regarding the state's economic role; nor is it meant to be an antonym of "conservative." It does imply that the state's interests cannot override those of the citizenry. Derived from a variety of secular and religious tenets, liberalism affirms the basic worth of individuals, their thoughts, and their desires. In the liberal canon no one, whether king or majority, has the right to tell people how to think, or even act (except in instances of imminent threat to social well-being). Although it has ancient foundations, liberalism is primarily the outgrowth of the efforts of political and social philosophers since the seventeenth century to free humanity from the fetters of unchecked state power and imposed religious dogma. Before the eighteenth century, liberal democracy's role in history was much less important than tribal democracy's.

It was liberal democracy that abolished political censorship, that eventually found it impossible to justify slavery of any kind, or torture for any reason, or the unequal position of women and minority races and ethnic groups. It is liberal democracy that is always teetering on the edge of denying that the individual has any substantial duty to sacrifice himself for the community if he chooses not to. It was liberal democracy that fascism and similar ideologies sought to destroy utterly. It was liberal democracy that the Marxist-Leninist regimes now dissolving in Eastern Europe found so repugnant in its individualism and inherent tendency to sacrifice group interests to individual interests.

The international human-rights movement is based on the tenets of liberal democracy, and is a natural product of this political system. Everywhere, these rights have become the hope of the oppressed, and the societies that support these rights become the natural allies of all peoples.

When the current democratic revolution is discussed, we should remember that we are referring to changes that represent the legacy of both these traditions, the tribal democratic and the liberal democratic. We must remember that their conjunction in modern democracies is the result of a long historical process, and far from automatic. Historically, democracies have tended to be more tribal than liberal. Regardless of the Constitution and the Bill of Rights and the values of the Founding Fathers, acceptance of liberal democracy came slowly to the American public. Even in recent years the United States has had periods in which tribal democracy rode roughshod over liberal democracy, as in the expulsion of the Japanese from the West Coast in the Second World War. Public-opinion polls continue to show that the tenets of liberal democracy may not be as thoroughly accepted in the United States and other democracies as we would like.

The slow pace of the liberalization of democracy, even in recent years, explains why as we go further back in history, the association of democracy and peace becomes more and more tenuous. Although the political systems of Athens and Sparta were far apart, both states were warlike; indeed, Athens became a specialist in imperial wars. The democratic Swiss cantons produced the mercenaries of Europe for several centuries. At the same time that democracy was being perfected in the West, its military forces conquered most of the world. Yet gradually the record has improved, as democracies have become more liberal. War became unfashionable in the democratic West after the First World War. Colonies became unfashionable after the Second World War. But if there is to be a "peace dividend" from the democratic revolution, it will occur only to the extent that tribal democracy has been overcome by liberal democratic attitudes that respect the rights of all peoples.

Today, as we contemplate a democratizing world, we must ask ourselves how strong the tribal and liberal elements actually are in the new democratic movements. We should recall that fascism in Italy, Japan, and Germany grew to maturity in democratizing societies, societies that provided the tools for free discussion and mobilization of small groups. Those groups were then able to use these privileges to overthrow the democratic system by capturing the attention and perhaps the majority support of peoples in whom the assumptions of liberal democracy were only weakly rooted.

Outside the West democracy is beset with the problem of incorporating basically illiberal peoples and movements into the democratic framework. In the recent Indian election the third most powerful party was a Hindu party dedicated to advancing the cause of the Hindu majority at the expense of both the rights of Muslims and the concept of the secular state. In some parts of India many Sikhs and Muslims and members of other groups are equally intolerant of those whose beliefs or backgrounds are different from their own. Pakistan's emergence as a democracy has been repeatedly delayed by the claims of Muslim movements against the rights of others, and these claims may again cause the collapse of democracy in Pakistan.

The clash of tribal democracy and liberal democracy has been particularly acute in the Middle East. It is either the case or feared to be the case that a really open electoral process in most Middle Eastern states would result in the establishment of an oppressive Muslim fundamentalism in place of the less oppressive current regimes. Sudan's most recent attempt at democracy was ultimately torn apart by tribalism, which made democracy as we know it impossible. We should note that Iran, under Islamic guidance, has had several contested elections with fair voting procedures since 1980. From the political-rights viewpoint it can be argued that Iran is now ruled by an elected democratic government, a government more democratic than most in the Third World. But its oppression of individuals or groups that lie beyond the boundaries of tribal morality or acceptance has been persistent. Its initial unwillingness, for example, to allow the Bahais any place in Iranian society, and its equally vicious destruction of the radical left, represented tribalisms that an elected parliament could overwhelmingly endorse. Despite the panoply of Western political institutions in Iran, it remains outside the democratic world that requires a commitment to civil liberties as well as political rights.

From one perspective, the demand for self-determination is a demand for freedom. From another, it is a demand for independence unrelated to the maintenance of those freedoms basic to liberal democracy. Too often the demand for self-determination is a tribalist demand that ends by narrowing rather than broadening the sphere of human rights. It is the demand that has torn Sri Lanka apart, destroying what was a functioning democratic system. It is the demand that came very close on several occasions to arresting the development of democracy in our own South. In itself, self-determination is a legitimate right, and should be recognized insofar as it does not threaten other rights. But this right should not be confused with those basic civil rights fundamental to liberal democracy, nor is it as important as they are.

It is with this consciousness that we must consider the prospects for democracy in those areas of the world that remain nondemocratic but may soon institute full political democracies if current trends continue. We must ask particularly what values we hold most dear. Do we want the establishment of democratic regimes that will soon come to deny those liberal, humanistic values we see as essential to a full human life? Do we want, for example, a politically more democratic but also more fundamentalist Egypt? Would we really want a "free Afghanistan" whose political system put women back in the Middle Ages? Would we still endorse the democracy of an India that ended up exacerbating religious or ethnic tensions to the point of new and endemic slaughter?

If we are lucky, we may be able to avoid facing such questions. But if the development of democracy in the Soviet Union, for example, proceeds as it has, with an increasing emphasis on self-determination at the popular level, will we not find larger and larger sections of the population developing independent political systems in which the desires and opinions and interests of the majority allow for the suppression of all those who disagree, or all those who belong to other "tribes"? Some years ago I regarded descriptions of the danger of the highly nationalistic Pamyat movement in the USSR as little more than the scare-mongering of scholars or anti-Soviets. Today I wonder if "pamyats" might not break out all over the Soviet world, fueled by the frustrations of failure in other sectors of life, much as fascism was fueled between the wars.

What do we bring away from this discussion? Certainly we should not conclude that because democratic movements are often less than thoroughly imbued with modern liberal ideals, we should stop pushing for the democratization of the world. We should continue the effort for several reasons. First, people do have democratic rights to self-determination, even if we do not like what they do with these rights. Second, the continued rolling of the democratic bandwagon may bring us closer to our overall goals. Third, nondemocratic regimes are often as illiberal as democratic ones. Fourth, since democratic systems are often initially more tribal than liberal, by denying the right of tribal democracy we may end up denying the right of a people to any democracy at all.

But the discussion suggests some dangers, and perhaps some changes in direction, in the pursuit of the millennium. It suggests that the campaign for liberal democracy, represented in part by the human-rights movement, should be continued and enhanced even as states become democratic in form. Also, we should develop educational programs that teach liberal values to broader and broader segments of the population in new democracies or states that have not yet become politically democratic. To avoid the arrest of this educational process we should in particular instances and for particular countries avoid pressing for the establishment of political democracy so long as the system in power takes an active role in developing and teaching the concepts of a liberal society.

I suspect that one reason for the collapse of communist systems in the Soviet sphere is that they appeared increasingly estranged from the world culture that has penetrated nearly everywhere since the Second World War. This culture simply no longer accepts the controls on movement and thought that characterized most of the world until recently. It no longer accepts discrimination for reasons of ideology, religion, gender, or ethnicity. It no longer accepts rulers that are not freely elected by their peoples. This culture has come upon the world rapidly, and may ultimately be destructive of essential values. But for now it advances the cause of the assumptions basic to liberal democracy, and therefore becomes an important aspect of the struggle for the extension of democracy.

In promoting democracy, governments and private organizations should place at least as much stress on the liberal underpinnings of modern democracy as on the forms of political democracy. The emphasis should be on the absolute value of the individual and the universal applicability of basic rights. We should support movements that undercut tribal thinking. We should refrain from insisting on rapid transitions to the political forms of democracy when establishing these forms appears likely to threaten the eventual attainment of the freedoms due every individual, and not just every group. We should be careful not to confuse the demand for self-determination with the demand for democracy. Thus the campaign for democracy, the campaign for human rights, and the campaign against war and armaments must become ever more closely identified with one another as we press on, both publicly and privately, toward a world of peace and freedom.

FROM COERCION TO CONSENT

See text p. 9

As the text notes, throughout the eighteenth and nineteenth century, governments moved away from direct coercion of their subjects. However, the relative absence of direct coercive measures does not mean that governments came to believe they could remain in power by simply relying on the goodwill of their subjects. In the United States, as in most other democratic regimes, efforts to create a base of support are continuous, even though those efforts may not be immediately recognized.

One of the most obvious forums for cultivating national unity is the public schools, as the text discusses in greater detail in succeeding chapters. From the inception of the public school system, it has always been understood that schools have an obligation to teach civic virtues, i.e., to create responsible citizens. One of the means by which children could be taught to respect the public order was to recite the pledge of allegiance on a daily basis.

The following case addresses the limits on the state's authority to generate feelings of national unity. In 1940, the U.S. Supreme Court considered a challenge to a flag salute requirement in the Pennsylvania schools, brought on behalf of two children whose religious beliefs prohibited them from saluting the flag. In that case, Minersville v. Gobitis, the Court upheld the right of a school board to require pupils to salute the flag as a legitimate exercise of its authority to instill "unifying [national] sentiment."

Shortly after Gobitis was decided, the Court reconsidered the flag salute issue. In an unprecedented reversal, the Court held that compelling a flag salute violated First Amendment freedoms, which included the freedom to dissent "as to things that touch the heart of the existing order."

Minersville School District v. *Gobitis* (1940)*

JUSTICE FRANKFURTER delivered the opinion of the Court.

A grave responsibility confronts this Court whenever in course of litigation it must reconcile the conflicting claims of liberty and authority. But when the liberty invoked is liberty of conscience, and the authority is authority to safeguard the nation's fellowship, judicial conscience is put to its severest test. Of such a nature is the present controversy.

Lillian Gobitis, aged twelve, and her brother William, aged ten, were expelled from the public schools of Minersville, Pennsylvania, for refusing to salute the national flag as part of a daily school exercise. The local Board of Education required both teachers and pupils to participate in this ceremony. The ceremony is a familiar one. The right hand is placed on the breast and the following pledge recited in unison: "I pledge allegiance to my flag, and to the Republic for which it stands; one nation indivisible, with liberty and justice for all." While the words are spoken, teachers and pupils extend their right hands in salute to the flag. The Gobitis family are affiliated with "Jehovah's Witnesses," for whom the Bible as the Word of God is the supreme authority. The children had been brought up conscientiously to believe that such a gesture of respect for the flag was forbidden by command of Scripture.

The Gobitis children were of an age for which Pennsylvania makes school attendance compulsory. Thus they were denied a free education, and their parents had to put them into private schools. To be relieved of the financial burden thereby entailed, their father, on behalf of the children and in his own behalf, brought this suit. . . .

Certainly the affirmative pursuit of one's convictions about the ultimate mystery of the universe and man's relation to it is placed beyond the reach of law. Government may not interfere with organized or individual expression of belief or disbelief. Propagation of belief—or even of disbelief—in the supernatural is protected, whether in church or chapel, mosque or synagogue, tabernacle or meeting-house. Likewise the Constitution assures generous immunity to the individual from imposition of penalties for offending, in the course of his own religious activities, the religious views of others, be they a minority or those who are dominant in government.

But the manifold character of man's relations may bring his conception of religious duty into conflict with the secular interests of his fellow-men. When does the constitutional guarantee compel exemption from doing what society thinks necessary for the promotion of some great common end, or from a penalty for conduct which appears dangerous to the general good? . . .

Our present task, then, as so often the case with courts, is to reconcile

*Minersville School District v. Gobitis, 310 U.S. 586, 1940.

two rights in order to prevent either from destroying the other. But, because in safeguarding conscience we are dealing with interests so subtle and so dear, every possible leeway should be given to the claims of religious faith.

In the judicial enforcement of religious freedom we are concerned with a historic concept.

[But in determining the authority of the state to take measures to maintain an orderly, tranquil, and free society, we] are dealing with an interest inferior to none in the hierarchy of legal values. National unity is the basis of national security. . . .

Situations like the present are phases of the profoundest problem confronting a democracy—the problem which Lincoln cast in memorable dilemma: "Must a government of necessity be too *strong* for the liberties of its people, or too *weak* to maintain its own existence?" No mere textual reading or logical talisman can solve the dilemma. And when the issue demands judicial determination, it is not the personal notion of judges of what wise adjustment requires which must prevail.

Unlike the instances we have cited, the case before us is not concerned with an exertion of legislative power for the promotion of some specific need or interest of secular society—the protection of the family, the promotion of health, the common defense, the raising of public revenues to defray the cost of government. But all these specific activities of government presuppose the existence of an organized political society. The ultimate foundation of a free society is the binding tie of cohesive sentiment. Such a sentiment is fostered by all those agencies of the mind and spirit which may serve to gather up the traditions of a people, transmit them from generation to generation, and thereby create that continuity of a treasured common life which constitutes a civilization. "We live by symbols." The flag is the symbol of our national unity, transcending all internal differences, however large, within the framework of the Constitution. This Court has had occasion to say that ". . . the flag is the symbol of the Nation's power, the emblem of freedom in its truest, best sense. . . . it signifies government resting on the consent of the governed; liberty regulated by law; the protection of the weak against the strong; security against the exercise of arbitrary power; and absolute safety for free institutions against foreign aggression."

The case before us must be viewed as though the legislature of Pennsylvania had itself formally directed the flag-salute for the children of Minersville; had made no exemption for children whose parents were possessed of conscientious scruples like those of the Gobitis family; and had indicated its belief in the desirable ends to be secured by having its public school children share a common experience at those periods of development when their minds are supposedly receptive to its assimilation, by an exercise appropriate in time and place and setting, and one designed to evoke in them appreciation of the nation's hopes and dreams, its sufferings and sacrifices. The precise issue, then, for us to decide is whether the legislatures of the various states and the authorities in a thousand counties and school districts of this country are barred from determining the appropriateness of various means to evoke that unifying sentiment without which there can ultimately be no liberties, civil or religious. To stigmatize legislative judgment in providing for this universal gesture of respect for the symbol of our national life in the setting of the common school as a lawless inroad on that freedom of conscience which the Constitution protects, would amount to no less than the pronouncement of pedagogical and psychological dogma in a field where courts possess no marked and certainly no controlling competence. The influences which help toward a common feeling for the common country are manifold. Some may seem harsh and others no doubt are foolish. Surely, however, the end is legitimate. And the effective means for its attainment are still so uncertain and so unauthenticated by science as to preclude us from putting the widely prevalent belief in flag-saluting beyond the pale of legislative power. It mocks reason and denies our whole history to find in the allowance of a requirement to salute our flag on fitting occasions the seeds of sanction for obeisance to a leader.

The wisdom of training children in patriotic impulses by those compulsions which necessarily pervade so much of the educational process is not for our independent judgment. Even were we convinced of the folly of such a measure, such belief would be no proof of its unconstitutionality. For ourselves, we might be tempted to say that the deepest patriotism is best engendered by giving unfettered scope to the most crochety beliefs. Perhaps it is best, even from the standpoint of those interests which ordinances like the one under review seek to promote, to give to the least popular sect leave from conformities like those here in issue. But the courtroom is not the arena for debating issues of educational policy. It is not our province to choose among competing considerations in the subtle process of securing effective loyalty to the traditional ideals of democracy, while respecting at the same time individual idiosyncracies among a people so diversified in racial origins and religious allegiances. So to hold would in effect make us the school board for the country. That authority has not been given to this Court, nor should we assume it.

We are dealing here with the formative period in the development of citizenship. Great diversity of psychological and ethical opinion exists among us concerning the best way to train children for their place in society. Because of these differences and because of reluctance to permit a single, iron-cast system of education to be imposed upon a nation compounded of so many strains, we have held that, even though public education is one of our most cherished democratic institutions, the Bill of Rights bars a state from compelling all children to attend the public schools. But it is a very different thing for this Court to exercise censorship over the conviction of legislatures that a particular program or exercise will best promote in the minds of children who attend the common schools an attachment to the institutions of their country.

What the school authorities are really asserting is the right to awaken in the child's mind considerations as to the significance of the flag contrary to those implanted by the parent. In such an attempt the state is normally at a disadvantage in competing with the parent's authority, so long—and this is the vital aspect of religious toleration—as parents are unmolested in their right to counteract by their own persuasiveness the wisdom and rightness of those loyalties which the state's educational system is seeking to promote. Except where the transgression of constitutional liberty is too plain for argument, personal freedom is best maintained—so long as the remedial channels of the democratic process remain open and unobstructed—when it is ingrained in a people's habits and not enforced against popular policy by the coercion of adjudicated law. That the flag-salute is an allowable portion of a school program for those who do not invoke conscientious scruples is surely not debatable. But for us to insist that, though the ceremony may be required, exceptional immunity must be given to dissidents, is to maintain that there is no basis for a legislative judgment that such an exemption might introduce elements of difficulty into the school discipline, might cast doubts in the minds of the other children which would themselves weaken the effect of the exercise.

The preciousness of the family relation, the authority and independence which give dignity to parenthood, indeed the enjoyment of all freedom, presuppose the kind of ordered society which is summarized by our flag. A society which is dedicated to the preservation of these ultimate values of civilization may in self-protection utilize the educational process for inculcating those almost unconscious feelings which bind men together in a comprehending loyalty, whatever may be their lesser differences and difficulties. That is to say, the process may be utilized so long as men's right to believe as they please, to win others to their way of belief, and their right to assemble in their chosen places of worship for the devotional ceremonies of their faith, are all fully respected.
Reversed.

CHAPTER 2

Constructing a Government: The Founding and the Constitution

THE FIRST FOUNDING: INTERESTS AND CONFLICTS

See text p. 17

Edmund Burke, a British statesman, is best known as the author of a political treatise entitled Reflections on the Revolution in France, *published in 1790. Burke was appalled by the bloodshed and chaos he observed during the French Revolution, which he attributed to the misguided attempts of the French revolutionaries to introduce an entirely new social order, without respect for traditional rights and liberties. Reflections on the Revolution in France is a classic in conservative political philosophy.*

Burke did not oppose the American Revolution, which took place while he was a member of British Parliament, with the vehemence he later exhibited during the French Revolution. Indeed, he suggested that the colonists' complaints had merit because the British government had disregarded their natural rights. In a speech before the House of Commons in 1770, Burke urged fellow members of Parliament to grant greater powers of self-government to the colonies. He pointed out that attempts to control the colonies from across the Atlantic, without any real understanding of the conditions under which the colonies operated, was doomed to failure. Every act of Parliament in governing the colonies was poorly thought out, with the result that the British government itself had to take the blame for the unrest that had resulted. He asserted: ". . . Your acts have not been listened to. . . . You have neither military nor civil power from the senseless manner in which you exercised them. A government without wisdom never will be without woe. All is shaken to the foundation by the entire absence of common sense."

By 1775, matters had gone from bad to worse. In the following excerpt from another speech given at that time, Burke urges the British government to attempt conciliation, restating his position that the situation called for "prudent management" rather than force of arms. In making out his case, he gives a detailed explanation of the American character—and the need to accommodate it—to convince his listeners that no other course of action would be likely to succeed.

Edmund Burke
"On Conciliation" (March 22, 1775)[*]

The proposition is peace. Not peace through the medium of war; not peace to be hunted through the labyrinth of intricate and endless negotiations; not peace to arise out of universal discord fomented from principle in all parts

*From Elliott Robert Barkan, ed., *Edmund Burke on the American Revolution* (Gloucester, MA: Peter Smith Publisher, Inc., 1972). Reprinted with permission.

of the empire; not peace to depend on the juridical determination of perplexing questions or the precise marking the shadowy boundaries of a complex government. It is simple peace, sought in its natural course, and in its ordinary haunts—it is peace sought in the spirit of peace, and laid in principles purely pacific. I propose, by removing the ground of the difference, and by restoring the *former unsuspecting confidence of the colonies in the mother country,* to give permanent satisfaction to your people; and (far from a scheme of ruling by discord) to reconcile them to each other in the same act, and by the bond of the very same interest which reconciles them to British government. . . .

[Burke explains in detail the economic advantages that had accrued to the British through trade with the colonies in North America; two-thirds of all British export trade alone was conducted with the North American and West Indian colonies.]

. . . America, gentlemen say, is a noble object. It is an object well worth fighting for. Certainly it is, if fighting a people be the best way of gaining them. Gentlemen in this respect will be led to their choice of means by their complexions and their habits. Those who understand the military art will of course have some predilection for it. Those who wield the thunder of the state may have more confidence in the efficacy of arms. But I confess, possibly for want of this knowledge, my opinion is much more in favour of prudent management than of force, considering force not as an odious, but a feeble instrument for preserving a people so numerous, so active, so growing, so spirited as this in a profitable and subordinate connection with us. . . .

[Burke argues that force is not a desirable alternative since its effect is temporary and Britain has no great experience with using force as its sole means of governance.]

. . . But there is still behind a third consideration concerning this object, which serves to determine my opinion on the sort of policy which ought to be pursued in the management of America, even more than its population and its commerce—I mean its *temper and character.*

In this character of the Americans, a love of freedom is the predominating feature which marks and distinguishes the whole; and as an ardent is always a jealous affection, your colonies become suspicious, restive, and untractable whenever they see the least attempt to wrest from them by force or shuffle from them by chicane what they think the only advantage worth living for. The fierce spirit of liberty is stronger in the English colonies probably than in any other people of the earth; and this from a great variety of powerful causes, which, to understand the true temper of their minds and the direction which this spirit takes, it will not be amiss to lay open somewhat more largely.

First, the people of the colonies are descendants of Englishmen. England, Sir, is a nation which still I hope respects, and formerly adored, her freedom. The colonists emigrated from you when this part of your character was most predominant, and they took this bias and direction the moment they parted from your hands. They are therefore not only devoted to liberty, but to liberty according to English ideas and on English principles. Abstract liberty, like other mere abstractions, is not to be found. Liberty inheres in some sensible object; and every nation has formed to itself some favourite point, which by way of eminence becomes the criterion of their happiness. It happened you know, Sir, that the great contests for freedom in this country were from the earliest times chiefly upon the question of taxing. . . . On this point of taxes the ablest pens and most eloquent tongues have been exercised; the greatest spirits have acted and suffered. . . .

[The British themselves have made it most clear that the people must have power over their own money.] The colonies draw from you, as with their life-blood, these ideas and principles. Their love of liberty, as with you, fixed and attached on this specific point of taxing. Liberty might be safe or might be endangered in twenty other particulars, without their being much pleased or alarmed. Here they felt its pulse, and as they found that beat they thought themselves sick or sound. . . . The fact is, that they did thus apply those general arguments; and your mode of governing them, whether through lenity or indolence, through wisdom or mistake, confirmed them in the imagination that they, as well as you, had an interest in these common principles.

They were further confirmed in this pleasing error by the form of their provincial legislative assemblies. Their governments are popular in a high degree, some are merely popular, in all the popular representative is the most weighty, and this share of the people in their ordinary government never fails to inspire them with lofty sentiments and with a strong aversion from whatever tends to deprive them of their chief importance.

If anything were wanting to this necessary operation of the form of government, religion would have given it a complete effect. Religion, always a principle of energy, in this new people is no way worn out or impaired, and their mode of professing it is also one main cause of this free spirit. The people are Protestants, and of that kind which is the most adverse to all implicit submission of mind and opinion. This is a persuasion not only favourable to liberty, but built upon it. . . . All Protestantism, even the most cold and passive, is a sort of dissent. But the religion most prevalent in our northern colonies is a refinement on the principle of resistance; it is the dissidence of dissent and the Protestantism of the Protestant religion. . . . The colonists left England when this spirit was high, and in the emigrants was the highest of all; and even that stream of foreigners, which has been constantly flowing into these colonies, has, for the greatest part, been composed of dissenters from the establishments of their several countries, and have brought with them a temper and character far from alien to that of the people with whom they mixed.

. . . It is [true] that in Virginia and the Carolinas they have a vast multitude of slaves. Where this is the case in any part of the world, those who are free are by far the most proud and jealous of their freedom. Freedom is to them not only an enjoyment, but a kind of rank and privilege. Not seeing there that freedom, as in countries where it is a common blessing and as broad and general as the air, may be united with much abject toil, with great misery, with all the exterior of servitude liberty looks amongst them like something that is more noble and liberal. I do not mean, Sir, to commend the superior morality of this sentiment, which has at least as much pride as virtue in it; but I cannot alter the nature of man. . . . In such a people, the haughtiness of domination combines with the spirit of freedom, fortifies it, and renders it invincible.

Permit me, Sir, to add another circumstance in our colonies, which contributes no mean part towards the growth and effect of this untractable spirit. I mean their education. In no country perhaps in the world is the law so general a study. The profession itself is numerous and powerful, and in most provinces it takes the lead. . . . [But] when great honours and great emoluments do not win over this knowledge [of law] to the service of the state, it is a formidable adversary to government. If the spirit be not tamed and broken by these happy methods, it is stubborn and litigious. *Abeunt studia in mores.*[1] This study renders men acute, inquisitive, dexterous, prompt in attack, ready in defence, full of resources. . . .

The last cause of this disobedient spirit in the colonies is hardly less powerful than the rest, as it is not merely moral, but laid deep in the natural constitution of things. Three thousand miles of ocean lie between you and them. No contrivance can prevent the effect of this distance in weakening government. Seas roll, and months pass, between the order and the execution, and the want of a speedy explanation of a single point is enough to defeat a whole system. . . . The Sultan gets such obedience as he can. He governs with a loose rein that he may govern at all. . . . This is the immutable condition, the eternal law, of extensive and detached empire.

Then, Sir, from these six capital sources: of descent, of form of government, of religion in the northern provinces, of manners in the southern, of education, of the remoteness of situation from the first mover of government—from all these causes a fierce spirit of liberty has grown up. It has grown with the growth of the people in your colonies, and increased with the increase of their wealth; a spirit that unhappily meeting with an exercise of power in England which, however lawful, is not reconcilable to any ideas of liberty, much less with theirs, has kindled this flame that is ready to consume us.

I do not mean to commend either the spirit in this excess or the moral causes which produce it. Perhaps a more smooth and accommodating spirit of freedom in them would be more acceptable to us. Perhaps ideas of liberty might be desired more reconcilable with an arbitrary and boundless authority. Perhaps we might wish the colonists to be persuaded that their liberty is more secure when held in trust for them by us (as their guardians during a perpetual minority) than with any part of it in their own hands. The question is, not whether their spirit deserves praise or blame, but—what, in the name of God, shall we do with it? . . . We are called upon to fix some rule and line

---

[1] "Pursuits influence character."

for our future conduct which may give a little stability to our politics and prevent the return of such unhappy deliberations as the present. . . . Until very lately, all authority in America seemed to be nothing but an emanation from yours. Even the popular part of the colony constitution derived all its activity, and its first vital movement, from the pleasure of the crown. We thought, Sir, that the utmost which the discontented colonists could do was to disturb authority; we never dreamt they could of themselves supply it, knowing in general what an operose business it is to establish a government absolutely new. . . . They have formed a government, sufficient for its purposes, without the bustle of a revolution or the troublesome formality of an election. Evident necessity and tacit consent have done the business in an instant. . . . The evil arising from hence is this: that the colonists, having once found the possibility of enjoying the advantages of order in the midst of a struggle for liberty, such struggles will not henceforward seem so terrible to the settled and sober part of mankind as they had appeared before the trial.

. . . In order to prove that the Americans have no right to their liberties, we are every day endeavouring to subvert the maxims which preserve the whole spirit of our own. To prove that the Americans ought not to be free, we are obliged to depreciate the value of freedom itself. . . .

. . . There are but three ways of proceeding relative to this stubborn spirit which prevails in your colonies and disturbs your government. These are: to change that spirit, as inconvenient, by removing the causes; to prosecute it as criminal; or, to comply with it as necessary. . . . [The first two ideas are unworkable in practice.]

The temper and character which prevail in our colonies are, I am afraid, unalterable by any human art. We cannot, I fear, falsify the pedigree of this fierce people, and persuade them that they are not sprung from a nation in whose veins the blood of freedom circulates. The language in which they would hear you tell them this tale would detect the imposition—your speech would betray you. An Englishman is the unfittest person on earth to argue another Englishman into slavery.

I think it is nearly as little in our power to change their republican religion as their free descent, or to substitute the Roman Catholic as a penalty, or the Church of England as an improvement. . . . The education of the Americans is also on the same unalterable bottom with their religion. You cannot persuade them to burn their books of curious science, to banish their lawyers from their courts of laws, or to quench the lights of their assemblies by refusing to choose those persons who are best read in their privileges. . . .

With regard to the high aristocratic spirit of Virginia and the southern colonies, it has been proposed, I know, to reduce it by declaring a general enfranchisement of their slaves. . . .

Slaves as these unfortunate black people are, and dull as all men are from slavery, must they not a little suspect the offer of freedom from that very nation which has sold them to their present masters?—from that nation, one of whose causes of quarrel with those masters is their refusal to deal any more in that inhuman traffic? An offer of freedom from England would come rather oddly, shipped to them in an African vessel, which is refused an entry into the ports of Virginia or Carolina, with a cargo of three hundred Angola negroes. . . .

If then the removal of the causes of this spirit of American liberty be, for the greater part, or rather entirely, impracticable; if the ideas of criminal process be inapplicable, or, if applicable, are in the highest degree inexpedient—what way yet remains? No way is open, but the third and last—to comply with the American spirit as necessary, or, if you please, to submit to it as a necessary evil.

THE SECOND FOUNDING: FROM COMPROMISE TO CONSTITUTION

See text p. 20

If the debates over the nature of the federal union seem to be of historical interest only, even a brief consideration of global conditions today should convince us otherwise. Current debates over the structure of the European Economic Community provide an insight into the critical importance of questions about the nature of union. The following article appeared in the British magazine, The Economist, *and invites readers to consider the implications of a federal system uniting Europe. Given the magazine's historically free-market position, it is not surprising that the article argues in favor of great caution in entering into any union of European states that might limit the ability of any single nation to secede at will.*

The Economist
"If You Sincerely Want to be a United States"*

Imagine a hot summer in Paris. By grace of a kindly time-warp, a group of European eminences have assembled for a conference. Charles de Gaulle is their chairman. Among those attending are John Maynard Keynes (who has a continent-wide reputation, though he is still only 29) and Albert Einstein. Bertrand Russell is not there—he is holidaying on Cape Cod—but he barrages the proceedings by fax. Russell is kept abreast of things by young King Juan Carlos of Spain, who, with Keynes, provides the driving force of the conference.

Impossible, except in one of those rosy early-morning dreams. Now remember the men who gathered at Philadelphia in the summer of 1787. George Washington was the chairman. Alexander Hamilton, whose short life never knew a dull moment, was there, as was James Madison, a pragmatic man of principle who would later become president. Together, they directed the conference. Benjamin Franklin was there too, though somewhat in his

*"If You Sincerely Want to be a United States," *The Economist* (March 23, 1991). © 1991 The Economist Newspaper, Limited, reprinted with permission.

dotage. Thomas Jefferson (compared with whom Bertrand Russell was a startlingly narrow fellow) was not there, but kept an eye on things from Paris.

It is no offence to Jacques Delors and his friends to say that the people now charged with trying to create a political union in Europe do not inspire such awe. Yet the job of the two intergovernmental conferences the European Community has assembled this year is not different in kind from that which faced America's constitutional convention 204 years ago. Constitution-writing is also in vogue in the Soviet Union, as that country's central government and its 15 surly republics struggle to redefine their relations with each other; though that is a matter of trying to stop a bad union falling apart, not creating a good new one. Might the most mature and successful constitutional settlement in the world have some lessons for these European parvenus?

They Were One, and They Knew It

Start with two great differences between America then and Europe now. The America that declared its independence from Britain in 1776 was, except for its black slaves, an extraordinarily homogeneous society.

Think of those huge distances, and those primitive communications, and wonder at the early Americans' sense of cohesion. Although North and South already showed the difference that had to be bridged by war in 1861–65, Americans shared some essential attributes. A few German and Dutch dissenters apart, their stock was solidly British. Their intellectual heroes (a nod to Montesquieu notwithstanding) were from the British tradition: Hobbes and Locke, Smith and Hume. Their language was English; their law was English law; their God an English God.

Wherever on the coast they settled, they had originally had to win the land by back breaking struggle (even in the Carolinas, whose plantations were far bigger than New England farms). Three thousand perilous miles from England, they had all learnt the same self-sufficiency. Most of them, or their fathers, had fought Indians.

And those who did not leave for Canada after the break with Britain had a second thing in common: they had all won their independence from an external power, by force of arms. Their successful war of liberation made them feel more clearly "American" than ever before.

Yet that war had been prosecuted by 13 states, not one; and it did not forge anything that, to modern eyes, looks like a nation-state. Indeed, this absence of unity was made explicit by the articles of confederation, which the 13 states signed in 1781. Article 2 said that the states retained their "sovereignty, freedom and independence." They merely (article 3) entered into a "firm league of friendship with each other."

After only six years, the articles of 1781 were deemed unsatisfactory enough to warrant revision. The result—today's constitution—provided a system of government that was federal in form, but with a much stronger central government than had existed before. So, if Europe wants to learn from America, it had better start with a look at the supposed defects of those articles.

In broad terms, critics of the confederation argued that it was unstable, an awkward half-way house between a collection of independent states and a truly single country. Their criticisms concentrated on two things: economics, in particular the internal market of the 13 states; and foreign policy, the ability of the states to fend off foreign dangers.

Take economics first. The monetary and fiscal policy of the America that had just chucked out the British was chaotic. Congress (the body of delegates that had, so far as possible, directed the war against Britain, and whose position was formalised by the articles) could not pay off its creditors. It had no taxing power, and could only issue "requisitions" (in effect, requests for money) to the states. Some paid; some did not. Some states took over the responsibility for the part of the national debt that was owed to their own citizens, and then paid this in securities they issued themselves. There was a shortage of sound money (coin). Some states issued paper money themselves; much of it soon lost its face value. The currency of one state was not normally legal tender in another.

Tariff policy was a particular bugbear. States with small towns and few ports, such as New Jersey and Connecticut, were at the mercy of big states like Pennsylvania and New York, through whose ports America's imports flowed. Tariffs levied by New York would be paid by consumers in (say) Connecticut; but Connecticut's treasury derived no benefit from these tariffs. In short, the internal barriers to trade were big.

Abroad, the 13 states faced a ring of dangers. Britain still held Canada and a string of forts to the west of the United States. If it wished, it could have encircled the 13 states; its troops burnt Washington in 1812. Spain controlled Florida and—worse—it presided over navigation on the Mississippi.

Americans with a sense of where history was taking them (meaning most Americans of the time) well knew that, in Europe, loose confederations were vulnerable to their enemies. Some members of Congress compared that body to the Polish parliament, whose every member had a veto. The comparison hurt: at that time, Poland was being divided three ways by its enemies. The German confederation, or Holy Roman Empire, was notoriously feeble. It was characterised, said Madison, by "the licentiousness of the strong and the oppression of the weak"—a "nerveless" body "agitated with unceasing fermentation in its bowels."

The Americans decided they wanted calmer bowels and a better circulation. In the Federalist Papers—the collection of essays written by Hamilton, Madison and John Jay after the convention of 1787—Hamilton was to weave together the economic and political arguments. Trade wars between the states, he suggested, would sooner or later turn into shooting wars. Given the lack of unity of the American states, European powers (with their "pernicious labyrinths of politics and wars") would divide and rule. The destiny to which God had pointed America would vanish in the ensuing strife.

That was putting it a bit high. Many historians today argue that, far from being on the edge of economic collapse, the America of 1780s was happy and rich. Peter Aranson of Emory University in Georgia says that, although there was little immigration, the new country's population grew as fast in that decade as at almost any time in American history. No sign of hardship there. Trade wars were ending as the states found ways to reduce or remove the tariffs on goods passing through their territory to another state. Had each state's currency been legal tender elsewhere, good money might sooner or later have driven out bad.

The Three Big Things of 1787

For all that, Hamilton and the others who wanted a stronger central government won the day in Philadelphia. The convention's report was adopted by the states, though not without a few close shaves. And America got the constitution it still has. How has it lasted so long? For three main reasons that should interest today's Europeans.

The first was that the constitution created an executive—the president—where none had existed before. The president embodied a response to those external threats. He was to be the commander-in-chief of the armed forces. Although Congress had the power to declare war (and jealously preserves it), the president, with the advice and consent of the Senate, could conclude treaties and appoint ambassadors. He was to be the instrument of a unified foreign policy. This was made explicit by the constitution's first article, which prohibited any of the states from entering into any treaty, alliance or confederation, and from keeping troops, and from engaging in war unless it was invaded or was in imminent danger.

Second, the constitution was a document of limited powers. It gave to the central government (or so went the theory) only those powers specifically allocated to it. The tenth amendment made plain what Hamilton and Madison though implicit: "The powers not delegated to the United States by the Constitution," it says, "nor prohibited to it by the states, are reserved to the states respectively, or to the people."

Third, the constitution recognised a "judicial power," and established a Supreme Court. The court, among other things, was to have jurisdiction over all cases arising "under the constitution" (and the constitution itself was declared to be "the supreme law of the land"). It also had jurisdiction over disputes between any one of the states and the United States, and between two or more states themselves. Members of the Supreme Court had no date of retirement. In other words, the Supreme Court was to be charged with deciding whether the practice of government conformed with the theory as laid down in the constitution.

How might modern Europeans use the American experience? Those who believe that the European Community is destined to be more than a collection of nation-states—an argument heard since the days of Monnet and Schuman—concentrate on the supposed instability of the original American confederation. Look at the Soviet Union, on the other hand, and you may conclude that that argument cuts the other way. It is the tight union of Stalin and Brezhnev that is unstable; it will survive, if it survives at all, only if it is converted into a much looser confederation.

Western Europe's federalists have a reply. In two respects, they argue, the Community has already learnt the lesson of the American constitution's success. Since the late 1950s the European Court of Justice has arrogated to itself the power to declare acts of member states or of Community institutions to have no effect if they contravene the Treaty of Rome, the EC's founding charter. And the notion of subsidiarity—that decisions in the Community should be taken at the lowest governmental level possible—is a rough-and-ready approximation to the American constitution's commitment to limited powers. Subsidiarity is not, or not yet, a matter of general Community law, but the idea is treated with growing respect.

Moreover, late 20th-century Europeans share the 18th-century American desire to create a single market and remove barriers to internal trade. Here the Americas found it necessary to make the states cede some sovereignty, and to grant the union some powers it had not previously possessed. The states were forbidden to levy their own external tariffs. In the so-called "commerce clause" of the constitution, the federal government was given the exclusive power to "regulate commerce with foreign nations, and among the several states."

In much the same way, Project 1992 is designed to realise the Community's dream of a single market, free of all internal impediments. European federalists would argue that the goal of monetary union is all of a piece with this. If a single trading block has 12 national currencies, the transactions costs of trade will always be higher than if there was but one. Americans at the 1787 convention would have recognised the force of this; the constitution they wrote forbids states to coin their own money. (Still, it was not until 1913 that America established a stable system for guiding national monetary policy.)

But that is not the whole of the American lesson. Those Europeans who doubt whether the American experience of federalism can be applied to Europe will find Americans ready to argue their case for them. One argument of America's own anti-federalists (still around, two centuries later) strikes a particular chord.

America's anti-federalists say the combination of a broad commerce clause and a powerful Supreme Court has been disastrous. It is a simple matter to show that almost anything is a matter of "inter-state commerce." Even if a company does almost all its business within one state, for instance, it may still use the federal postal service. Once interstate commerce has been proved, the central government can easily decide that such commerce is within its regulatory competence. As Mr. Aranson has pointed out, as early as 1870 the Supreme Court held that Congress could insist on the inspection of steamships travelling entirely within the waters of one state, if other vessels on those waters carried goods bound for other states.

According to the anti-federalists, the breadth of the commerce clause means that an activist Supreme Court, given an inch, takes a mile. The power of states to regulate their own affairs has been diminished, and the power of the central government has been allowed to increase excessively.

Non-Americans living in America, wrapped in the red tape of federalism (try working out where to get your car exhaust tested each year if you bought the car in Virginia, live in Maryland and work in the District of Columbia), may think the argument over-done; they usually pray for less power for the individual states, no more. But many Americans still worry about excessive centralisation. So do people on the other side of the Atlantic.

Europeans fearful of being turned into "identikit Europeans," the Margaret Thatcher's phrase, therefore have American allies. Such Europeans will note Mr. Aranson's warning that America's commerce clause "sustains national cartels that cross state boundaries and empower states, often with federal assistance, to cartelise markets." These Europeans suspect that a Community "social charter" will mean all European states sooner or later being required to have the same laws on health and welfare.

The Right to Opt Out

Europe's anti-federalists can draw further succour from America. The part of a future Europe that most Europeans find it hardest to picture clearly is the idea of Europe acting towards the outside world with a united mind, a single will.

Different Europeans, faced with a challenge abroad, can behave in radically different ways. This partly because Europe is still far from being the homogeneous society that America was from the start. Europe is still a place of separate nationalisms, to an extent that America never was; those nationalisms have grown milder in the past half-century, but they have not vanished. Although almost all of Europe suffered the same frightful war 50 years ago, the various Europeans have very different memories of it. And this past year they have displayed very different feelings about such things as standing up to Saddam Hussein, and rebuking Mikhail Gorbachev for re-embracing his country's old guard.

This has a direct constitutional implication. Recall how important foreign policy, the threat abroad, was to Madison and Hamilton. They would have considered a union without a single foreign and defence policy to be a nonsense on stilts. So they created a powerful executive, independent of the states, to take control of that policy. Even those Europeans who want a single foreign policy shy away from a European equivalent of the American presidency. Yet without a president, embodying within his person a common will towards the world outside, it is hard to see how Europeans can create what Americans would regard as a federal Europe.

The non-homogeneity, and the hesitation about a European president as powerful as America's, will not necessarily remain as influential as they are today. But one awkward lesson from America is permanent. This is the fact that America did not take its final political shape in 1787; three-quarters of a century later, the founding fathers' structure blew up.

Most non-Americans do not realise how large the civil war of 1861–65 looms in America's collective memory. It killed more than 600,000 people, foreshadowing the efficient slaughter that Europe did not experience until Verdun and the Somme 50 years later. In its last year when the North's armies under Grant and Sherman marched into the South's heartland, it became unbearably brutal. If you are going to have a constitution linking several states that cherish their sovereignty, it is worth making sure in advance that it does not lead to the kind of war America's constitution led to.

Unfair! yell Northern historians, for whom it is an article of faith that the civil war was fought not over a constitutional principle (the right of states to secede from the union) but over a social injustice (slavery). The Northerners have a case, even though—as Southerners never tire of pointing out—the abolition of slavery was not formally an original aim of the war: the fact is that, without slavery, the Southerners would not have wanted to secede. Since Europe's federalists would argue that nothing divides European countries from each other as passionately as slavery divided North and South, they may feel justified in ignoring the terrible warning of the civil war.

They would be wrong. Nobody knows what explosive arguments the future of Europe will bring. Some countries may see relations with Russia as the right centrepiece for Europe's foreign policy; others may put relations with America in that place; still others will focus on the Arab world to Europe's south. Some Europeans may want far more restrictive immigration policies than others, which could lead to some sharp intra-European border tensions. Country X will favour fewer controls on arms sales abroad than Country Y. Europe's capacity to speak and act as one is still almost entirely theoretical. If Europeans are genuinely interested in learning from the American experience, this lesson should be taken to heart: make it clear in advance that, whatever union is to be forged, states can leave it, unhindered, at will.

THE CONSTITUTION

See text p. 34

In The Federalist No. 10, James Madison observed that the strength of the new union—the division of its powers between state and federal governments and among different branches at the same level of government—lay in its ability to limit the power of factions, which, he observed, arise naturally where any collection of human beings occurs. The elaborate limiting of powers means, at the same time, that government tends to be fairly cumbersome and exasperatingly slow.

James Madison
The Federalist No. 10

Among the numerous advantages promised by a well-constructed Union, none deserves to be more accurately developed than its tendency to break and control the violence of faction. The friend of popular governments never finds himself so much alarmed for their character and fate as when he contemplates their propensity to this dangerous vice. He will not fail, therefore, to set a due value on any plan which, without violating the principles to which he is attached, provides a proper cure for it. The instability, injustice, and confusion introduced into the public councils have, in truth, been the mortal diseases under which popular governments have everywhere perished, as they continue to be the favorite and fruitful topics from which the adversaries to liberty derive their most specious declamations. The valuable improvements made by the American constitutions on the popular models, both ancient and modern, cannot certainly be too much admired; but it would be an unwarrantable partiality to contend that they have as effectually obviated the danger on this side, as was wished and expected. Complaints are everywhere heard from our most considerate and virtuous citizens, equally the friends of public and private faith and of public and personal liberty, that our governments are too unstable, that the public good is disregarded in the conflicts of rival parties, and that measures are too often decided, not according to the rules of justice and the rights of the minor party, but by the superior force of an interested and overbearing majority. However anxiously we may wish that these complaints had no foundation, the evidence of known facts will not permit us to deny that they are in some degree true. It will be found, indeed, on a candid review of our situation, that some of the distresses under which we labor have been erroneously charged on the operation of our governments; but it will be found, at the same time, that other causes will not alone account for many of our heaviest misfortunes; and, particularly, for that prevailing and increasing distrust of public engagements and alarm for private rights which are echoed from one end of the continent to the other. These must be chiefly, if not wholly, effects of the unsteadiness and injustice with which a factious spirit has tainted our public administration.

By a faction I understand a number of citizens, whether amounting to a majority or minority of the whole, who are united and actuated by some common impulse of passion, or of interest, adverse to the rights of other citizens, or to the permanent and aggregate interests of the community.

There are two methods of curing the mischiefs of faction: the one, by removing its causes; the other, by controlling its effects.

There are again two methods of removing the causes of faction: the one, by destroying the liberty which is essential to its existence; the other, by

*James Madison, *The Federalist No. 10,* ed. Clinton Rossiter (New York: NAL, 1961).

giving to every citizen the same opinions, the same passions, and the same interests.

It could never be more truly said than of the first remedy that it was worse than the disease. Liberty is to faction what air is to fire, an aliment without which it instantly expires. But it could not be a less folly to abolish liberty, which is essential to political life, because it nourishes faction than it would be to wish the annihilation of air, which is essential to animal life, because it imparts to fire its destructive agency.

The second expedient is as impracticable as the first would be unwise. As long as the reason of man continues fallible, and he is at liberty to exercise it, different opinions will be formed. As long as the connection subsists between his reason and his self-love, his opinions and his passions will have a reciprocal influence on each other; and the former will be objects to which the latter will attach themselves. The diversity in the faculties of men, from which the rights of property originate, is not less an insuperable obstacle to a uniformity of interests. The protection of these faculties is the first object of government. From the protection of different and unequal faculties of acquiring property, the possession of different degrees and kinds of property immediately results; and from the influence of these on the sentiments and views of the respective proprietors ensues a division of the society into different interests and parties.

The latent causes of faction are thus sown in the nature of man; and we see them everywhere brought into different degrees of activity, according to the different circumstances of civil society. A zeal for different opinions concerning religion, concerning government, and many other points, as well of speculation as of practice; an attachment to different leaders ambitiously contending for pre-eminence and power; or to persons of other descriptions whose fortunes have been interesting to the human passions, have, in turn, divided mankind into parties, inflamed them with mutual animosity, and rendered them much more disposed to vex and oppress each other than to co-operate for their common good. So strong is this propensity of mankind to fall into mutual animosities that where no substantial occasion presents itself the most frivolous and fanciful distinctions have been sufficient to kindle their unfriendly passions and excite their most violent conflicts. But the most common and durable source of factions has been the various and unequal distribution of property. Those who hold and those who are without property have ever formed distinct interests in society. Those who are creditors, and those who are debtors, fall under a like discrimination. A landed interest, a manufacturing interest, a mercantile interest, a moneyed interest, with many lesser interests, grow up of necessity in civilized nations, and divide them into different classes, actuated by different sentiments and views. The regulation of these various and interfering interests forms the principal task of modern legislation and involves the spirit of party and faction in the necessary and ordinary operations of government.

No man is allowed to be judge in his own cause, because his interest would certainly bias his judgment and, not improbably, corrupt his integrity. With equal, nay with greater reason, a body of men are unfit to be both judges and parties at the same time; yet what are many of the most important acts of legislation but so many judicial determinations, not indeed concerning the rights of single persons, but concerning the rights of large bodies of citizens? And what are the different classes of legislators but advocates and parties to the causes which they determine? Is a law proposed concerning private debts? It is a question to which the creditors are parties on one side and the debtors on the other. Justice ought to hold the balance between them. Yet the parties are, and must be, themselves the judges; and the most numerous party, or in other words, the most powerful faction must be expected to prevail. Shall domestic manufacturers be encouraged, and in what degree, by restrictions on foreign manufacturers? are questions which would be differently decided by the landed and the manufacturing classes, and probably by neither with a sole regard to justice and the public good. The apportionment of taxes on the various descriptions of property is an act which seems to require the most exact impartiality; yet there is, perhaps, no legislative act in which greater opportunity and temptation are given to a predominant party to trample on the rules of justice. Every shilling with which they overburden the inferior number is a shilling saved to their own pockets.

It is in vain to say that enlightened statesmen will be able to adjust these clashing interests and render them all subservient to the public good. Enlightened statesmen will not always be at the helm. Nor, in many cases, can such an adjustment be made at all without taking into view indirect and remote considerations, which will rarely prevail over the immediate interest which one party may find in disregarding the rights of another or the good of the whole.

The inference to which we are brought is that the *causes* of faction cannot be removed and that relief is only to be sought in the means of controlling its *effects*.

If a faction consists of less than a majority, relief is supplied by the republican principle, which enables the majority to defeat its sinister views by regular vote. It may clog the administration, it may convulse the society; but it will be unable to execute and mask its violence under the forms of the Constitution. When a majority is included in a faction, the form of popular government, on the other hand, enables it to sacrifice to its ruling passion or interest both the public good and the rights of other citizens. To secure the public good and private rights against the danger of such a faction, and at the same time to preserve the spirit and the form of popular government, is then the great object to which our inquiries are directed. Let me add that it is the great desideratum by which alone this form of government can be rescued from the opprobrium under which it has so long labored and be recommended to the esteem and adoption of mankind.

By what means is this object attainable? Evidently by one of two only. Either the existence of the same passion or interest in a majority at the same time must be prevented, or the majority, having such coexistent passion or interest, must be rendered, by their number and local situation, unable to concert and carry into effect schemes of oppression. If the impulse and the opportunity be suffered to coincide, we well know that neither moral nor religious motives can be relied on as an adequate control. They are not found to be such on the injustice and violence of individuals, and lose their efficacy in proportion to the number combined together, that is, in proportion as their efficacy becomes needful.

From this view of the subject it may be concluded that a pure democracy, by which I mean a society consisting of a small number of citizens, who assemble and administer the government in person, can admit of no cure for the mischiefs of faction. A common passion or interest will, in almost every case, be felt by a majority of the whole; a communication and concert results from the form of government itself; and there is nothing to check the inducements to sacrifice the weaker party or an obnoxious individual. Hence it is that such democracies have ever been spectacles of turbulence and contention; have ever been found incompatible with personal security or the rights of property; and have in general been as short in their lives as they have been violent in their deaths. Theoretic politicians, who have patronized this species of government, have erroneously supposed that by reducing mankind to a perfect equality in their political rights, they would at the same time be perfectly equalized and assimilated in their possessions, their opinions, and their passions.

A republic, by which I mean a government in which the scheme of representation takes place, opens a different prospect and promises the cure for which we are seeking. Let us examine the points in which it varies from pure democracy, and we shall comprehend both the nature of the cure and the efficacy which it must derive from the Union.

The two great points of difference between a democracy and a republic are: first, the delegation of the government, in the latter, to a small number of citizens elected by the rest; secondly, the greater number of citizens and greater sphere of country over which the latter may be extended.

The effect of the first difference is, on the one hand, to refine and enlarge the public views by passing them through the medium of a chosen body of citizens, whose wisdom may best discern the true interest of their country and whose patriotism and love of justice will be least likely to sacrifice it to temporary or partial considerations. Under such a regulation it may well happen that the public voice, pronounced by the representatives of the people, will be more consonant to the public good than if pronounced by the people themselves, convened for the purpose. On the other hand, the effect may be inverted. Men of factious tempers, of local prejudices, or of sinister designs, may, by intrigue, by corruption, or by other means, first obtain the suffrages, and then betray the interests of the people. The question resulting is, whether small or extensive republics are most favorable to the election of proper guardians of the public weal; and it is clearly decided in favor of the latter by two obvious considerations.

In the first place it is to be remarked that however small the republic may be the representatives must be raised to a certain number in order to guard against the cabals of a few; and that however large it may be they must be limited to a certain number in order to guard against the confusion of a multitude. Hence, the number of representatives in the two cases are not being in proportion to that of the constituents, and being proportionally greatest in the small republic, it follows that if the proportion of fit characters be not less in the large than in the small republic, the former will present a greater option, and consequently a greater probability of a fit choice.

In the next place, as each representative will be chosen by a greater number of citizens in the large than in the small republic, it will be more difficult for unworthy candidates to practise with success the vicious arts by which elections are too often carried; and the suffrages of the people being more free, will be more likely to center on men who possess the most attractive merit and the most diffusive and established characters.

It must be confessed that in this, as in most other cases, there is a mean, on both sides of which inconveniencies will be found to lie. By enlarging too much the number of electors, you render the representative too little acquainted with all their local circumstances and lesser interests; as by reducing it too much, you render him unduly attached to these, and too little fit to comprehend and pursue great and national objects. The federal Constitution forms a happy combination in this respect; the great and aggregate interests being referred to the national, the local and particular to the State legislatures.

The other point of difference is the greater number of citizens and extent of territory which may be brought within the compass of republican than of democratic government; and it is this circumstance principally which renders factious combinations less to be dreaded in the former than in the latter. The smaller the society, the fewer probably will be the distinct parties and interests composing it; the fewer the distinct parties and interests, the more frequently will a majority be found of the same party; and the smaller the number of individuals composing a majority, and the smaller the compass within which they are placed, the more easily will they concert and execute their plans of oppression. Extend the sphere and you take in a greater variety of parties and interests; you make it less probable that a majority of the whole will have a common motive to invade the rights of other citizens; or if such a common motive exists, it will be more difficult for all who feel it to discover their own strength and to act in unison with each other. Besides other impediments, it may be remarked that, where there is a consciousness of unjust or dishonorable purposes, communication is always checked by distrust in proportion to the number whose concurrence is necessary.

Hence, it clearly appears that the same advantage which a republic has over a democracy in controlling the effects of faction is enjoyed by a large over a small republic—is enjoyed by the Union over the States composing it. Does this advantage consist in the substitution of representatives whose enlightened views and virtuous sentiments render them superior to local prejudices and to schemes of injustice? It will not be denied that the representation of the Union will be most likely to possess these requisite endowments. Does it consist in the greater security afforded by a greater variety of parties, against the event of any one party being able to outnumber and oppress the rest? In an equal degree does the increased variety of parties comprised within the Union increase this security? Does it, in fine, consist in the greater obstacles opposed to the concert and accomplishment of the secret wishes of an unjust and interested majority? Here again the extent of the Union gives it the most palpable advantage.

The influence of factious leaders may kindle a flame within their particular States but will be unable to spread a general conflagration through the other States. A religious sect may degenerate into a political faction in a part of the Confederacy; but the variety of sects dispersed over the entire face of it must secure the national councils against any danger from that source. A rage for paper money, for an abolition of debts, for an equal division of property, or for any other improper or wicked project, will be less apt to pervade the whole body of the Union than a particular member of it, in the same proportion as such a malady is more likely to taint a particular county or district than an entire State.

In the extent and proper structure of the Union, therefore, we behold a republican remedy for the diseases most incident to republican government. And according to the degree of pleasure and pride we feel in being republicans ought to be our zeal in cherishing the spirit and supporting the character of federalist.

PUBLIUS

See text p. 34

The two-hundredth anniversary of the Constitution was in 1987. As Americans pondered the meaning of that anniversary, they also thought about whether it was time to overhaul the system; after all, Thomas Jefferson once suggested that a constitution ought to be revised approximately once every twenty years. In the following article from a special issue of the Los Angeles Times *celebrating the Constitution's birthday, commentator David Lauter reviews some of the arguments that have been made for and against an overhaul of the Constitution.*

David Lauter
"We the People: The American Constitution After 200 Years: Celebrating the Nation's Charter as Problem and Solution"*

The traveler wandered the rutted roads from New England south to the Carolinas and rode the mule-drawn canal barges west through the mountains toward the Mississippi, all the while taking notes on the strange young country spread out before him.

When he returned to France, Alexis de Tocqueville wrote in 1835, "I have never been more struck by the good sense and the practical judgment of the Americans than in the manner in which they elude the numberless difficulties resulting from their federal Constitution."

A century-and-a-half later, the nation de Tocqueville viewed in adolescence has grown to adulthood. The Constitution, signed by its framers in Philadelphia on Sept. 17, 1787, is now the oldest written national charter of government in effect anywhere in the world. And Americans are still demonstrating a pragmatic genius for overcoming what de Tocqueville took to be the Constitution's "numberless difficulties."

Americans themselves complain ceaselessly about the inefficiencies and frustrations it entails, from the Fifth Amendment's protection of criminals to the seemingly archaic checks and balances that almost paralyze modern government. Critics of the Constitution yearn for the more streamlined decision making of parliamentary systems in which prime ministers have extraordinary freedom of action and are quickly replaced if they lose popular support.

Why, then, with all the manifest burdens it imposes, has the Constitution been so widely admired and so little changed in 200 years? Why did British Prime Minister William Gladstone declare, in 1878, that "the American Constitution is the most wonderful work ever struck off at a given time by the brain and purpose of man"?

The answer appears to be that the mechanisms designed by the Founding Fathers, while maddeningly slow and cumbersome, have proven remarkably effective at enabling the people of a huge and heterogeneous nation to preserve the pattern of "conflict within consensus" that historians identify as the unique feature of America's politics.

With one terrible exception, the Civil War, the constitutional process has enabled Americans to pass through periods of profound change, to disagree, struggle ferociously and sometimes violently over policies, yet ultimately reach decisions that most can support and almost all accept—without plunging into the abyss of fanaticism that has torn and destroyed so many societies.

*David Lauter, "We the People: The American Constitution After 200 Years: Celebrating the Nation's Charter as Problem and Solution," *Los Angeles Times* (September 13, 1987). Reprinted with permission.

'Intense Disagreements'

A constitution should "allow very intense disagreements to be handled without violence and without loss of legitimacy" of the nation's institutions, said UC Berkeley political scientist Raymond Wolfinger. By that measure, the Constitution has been a resounding success.

Unlike Marx and other more theoretical political thinkers, the framers of the Constitution started with human nature, which they saw as severely flawed and limited, then tried to design a government that would guarantee "the blessings of liberty" to the maximum extent possible within those limitations. After all, Madison wrote in the Federalist papers, "If men were angels, no government would be necessary. If angels were to govern men, neither external nor internal controls on government would be necessary."

Reinforcing such pragmatism, a tradition of almost-religious veneration has grown up around the Constitution. One 19th-Century President called it the "ark of the people's covenant" and said it must be "shield(ed) . . . from impious hands." Advocates of sundry causes claim the Constitution's support, and tourists line up in droves to see its first and last pages encased in bulletproof glass at the National Archives.

The American lexicon contains few political epithets more powerful than "unconstitutional."

Bending the System

To be sure, this veneration has not eliminated the frustrations inherent in the system. Nor has it always been strong enough to prevent abuses of the rights and values embodied in the Constitution and the Bill of Rights. In race relations particularly, as well as in periods of national crisis and in circumstances when public passions ran out of control, events have occurred that dishonored the Constitution's high ideals.

The importance of those ideals has become so ingrained in the nation's consciousness, however, that the system has shown a remarkable tendency to right itself and return to its intended course.

"Though written constitutions may be violated in moments of passion or delusion, yet they furnish a text to which those who are watchful may again rally and recall the people," Jefferson wrote to a friend in 1802, "they fix too for the people the principles of their political creed."

Within the framework of the Constitution, strong national leaders have tried to bend the system to their will—including Jefferson himself, who entered the White House with a restrictive view of presidential power but pushed his authority to the limit when the opportunity arose in 1803 to make the Louisiana Purchase and double the size of the nation.

Abraham Lincoln suspended portions of the Constitution during the Civil War. Theodore Roosevelt complained that the Constitution "permit(s) one set of people to hoist sails for their own amusement, and another set of people to put down anchors for their own purposes."

"The result from the standpoint of progress has not been happy," he said.

In contemporary times, writers, political scientists and practicing politicians all have advocated overhauls of the Constitution, arguing that the intricate system of checks and balances designed under 18th-Century theory will not do for the practice of the 21st.

Revision of Old Charter

Said political scientist Robert A. Dahl: "I'm increasingly doubtful that the Constitution is functioning really well. . . . I find it hard to engage in this year of celebrating the Constitution as if it were somehow a perfect document."

Indeed, over recent years, 32 states have called for a new Constitutional Convention to revise the old charter, mostly responding to popular frustration with the federal deficit. Two more states joining the call would suffice to bring a convention into being for the first time since the one that ended 200 years ago this week. While no such conventions have been held since the first one, the Constitution has been amended 26 times. The 10 amendments constituting the Bill of Rights were added in 1791, and later amendments introduced such far-reaching changes as ending slavery, creating national guarantees of due process and individual rights, granting women the vote and providing for direct popular election of senators.

Important as such changes have been and wracking as was the history that produced them, all can be seen as extending and intensifying the nation's commitment to the values and ideas underlying the original Constitution and, before it, the Declaration of Independence.

Many factors—including economic, regional and cultural differences—led to the cataclysm of the Civil War, for example. But one of the things that ultimately made a confrontation unavoidable was the inherent contradiction between the institution of slavery and the ideas of equality and fairness implicit in the Constitution.

Though the Founding Fathers had made clear their intention to create a national government superior to the states, they had sidestepped and compromised on what Madison called the "powder keg" of slavery—which many delegates even then saw in starkly moral terms.

In the end, more than 500,000 Americans died—more than in World War I and World War II combined—to meet the issue head-on. Henceforth, no state would have the right to abridge freedoms guaranteed to individuals by the national Constitution, and no institution or practice could stand permanently unchallenged if it contradicted the nation's fundamental values.

What accounts for the relative stability of the American system during two centuries in which the governments of so many other countries were ripped apart and radically changed not once but several times? Scholars point to several factors:

- A nation that seems always in the midst of rapid change in its social rules and economic relationships has been correspondingly conservative in changing the political framework within which those changes occur.

- A people who concentrate in overwhelming numbers on the pragmatic and immediate problems of their private lives have been highly resistant to the fanatical approaches to politics and religion that have shattered other societies. "The great middle-of-road-consensus impulse of Americans," one historian called it.

Indeed, American politics has tended to become most turbulent when large numbers of people believed that their personal lives—and hopes for the future—were threatened.

- A society that lacked an established church, a native aristocracy and a universal culture has clung to the Constitution as a symbol of unity.

"The Constitution has been to us what a king has often been to other nationalities," Harvard President A. Lawrence Lowell said in 1886.

The Constitution, of course, can neither be credited with all that has gone well in American history nor blamed for all failures. "There are other things in society" that help determine the fates of government and that can overwhelm even the most flexible of constitutions, as shown by the experience of numerous Latin American nations, political scientist Wolfinger pointed out.

Isolated Country

America has been both wealthy and physically isolated. The nation's wealth—natural resources, abundant land and salubrious climate—tended to reduce social conflict by holding out the hope of improving standards of living for most citizens most of the time. Politics in America has most often—though not always—been fought out on a relatively narrow middle ground of shared assumptions, values and symbols, lacking the intense, class-based politics that in France, for example, have caused three revolutions and nine different systems in the last 200 years.

U.S. institutions also have been free to develop without the distortions caused by fear of external enemies.

The importance of such natural advantages cannot be underestimated: Even with them, World War I, which brought widespread jailing of socialists and pacifists, World War II, with its internment of Japanese-Americans, and the McCarthy-era assaults on civil liberties in the 1950s all hinted at how fragile constitutional liberties can be when war or other threats convulse a nation.

At the same time, the nation's wealth and size have posed unusual problems for the constitutional system. When the Constitution was written, many doubted that a republic could survive except in a geographically small unit.

In devising a system for a nation of continental proportions, "what's at stake is the difference between trying to turn the Queen Mary around and trying to turn a rowboat," UC Berkeley political scientist Nelson W. Polsby said.

The image of the Queen Mary is exactly what most of the Constitution's current critics seize on. Just like an ocean liner, they claim, the constitutional system is simply too slow to respond to the accelerating pace of life in the age of instant global communications, instant food and instant nuclear annihilation.

The system has been strained still further, many political scientists say, by the decline of effective political parties, which helped for many years to knit Presidents and Congress together and thereby counterbalance the system's tendency toward fractionation.

For all those reasons, "the fragmentation of power institutionalized in the system of checks and balances poses very severe questions for the constitutional system," political scientist James McGregor Burns said.

Source of Stability

But the separation of powers, the inefficiency that so often makes government cumbersome, may, in fact, have been the greatest source of the Constitution's stability.

"Most of the founders believed the idea that, given power, men would abuse it," Degler said. Because of that belief, the governmental structure was built for distance, not for speed. To the Founding Fathers, a government that could handle day-to-day problems easily was less important than a government that could assure freedom and stability to generation after generation.

"Democratical states must always feel before they can see," George Washington wrote in 1785 to his Revolutionary War aide, the Marquis de Lafayette. "It is this that makes their governments slow, but the people will be right at last."

"The heterogeneity of the nation demands that we pay attention to the opinions of others," Polsby said. "It's a strength of our Constitution that a consensus is necessary to do large things."

The relationship between the Constitution and periods of national crisis has illustrated that point from the beginning.

While some states ratified the new charter quickly, in others the debates were long and arduous.

New Consensus

The unusual aspect of the debate, however, is that once it ended, so did serious opposition to the Constitution. Through the process of debate, a new consensus had been formed, and even those who had so strongly opposed the Constitution decided to accept it.

A more drawn-out, sometimes brutal process of consensus building centered on the nation's attempts, beginning in the late 19th Century, to strengthen the rights and protect the welfare of individuals by bridling the powers of massive corporations and their owners—"the malefactors of great wealth," as President Theodore Roosevelt called them.

As the Industrial Revolution transformed a country of villages, farms and small businesses into a nation of cities and giant factories, wrenching struggles took place—marked by political radicalism, riots, bloody confrontations, even anarchists' bombs.

Yet the period illustrates the way the system works for long-term stability, even at the price of near-term upheaval.

Over time, Congress and Presidents responded to the rising demand for economic and social reform; new laws were passed providing for collective bargaining of labor contracts, regulations of wages and hours, restrictions on child labor and similar reforms.

The establishment of an oversight role for the federal government in the realm of economics and commerce represented a dramatic change. Few nations have so fundamentally changed their economic systems except in a revolution or the aftermath of a war.

Universal Problems

"The underlying problems faced by human communities everywhere have to do with the intractable primordial differences that people have over race, religion and language," Berkeley's Polsby said.

"Religion was something they (the authors of the Constitution) solved right at the beginning," language has never yet become the serious social division for the United States that it is, for example, in Canada, and, he said, "we're on the road to doing something meaningful about race."

The Constitution no doubt will face challenges in the next 200 years, but having handled those three "primordial differences," perhaps it will continue to justify the boast of 19th-Century orator Sen. Henry Clay of Kentucky: "The Constitution of the United States was made not merely for the generation that then existed, but for posterity—unlimited, undefined, endless, perpetual posterity."

CHAPTER 3

The Constitutional Framework: Federalism and the Separation of Powers

THE FIRST PRINCIPLE: THE FEDERAL FRAMEWORK

See text p. 39 and 43

The federal structure of the American government has become increasingly difficult to discern as the powers of the national government have expanded in the past half century. Nonetheless, as the text points out, the concept of federalism lies at the heart of the American political system.

Early in the nation's history, the United States Supreme Court interpreted the powers of the national government expansively. The first Supreme Court case to directly address the scope of federal authority under the Constitution was McCulloch v. Maryland (1819). The facts, recited in the text, were straightforward: Congress created the Bank of the United States—to the dismay of many states who viewed the creation of a national bank as a threat to the operation of banks within their own state borders. As a result, when a branch of the Bank of the United States was opened in Maryland, that state attempted to limit the bank's ability to do business under a law that imposed taxes on all banks not chartered by the state.

In an opinion authored by Chief Justice Marshall, the Court considered two questions: whether Congress had the authority to create a national bank; and whether Maryland could in turn tax it. Marshall's answer to these two questions defends an expansive theory of implied powers for the national government and propounds the principle of national supremacy with an eloquence rarely found in judicial decisions.

McCulloch v. Maryland (1819)*

CHIEF JUSTICE JOHN MARSHALL delivered the opinion of the Court.

The first question made in the cause is, has Congress power to incorporate a bank? The power now contested was exercised by the first Congress elected under the present constitution. The bill for incorporating the Bank of the United States did not steal upon an unsuspecting legislature, and pass unobserved. Its principle was completely understood, and was opposed with equal zeal and ability. . . . In discussing this question, the counsel for the state of Maryland have deemed it of some importance, in the construction of the constitution, to consider that instrument not as emanating from the people, but as the act of sovereign and independent states. The powers of

*McCulloch v. Maryland, 17 U.S. 316, 1819.

the general government, it has been said, are delegated by the states, who alone are truly sovereign; and must be exercised in subordination to the states, who alone possess supreme dominion. . . . No political dreamer was ever wild enough to think of breaking down the lines which separate the states, and of compounding the American people into one common mass. Of consequence, when they act, they act in their states. But the measures they adopt do not, on that account, cease to be the measures of the people themselves, or become the measures of the state governments.

From these conventions the constitution derives its whole authority. The government proceeds directly from the people; is "ordained and established" in the name of the people; and is declared to be ordained, "in order to form a more perfect union, establish justice, insure domestic tranquility, and secure the blessings of liberty to themselves and to their posterity." The assent of the states, in their sovereign capacity, is implied in calling a convention, and thus submitting that instrument to the people. But the people were at perfect liberty to accept or reject it; and their act was final. It required not the affirmance, and could not be negatived, by the state governments. The constitution, when thus adopted, was of complete obligation, and bound the state sovereignties.

The government of the Union, then (whatever may be the influence of this fact on the case), is, emphatically, and truly, a government of the people. In form and in substance it emanates from them. Its powers are granted by them, and are to be exercised directly on them, and for their benefit.

This government is acknowledged by all to be one of enumerated powers. The principle, that it can exercise only the powers granted to it, is now universally admitted. But the question respecting the extent of the powers actually granted, is perpetually arising, and will probably continue to arise, as long as our system shall exist. The government of the United States though limited in its powers, is supreme; and its laws, when made in pursuance of the constitution, form the supreme law of the land, "anything in the constitution or laws of any state to the contrary notwithstanding." . . .

A constitution, to contain an accurate detail of all the subdivisions of which its great powers will admit, and of all the means by which they may be carried into execution, would partake of the prolixity of a legal code, and could scarcely be embraced by the human mind. It would probably never be understood by the public. Its nature, therefore, requires, that only its great outlines should be marked, its important objects designated, and the minor ingredients which compose those objects be deduced from the nature of the objects themselves. . . . in considering this question, then, we must never forget, that it is a constitution we are expounding.

Although, among the enumerated powers of government, we do not find the word "bank" or "incorporation," we find the great powers to lay and collect taxes; to borrow money; to regulate commerce; to declare and conduct a war; and to raise and support armies and navies. The sword and the purse, all the external relations, and no inconsiderable portion of the industry of the nation, are entrusted to its government. . . . [I]t may with great reason be contended, that a government, entrusted with such ample powers, on the due execution of which the happiness and prosperity of the nation so vitally depends, must also be entrusted with ample means for their execution. The power being given, it is the interest of the nation to facilitate its execution. It can never be their interest, and cannot be presumed to have been their intention, to clog and embarrass its execution by withholding the most appropriate means. . . . It is, then, the subject of fair inquiry, how far such means may be employed.

The government which has a right to do an act, and has imposed on it the duty of performing that act, must, according to the dictates of reason, be allowed to select the means. . . .

But the constitution of the United States has not left the right of Congress to employ the necessary means, for the execution of the powers conferred on the government, to general reasoning. To its enumeration of powers is added that of making "all laws which shall be necessary and proper, for carrying into execution the foregoing powers, and all other powers vested by this constitution, in the government of the United States, or in any department [or officer] thereof."

The counsel for the state of Maryland have urged various arguments, to prove that this clause . . . is really restrictive of the general right, which might otherwise be implied, of selecting means for executing the enumerated powers.

. . . [Maryland argues that] Congress is not empowered by it to make all laws, which may have relation to the powers conferred on the government, but such only as may be "necessary and proper" for carrying them into execution. The word "necessary" is considered as controlling the whole sentence, and as limiting the right to pass laws for the execution of the granted powers, to such as are indispensable, and without which the power would be nugatory. That it excludes the choice of means, and leaves to Congress, in each case, that only which is most direct and simple.

Is it true, that this is the sense in which the word "necessary" is always used? . . . We think it does not. If reference be had to its use, in the common affairs of the world, or in approved authors, we find that it frequently imports no more than that one thing is convenient, or useful, or essential to another. To employ the means necessary to an end, is generally understood as employing any means calculated to produce the end, and not as being confined to those single means, without which the end would be entirely unattainable.

Let this be done in the case under consideration. The subject is the execution of those great powers on which the welfare of a nation essentially depends. It must have been the intention of those who gave these powers, to insure, as far as human prudence could insure, their beneficial execution. This could not be done by confiding the choice of means to such narrow limits as not to leave it in the power of Congress to adopt any which might be appropriate, and which were conducive to the end. This provision is made in a constitution intended to endure for ages to come, and consequently, to be adapted to the various crises of human affairs. To have prescribed the means by which government should, in all future time, execute its powers, would have been to change, entirely, the character of the instrument, and give it the properties of a legal code. It would have been an unwise attempt to provide, by immutable rules, for exigencies which, if foreseen at all, must have been seen dimly, and which can be best provided for as they occur. To have declared that the best means shall not be used, but those alone without which the power given would be nugatory, would have been to deprive the legislature of the capacity to avail itself of experience, to exercise its reason, and to accommodate its legislation to circumstances. If we apply this principle of construction to any of the powers of the government, we shall find it so pernicious in its operation that we shall be compelled to discard it. . . .

We admit, as all must admit, that the powers of the government are limited, and that its limits are not to be transcended. But we think the sound construction of the constitution must allow to the national legislature that discretion, with respect to the means by which the powers it confers are to be carried into execution, which will enable that body to perform the high duties assigned to it, in the manner most beneficial to the people. Let the end be legitimate, let it be within the scope of the constitution, and all means which are appropriate, which are plainly adapted to that end, which are not prohibited, but consist with the letter and spirit of the constitution, are constitutional. . . .

It being the opinion of the court that the act incorporating the bank is constitutional, and that the power of establishing a branch in the state of Maryland might be properly exercised by the bank itself, we proceed to inquire: Whether the state of Maryland may, without violating the constitution, tax that branch?

That the power of taxation is one of vital importance; that it is retained by the states; that it is not abridged by the grant of a similar power to the government of the Union; that it is to be concurrently exercised by the two governments; are truths which have never been denied. But, such is the paramount character of the constitution that its capacity to withdraw any subject from the action of even this power, is admitted. . . . [T]he paramount character [of the Constitution] would seem to restrain, as it certainly may restrain, a state from such other exercise of this power as is in its nature incompatible with, and repugnant to, the constitutional laws of the Union. A law, absolutely repugnant to another, as entirely repeals that other as if express terms of repeal were used. . . .

This great principle is, that the constitution and the laws made in pursuance thereof are supreme; that they control the constitution and laws of the respective states, and cannot be controlled by them. From this, which may be almost termed an axiom, other propositions are adduced as corollaries, on the truth or error of which, and on their application to this case, the cause has been supposed to depend. These are, 1st. That a power to create implies a power to preserve. 2d. That a power to destroy, if wielded by a different hand, is hostile to, and incompatible with, these powers to create and to preserve. 3d. That where this repugnance exists, that authority which is supreme must control, not yield to that over which it is supreme.

. . . [T]axation is said to be an absolute power, which acknowledges no other limits than those expressly prescribed in the constitution, and like sovereign powers of every other description, is trusted to the discretion of those who use it. But the very terms of this argument admit that the sovereignty of the state, in the article of taxation itself, is subordinate to, and may be controlled by the constitution of the United States. How far it has been controlled by that instrument must be a question of construction. In making this construction, no principle not declared can be admissible, which would defeat the legitimate operations of a supreme government. . . .

All subjects over which the sovereign power of a state extends, are objects of taxation; but those over which it does not extend, are, upon the soundest principles, exempt from taxation. . . . The sovereignty of a state extends to everything which exists by its own authority, or is introduced by its permission; but does it extend to those means which are employed by Congress to carry into execution—powers conferred on that body by the people of the United States? We think it demonstrable that it does not. Those powers are not given by the people of a single state. They are given by the people of the United States, to a government whose laws, made in pursuance of the constitution, are declared to be supreme. Consequently, the people of a single state cannot confer a sovereignty which will extend over them.

If we apply the principle for which the state of Maryland contends, to the constitution generally, we shall find it capable of changing totally the character of that instrument. We shall find it capable of arresting all the measures of the government, and of prostrating it at the foot of the states. The American people have declared their constitution, and the laws made in pursuance thereof, to be supreme; but this principle would transfer the supremacy, in fact, to the states. If the controlling power of the states be established; if their supremacy as to taxation be acknowledged; what is to restrain their exercising this control in any shape they may please to give it? Their sovereignty is not confined to taxation. That is not the only mode in which it might be displayed. The question is, in truth, a question of supremacy; and if the right of the states to tax the means employed by the general government be conceded, the declaration that the constitution, and the laws made in pursuance thereof, shall be the supreme law of the land, is empty and unmeaning declamation. . . .

We are unanimously of opinion, that the law passed by the legislature of Maryland, imposing a tax on the Bank of the United States, is unconstitutional and void. This opinion does not deprive the states of any resources which they originally possessed. It does not extend to a tax paid by the real property of the bank, in common with other real property within the state, nor to a tax imposed on the interest which the citizens of Maryland may hold in this institution, in common with other property of the same description throughout the state. But this is a tax on the operations of the bank, and is, consequently, a tax on the operation of an instrument employed by the government of the Union to carry its powers into execution. Such a tax must be unconstitutional.

Reversed.

THE SECOND PRINCIPLE: THE SEPARATION OF POWERS

See text p. 52

The term "separation of powers," as the text points out, is something of a misnomer, because the American system is one of separate institutions sharing power, rather than a system in which each branch of government exercises separate powers. The idea of shared powers was central to the Federalists' conception of the constitutional framework.

In The Federalist No. 51, *Madison makes his strongest case for erecting a framework that will provide the motives for each branch to limit the powers of the others. It is in this paper that Madison makes some of his most famous statements about how to contrive a government that will control itself. "In framing a government which is to be administered by men over men, the great difficulty lies in this: you must first enable the government to control the governed; and in the next place oblige it to control itself." After discussing internal controls on the powers of each branch of government, Madison returns to his central theme, set out in* The Federalist No. 10: *that the strength of the federal system proposed by the Constitution lies in the fragmenting of power, not only among different branches of the national government but also between the state and federal governments and between different interest groups in the citizenry at large.*

James Madison
The Federalist No. 51[*]

To what expedient, then, shall we finally resort, for maintaining in practice the necessary partition of power among the several departments as laid down in the Constitution? The only answer that can be given is that as all these exterior provisions are found to be inadequate the defect must be supplied, by so contriving the interior structure of the government as that its several constituent parts may, by their mutual relations, be the means of keeping each other in their proper places. Without presuming to undertake a full development of this important idea I will hazard a few general observations which may perhaps place it in a clearer light, and enable us to form a more correct judgment of the principles and structure of the government planned by the convention.

In order to lay a due foundation for that separate and distinct exercise of the different powers of government, which to a certain extent is admitted on all hands to be essential to the preservation of liberty, it is evident that each department should have a will of its own; and consequently should be so constituted that the members of each should have as little agency as possible in the appointment of the members of the others. Were this principle rigorously adhered to, it would require that all the appointments for the supreme executive, legislative, and judiciary magistracies should be drawn from the same fountain of authority, the people, through channels having

[*]James Madison, *The Federalist No. 51*, ed. Clinton Rossiter (New York: NAL, 1961).

no communication whatever with one another. Perhaps such a plan of constructing the several departments would be less difficult in practice than it may in contemplation appear. Some difficulties, however, and some additional expense would attend the execution of it. Some deviations, therefore, from the principle must be admitted. In the constitution of the judiciary department in particular, it might be inexpedient to insist rigorously on the principle: first, because peculiar qualifications being essential in the members, the primary consideration ought to be to select that mode of choice which best secures these qualifications; second, because the permanent tenure by which the appointments are held in that department must soon destroy all sense of dependence on the authority conferring them.

It is equally evident that the members of each department should be as little dependent as possible on those of the others for the emoluments annexed to their offices. Were the executive magistrate, or the judges, not independent of the legislature in this particular, their independence in every other would be merely nominal.

But the great security against a gradual concentration of the several powers in the same department consists in giving to those who administer each department the necessary constitutional means and personal motives to resist encroachments of the others. The provision for defense must in this, as in all other cases, be made commensurate to the danger of attack. Ambition must be made to counteract ambition. The interest of the man must be connected with the constitutional rights of the place. It may be a reflection on human nature that such devices should be necessary to control the abuses of government. But what is government itself but the greatest of all reflections on human nature? If men were angels, no government would be necessary. If angels were to govern men, neither external nor internal controls on government would be necessary. In framing a government which is to be administered by men over men, the great difficulty lies in this: you must first enable the government to control the governed; and in the next place oblige it to control itself. A dependence on the people is, no doubt, the primary control on the government; but experience has taught mankind the necessity of auxiliary precautions.

This policy of supplying, by opposite and rival interests, the defect of better motives, might be traced through the whole system of human affairs, private as well as public. We see it particularly displayed in all the subordinate distributions of power, where the constant aim is to divide and arrange the several offices in such a manner as that each may be a check on the other—that the private interest of every individual may be a sentinel over the public rights. These inventions of prudence cannot be less requisite in the distribution of the supreme powers of the State.

But it is not possible to give to each department an equal power of self-defense. In republican government, the legislative authority necessarily predominates. The remedy for this inconveniency is to divide the legislature into different branches; and to render them, by different modes of election and different principles of action, as little connected with each other as the nature of their common functions and their common dependence on the society will admit. It may even be necessary to guard against dangerous encroachments by still further precautions. As the weight of the legislative authority requires that it should be thus divided, the weakness of the executive may require, on the other hand, that it should be fortified. An absolute negative on the legislature appears, at first view, to be the natural defense with which the executive magistrate should be armed. But perhaps it would be neither altogether safe nor alone sufficient. On ordinary occasions it might not be exerted with the requisite firmness, and on extraordinary occasions it might be perfidiously abused. May not this defect of an absolute negative be supplied by some qualified connection between this weaker branch of the stronger department, by which the latter may be led to support the constitutional rights of the former, without being too much detached from the rights of its own department?

If the principles on which these observations are founded be just, as I persuade myself they are, and they be applied as a criterion to the several State constitutions, and to the federal Constitution, it will be found that if the latter does not perfectly correspond with them, the former are infinitely less able to bear such a test.

There are, moreover, two considerations particularly applicable to the federal system of America, which place that system in a very interesting point of view.

First. In a single republic, all the power surrendered by the people is submitted to the administration of a single government; and the usurpations are guarded against by a division of the government into distinct and separate departments. In the compound republic of America, the power surrendered by the people is first divided between two distinct governments, and then the portion allotted to each subdivided among distinct and separate departments. Hence a double security arises to the rights of the people. The different governments will control each other, at the same time that each will be controlled by itself.

Second. It is of great importance in a republic not only to guard the society against the oppression of its rulers, but to guard one part of the society against the injustice of the other part. Different interests necessarily exist in different classes of citizens. If a majority be united by a common interest, the rights of the minority will be insecure. There are but two methods of providing against this evil: the one by creating a will in the community independent of the majority—that is, of the society itself; the other, by comprehending in the society so many separate descriptions of citizens as will render an unjust combination of a majority of the whole very improbable, if not impracticable. The first method prevails in all governments possessing an hereditary or self-appointed authority. This, at best, is but a precarious security; because a power independent of the society may as well espouse the unjust views of the major as the rightful interests of the minor party, and may possibly be turned against both parties. The second method will be exemplified in the federal republic of the United States. Whilst all authority in it will be derived from and dependent on the society, the society itself will be broken into so many parts, interests and classes of citizens, that the rights of individuals, or of the minority, will be in little danger from interested combinations of the majority. In a free government the security for civil rights must be the same as that for religious rights. It consists in the one case in the multiplicity of interests, and in the other in the multiplicity of sects. The degree of security in both cases will depend on the number of interests and sects; and this may be presumed to depend on the extent of country and number of people comprehended under the same government. This view of the subject must particularly recommend a proper federal system to all the sincere and considerate friends of republican government, since it shows that in exact proportion as the territory of the Union may be formed into more circumscribed Confederacies, or States, oppressive combinations of a majority will be facilitated; the best security, under the republican forms, for the rights of every class of citizen, will be diminished; and consequently the stability and independence of some member of the government, the only other security, must be proportionally increased. Justice is the end of government. It is the end of civil society. It ever has been and ever will be pursued until it be obtained, or until liberty be lost in the pursuit. In a society under the forms of which the stronger faction can readily unite and oppress the weaker, anarchy may as truly be said to reign as in a state of nature, where the weaker individual is not secured against the violence of the stronger; and as, in the latter state, even the stronger individuals are prompted, by the uncertainty of their condition, to submit to a government which may protect the weak as well as themselves; so, in the former state, will the more powerful factions or parties be gradually induced, by a like motive, to wish for a government which will protect all parties, the weaker as well as the more powerful. It can be little doubted that if the State of Rhode Island was separated from the Confederacy and left to itself, the insecurity of rights under the popular form of government within such narrow limits would be displayed by such reiterated oppressions of factious majorities that some power altogether independent of the people would soon be called for by the voice of the very factions whose misrule had proved the necessity of it. In the extended republic of the United States, and among the great variety of interests, parties, and sects which it embraces, a coalition of a majority of the whole society could seldom take place on any other principles than those of justice and the general good; whilst there being thus less danger to a minor from the will of a major party, there must be less pretext, also, to provide for the security of the former, by introducing into the government a will not dependent on the latter, or, in other words, a will independent of the society itself. It is no less certain than it is important, notwithstanding the contrary opinions which have been entertained, that the larger the society, provided it lie within a practicable sphere, the more duly capable it will be of self-government. And happily for the *republican cause,* the practicable sphere may be carried to a very great extent by a judicious modification and mixture of the *federal principle.*

PUBLIUS

CHANGING THE FRAMEWORK

See text p. 59

From time to time, there are movements calling for a constitutional convention to amend the Constitution on a variety of issues. In recent years, proponents of the Equal Rights Amendment have attempted to convene a constitutional congress to consider gender equality issues; opponents of abortion rights have sought constitutional recognition of a fetal right to life; citizens concerned about the country's dismal domestic financial situation have rallied for a balanced budget amendment; and the Supreme Court's decision invalidating statutes prohibiting the desecration of the United States flag prompted a call for a flag protection amendment.

Arguments for and against a constitutional convention abound: proponents cite Thomas Jefferson's arguments that a constitution should be reconsidered at relatively frequent intervals, while opponents express fear that any convention would "run away" from its original premises, with the result that we might find ourselves stripped of significant rights.

In the following article published during the bicentenary of the Constitution, Mary Frances Berry, a professor at the University of Pennsylvania and author of Why ERA Failed, *discusses the arguments surrounding the calling of a constitutional convention. Barry concludes that the limitations upon the calling of such a convention are ultimately well-considered, and outweigh the potential benefits that such a reconsideration might produce.*

Mary Frances Berry
"Amending the Constitution: How Hard It Is to Change"*

I worked hard for many years to change the United States Constitution— and I failed. Like so many others, I wanted the Constitution to assert the principle of equal rights without regard to gender. I had high hopes for the equal rights amendment, but I knew from the beginning that a constitutional amendment is difficult to obtain. So I was not surprised when the measure failed.

I was disappointed at the defeat but no less glad that the Constitution is so hard to change. I appreciate even more deeply now the obstacles the framers of the Constitution put in the way of the amendment process. The reason is simple: even though my efforts were unsuccessful, and there is no E.R.A. in the Constitution, there is also no official school prayer amendment or anti-abortion amendment.

Article V of the Constitution—the amending article—plays no favorites. It disciplines even the most ardent proponents to its commands and occasionally turns opponents into allies. There is an irony of sorts, for instance, that Phyllis Schlafly, who did so much to stop the E.R.A., and I now find ourselves in agreement in opposing a constitutional convention that has lately been proposed to consider a balanced budget amendment. I'll get to our unlikely alliance a little later.

The makers of the Constitution wanted to create a firm basis for the exercise of governmental power. However, they were wise enough to know that if they made their document too rigid, if they wrote it so that it could not be revised to suit future times and events, they were inviting future revolution. They would be creating a situation in which the only method to effect change would be to cast aside the Constitution itself. As George Mason noted at the 1787 convention, changes would be necessary, and it would be "better to provide for them in an easy, regular and constitutional way than to trust to chance and violence."

So they made it open to change—but not open to change without great effort. James Madison was among those who warned against making things too easy. It was important, he said, to guard "against that extreme facility which would render the Constitution too mutable." For if it could be altered easily, the Constitution would be mere temporary law, not a document for the ages.

The great idea in Article V is that change requires two elements: consensus and necessity. There must be substantive national agreement, as well as agreement in most of the states, that an urgent problem exists that cannot be remedied by the courts, legislatures or Congress, and which can be solved only if the Constitution is changed.

The public expression of consensus and necessity that Article V requires can come to light in two ways.

In the first, an amendment may be proposed by a two-thirds vote in each house of Congress. The approved amendment then must be ratified by majority votes in the legislatures or conventions of three-fourths of the states before it can become part of the Constitution. The second way is that, if two-thirds of the states ask for a constitutional convention to consider amendments, Congress should be obliged to call one. Any changes such a convention passes must then be ratified by three-fourths of the states. This second path has, so far, gone untried in United States history: no constitutional convention, since the first one in 1787, has ever been called.

Meanwhile, the first route to constitutional amendments has been well traveled. Almost 10,000 of them have been proposed in the Congress since Article V became law. Only 26 have been ratified. Of these, the Bill of Rights, the 13th, 14th and 15th Amendments resulting from the Civil War, and the 19th, permitting women to vote, remedied major defects in the original document. Most of the others smoothed out procedural difficulties. One, Prohibition, was the result of an artificial consensus and was soon repealed.

Six other amendments have been approved by Congress but not ratified by the states. These include the E.R.A., an amendment to prohibit child labor and an amendment that would have given the District of Columbia a voting member of the House and two Senators. It is easy to see why so many amendments have been proposed in Congress.

For politicians, advocating solution by amendment is a convenient response to hot political problems. For instance, whenever the Supreme Court makes a widely publicized decision on a controversial issue, there are Congressional proposals to limit the power of the Justices. The legislator can thereby show concerned voters back home that action, however ineffectual, has been taken, something has been done.

It is clear that a strong effort to gain an amendment can influence government even when it fails. It acts as a brooding omnipresence in the sky, signaling to politicians that they must act. Some proposals that fail as amendments result in legislation. Proposed amendments reflecting public opposition to busing for desegregation purposes led to a 1972 education law restricting Federal involvement in busing. More recently, official school prayer amendment proposals led to the passage of the Equal Access Act of 1984, which provides that religious activities may not be excluded from among any extracurricular activities allowed on a public school's premises. Instead of passing an amendment requiring the balancing of the Federal budget, Congress in 1985 tried the expedient of enacting the Gramm-Rudman-Hollings Act to achieve a balanced budget in stages. In each of these cases, the stringent requirements for ratification of an amendment have prevented changing the Constitution. But politicians who needed to do so could show constituents that they were responding to their concerns.

In the case of an amendment calling for a balanced budget, however, apprehensions about the Federal deficit have created a feeling of necessity that may not be satisfied by legislation. The issue may well bring about the first constitutional convention since 1787. Already, 32 states (only two fewer than required) have called for a convention to consider a budget-balancing amendment, and President Reagan supports the idea. Proponents of the convention say it would be a fast, easy assembly that would simply meet, adopt an amendment, send it to the states to ratify, and then go home.

Those who oppose the convention, including myself, are not sure. Ordinarily disparate forces such as Phyllis Schlafly's Eagle Forum, the National Organization for Women, the American Civil Liberties Union and the John Birch Society are all opposed, because they fear the convention has the potential of putting the Constitution at risk.

The fact is, nothing in the language of Article V limits the subjects to be considered at a constitutional convention, nothing establishes rules of procedure to be followed or precludes scrapping the entire Constitution. The sole convention we have had, in 1787, was called only for the purpose of amending our first constitution, the Articles of Confederation. But the Founding Fathers discarded the Articles altogether and drafted a new document. They even modified the ratification procedure to insure success. That could happen again.

The purpose of Article V's convention provision is to make it possible for amendments to be proposed that Congress does not want proposed, and it would be illogical indeed to assume that Congress could bind a convention's agenda. Even if the Congress decided to call a convention for the sole purpose of proposing amendments to balance the budget, and even if the convention agreed to this overall goal, the gathering would still have great freedom. The participants might decide that Congressional budgetary authority should be limited to support for the national defense. They could delete support for the general welfare from the Constitution, thus precluding such items as Social Security, Medicaid and Medicare. They could decide to amend Congressional power to regulate commerce, which now allows for such activities as environmental regulation, labor regulation and antitrust enforcement. This would, after all, abolish a whole series of Federal agencies and decrease the budget.

But if the participants decided to ignore any instructions controlling their agenda—and who could stop them—they could decide to ban abortion and void the First Amendment, require the government to provide jobs, housing and education for all Americans, or any other proposal that gained approval by whatever majority they decided to require. Any proposals that gained ratification by three-fourths of the states would become part of the nation's fundamental law. However, the convention might decide, as the original convention did, to change the mode of ratification, perhaps to require only a simple majority of the states. Given this very real possibility for wide-ranging action and unprecedented mischief, the pertinent question is not whether we want a constitutional convention to require a balanced budget, but whether we want to risk a convention at all.

I am tempted by the argument that believers in pure democracy and majoritarian rule ought to favor a convention in order to let the people reign and make whatever decisions they choose. However, the Founding Fathers created not pure democracy, but a republican form of government in which the people govern through their representatives and with checks and balances, including a check on the majority's impulses.

I am reminded in my service on the United States Commission on Civil Rights, whenever issues such as voting rights or affirmative action come before us, of how dangerous it would be to define civil rights by the will of an administration elected by a political majority. In our system of government, the rights of all, liberals and conservatives, people of all races and both sexes, the majority and minority groups, are accorded constitutional protection.

The amendment process set up in Article V allows our government to adapt itself to social change. At the same time, it gives us a check against beliefs that may be strongly held but are not widely approved. Because our Constitution can be amended, we can repair tears in our social fabric and try different strategies and tactics to resolve problems. Because our Constitution cannot be amended easily, we can preserve the stability and continuity that lasting republican government requires.

CHAPTER 4

The Constitution and the Individual: The Bill of Rights, Civil Liberties, and Civil Rights

CIVIL LIBERTIES: NATIONALIZING THE BILL OF RIGHTS

See text p. 68

The declaration made in Barron v. Baltimore *(1833) that citizenship had a dual aspect—state and national—set the terms of the Supreme Court's interpretation of the Bill of Rights for nearly 150 years. The reasoning of the case proved persuasive even after the adoption of the Fourteenth Amendment, as the federal courts refused to extend the protections of the federal Constitution to citizens aggrieved by the actions of state or local governments.*

Barron v. Baltimore (1833)*

[Barron brought suit in a federal court claiming that the city of Baltimore had appropriated his property for a public purpose without paying him just compensation. He asserted that the Fifth Amendment to the Constitution operated as a constraint upon both state and federal governments.]

CHIEF JUSTICE JOHN MARSHALL delivered the opinion of the court.

. . . The question presented is, we think, of great importance, but not of much difficulty. The constitution was ordained and established by the people of the United States for themselves, for their own government, and not for the government of the individual states. Each state established a constitution for itself, and in that constitution, provided such limitations and restrictions on the powers of its particular government, as its judgment dictated. The people of the United States framed such a government for the United States as they supposed best adapted to their situation and best calculated to promote their interests. The powers they conferred on this government were to be exercised by itself; and the limitations on power, if expressed in general terms, are naturally, and, we think, necessarily, applicable to the government created by the instrument. They are limitations of power granted in the instrument itself; not of distinct governments, framed by different persons and for different purposes.

If these propositions be correct, the fifth amendment must be understood as restraining the power of the general government, not as applicable

*Barron v. Baltimore, 32 U.S. 243, 1833.

to the states. In their several constitutions, they have imposed such restrictions on their respective governments, as their own wisdom suggested; such as they deemed most proper for themselves. It is a subject on which they judge exclusively, and with which others interfere no further than they are supposed to have a common interest. . . .

Had the people of the several states, or any of them, required changes in their constitutions; had they required additional safe-guards to liberty from the apprehended encroachments of their particular governments; the remedy was in their own hands, and could have been applied by themselves. A convention could have been assembled by the discontented state, and the required improvements could have been made by itself.

. . . Had congress engaged in the extraordinary occupation of improving the constitutions of the several states, by affording the people additional protection from the exercise of power by their own governments, in matters which concerned themselves alone, they would have declared this purpose in plain and intelligible language.

But it is universally understood, it is a part of the history of the day, that the great revolution which established the constitution of the United States, was not effected without immense opposition. Serious fears were extensively entertained, that those powers which the patriot statesmen, who then watched over the interests of our country, deemed essential to union, and to the attainment of those unvaluable objects for which union was sought, might be exercised in a manner dangerous to liberty. In almost every convention by which the constitution was adopted, amendments to guard against the abuse of power were recommended. These amendments demanded security against the apprehended encroachments of the general government—not against those of the local governments. In compliance with a sentiment thus generally expressed, to quiet fears thus extensively entertained, amendments were proposed by the required majority in congress, and adopted by the states. These amendments contain no expression indicating an intention to apply them to the state governments. This court cannot so apply them.

We are of opinion, that the provision in the fifth amendment to the constitution, declaring that private property shall not be taken for public use, without just compensation, is intended solely as a limitation on the exercise of power by the government of the United States, and is not applicable to the legislation of the states. We are, therefore, of opinion, that there is no repugnancy between the several acts of the general assembly of Maryland, given in evidence by the defendants at the trial of this cause, in the court of that state, and the constitution of the United States. This court, therefore, has no jurisdiction of the cause, and it is dismissed.

This cause came on to be heard, on the transcript of the record from the court of appeals for the western shore of the state of Maryland, and was argued by counsel: On consideration whereof, it is the opinion of this court, that there is no repugnancy between the several acts of the general assembly of Maryland, given in evidence by the defendants at the trial of this cause in the court of that state, and the constitution of the United States; whereupon,

it is ordered and adjudged by this court, that this writ of error be and the
same is hereby dismissed, for the want of jurisdiction.

See text p. 74

*One of the most significant changes in constitutional interpretation in the last
twenty-five years has been the Court's willingness to look beyond the explicit language
of the Bill of Rights to find unenumerated rights, such as the right to privacy. In discovering such rights, the Court has engaged in what is known as substantive due process
analysis—defining and articulating fundamental rights—distinct from its efforts to define
the scope of procedural due process, when it decides what procedures the state and
federal governments must follow to be fair in their treatment of citizens. The Court's
move into the substantive due process area has generated much of the political discussion over the proper role of the Court in constitutional interpretation, as discussed in
further detail in Chapter 9 of your textbook.*

The case that has been the focal point for this debate is Roe v. Wade, *the 1972 case
which held that a woman's right to privacy protected her decision to have an abortion.
The right to privacy in matters relating to contraception and childbearing had been
recognized in the 1965 decision of* Griswold v. Connecticut, *and was extended in
subsequent decisions culminating in* Roe. *The theoretical issue of concern here relates
back to the incorporation issue: Should the Supreme Court be able to prohibit the states
not only from violating the express guarantees contained in the Bill of Rights, but its
implied guarantees as well?*

Roe v. Wade (1973)*

*[Texas law prohibited abortions except for "the purpose of saving the life of the
mother." Plaintiff challenged the constitutionality of the statute, claiming that it
infringed upon her substantive due process right to privacy.]*

JUSTICE BLACKMUN delivered the opinion of the Court.

. . . [We] forthwith acknowledge our awareness of the sensitive and emotional nature of the abortion controversy, of the vigorous opposing views,
and the deep and seemingly absolute convictions that the subject inspires.
One's philosophy, one's experiences, one's exposure to the raw edges of
human existence, one's religious training, one's attitudes toward life and
family and their values, and the moral standards one establishes and seeks
to observe, are all likely to affect one's thinking [about] abortion. In addition, population growth, pollution, poverty, and racial overtones tend to
complicate and not to simplify the problem. Our task, of course, is to resolve
the issue by constitutional measurement, free of emotion and of predilec-

*Roe v. Wade, 410 U.S. 113, 1973.

tion. We seek earnestly to do this, and, because we do, we have inquired into, and in this opinion place some emphasis upon, medical and medical-legal history and what that history reveals about man's attitudes toward the abortion procedure over the centuries. . . .

[The Court here reviewed ancient and contemporary attitudes toward abortion, observing that restrictive laws date primarily from the late nineteenth century. The Court also reviewed the possible state interests in restricting abortions, including discouraging illicit sexual conduct, limiting access to a hazardous medical procedure, and the states' general interests in protecting fetal life. The Court addressed only the third interest as a current legitimate interest of the state.]

. . . The Constitution does not explicitly mention any right of privacy. In a line of decisions, however, . . . the Court has recognized that a right of personal privacy, or a guarantee of certain areas or zones of privacy, does exist under the Constitution. . . . This right of privacy, whether it be founded in the Fourteenth Amendment's concept of personal liberty and restrictions upon state action, as we feel it is, or, as the District Court determined, in the Ninth Amendment's reservation of rights to the people, is broad enough to encompass a woman's decision whether or not to terminate her pregnancy. The detriment that the State would impose upon the pregnant woman by denying this choice altogether is apparent. Specific and direct harm medically diagnosable even in early pregnancy may be involved. Maternity, or additional offspring, may force upon the woman a distressful life and future. Psychological harm may be imminent. Mental and physical health may be taxed by child care. There is also the distress, for all concerned, associated with the unwanted child, and there is the problem of bringing a child into a family already unable, psychologically and otherwise, to care for it. In other cases, as in this one, the additional difficulties and continuing stigma of unwed motherhood may be involved. All these are factors the woman and her responsible physician necessarily will consider in consultation.

On the basis of elements such as these, appellants and some amici argue that the woman's right is absolute and that she is entitled to terminate her pregnancy at whatever time, in whatever way, and for whatever reason she alone chooses. With this we do not agree. Appellants' arguments that Texas either has no valid interest at all in regulating the abortion decision, or no interest strong enough to support any limitation upon the woman's sole determination, is unpersuasive. The Court's decisions recognizing a right of privacy also acknowledge that some state regulation in areas protected by that right is appropriate. As noted above, a State may properly assert important interests in safeguarding health, in maintaining medical standards, and in protecting potential life. At some point in pregnancy, these respective interests become sufficiently compelling to sustain regulation of the factors that govern the abortion decision. The privacy right involved, therefore, cannot be said to be absolute. In fact, it is not clear to us that the claim asserted by some amici that one has an unlimited right to do with one's body as one pleases bears a close relationship to the right of privacy previously articulated in the Court's decisions. . . .

We therefore conclude that the right of personal privacy includes the abortion decision, but that this right is not unqualified and must be considered against state interests in regulation.

Where certain "fundamental rights" are involved, the Court has held that regulation limiting these rights may be justified only by a "compelling state interest," and that legislative enactments must be narrowly drawn to express only the legitimate state interests at stake.

. . . The District Court held that the appellee failed to meet his burden of demonstrating that the Texas statute's infringement upon Roe's rights was necessary to support a compelling state interest. . . . Appellee argues that the State's determination to recognize and protect prenatal life from and after conception constitutes a compelling state interest. As noted above, we do not agree fully with either formulation.

The appellee and certain amici argue that the fetus is a "person" within the language and meaning of the Fourteenth Amendment. In support of this they outline at length and in detail the well-known facts of fetal development. If this suggestion of personhood is established, the appellant's case, of course, collapses, for the fetus' right to life is then guaranteed specifically by the Amendment. The appellant conceded as much on reargument. On the other hand, the appellee conceded on reargument that no case could be cited that holds that a fetus is a person within the meaning of the Fourteenth Amendment.

The Constitution does not define "person" in so many words. Section 1 of the Fourteenth Amendment contains three references to "person." The first, in defining "citizens," speaks of "persons born or naturalized in the United States." The word also appears both in the Due Process Clause and in the Equal Protection Clause. "Person" is used in other places in the Constitution. . . . But in nearly all these instances, the use of the word is such that it has application only postnatally. None indicates, with any assurance, that it has any possible pre-natal application.

All this, together with our observation, that throughout the major portion of the 19th century prevailing legal abortion practices were far freer than they are today, persuades us that the word "person," as used in the Fourteenth Amendment, does not include the unborn.

. . . The pregnant woman cannot be isolated in her privacy. She carries an embryo and, later, a fetus, if one accepts the medical definitions of the developing young in the human uterus. . . . The situation therefore is inherently different from marital intimacy, or bedroom possession of obscene material, or marriage, or procreation, or education, with which [earlier cases defining the right to privacy] were concerned. As we have intimated above, it is reasonable and appropriate for a State to decide that at some point in time another interest, that of health of the mother or that of potential human life, becomes significantly involved. The woman's privacy is no longer sole and any right of privacy she possesses must be measured accordingly.

Texas urges that, apart from the Fourteenth Amendment, life begins at conception and is present throughout pregnancy, and that, therefore, the

State has a compelling interest in protecting that life from and after conception. We need not resolve the difficult question of when life begins. When those trained in the respective disciplines of medicine, philosophy, and theology are unable to arrive at any consensus, the judiciary, at this point in the development of man's knowledge, is not in a position to speculate as to the answer.

. . . In view of all this, we do not agree that, by adopting one theory of life, Texas may override the rights of the pregnant woman that are at stake. We repeat, however, that the State does have an important and legitimate interest in preserving and protecting the health of the pregnant woman, whether she be a resident of the State or a nonresident who seeks medical consultation and treatment there, and that it has still *another* important and legitimate interest in protecting the potentiality of human life. These interests are separate and distinct. Each grows in substantiality as the woman approaches term and, at a point during pregnancy, each becomes "compelling."

With respect to the State's important and legitimate interest in the health of the mother, the "compelling" point, in the light of present medical knowledge, is at approximately the end of the first trimester. This is so because of the now established medical fact . . . that until the end of the first trimester mortality in abortion is less than mortality in normal childbirth. It follows that, from and after this point, a State may regulate the abortion procedure to the extent that the regulation reasonably relates to the preservation and protection of maternal health. Examples of permissible state regulation in this area are requirements as to the qualifications of the person who is to perform the abortion; as to the licensure of that person; as to the facility in which the procedure is to be performed, that is, whether it must be a hospital or may be a clinic or some other place of less-than-hospital status; as to the licensing of the facility; and the like.

This means, on the other hand, that, for the period of pregnancy prior to this "compelling" point, the attending physician, in consultation with his patient, is free to determine, without regulation by the State, that in his medical judgment the patient's pregnancy should be terminated. If that decision is reached, the judgment may be effectuated by an abortion free of interference by the State.

With respect to the State's important and legitimate interest in potential life, the "compelling" point is at viability. This is so because the fetus then presumably has the capability of meaningful life outside the mother's womb. State regulation protective of fetal life after viability thus has both logical and biological justifications. If the State is interested in protecting fetal life after viability, it may go so far as to proscribe abortion during that period except when it is necessary to preserve the life or health of the mother.

Measured against these standards, the Texas Penal Code, in restricting legal abortions to those "procured or attempted by medical advice for the purpose of saving the life of the mother," sweeps too broadly. The statute makes no distinction between abortions performed early in pregnancy and

those performed later, and it limits to a single reason, "saving" the mother's life, the legal justification for the procedure. The statute, therefore, cannot survive the constitutional attack made upon it here. . . .
Reversed.

See text p. 75

Over the last decade, the appointment of Justices O'Connor, Scalia, Kennedy, Souter, and Thomas by Presidents Ford, Reagan, and Bush, have shifted the balance of power on the Supreme Court; together with Chief Justice Rehnquist and the less consistently categorized Justice White, these justices constitute a strong conservative bloc. While positions among the justices vary on specific issues, the Court as a whole has changed its voice. There is a great deal more deference being accorded to state legislative schemes than in the last thirty years, and rights that seemed to be firmly in place—primarily because they had not been overturned by the Burger Court—are now open to question. The following article points out that the Court has now completed a transition, and that there may now be an open season on the rights articulated during the Warren and Burger eras.

Linda Greenhouse
"Conservatively Speaking, It's an Activist Supreme Court"*

In approach as well as content, the Supreme Court's sweeping decision [in late May 1991] upholding Federal restrictions on abortion counseling brought the Court itself into sharp focus. Nearly five years into the tenure of Chief Justice William H. Rehnquist and 10 months after the retirement of Justice William J. Brennan Jr., the Supreme Court is no longer in transition. It has become the Court it will most likely be for the next generation.

A series of rulings this term has made clear that this is a Court with an activist's appetite and reach. Increasingly reflecting the style and aims of the Chief Justice, the Court is not interested in taking tentative or incremental steps, in deferring hard questions, in playing the passive role usually identified with the label "judicial restraint."

Whether intentionally or not, Justice Sandra Day O'Connor took the Court's measure in a blandly worded, three-paragraph opinion. . . . She was dissenting from Chief Justice Rehnquist's opinion for a 5-to-4 majority in *Rust* v. *Sullivan*, which upheld Federal regulations barring all discussion of abortion in family-planning clinics that receive Federal money. "It is a fundamental rule of judicial restraint," she said, quoting a series of Supreme Court decisions dating to 1885, "that this Court will not reach constitutional questions in advance of the necessity of deciding them."

A preliminary question in the case was whether the challenged regulations were authorized by the 1970 Federal law that established the family-planning program. The regulations, issued by the Reagan Administration in 1988, represented a sharp administrative departure, replacing rules that for the first 18 years of the statute's life had in fact required clinic employees to provide information about abortion.

Justice O'Connor's Dissent

If the Court had found that the regulations were inconsistent with Congressional intent, that would have ended the case, without requiring the Court to address the free-speech questions that formed the heart of the constitutional challenge. The majority acknowledged that the 1970 law was ambiguous, but said that the new regulations were at least a plausible interpretation of what Congress intended. While conceding that the constitutional arguments had some force, the Court went on to declare the regulations constitutional in all respects. Justices Byron R. White, Antonin Scalia, Anthony M. Kennedy and David H. Souter joined this opinion.

In her dissent, Justice O'Connor said that the Court should not have addressed the constitutional issues at all. She invoked a line of Supreme Court precedents that counsel restraint in just such a situation, holding that when one possible interpretation of a statute raises serious constitutional problems, the Court should avoid the difficulties by using a different interpretation. Applied in this case, Justice O'Connor said, the rule meant that regulations that were both constitutionally problematic and not explicitly required by the terms of the statute should be deemed unauthorized; if that conclusion was incorrect, she said, "Congress retains the power to force the constitutional question by legislating more explicitly."

Chief Justice Rehnquist, however, has shown little patience with Congress. Last year, he publicly urged Congress to amend the Federal habeas corpus statute, which gives the Federal courts jurisdiction to hear state prisoners' constitutional challenges to their convictions or sentences. The Chief Justice wanted strict limits placed on an inmate's ability to bring second or "successive" petitions.

The bill that he supported did not pass. But the Supreme Court accomplished much the same objective in a case this term. In a 6-to-3 decision, *McCleskey* v. *Zant,* the Court reinterpreted an aspect of habeas corpus law known as the "abuse of the writ" doctrine to bar almost all petitions after the initial one. The *McCleskey* decision was written by Justice Kennedy, who said the limitation was needed to "vindicate the state's interest in the finality of its criminal judgments." A dissent by Justices Thurgood Marshall, Harry A. Blackmun and John Paul Stevens said the Court was improperly seeking to "function as a backup legislature."

The question in another case [in the 1991] term, *Arizona* v. *Fulminante*, was whether a defendant's confession was coerced and, if so, whether it could still be admitted as evidence in his trial. In an opinion by Justice White, the Court ruled that the confession was coerced and that it had to be kept out of the trial because it was not "harmless," that is, it supplied proof of guilt that could not be derived from the prosecution's other evidence.

Ordinarily, that conclusion would have ended the case. But Chief Justice Rehnquist, over Justice White's dissent, went further. He put together a 5-to-4 majority for a separate section of the opinion, ruling for the first time that coerced confessions can sometimes be admitted at trial as "harmless error." Since the majority of the Court held that the use of this confession was not harmless, the added declaration had no bearing on the outcome of this particular case. It was the sort of gratuitous advisory opinion that judicial conservatives have long condemned.

There is a distinct sense at the Court now of completing long-held agendas. The Chief Justice and his allies appear to believe that for much of their adult lifetimes, the Court went seriously astray in ways that can finally be rectified, by conventionally conservative means if possible, by activist methods if necessary.

At his confirmation hearing last fall, David Souter seemed to take pains to distance himself from this stance. He indicated that while he might not have chosen many of the Warren Court's expansive departures, he now regarded that legacy not as an aberration but as part of the law's modern fabric. But if he is troubled by the developments this term, he has not indicated so either by his vote or by his voice. If his silent assent indicates that he is comfortable in the Rehnquist camp, it is hard to see what obstacles remain in the way of the Court's activist course.

CIVIL RIGHTS

See text p. 77

Brown v. Board of Education *(1954) was a momentous opinion, invalidating the system of apartheid that had been established under* Plessy v. Ferguson *(1896). As the text points out, however, the constitutional pronouncement only marked the beginning of the struggle for racial equality, as federal courts got more and more deeply involved in trying to prod recalcitrant state and local governments into taking steps to end racial inequalities. The* Brown *decision follows. The second reading is an excerpt from the appendix to the fifty-page school busing decision issued twenty-one years later by Judge Garrity in* Morgan v. Kerrigan *(1975) in the continuing effort to desegregate the Boston school system. Repeated here are only a few of the paragraphs from the court's plan to revamp the school system. The* Morgan v. Kerrigan *decision illustrates the extent to which the courts have found themselves enmeshed in such intricacies as running a school system in their efforts to have their decisions enforced.*

Brown v. Board of Education (1954)*

[The Brown *case involved appeals from several states. In each case, the plaintiffs had been denied access to public schools designated only for white children under a variety of state laws. They challenged the* Plessy v. Ferguson *(1896) "separate but equal" doctrine, contending that segregated schools were by their nature unequal.*

Chief Justice Warren first discussed the history of the Fourteenth Amendment's equal protection clause, finding it too inconclusive to be of assistance in determining how the Fourteenth Amendment should be applied to the question of public education.]

CHIEF JUSTICE WARREN writing for the majority.

. . . The doctrine of "separate but equal" did not make its appearance in this Court until 1896, in the case of Plessy v. Ferguson, involving not education but transportation. American courts have since labored with the doctrine for over half a century. In this Court, there have been six cases involving the "separate but equal" doctrine in the field of public education. . . .

In the instant cases, [the question of the application of the separate but equal doctrine to public education] is directly presented. Here, . . . there are findings below that the Negro and white schools involved have been equalized, or are being equalized, with respect to buildings, curricula, qualifications and salaries of teachers, and other "tangible" factors. Our decision, therefore, cannot turn on merely a comparison of these tangible factors in the Negro and white schools involved in each of the cases. We must look instead to the effect of segregation itself on public education.

In approaching this problem, we cannot turn the clock back to 1868 when the [Fourteenth] Amendment was adopted, or even to 1896 when Plessy v. Ferguson was written. We must consider public education in the light of its full development and its present place in American life throughout the Nation. Only in this way can it be determined if segregation in public schools deprives these plaintiffs of the equal protection of the laws.

Today, education is perhaps the most important function of state and local governments. Compulsory school attendance laws and the great expenditures for education both demonstrate our recognition of the importance of education to our democratic society. It is required in the performance of our most basic public responsibilities, even service in the armed forces. It is the very foundation of good citizenship. Today it is a principal instrument in awakening the child to cultural values, in preparing him for later professional training, and in helping him to adjust normally to his environment. In these days, it is doubtful that any child may reasonably be expected to succeed in life if he is denied the opportunity of an education. Such an opportunity, where the state has undertaken to provide it, is a right which must be made available to all on equal terms.

*Brown v. Board of Education of Topeka, Kansas, 347 U.S. 483, 1954.

We come then to the question presented: Does segregation of children in public schools solely on the basis of race, even though the physical facilities and other "tangible" factors may be equal, deprive the children of the minority group of equal educational opportunities? We believe that it does.

In Sweatt v. Painter, in finding that a segregated law school for Negroes could not provide them equal educational opportunities, this Court relied in large part on "those qualities which are incapable of objective measurement but which make for greatness in a law school." In McLaurin v. Oklahoma State Regents, the Court, in requiring that a Negro admitted to a white graduate school be treated like all other students, again resorted to intangible considerations: ". . . his ability to study, to engage in discussions and exchange views with other students, and, in general, to learn his profession." Such considerations apply with added force to children in grade and high schools. To separate them from others of similar age and qualifications solely because of their race generates a feeling of inferiority as to their status in the community that may effect their hearts and minds in a way unlikely ever to be undone. The effect of this separation on their educational opportunities was well stated by a finding in the Kansas case by a court which nevertheless felt compelled to rule against the Negro plaintiffs:

"Segregation of white and colored children in public schools has a detrimental effect upon the colored children. The impact is greater when it has the sanction of the law; for the policy of separating the races is usually interpreted as denoting the inferiority of the Negro group. A sense of inferiority affects the motivation of a child to learn. Segregation with the sanction of law, therefore, has a tendency to [retard] the educational and mental development of Negro children and to deprive them of some of the benefits they would receive in a racial[ly] integrated school system." Whatever may have been the extent of psychological knowledge at the time of Plessy v. Ferguson, this finding is amply supported by modern authority. Any language in Plessy v. Ferguson contrary to this finding is rejected.

We conclude that in the field of public education the doctrine of "separate but equal" has no place. Separate educational facilities are inherently unequal. Therefore, we hold that the plaintiffs and others similarly situated for whom the actions have been brought are, by reason of the segregation complained of, deprived of the equal protection of the laws guaranteed by the Fourteenth Amendment. This disposition makes unnecessary any discussion whether such segregation also violates the Due Process Clause of the Fourteenth Amendment.

Because these are class actions, because of the wide applicability of this decision, and because of the great variety of local conditions, the formulation of decrees in these cases presents problems of considerable complexity. On reargument, the consideration of appropriate relief was necessarily subordinated to the primary question—the constitutionality of segregation in public education. We have now announced that such segregation is a denial of the equal protection of the laws.

Morgan v. Kerrigan (1975)*

JUSTICE GARRITY writing for the majority.

V. Excerpts from Student Desegregation Plan

The Community School Districts

Definition and Purposes

A Community School District is an area of the city, clearly bounded by identifiable lines on a map, within which all residents are entitled to attend the public schools in that area, as seat capacities may allow. Maps, geocodes and facilities tables of the eight community districts appear *infra*. The purposes of these Districts are: (a) To accomplish desegregation of the schools in conformance with constitutional principles; (b) To correlate the programs and operations of public educational services with the needs and interests of residents and students within a natural unit or combination of units of the residential communities of Boston; (c) To enable parents and students to plan a coherent sequence of learning experiences within an identifiable series of schools that culminate in Community District High Schools; (d) To minimize the costs and burdens of transporting students, staff, and material between distant points in the city; and (e) To utilize existing facilities fully and efficiently.

No Community District boundary shall be modified except on notice to the parties with the review and approval of the court. Community District schools shall be equal in quality and status in all respects to Citywide schools and programs. No teacher or school administrator in a Citywide school may remand a student to a district school as unsuitable for the Citywide school or as a punishment. Neither may schools in any Community District develop alternative programs which operate *de facto* as preventive detention or short-term segregation facilities. There shall be no segregation of students within schools, classrooms, or programs in the school system.

Curriculum and Grade Structure

Within the limits established by state standards, the policies of the School Department, and contractual obligations entered into with a paired college or university, each Community School District shall develop its curriculum and programs of instruction and extra-curricular activities in response to

*Morgan v. Kerrigan, 401 U.S. 216, 1975.

the needs and interests of the parents and students resident within the District, so that programs are non-discriminatory and inclusive of all ethnic groups. All extra-curricular activities and athletic programs shall be available and conducted on a desegregated basis. These responses shall be coherent from grade to grade and from school to school. Programs of instruction at all levels shall be planned to reinforce the quality of learning within the District High School. Each high school shall be a four year, comprehensive institution which serves with equal and uniform excellence of instruction, students seeking general culminating education, those seeking vocational training or experience, and those seeking preparation for post-secondary study. Each District High School shall also serve as an Adult or Multipurpose Community Education facility.

Community District school grade structures shall be uniform. Schools shall be 1–5 at the elementary level, and 9–12 at the high school level. They may enroll 13th graders. Most but not all elementary schools shall contain kindergartens. Kindergarten assignments shall be made by the School Department to appropriate facilities, and may include inter-district assignments. Kindergarten classes shall be desegregated wherever possible. If kindergarten students must be assigned to schools outside their home neighborhoods, the assignments shall be made in accordance with two principles: (1) The resulting student bodies shall be desegregated, and (2) the burdens of distance and transportation shall be distributed equitably across ethnic groups.

Bilingual Students

Schools where bilingual programs shall be provided are shown in the school tables which are part of this plan. Where 20 or more kindergarten students attend a school and are found to be in *need* of bilingual instruction, the School Department shall provide it. Parents who seek bilingual instruction for their children at any grade level shall note this on the enrollment application form which the School Department shall mail to them. However, the School Bilingual Department staff shall make the decision to *assign* students to programs, but not to specific schools within Community Districts. Bilingual program assignments will be the first made by the Assignment Unit.

See text p. 86

In American society, with its ideal of equal opportunity, it is sometimes difficult to grasp the structural problems that limit opportunity for a large number of citizens. In recent decades, the gap between the rich and the poor has widened, and promises to continue to increase in the future. In the following article written for The Nation, *Paul*

Savoy argues that Americans cannot begin to address problems of poverty and inequality until they recognize the right of all Americans to a minimum quality of life. Until that change of attitude occurs, he argues, the concept of equal opportunity will be an empty phrase. As you read the article, you should consider the implications raised by his proposals: if Americans amended the Constitution to include an economic Bill of Rights similar to that suggested by Savoy, would that mean restructuring the entire system of government?

Paul Savoy
"Time for a Second Bill of Rights: An Economic One"*

This year the nation will celebrate the 200th anniversary of the ratification of the Bill of Rights. The occasion provides a timely opportunity for liberals and progressives to consider constitutional reform as a means for achieving what the political process has so far failed to accomplish: closing the widening gap between the rich and the poor, and assuring every person the means with which to secure a quality of life worthy of human dignity. It is time to seriously consider adopting an economic Bill of Rights. . . . In a nation endowed with such enormous private and public wealth, one out of every five infants is born into poverty, 30 million Americans are living below the poverty line, major cities in the United States are experiencing a 20 to 25 percent rise in hunger and homelessness, some 32 million Americans have no health coverage and more than 5 million children go to bed hungry every night. If Americans have become numb to these statistics, it is not because of the atrophy of the human heart but rather because of a radical failure of political will and moral vision. . . .

Our civil rights and civil liberties are rights in the negative sense. The provisions of the Bill of Rights guaranteeing freedom of speech and religion and due process of law are protections from government. They do not include affirmative obligations on government. We do not have a constitutional right to have the state provide us with health care, or give us shelter if we are homeless, or prevent a child from being beaten or from starving to death. This is what Columbia University law professor Louis Henkin describes as one of "the serious genetic defects" of our Bill of Rights. Professor Henkin, who is co-director of the Center for the Study of Human Rights at Columbia, points out that the "international human rights movement that developed after the Second World War gives equal place to economic and social rights, but these human rights have no constitutional status in the U.S." We have developed a broad range of legislative programs in America to provide aid to dependent children, health and nutrition services, housing

---

*Paul Savoy, "Time for a Second Bill of Rights: An Economic One," *The Nation* (June 17, 1991). This article is reprinted from *The Nation* magazine/The Nation Company, Inc., © 1991.

allowances, unemployment and disability insurance, and other social protections for individuals. However, since they have not been put into the Constitution, these benefits are not fundamental entitlements but are subject to budgetary constraints, the shifting winds of the political process, and the competing demands of defense spending and other federal programs.

Moreover, the beneficiaries of most social welfare programs continue to be treated as charity recipients rather than rights-holders in the same sense that we regard the *New York Times* as the holder of a right to freedom of the press. Why, aside from a long history of social prejudice, should this be so? Why does a person have a constitutional right to free speech, or a right to a lawyer if charged with a crime, but no right to be fed if he or she is starving? By expanding the concept of constitutional rights to include the affirmative right to a decent standard of living, it is possible to create an entirely new form of politics out of what Vaclav Havel has called "the phenomenon of the human conscience."

The great challenge for men and women of conscience and vision in America is to build a politics that will elevate progressive causes to constitutional status. It is a politics that speaks to the fundamental right to live in a just and humane society, free not only from discrimination on the basis of race, sex, age, sexual orientation, health condition or physical disability but free from hunger, homelessness, unemployment, illiteracy, drug abuse, high infant mortality, inadequate health care and a toxic environment. It is a politics of institutional transformation that can begin with a call for a Bill of Human Rights and Services that would expand our existing constitutional rights to include:

- the right to a quality of life worthy of human dignity, including adequate nutrition, clothing, housing, public transportation, health care and other social services necessary to satisfy basic human needs.

- the right of families to special protection, guaranteeing prenatal care, child care, and a reasonable period of leave for family illness or the birth of a child, and family planning assistance, including the right to choose an abortion.

- the right to an education sufficient to prepare individuals for suitable occupations or professions of their own choosing and to enable them to participate in the cultural life of their community.

- the right to employment, with guaranteed public-sector jobs for those who cannot find work in the private sector, at fair and favorable wages, with equal pay for equal work.

- the right to adequate income maintenance in the event of unemployment, illness, disability or other lack of livelihood in circumstances beyond the control of the individual.

- the right to clean air, clean water and renewable sources of energy, with citizen-plaintiffs granted standing to represent the interests of an endangered planet.

- the right to economic and social security for future generations of older Americans.

No constitutional plan can or should dictate a particular means for implementing economic and social rights. It would be up to Congress to decide, for example, how a constitutional guarantee of employment and job training should be apportioned between public-works programs and government contracts with private employers. Similarly, Congress would have latitude to decide whether the basic necessities of life should be provided by supplementing a full-employment plan with a guaranteed-income program or with an assistance program similar to the existing welfare system. Congress also would have discretion to determine whether a guarantee of universal health care should be implemented according to the Canadian model of public insurance, which uses tax dollars to provide essential medical care to everyone at no charge, or by allocating responsibility between government programs and publicly mandated employer contributions to private insurance plans. However, without a constitutional mandate for socializing economic opportunities and correcting the failures of the nation's system of health and social services, such proposals will be treated by Congress as so much pie-in-the-sky that can be ignored as too costly.

By requiring Congress to put human needs before military needs, a bill of economic and social rights would compel reductions in the defense budget and yield a substantial portion of the revenue needed to pay the bill. A 25 percent cut in defense spending would produce a quarter of a trillion dollars over a three-year period at current spending levels. The cost of launching two Patriot missiles would provide health care for 13,000 homeless children through a mobile medical outreach program. The cost of feeding U.S. troops in the Persian Gulf for one month would provide meals for a million children for a year through the National School Lunch Program. The cost of chemical protection suits ordered by the Pentagon would provide health, education and medical services for 4 million women a year through Planned Parenthood. . . . This is an economy in which our cities are in danger of becoming embattled citadels resembling scenes from Escape From New York. This is a nation in which a Democratic-controlled Congress lacks the political will to enact a strong civil rights bill or a comprehensive system of national health insurance. This is a democracy that, as a practical matter, is governed to a far greater extent by a one-party system than most countries in Eastern Europe; a democracy in which electoral politics has become so dominated by the power of money that civil rights and social programs are endangered as never before.

How a new Bill of Rights should be enacted—whether by constitutional amendment or, as some have suggested, by new civil rights legislation expanding the constitutional ideal of equality to include economic and social security, or by other means—is an issue that is likely to stir considerable controversy. What is essential is that a wide-ranging national debate begin and that we begin to chart the road toward establishing an adequate standard of living as an entitlement of all Americans.

The average citizen makes the mistake of leaving the Constitution to lawyers and matters of the common good to special interests. This is unfortunate because lawyers are not commonly advocates for constitutional reform and the public good is no gift of government lobbyists. As the country slides deeper into a recession of the economy and the human spirit, progressives confront a fateful choice: A broad coalition of civil rights groups, feminists, labor organizations, environmentalists, health activists, children's rights advocates and lower-income constituencies can either build a second civil rights movement—this one aimed at ending economic as well as racial apartheid in America—or we must learn to accept the consequences of politics as usual, with less blaming of our political representatives and fewer illusions. . . . However difficult such a task may be, there are fair, progressive and dignified ways to share the burdens of our fundamental human vulnerability, and we should not shrink from finally declaring that this is one of the great purposes for which our Constitution should be reordained and rededicated.

CHAPTER 5

Congress: the First Branch

MAKING LAW

See text p. 93

The Federalist No. 10, (on pp. 29–34), should be reread at this time. In that document, undoubtedly the best known of The Federalist Papers, James Madison outlines the theory of representation that is the foundation of the structure of the American political system. Viewing faction as inevitable in a democracy, Madison argues for a representative government, one which could "refine and enlarge the public views by passing them through the medium of a chosen body of citizens, whose wisdom may best discern the true interest of their country."

This metaphor of the filter is critical to understanding the political theory of the Federalists, and, as might be expected, was one of the key issues of contention between the Federalists and the Antifederalists. The Antifederalists objected strongly to the idea that the views of the people should be filtered through an elite representative body; they argued instead that representatives ought to mirror their constituents' views.

See text p. 94

What may a member of Congress do in the service of constituents? In large measure, the answer depends upon how the representative views his or her role in representing a constituency. Despite the best of intentions, most members of Congress find little time for pondering the larger affairs of state because they are swamped with the everyday details of representing the folks back home; political analyst Fred Barnes recently described the life of most representatives as "mindlessly hectic and stupefyingly dull."

In recent years, several ethics scandals have erupted concerning the manner in which members of Congress act simply as agents of constituents. In the following article, political writer Michael Waldman discusses the kinds of limits that ought to be imposed on congressional influence peddling. But while many of the ethics scandals can be attributed to the personal failings of the senator or representative directly involved, part of the problem lies in the structure of the institution of Congress itself. In reading the Waldman piece, therefore, it is important to think not only about what members of Congress may or may not be doing right, but also about what constraints may be placed upon them by the expectations of the job itself.

Michael Waldman
"Quid Pro Whoa: What Your Congressman Shouldn't Do for You: Ethics of Influence, Policy and Campaign Funds"

It was late 1988, and the worm-probe industry was up in arms. Worm probes, which resemble straightened-out wire coat hangers, are thrust into the ground by earthworm breeders; a jolt of electricity sends the creatures wriggling to the surface for harvest. Unfortunately, according to the Consumer Product Safety Commission, worm probes led to the electrocution of at least twenty-eight people; the agency was trying to remove the product from the shelves. But that might put the manufacturer of Worm Gett'rs, located in Caldwell, Idaho, out of business. So Republican Senators Steve Symms and James McClure of Idaho quietly blocked reauthorization of the CPSC, which had lacked a full legal mandate for nearly a decade. Consumer groups struggled to break the worm-probe filibuster, but to no avail. The legislation died, the agency remained crippled, and Worm Gett'rs stayed on the market.

As the saga of these hayseed Charles Keatings indicates, dubious constituent service is a problem not confined to the S&L and HUD scandals. Nonetheless, the senators now in the dock for their activities in these debacles have innocently protested that they are merely giving the voters what they want. . . .

Like metal filings to a magnet, congressional offices inevitably attract pleas for help. We want our representative to pummel the bureaucracy on our behalf for a veterans check, disability benefit, small business loan. But some requests clearly cross the line, elevating the interest of constituents— or worse, contributors—over the public weal. With more than 100,000 people working directly or indirectly for business lobbies in Washington, D.C., pressures can grow intense.

What's a senator of average intelligence, ethics, and backbone to do? "The system is wrong, it's bad, it's corrupting," says William Proxmire, former chairman of the Senate Banking Committee. "But there's nothing developed to help. I feel sympathetic for [John] Glenn and those fellows— there is so little in the way of guidance." Most attention has rightly focused on campaign finance laws. But Congress also desperately needs some new, explicit rules to help distinguish appropriate intervention from sleazy shilling.

. . . Here are a few: Don't handcuff the cops. Members of Congress should not interfere with ongoing individual criminal investigations or prosecutions. Sounds obvious, but recall that at least two of [Charles] Keat-

*Michael Waldman, "Quid Pro Whoa: What Your Congressman Shouldn't Do for You," *New Republic* (March 19, 1990). Reprinted by permission of The New Republic, © 1990, The New Republic, Inc.

ing's supporters continued their advocacy after being informed by regulators in 1987 that a criminal referral would be made to the Justice Department. [Keating and a number of members of Congress were implicated in the Savings and Loan Crises of the late 1980s.] As late as two years later Arizona's Dennis DeConcini and California's Alan Cranston urgently phoned regulators in an effort to block the seizure of the S&L. And D'Amato phoned Rudolph Giuliani to ask the U.S. Attorney to review sentences for two mobsters, according to *The Village Voice* and *New York Daily News*. . . . "What the Keating Five did different was the scale," argues Harvard political scientist Morris Fiorina. "Other than that, they did what other members of Congress do all the time, and have been doing for 200 years." Well, yes and no. Every day lawmakers carry water for big contributors, through tax loopholes, trade provisions, and liability limitations. But when Keating's allies summoned regulators to the two now notorious meetings on Capitol Hill in April 1987, the goal was to get an independent agency to back off from an ongoing enforcement proceeding. That's not only wrong; more unusual for Washington, it's rare. At the first meeting, Edwin Gray has testified under oath, DeConcini offered him a deal on behalf of Keating. A week later they met again, this time with regulators from San Francisco who were conducting the Lincoln examination. Many of the senators' assertions were couched as questions, but the message was unmistakable. Gray and other former regulators who served in the Carter and Reagan administrations say they can't remember anything like it.

"Once a regulatory body is established as an independent body, it is as wrong to lean on them as it is a judge," argues Proxmire. "Even if there are no campaign contributions whatsoever, if a legislator has influence because he's a chairman of a committee or because he's an influential member of a committee, he shouldn't be putting pressure on an independent or semi-independent agency on behalf of a constituent." Former Arizona Governor Bruce Babbitt, who turned down a Keating request to lobby for Lincoln, agrees. "Where an administrative proceeding is in the nature of a law enforcement proceeding, as most of these bank procedures are, then I believe it is improper to intervene," he said. Even most politicians doing favors for their donors understand this unwritten rule. This standard too involves nuances. On-the-record comments by members of Congress in an agency rulemaking—as opposed to enforcement proceeding—can enhance policymaking. And any standard should encourage legitimate congressional oversight—such as when a senator, in the course of a public hearing urges vigorous enforcement of the law. But the opportunity for inappropriate congressional special pleading increases the more an agency action focuses on a specific company or person.

. . . "You can't control the problem by saying, 'Congressman, you can't call an agency about a grant for your district,' " notes Babbitt. "The question is at what point does it become extortionate." Wherever that point is, there you will find Al D'Amato. New York's junior senator stands out not because his was the only congressional name on the HUD phone logs, but because of the relentlessness of his quids and quos. In case after case, D'Amato demanded HUD funds for projects built by developers who had contributed to his campaigns, or who had retained as counsel the senator's brother, Armand. HUD officials, mostly hand-picked patronage employees, readily complied; if not, D'Amato hounded the agency until it did. (One top regional official had a speed-dial button on his phone that enabled him to contact his mentor quickly.) In essence, D'Amato operated the New York region of HUD as a classic protection racket: first, monopolize the supply (through control of the agency); then extract your monopolist's fee. . . .

Standards are inevitably murkier when it comes to everyday contract hustling and grantsmanship. Still, some rules, if followed, could purify the process. Consider a congressman who is asked by a developer to help win a HUD grant for a hometown project. At a bare minimum, the lawmaker should conduct an independent investigation, even a cursory one, to see if the constituent's claims are valid or self-serving. "You can usually find out with just one phone call what's going on," said one Democratic administrative assistant. "And that will often be to the agency itself, so it accomplishes the mission of letting them know you're watching." And most intervention should be limited to inquiring about the status of a proceeding, rather than thumping for a result.

More important would be a requirement that lawmakers do all their advocacy for private citizens in public. Members of Congress, like other citizens, are not supposed to make secret contracts with regulators during a formal proceeding. Executive branch officials in many agencies are required to log any contacts they have with the public; Congress should be subject to the same standard. Quietly sleazy help for financial contributors, not workaday assistance for veterans, would potentially embarrass members of Congress under a full disclosure system. . . .

Finally, solons should refrain from pushing for the district's interests if they differ from those of the country. Today, too many lawmakers see their job as being similar to that of a lawyer—represent the client, no matter what the cost. Civics-text earnestness of this sort might be no match for hard political reality, but DeConcini's defense of his actions in the Keating case illustrates why it is needed. "Did we do anything wrong by interceding? That's what I do for you, ladies and gentlemen," he told an Arizona audience recently. "That's my job." He pointed proudly to another recent intervention: when the Department of Defense wanted to buy sixty Apache helicopters, manufactured in Arizona, DeConcini and other legislators met with Secretary Dick Cheney and forced the agency to buy more. Maybe this was good for some residents of Arizona (though that state's citizens pay taxes, too), but it's a lousy way to construct coherent budget policy and the main reason that dovish Democrats are as great an obstacle to arms reductions as the administration. . . .

Only scandals produce seismic changes in congressional rules, if not mores. We may be at that point now. Let's hope so. Otherwise, the dominant ethos will continue to be that of the senator's aide who referred to a favored firm as her boss's "client." Client? "Client, constituent," she told startled consumer lobbyists. "It's the same thing in this context, right?"

THE COMMITTEE SYSTEM: THE CORE OF CONGRESS

See text p. 101

As the text notes, committees have traditionally been the backbone of Congress, providing the structure upon which the actual work of legislating is carried out. The importance of committees lies largely in their function as a forum in which legislative proposals can be brought forth and discussed by members of both parties with expertise in the particular subject matter at issue.

In recent years, however, the power of committees has been dramatically undercut. As Kenneth Shepsle has pointed out in The Changing Textbook Congress, Congress in the 1940s and 1950s operated on a committee-based equilibrium. Beginning in the 1970s, however, broad, demographic changes created a different external environment, while internal changes in rules governing seniority allowed less experienced congressional members to chair committees. Subcommittees proliferated, draining power from committee chairs, legislation became increasingly complex, and deep divisions developed both within the parties and between Congress and the executive branch. Each of these factors contributed to the decreasing efficiency of the committee system. The result, according to Richard Cohen, a political commentator for the National Journal, is that committees have proved largely unable to initiate and move along legislative proposals, shifting that responsibility to party leaders by default.

Richard E. Cohen
"Crumbling Committees"*

Woodrow Wilson would hardly recognize Congress these days.

"Congress in its committee rooms is Congress at work," the 32nd President, while a graduate student in 1885, wrote in *Congressional Government.*

Wilson's book, still a political science classic a century later, talked of how Congress handled most legislation through a hierarchical system dominated by committee chairmen.

In recent years, however, internal changes have quietly revolutionized the sources of legislative power on Capitol Hill, eroding the influence of once all-powerful committees and of their bosses. Today, committees are often irrelevant or, worse yet, obstacles.

Congress has turned to these new arrangements, in part, to ease the lawmakers' burden. "The erosion of the committee process has made life more difficult in the Senate," said a former top Senate aide who is now a corporate lobbyist. But the informal, closed-door sessions that have resulted from this erosion "may be an attribute for Senators working in a fish-bowl, where every lobbyist knows what is happening before he does."

There are other reasons for the new procedures, including the reforms of the 1970s that some blame for exacerbating committee turf battles and producing too many subcommittee chairmen. The move away from commit-

*Richard E. Cohen, "Crumbling Committees," *National Journal* (August 4, 1990). Reprinted with permission.

tee dominance is also driven by nonlegislative concerns: On some politically volatile issues, party leaders have simply concluded that the committee process doesn't work.

. . .[C]ongress, especially the Senate [repeatedly went] outside the committee system to handle key legislation during [1990]. . . . [Through] informal arrangements, [legislation] took shape behind closed doors, with party leaders controlling the process. In at least one aspect, therefore, Wilson's portrayal of Congress remains valid. "One very noteworthy result of this system," he wrote, "is to shift the theater of debate upon legislation from the floor of Congress to the privacy of the committee rooms."

Shifting Power

This topsy-turvy handling of major issues reflects some broader internal changes. They include the breakdown of the seniority system, an erosion of party discipline, the paralysis resulting from divided party control of the White House and Congress, increased partisan sloganeering and the growing influence of 30-second campaign spot commercials.

The new, less formal procedures have led to other shortcomings in the legislative work product. "The committee process is designed to weed out problems," J. Thomas Sliter, a former top Senate Democratic aide, said. "But when bills are put together on an ad hoc basis, the trouble can be that there are no hearings and more staff control, which increases the risk of unintended consequences."

Members of Congress have complained that they have little idea what they are voting on when they are presented on the floor with an anticrime or an environmental bill, for example, that runs several hundred pages. Although tax bills are typically written inside the Ways and Means and Finance Committees, even those panels assign the task of writing the details to the committee staffs. The committees have been embarrassed occasionally when they have learned about the impact of the bills that have emerged.

. . . "In the not-distant past, the hallmark of the Senate was weak leaders and strong chairmen," said Robert G. Liberatore, who was staff director of the Senate Democratic Policy Committee from 1981–84. "The loss of power by committee chairmen and the increased chaos in the use of Senate rules to promote a Senator's views have required leadership to be more involved in keeping things going."

The altered power relationships have come in response to the often tumultuous political changes of the 1980s—notably, the division of political power between the White House and Congress and the shifts in control of the Senate in 1980 and again in 1986.

"The institution is groping to find ways to get things done when it's difficult to do anything," said Norman J. Ornstein, a congressional scholar at the American Enterprise Institute for Public Policy Research.

Congress is resorting more frequently to the informal procedures in part because the Bush Administration has been "more aggressive in arguing its views," Sen. Wendell H. Ford, D-Ky., said. "With the Administration leading the [Senate] Republicans almost in lockstep, that means that even if a bill is reported by a committee, the bill often won't move" without further negotiations. The President's effective use of the veto . . . has enhanced his influence at Congress's expense.

In the Senate more than in the House, Democrats have been forced to improvise because of turnover in the ranks of committee chairmen and party leaders. "Prior to 1980, there was an entrenched senior member staff structure in the Senate that had been there for more than a decade," said Leon G. Billings, a lobbyist who was a top aide to then-Senator Edmund S. Muskie, D-Maine. "That was seriously disrupted for Democrats in the six year hiatus [of 1981–87, when the GOP controlled the Senate]. More junior Senators, who were less well versed on specific issues, took over."

. . . "The problems we face are becoming more complex, and the solutions don't fit neatly into the baskets represented by the committee system," said David E. Johnson, a former top aide to [Senate Majority Leader George J.] Mitchell who is now a Washington lobbyist and an informal adviser to the Majority Leader. "When I started working for Muskie in 1973, the Senate was a much different place. There was more respect for seniority and learning your committee assignment. Now, it seems that there is more of an entrepreneurial spirit in the Senate and in politics, generally."

Constituent Committees

Wilson's observation in 1885 that committees predominate because "the House is conscious that time presses" remains apt.

Congress functions most smoothly when bills are written in committee with bipartisan support. On most committees, the members generally seek that approach, if only because what they produce is more likely to win support on the House or Senate floor if a consensus has developed.

"Task forces usually are created only after a committee has run into a problem moving a bill," said Thomas A. Daschle of South Dakota, the co-chairman with Mitchell of the Senate Democratic Policy Committee. "They may enhance the influence of a chairman if they can improve his ability to move a bill through the floor."

Members often seek assignments to committees that deal with the issues in which they and their constituents are most interested. And that means that the committees can become captives of the interest groups most affected by their work. Seats on the Agriculture Committees tend to be filled by lawmakers representing farmers, for example, and western and southern Senators gravitate toward the Energy and Natural Resources Committee.

"On the key committees that Senators want to be on—Finance, Appropriations, Armed Services—there tend to be more balanced views," said Liberatore, who is a lobbyist for Chrysler Corp. "Many of the others are constituent committees, which generally have more staff control, and there is less interest by members in the details of programs."

. . . "There is no concerted effort to bypass committees," said Senator Wyche Fowler Jr., D-Ga., whom Mitchell tapped as assistant floor leader. "That's much more difficult for leadership to manage." The need for informal mechanisms, in part, "has to do with the personalities and effectiveness" of chairmen, Fowler added.

Even seemingly routine action on bills can often become snarled. When the Senate in June 1989 acted on the child care bill—one of the Democrats' top domestic priorities—it was initially written by Labor and Human Resources Committee Democrats, who are mostly sympathetic to organized labor and child care groups. Before the measure could win Senate passage, however, Mitchell was forced to file a floor substitute that substantially watered down the original version and added provisions that the Finance Committee had prepared. Because most Republicans opposed the measure, the support of Orrin G. Hatch of Utah, the Labor Committee's senior Republican, was vital to Senate passage.

Hatch took a more traditional minority role when his strong opposition triggered an angry debate on the pending Civil Rights Act, which the Labor Committee drafted. As a result, committee chairman Edward M. Kennedy, D-Mass., sought but ultimately failed to work out differences directly with White House chief of staff John H. Sununu. Kennedy and Sununu had conducted similar negotiations a year ago to expedite Senate passage of landmark legislation expanding the rights of disabled persons.

. . . Some committees and committee chairmen have been ill-equipped to deal with . . . controversial topics requiring quick action and a sensitivity to partisan implications.

Pay raise and campaign finance bills, for example, have become known as "leadership issues." They require party leaders' extensive participation because "they involve the Members themselves and need bipartisan support," said Rep. Martin Frost, D-Texas, who has served on informal leadership panels dealing with both issues. . . .

"These are issues that require the leadership to play a critical role to overcome the parochial interests of individual Members," Common Cause president Fred Wertheimer said. "After 15 years of the parties' battling each other and incumbents benefiting from the current system, that makes it harder to resolve. . . . On these issues, accountability is not with the committee system, it's with the party leaders."

. . . Sometimes, overlapping committee jurisdictions are obstacles to moving legislation to the floor. Issues such as education, trade and drug control may be in the jurisdiction principally of a single committee of the House or Senate. But several other committees can and often do argue for a share of the jurisdiction so that their members can get a piece of the action.

"There are so many overlapping jurisdictions, which create difficulties in working out problems," Daschle said. "And many more Members desire to be involved, even though they are not on the committee with jurisdiction." That helps to explain, for example, why eight Senate committees and nine House committees worked on parts of the 1988 Trade Act.

Reformers made several efforts in the 1970s to overhaul committee jurisdiction but failed, for the most part, because of opposition from Members who feared a loss of influence. . . .

"It's not possible for many bills to go through the committee system until Congress redoes itself," said Bolling, who has become an adviser to Gephardt. "It's nutty now. But this is not the time to reform, either strategically or politically."

Other major changes in the mid-1970s, which were the culmination of lengthy efforts by Bolling and other Democratic reformers, served to weaken the roles of the once-autocratic committee chairmen. They included the adoption of the new congressional budget process; the election in 1974 of the "Watergate babies," nationally oriented House Democrats with little respect for their elders or for House traditions; and the strengthening of the House Democratic Caucus, which demonstrated its new muscle in 1975 by ousting three senior committee chairmen. Intentionally or not, these changes contributed to Congress's internal gridlock. . . .

"Congress prefers strong chairmen," Fowler said. "But the proliferation of chairmen has weakened the committee system. You no longer have the whales on any complex issues. You usually have two to three committee chairmen and eight or nine subcommittee chairmen, all jealous of their turf.". . .

Flexible Leaders

New procedures intended to supplement the work of the committees may enhance the power of congressional leaders, especially those in the Senate. "By picking who is on the team and putting a spin on the outcome, leadership can exert more control," a Senate Democratic source said.

At the same time, the added responsibilities can complicate the lives of party leaders, who already have to balance a range of legislative and political demands. Increasingly, however, Members are selecting leaders—such as Mitchell, Gephardt, Dole and House Minority Whip Newt Gingrich—who have demonstrated that they can not only speak to national constituencies but can also deal with internal pressures.

In addition, Bush and top White House officials have been more interested in resolving legislative details with congressional leaders than their recent predecessors have—in part, congressional sources suggest, because Bush spends less time than other Presidents did developing a White House legislative agenda.

Until recent years, active Presidents did not have to contend with strong congressional leaders seeking their own podiums. Sam Rayburn of Texas, who was House Speaker in 17 of the years from 1940–61 and was probably the century's most skillful lawmaker, prided himself on his ability to work closely with Presidents and committee chairmen. But to the public at large, he was not very well known.

"Rayburn had half the power" of later Speakers, said Bolling, whom many regarded as Rayburn's protege. "But he had enormous prestige from the ability to understand what could be done and how to tell a President."

Mitchell may be setting a new model for Senate leaders as he tries to combine the roles of legislative agenda-setter and national party spokesman. Last fall, for example, he engaged in public and private lobbying to kill, virtually single-handedly, Bush's proposed cut in the capital gains tax rate, which was backed by a majority of Senators, including members of the Finance Committee.

"George Mitchell takes a much more flexible approach to leadership," Ornstein said. "This is an era when leaders use whatever tools work and seek new ones, where necessary. . . . They have to be more creative and improvisational." . . .

Whether it is the budget or other issues, party leaders have often said that they do not want to put their own "stamp" on issues. In an increasing number of cases, however, they have found that if they don't no one else can.

CONGRESS AND THE FUTURE

See text p. 126

See text p. 126

Few issues have tested the relationship between Congress and the president as sorely as the budget deficit. Congress and the president point fingers at one another during budget time, allowing the deficit to grow at a rate that is beyond the ability of most human minds to conceive. In the following 1990 article, Lawrence Haas, writing for the National Journal, *looks at President Bush's proposals for line-item veto power, which would increase the president's power vis-a-vis Congress in the budget process. Legislation, however, was never introduced for the line-item veto on a federal level, and consequently the debate goes on.*

Lawrence J. Haas
"Line-Item Logic"*

Let's help ensure our future of prosperity by giving the President a tool that—though I will not get to use it—is one I know future Presidents of either party must have," President Reagan told Congress in January 1988, in his last State of the Union message. "Give the President the same authority that 43 governors use in their states, the right to reach into massive appropriations bills, pare away the waste and enforce budget discipline. Let's approve the line-item veto."

To show how powerful this tool could be, Reagan said he would send Congress a list of items that, had he been given the chance, he would have

*Lawrence J. Haas, "Line-Item Logic," *National Journal* (June 9, 1990). Reprinted with permission.

struck from the $600 billion fiscal 1988 continuing resolution that had been enacted a month earlier. He proceeded to ask Congress to strike those items. "What an example we can set," the President said, "that we are serious about getting our financial accounts in order."

When the list arrived on Capitol Hill, however, it seemed almost a parody of Reagan's words. With Washington running annual deficits of about $150 billion, the 107 items that then-Office of Management and Budget (OMB) director James C. Miller III suggested should be struck added up to just $1.15 billion in 1988 outlays.

No, a line-item veto isn't going to solve America's fiscal problems. . . .

But the real issue here is power—that of the President in relation to Congress. Where you stand on the line-item veto or related measures depends a lot on what you think has happened to presidential power over the years. The line-item veto's supporters argue that for one reason or another, the President isn't as powerful in shaping fiscal policy as he once was. Critics of the proposal contend that the President is quite powerful, thank you, and should not be given extra authority that could upset the Constitution's delicate balance between the branches.

The line-item veto is not the only new power President Bush is seeking as a way to control spending. As part of the continuing budget summit between White House aides and congressional leaders, Bush's team is expected to propose altering the budget process to try to prevent any tax hikes he might accept from being diverted from deficit cutting to new spending. . . .

[Other proposals by Bush's administration include requiring Congress to vote to override the president's requests to withhold funding, to include the president in the budget process by requiring his signature on a joint budget resolution, and to limit Congress's ability to spend money if the OMB drags its feet on making across the board cuts.]

Bush's prospects for winning any of these new powers are debatable. Many Democrats and some high-profile Republicans are dead-set against the line-item veto, which probably would require a constitutional amendment. . . .

A Bigger Bully Pulpit

The Bush Administration engaged itself in the debate over presidential power soon after taking office. [Budget Director Richard] Darman told the Senate Governmental Affairs Committee in early 1989 why a new President these days needs to avoid important losses in his battles with Congress: "The presidency is a much, much weaker institution than I think most people assume it is, and I think if you start an Administration with a highly visible, highly advertised loss, you permanently weaken the presidency for whatever else it might do."

Many historians scoff at this view. "Increasingly, the question of whether the President is or isn't strong enough has become a polemical issue," said Fred I. Greenstein, a scholar of the presidency at Princeton University. When a Republican occupies the White House, supporters complain about the encumbrances placed upon him, particularly by a Democratic-controlled Congress. It's no coincidence, Greenstein and others say, that the conservative American Enterprise Institute for Public Policy Research (AEI) last year published *The Fettered Presidency,* a set of essays about such constraints.

. . . In the grand sweep of history, the presidency does not seem weakened in the area of fiscal policy. Before 1921, the President did not even propose his own budget; instead, executive agencies sent separate requests to the relevant congressional committees.

Even during the New Deal, the federal budget equaled barely 10 per cent of the gross national product, compared with more than 20 per cent since the late 1970s. In a sense when it comes to shaping the economy through fiscal policy, the President and Congress are both stronger than they used to be.

Whether in more recent years legal and other types of changes have tied the President's hands a bit is more debatable. Unquestionably, the 1974 Congressional Budget and Impoundment Control Act was important in establishing Congress as a competing force on fiscal policy. For one thing, it created the Budget Committees and, through them, the process by which Congress adopts a budget resolution. Until that point, Congress had no mechanism for making over-all decisions about fiscal policy. Nor could it offer a single, comprehensive alternative to the President's budget.

For another, the 1974 law institutionalized the concept of a "current services" baseline. Since then, instead of just comparing its tax and spending decisions with presidential proposals, as it had traditionally done. Congress has downgraded the President's budget by comparing legislative decisions with a new measurement that factors in inflation, past budget authority and other variables.

But to those worried about the President's power to control spending, the more important provisions of the 1974 law were designed to counter President Nixon's impoundment—withholding—of urban aid and other funds. . . . Nixon broke new ground by deciding that he would not spend funds on programs he did not like.

[Republican] Senator Dan Coats [of Indiana. . .] argues that the 1974 Budget Act tied the President's hands. "I think the scales were tipped too far in the other direction, to limit the presidency in terms of its impact on unnecessary spending," he said.

Coats and others point to Congress's record in accepting request for rescissions. In 1986 and 1987, Congress rescinded just 1 per cent of the money Reagan requested. A year later, Reagan didn't bother to request rescissions.

But Congress's record may have less to do with budget rules than with the political climate. . . . In 1981, when Reagan was flying high and the public clearly supported his desire to cut domestic "waste, fraud and abuse," Congress rescinded 71 per cent of his requested $16.5 billion. . . .

History's Record

Historically, the push to increase presidential power to control spending is a familiar struggle. President Grant requested a line-item veto in 1873, and lawmakers have proposed it from time to time since. . . .

This more recent push seems to derive from two sources: widespread exasperation over the stubborn budget deficit and complaints about an omnipotent Congress.

The deficit, many argue, might be much smaller if the President had enhanced rescission power. . . . If the President could force Members to vote on his rescission requests, Coats and others believe, he could publicly embarrass the sponsors of "pork" [proposed funds, appointments, and legislation offered in return for political support and patronage].

That is debatable, given the experience of the 43 states whose governors have line-item power. "The history of item vetoes at the state level reveals that legislatures are willing to appropriate excessive funds to please their constituents and place the onus of deficit reduction on the governor," constitutional scholars Louis Fisher and Neal Devins wrote in the *Georgetown Law Journal* in 1986. . . .

But the experiences of states may not be relevant. In the states there has been a stronger tradition of resistance to legislatures than there has been in Washington, according to scholars, and governors have been viewed as the citizens' bulwark against irresponsible state legislators.

How a line-item veto might work at the federal level is anyone's guess. . . .

But the most important questions seem to be governmental, not fiscal. One of the Constitution's hallmarks is the delicate system of checks and balances between the three branches. That a line-item veto would shift power to the executive is disputed by few on either side of the debate. The only question is whether it is a good idea.

Those who favor it tend to complain about congressional practices that, they say, have effectively disenfranchised the executive from fiscal decision making. Their pet peeve is the omnibus spending bill, a package containing as many as 13 appropriations bills that Congress sometimes sends to the President at the end of the session.

Under these circumstances, supporters of a line-item veto have maintained, the President has little choice but to sign the bill. . . .

True enough. But omnibus spending bills have been around longer than the Republic itself. As Rep. Edwards wrote in "Of Conservatives and Kings," an article for *Policy Review* early last year, "both omnibus appropriations and non-germane riders were common nearly 300 years ago and were well-known to the nation's Founding Fathers." So it is hard to argue that the presidency is somehow weaker today because of them. . . .

Where the danger arises, critics of the line-item veto say, is with the President's leverage over individual lawmakers. With the threat of striking funds for Members' pet projects—and making his line-item veto stick—he could entice them into voting for other things he wants, such as foreign aid, in exchange for presidential acquiescence in the pork. . . .

Why Bush really wants more fiscal power at a time of high deficits baffles more than a few observers. In a sense, the budget process in its current form is quite convenient for him.

Here's why. After the President sends his budget to Congress, usually in January, attention turns to Capitol Hill. The President has no legislative responsibility over the budget resolution, or over the resulting tax and spending measures, until they reach his desk. As a result, he can blame Congress for the annual fiscal havoc with some justification, simply by pointing out that he had little to do with it. This was one of Reagan's time-honored tactics, and Bush has occasionally adopted it for his own use. . . .

If the current arrangement is really so convenient, the White House could be leading itself into an uncomfortable position, particularly if this year's budget summit does not solve the deficit problem. With a victory on any of the budget process changes that he's pushing, Bush could find himself with a bit more power to cut spending—and a lot more public blame for the problem.

See text p. 127

While some of the decline in congressional power is attributable to the growth in the power of the executive branch, Congress still has at its disposal the tools necessary to rebuild itself. But some of the hurdles Congress must jump to reclaim its status have more to do with reputation rather than any concrete loss of power. As Washington Post commentator David Broder points out in the following article, Congress has lost its credibility on several fronts: it is disorganized and its members are seen as more inter-ested in themselves and their personal futures than the future of the nation. Broder notes that suggestions for improving congressional stature range from calls for campaign finance reform, to increasing party discipline and restructuring the staff and committee systems.

David S. Broder
"How to Fix Congress—Advice from the Alumni"*

The alumni are worried that dear old Alma Mater is getting a bad name.

It's the Congress of the United States we're talking about, not Old Siwash or Winsockie or Euphoria State. . . .

Former Senate Republican leader Howard H. Baker Jr., of Tennessee, whose father, mother and father-in-law all served in Congress before him,

*David S. Broder, "How to Fix Congress—Advice from the Alumni," *Washington Post* (January 6, 1991). Copyright © 1991, The Washington Post. Reprinted with permission.

summed up the general sentiment by saying, "I've seen Congress's reputation go up and down for many, many years. But I've never seen it lower than it is now. I think there will be a massive wave of anti-incumbent sentiment unless the problem is addressed."

The definition of "the problem" varies from person to person. And when the old grads are asked what practical steps Congress could take to improve its standing with the public, they offer a variety of suggestions. But in this unscientific sampling of notable alumni, the single action most often mentioned is to change the way the campaigns for Congress are financed.

"I cannot say how important I think it is," said former representative Dick Bolling, who believes that financing lies at the heart of most of Congress's other problems. Agreeing, former senator Thomas Eagleton said, "I don't care what ethics bills you pass, if you don't do anything about campaign-spending reform, you haven't done anything at all."

Bolling and Eagleton are both liberal Democrats from Missouri. But this is no longer just a liberal lament. Former Nevada senator Paul Laxalt, the chairman of Ronald Reagan's presidential campaigns, said, "There's far too much emphasis on money and far too much time spent collecting it. It's the most corrupting thing I see on the congressional scene."

Laxalt said, "The problem is so bad we ought to start thinking about federal financing" of House and Senate campaigns. "It was anathema to me," as it has been to most conservatives, he said, "but in my experience with the [Reagan] presidential campaigns, it worked, and it was like a breath of fresh air. . . . A lot of us who retired [from Congress] did so because we just didn't have the stomach to go out and hustle for money the way you have to do now." . . .

Two prominent Republican alumni—former senator Bill Brock of Tennessee and former representative Melvin R. Laird of Wisconsin—argue that the best way to insulate Congress from special-interest PAC (political action committee) money is to route all such campaign funds through the parties. Laird argues that most organized giving today is "really to buy access" to the lawmakers. Brock, a former national GOP chairman, agrees that allowing the PACs to contribute only to the parties would reduce the access game—and strengthen party discipline. Tighter party control is necessary if Congress is to tackle the tough problems, several alums say. . . .

Former senator William Proxmire (D) of Wisconsin, a maverick who prided himself on his low-cost campaigns, is critical of the focus on reelection. "Being a senator is such a marvelous job," he said, "they do whatever they can to hold onto it. It becomes a priority for them, and their families, and their staffs, and even their colleagues pressure them, because their chairmanships depend on their party staying in control. And once the No. 1 objective becomes being reelected, you can rationalize all sorts of things. . . ." If reelection pressures are the problem, is term-limitation the answer? Some alumni say yes. Conservatives [James J.] Broyhill and [William H.] Hudnut III are for the idea, and so is liberal former representative Shirley Chisholm (D) of New York. "There's anger and a lack of trust I've not seen before," she said, describing her sense of the public attitude toward Congress. "We need new blood—a new transfusion. Too many of them have Potomac fever and forgot how they got there."

But even those who voluntarily cut short their own congressional careers tend to reject the idea of limiting tenure by law. "When you decrease the tenure," said Rhodes, "the influence of unelected staff members goes up." Laird calls term limits "a repudiation of our whole philosophy of representative government." Former representative James R. Jones (D), whose home state of Oklahoma has passed term-limits for the legislature, calls them "crazy," but adds, "The only way to avoid them is for members of Congress to start acting as if the Constitution already included a limit on terms. If they would show more courage and candor, it would do wonders."

Finally, some alumni suggest that the public itself may have to take responsibility for Congress and its flaws. "From my perspective," said John Culver, "term-limitation is the latest manifestation of public irresponsibility. Many people don't vote. Most of those who do vote don't want to vote against their own congressman. So they look on term-limitations as a way of changing people without the bother—or the responsibility—of voting them out."

Culver said he agreed that today's Congress—"made up of wonderfully attractive people"—seems "more preoccupied with reelection than the old Congresses made up of people who were, frankly, less than distinguished." But, he said, "an informed electorate is the cornerstone of a democracy, and that's the responsibility of the people, not of the members of Congress. In the end, the public is going to get what it demands. This Congress is about what the people deserve—maybe a little better."

CHAPTER 6

The President and the Executive Branch

THE CONSTITUTIONAL BASIS OF THE PRESIDENCY

See text p. 135

The Supreme Court has had few occasions to rule on the constitutional limits of executive authority. The Court is reluctant to issue opinions on matters that are better resolved by a different branch, and the scope of the president's power is typically just such an issue. In the two cases that follow, however, the Court did decide to look at the relationship between the exercise of presidential prerogative and the limits imposed by the Constitution.

In Youngstown Sheet and Tube Co. v. Sawyer *(1952), the owners of a number of steel mills contested President Truman's authority to order the secretary of commerce to operate the nation's steel mills, an order that had been issued in an effort to avert strikes that would disrupt steel production while the country was engaged in the Korean War. The issue before the Court was whether the Constitution permitted the president to take such a unilateral action; the Court decided that it did not.*

United States v. Nixon *(1974), involves a different set of claims to executive authority. President Nixon had been implicated in a conspiracy to coverup a burglary of the Democratic Party Headquarters at the Watergate Hotel in Washington, D.C., during the 1972 election campaign. The United States ordered the president to produce a number of documents and tapes related to the coverup. Nixon produced some edited versions of some of the materials, but refused to comply with much of the request, asserting that he was entitled to withhold the information under a claim of "executive privilege."*

Youngstown Sheet & Tube Co. v. Sawyer (1952)*
[The Steel Seizure Case]

JUSTICE BLACK delivered the opinion of the Court.

We are asked to decide whether the President was acting within his constitutional power when he issued an order directing the Secretary of Commerce to take possession of and operate most of the Nation's steel mills. The mill owners argue that the President's order amounts to lawmaking, a legislative function which the Constitution has expressly confided to the Congress and not to the President. The Government's position is that the order was made on findings of the President that his action was necessary to avert a national

---

*Youngstown Sheet and Tube Company v. Sawyer, 343 U.S. 579, 1952.

catastrophe which would inevitably result from a stoppage of steel production, and that in meeting this grave emergency the President was acting
within the aggregate of his constitutional powers as the Nation's Chief
Executive and the Commander in Chief of the Armed Forces of the United
States. . . .

The President's power, if any, to issue the order must stem either from
an act of Congress or from the Constitution itself. There is no statute that
expressly authorizes the President to take possession of property as he did
here. Nor is there any act of Congress to which our attention has been
directed from which such a power can fairly be implied. Indeed, we do not
understand the Government to rely on statutory authorization for this seizure. . . .

It is clear that if the President had authority to issue the order he did,
it must be found in some provisions of the Constitution. And it is not
claimed that express constitutional language grants this power to the President. The contention is that presidential power should be implied from the
aggregate of his powers under the Constitution. Particular reliance is placed
on provisions in Article II which say that "The executive Power shall be
vested in a President"; that "he shall take Care that the Laws be faithfully
executed"; and that he "shall be Commander in Chief of the Army and Navy
of the United States."

The order cannot properly be sustained as an exercise of the President's
military power as Commander in Chief of the Armed Forces. The Government attempts to do so by citing a number of cases upholding broad powers
in military commanders engaged in day-to-day fighting in a theater of war.
Such cases need not concern us here. Even though "theater of war" be an
expanding concept, we cannot with faithfulness to our constitutional system
hold that the Commander in Chief of the Armed Forces has the ultimate
power as such to take possession of private property in order to keep labor
disputes from stopping production. This is a job for the Nation's lawmakers,
not for its military authorities.

Nor can the seizure order be sustained because of the several constitutional provisions that grant executive power to the President. In the framework of our Constitution, the President's power to see that the laws are
faithfully executed refutes the idea that he is to be a lawmaker. The Constitution limits his functions in the lawmaking process to the recommending
of laws he thinks wise and the vetoing of laws he thinks bad. And the
Constitution is neither silent nor equivocal about who shall make laws which
the President is to execute.

The President's order does not direct that a congressional policy be
executed in a manner prescribed by Congress—it directs that a presidential
policy be executed in a manner prescribed by the President. The power of
Congress to adopt such public policies as those proclaimed by the order is
beyond question. It can authorize the taking of private property for public
use. It can make laws regulating the relationships between employers and
employees, prescribing rules designed to settle labor disputes, and fixing
wages and working conditions in certain fields of our economy. The Consti-

tution did not subject this lawmaking power of Congress to presidential or military supervision or control. . . .

The Founders of this Nation entrusted the lawmaking power to the Congress alone in both good and bad times. It would do no good to recall the historical events, the fears of power and the hopes for freedom that lay behind their choice. Such a review would but confirm our holding that this seizure order cannot stand. The judgment of the District Court is Affirmed.

JUSTICE FRANKFURTER, concurring.

The powers of the President are not as particularized as are those of Congress. But unenumerated powers do not mean undefined powers. The separation of powers built into our Constitution gives essential content to undefined provisions in the frame of our government.

To be sure, the content of the three authorities of government is not to be derived from an abstract analysis. The areas are partly interacting, not wholly disjointed. The Constitution is a framework for government. Therefore the way the framework has consistently operated fairly establishes that it has operated according to its true nature. Deeply embedded traditional ways of conducting government cannot supplant the Constitution or legislation, but they give meaning to the words of a text or supply them. It is an inadmissibly narrow conception of American constitutional law to confine it to the words of the Constitution and to disregard the gloss which life has written upon them. In short, a systematic, unbroken, executive practice, long pursued to the knowledge of the Congress and never before questioned, engaged in by Presidents who have also sworn to uphold the Constitution, making as it were such exercise of power part of the structure of our government, may be treated as a gloss on "executive Power" vested in the President by § 1 of Art. II.

JUSTICE JACKSON, concurring in the judgment and opinion of the Court.

The actual art of governing under our Constitution does not and cannot conform to judicial definitions of the power of any of its branches based on isolated clauses or even single Articles torn from context. While the Constitution diffuses power the better to secure liberty, it also contemplates that practice will integrate the dispersed powers into a workable government. It enjoins upon its branches separateness but interdependence, autonomy but reciprocity. Presidential powers are not fixed but fluctuate, depending upon their disjunction or conjunction with those of Congress. We may well begin by a somewhat oversimplified grouping of practical situations in which a President may doubt, or others may challenge, his powers, and by distinguishing roughly the legal consequences of this factor of relativity.

1. When the President acts pursuant to an express or implied authorization of Congress, his authority is at its maximum, for it includes all that he possesses in his own right plus all that Congress can delegate. In these

circumstances, and in these only, may he be said (for what it may be worth) to personify the federal soverignty. If this act is held unconstitutional under these circumstances, it usually means that the Federal Government as an undivided whole lacks power. . . .

2. When the President acts in absence of either a congressional grant or denial of authority, he can only rely upon his own independent powers, but there is a zone of twilight in which he and Congress may have concurrent authority, or in which its distribution is uncertain. Therefore, congressional inertia, indifference or quiescence may sometimes, at least as a practical matter, enable, if not invite, measures on independent presidential responsibility. In this area, any actual test of power is likely to depend on the imperatives of events and contemporary imponderables rather than on abstract theories of law.

3. When the President takes measures incompatible with the expressed or implied will of Congress, his power is at its lowest ebb, for then he can rely only upon his own constitutional powers minus any constitutional powers of Congress over the matter. Courts can sustain exclusive presidential control in such a case only by disabling the Congress from acting upon the subject. Presidential claim to a power at once so conclusive and preclusive must be scrutinized with caution, for what is at stake is the equilibrium established by our constitutional system.

[In this case, the actions of the president fit into neither of the first two situations, and must be sustained, if at all, under the third. In this case, there is no basis for concluding that Congress could not act in this case.]

United States v. Nixon (1974)*

CHIEF JUSTICE BURGER delivered the opinion of the Court.

In the District Court, the President's counsel argued that the court lacked jurisdiction to issue the subpoena because the matter was an intra-branch dispute between a subordinate and superior officer of the Executive Branch and hence not subject to judicial resolution. That argument has been renewed in this Court with emphasis on the contention that the dispute does not present a "case" or "controversy" which can be adjudicated in the federal courts. The President's counsel argues that the federal courts should not intrude into areas committed to the other branches of Government. He views the present dispute as essentially a "jurisdictional" dispute within the Executive Branch which he analogizes to a dispute between two congressional committees. Since the Executive Branch has exclusive authority and absolute discretion to decide whether to prosecute a case, it is contended

*United States v. Nixon, 418 U.S. 683, 1974.

that a President's decision is final in determining what evidence is to be used in a given criminal case.

. . . Although his counsel concedes the President has delegated certain specific powers to the Special Prosecutor, he has not "waived nor delegated to the Special Prosecutor the President's duty to claim privilege as to all materials which fall within the President's inherent authority to refuse to disclose to any executive officer." The Special Prosecutor's demand for the items therefore presents, in the view of the President's counsel, a political question since it involves a "textually demonstrable" grant of power under Art. II. . . .

The demands of and the resistance to the subpoena present an obvious controversy in the ordinary sense, but that alone is not sufficient to meet constitutional standards. In the constitutional sense, controversy means more than disagreement and conflict; rather it means the kind of controversy courts traditionally resolve. Here at issue is the production or nonproduction of specified evidence deemed by the Special Prosecutor to be relevant and admissible in a pending criminal case. It is sought by one official of the Government within the scope of his express authority; it is resisted by the Chief Executive on the ground of his duty to preserve the confidentiality of the communications of the President. Whatever the correct answer on the merits, these issues are "of a type which are traditionally justiciable." . . .

. . . We turn to the claim that the subpoena should be quashed because it demands "confidential conversations between a President and his close advisors that it would be inconsistent with the public interest to produce." The first contention is a broad claim that the separation of powers doctrine precludes judicial review of a President's claim of privilege. The second contention is that if he does not prevail on the claim of absolute privilege, the court should hold as a matter of constitutional law that the privilege prevails over the subpoena *duces tecum.* . . .

[The Court discussed its authority to interpret the Constitution, concluding that it had full power to interpret a claim of executive privilege.]

In support of his claim of absolute privilege, the President's counsel urges two grounds one of which is common to all governments and one of which is peculiar to our system of separation of powers. The first ground is the valid need for protection of communications between high government officials and those who advise and assist them in the performance of their manifold duties; the importance of this confidentiality is too plain to require further discussion. Human experience teaches that those who expect public dissemination of their remarks may well temper candor with a concern for appearances and for their own interests to the detriment of the decisionmaking process. Whatever the nature of the privilege of confidentiality of presidential communications in the exercise of Art. II powers the privilege can be said to derive from the supremacy of each branch within its own assigned area of constitutional duties. Certain powers and privileges flow from the nature of enumerated powers; the protection of the confidentiality of presidential communications has similar constitutional underpinnings.

The second ground asserted by the President's counsel in support of the claim of absolute privilege rests on the doctrine of separation of powers. Here it is argued that the independence of the Executive Branch within its own sphere, insulates a president from a judicial subpoena in an ongoing criminal prosecution, and thereby protects confidential presidential communications.

However, neither the doctrine of separation of powers, nor the need for confidentiality of high level communications, without more, can sustain an absolute, unqualified presidential privilege of immunity from judicial process under all circumstances. The President's need for complete candor and objectivity from advisers calls for great deference from the courts. However, when the privilege depends solely on the broad, undifferentiated claim of public interest in the confidentiality of such conversations, a confrontation with other values arises. Absent a claim of need to protect military, diplomatic or sensitive national security secrets, we find it difficult to accept the argument that even the very important interest in confidentiality of presidential communications is significantly diminished by production of such material for *in camera* inspection with all the protection that a district court will be obliged to provide.

The impediment that an absolute, unqualified privilege would place in the way of the primary constitutional duty of the judicial branch to do justice in criminal prosecutions would plainly conflict with the function of the courts under Art. III. In designing the structure of our Government and dividing and allocating the sovereign power among three coequal branches, the Framers of the Constitution sought to provide a comprehensive system, but the separate powers were not intended to operate with absolute independence. To read the Art. II powers of the President as providing an absolute privilege as against a subpoena essential to enforcement of criminal statutes on no more than a generalized claim of the public interest in confidentiality of nonmilitary and nondiplomatic discussions would upset the constitutional balance of "a workable government" and gravely impair the role of the courts under Art. III.

Since we conclude that the legitimate needs of the judicial process may outweigh presidential privilege, it is necessary to resolve those competing interests in a manner that preserves the essential functions of each branch. The right and indeed the duty to resolve that question does not free the judiciary from according high respect to the representations made on behalf of the President. The expectation of a President to the confidentiality of his conversations and correspondence, like the claim of confidentiality of judicial deliberations, for example, has all the values to which we accord deference for the privacy of all citizens and added to those values the necessity for protection of the public interest in his responsibilities against the inroads of such a privilege on the fair administration of criminal justice. The interest in preserving confidentiality is weighty indeed and entitled to great respect. However we cannot conclude that advisers will be moved to temper the candor of their remarks by the infrequent occasions of disclosure because of the possibility that such conversations will be called for in the context of a criminal prosecution.

On the other hand, the allowance of the privilege to withhold evidence that is demonstrably relevant in a criminal trial would cut deeply into the guarantee of due process of law and gravely impair the basic function of the courts. A President's acknowledged need for confidentiality in the communications of his office is general in nature, whereas the constitutional need for production of relevant evidence in a criminal proceeding is specific and central to the fair adjudication of a particular criminal case in the administration of justice. Without access to specific facts a criminal prosecution may be totally frustrated. The President's broad interest in confidentiality of communications will not be vitiated by disclosure of a limited number of conversations preliminarily shown to have some bearing on the pending criminal cases.

We conclude that when the ground for asserting privilege as to subpoenaed materials sought for use in a criminal trial is based only on the generalized interest in confidentiality, it cannot prevail over the fundamental demands of due process of law in the fair administration of criminal justice. The generalized assertion of privilege must yield to the demonstrated, specific need for evidence in a pending criminal trial. . . .

In this case the President challenges a subpoena served on him as a third party requiring the production of materials for use in a criminal prosecution on the claim that he has a privilege against disclosure of confidential communications. He does not place his claim of privilege on the ground they are military or diplomatic secrets. As to these areas of Art. II duties the courts have traditionally shown the utmost deference to presidential responsibilities. No case of the Court, however, has extended this high degree of deference to a President's generalized interest in confidentiality. Nowhere in the Constitution, as we have noted earlier, is there any explicit reference to a privilege of confidentiality; yet to the extent this interest relates to the effective discharge of a President's powers, it is constitutionally based. . . .

[The Court distinguished this case from cases involving claims against the president while acting in an official capacity.]

Mr. Chief Justice Marshall sitting as a trial judge in the *Burr* case was extraordinarily careful to point out that: "[I]n no case of this kind would a Court be required to proceed against the President as against an ordinary individual." Marshall's statement cannot be read to mean in any sense that a President is above the law, but relates to the singularly unique role under Art. II of a President's communications and activities, related to the performance of duties under that Article. Moreover, a President's communications and activities encompass a vastly wider range of sensitive material than would be true of any "ordinary individual." It is therefore necessary in the public interest to afford presidential confidentiality the greatest protection consistent with the fair administration of justice. The need for confidentiality even as to idle conversations with associates in which casual reference might be made concerning political leaders within the country or foreign statesmen is too obvious to call for further treatment. We have no doubt that the District Judge will at all times accord to presidential records that high degree of deference suggested in *United States v. Burr,* and will discharge his responsibility to see to it that until released to the Special Prosecutor no *in camera* material is revealed to anyone. This burden applies with even greater force to excised material; once the decision is made to excise, the material is restored to its privileged status and should be returned under seal to its lawful custodian.

Affirmed.

THE RISE OF PRESIDENTIAL GOVERNMENT

See text p. 139

The term "presidential government" would no doubt have sounded strange to the ears of the Founders, who designed a governmental framework with the legislative branch firmly holding the upper hand. Since the 1930s, as the text points out, the presidency has grown in stature. Given the number and complexity of tasks now delegated to the executive branch, there seems to be little possibility of decreasing the authority vested there. In the following article, Professor Theodore Lowi talks about the growth in presidential power since the 1930s, and suggests "building down" the presidency, both in terms of limiting its formal powers and our own expectations of the possibilities of the office.

Theodore J. Lowi
"Presidential Power: Restoring the Balance"*

The system of a large positive national government in the United States was deliberately constructed in the 1930s. The urgency of the times and the poverty of government experience meant that the building was done exuberantly but improvisationally, without much concern for constitutional values or history. The modern presidency is the centerpiece of that construction. Considered by many a triumph of democracy, the modern American presidency is also its victim.

The gains from presidential government were immediate. Presidential government energized the executive; it gave the national government direction; it enhanced the capacity of presidential leadership to build national consensus and to overcome the natural inertia of a highly heterogeneous society. The costs of presidential government were cumulative. Most of the costs result from the fact that the expectations of the masses have grown faster than the capacity of presidential government to meet them. This imbalance has produced a political cycle, running on a regular course from boom to bust and back again. . . .

*Theodore J. Lowi, "Presidential Power: Restoring the Balance," in *The Personal President* (Ithaca, NY: Cornell University Press, 1985). Reprinted with permission.

Ten years after Watergate the received wisdom seems to be that it was a low point in the history of the presidency and a high point in the history of the genius of the American system for self-correction. . . . [But] an examination of the specific results of Watergate will simply not sustain that kind of conclusion. . . . Before jumping to any larger conclusions . . . let us review the direct lessons that can definitively be learned from the outcome of Watergate. *If you are president:* Don't commit a crime. Don't encourage members of your staff to commit a crime—that is itself a commission of a crime. Don't keep records—written or on tape—of actions or discussions remotely connected to the commission of a crime. Dispose of any such records well before allegations of possible crimes can be made, because executive privilege does not protect confidential records that bear on such allegations. *If you are a member of the president's staff:* Don't burgle for the president. Don't engage in forgery for the president. Don't engage in illegal wiretapping and electronic surveillance for the president. Don't lie for the president, and in particular don't permit your president to encourage you to lie. Don't encourage or participate in the obstruction of justice. Don't destroy evidence. Don't offer or accept bribes. Don't try to encourage persons or government agencies to engage in actions that violate federal laws. And if any of these activities should take place, be absolutely certain of deniability—that proof can be rendered up that the president was truly and absolutely ignorant of the illegal activities that were taking place.

In other words, no substantial direct lesson can be learned from Watergate except not to engage in illegal activities or be caught doing so. No general lesson can be drawn about the imperial presidency or the plebiscitary presidency that could not have been drawn before Watergate or in ignorance of its events and results. . . . In every respect other than the extent of illegal activities, there is a Watergate of some kind every day in the life of a president. The scale of presidential power and of mass expectation about presidential power is so great that presidents must, as in Watergate, attempt to control their environment to the maximum, especially those aspects of it that might tend to be barriers in the way of meeting presidential responsibilities. Those responsibilities are so pressing and so close to unmeetable that presidents must have vast contingency plans to make up the difference between expectations and realities. Presidents must first . . . find a way to control events themselves. But because of the near certainty of failure, presidents must have contingency plans for what to do if they cannot control events. This means they must have contingency plans for controlling the news about the events. That requires an army of public relations people . . . to try to create the appearance of success. But since the White House cannot control the way events are interpreted as news, there must also be contingency plans for controlling what gets into the public domain in the first place. . . .

The Imperial/Plebiscitary Presidency

Richard Nixon was brought up on the imperial presidency and had no serious misgivings about it. Imperial meant something established, neither extreme nor extraordinary. . . . *Imperial* . . . connotes a strong state with sovereignty and power over foreigners, as well as rank, status, privilege, and authority, and it also connotes the president's power and responsibility to do whatever he judges necessary to maintain the sovereignty of the state and its ability to keep public order, both international and domestic. The imperial presidency turns out on inspection, therefore, to be nothing more nor less than the discretionary presidency grounded in national security rather than domestic government. Characterizing the presidency as plebiscitary is not at all inconsistent; it is an attempt to capture the same factors and at the same time to tie them to the greatest source of everyday pressure on the presidency—not the Soviet Union, not world leadership, but the American people and their expectations. Nixon's understanding of this situation in all its aspects was probably more extensive and complete than that of any other modern president. He understood it to a fault. If so, he was operating logically and sanely under the following assumptions:

The first assumption is that the president and the state are the same thing, that president is state personified. The second is that powers should be commensurate with responsibilities. Since most of the responsibilities of state were intentionally delegated to the president, there is every reason to assume that Congress and the people intended that there be a capacity to carry them out.

The third assumption, intimately related to the second, is that the president should not and cannot be bound by normal legal restrictions. To put this indelicately, the president's actions must be considered above the law or subject to a different kind of law from those of ordinary citizens. While not free to commit any crime merely for the sake of convenience, the president nevertheless cannot be constantly beset by considerations of legality when the state itself is or seems to be at issue.

The first three assumptions head inexorably toward a fourth, which is that any *deliberate* barriers to presidential action must be considered tantamount to disloyalty. Barriers to presidential action can be tolerated up to a point, and it is probable that most presidents, including Richard Nixon, have prided themselves on their uncommon patience with organized protests, well-meaning but embarrassing news leaks, journalistic criticism, and organized political opposition. But there is a point beyond which such barriers cannot be tolerated, and as that point is approached, confidential knowledge of the identities and contentions of the organizers of obstructions must be gathered. When the intentions of these organizers are determined, to the president's satisfaction, to be malicious, it would be foolish for the president to wait. . . .

Restoring the Balance: Some False Starts and Panaceas

The War Powers Resolution.   The War Powers Resolution was passed in November 1973, by a Congress that wanted to put an end to what its members deemed usurpation, the assertion of presidential power to make presidential war. . . . The purpose of the War Powers Resolution was to "fulfill the intent of the framers of the Constitution" (Section 2) by reintroducing a balancing role for Congress. The resolution is in largest part a failure, however, in at least two respects. First, it does not give Congress any substantial powers to check the president or any substantial new opportunities to participate in foreign policy that it did not already have or could not exercise without the resolution. Second, presidents since 1974 have not regarded themselves as bound by the resolution, at least not in the sense Congress seems to have intended. . . .

Even the president with the weakest constitutional authority in American history, the appointed Gerald Ford, was able to play fast and loose with the War Powers Resolution within a year after its passage. . . .

Budget Reform.   The Congressional Budget and Impoundment Control Act of 1974 also had as its intention the restoration of a balance between the president and Congress. The purpose of the act was to centralize the budgetary process in Congress and to bring appropriations decisions closer to revenue decisions. . . .

There are few disagreements with the contention that the reformed budget process is an improvement. The CBO has turned out to be a definite asset for Congress and a tremendously important source of fiscal information independent of and often in contention with that of the White House and the OMB. However, there are few who would argue that the new arrangements have substantially changed the imbalances of power between the executive branch and Congress. Even where Congress permits itself to be influenced by its own ceilings as established in the first Concurrent Resolution, the second Concurrent Resolution has been late every year since the first year (1976) and is, therefore, not available at the most significant times when commitments are made. Moreover, Congress has not yet been able to use the reformed budgetary process to improve its ability to make real "program budget" decisions, wherein priorities between and among programs and appropriations are actually set. . . .

Assessment of the budget reform's success in reducing constitutional imbalances can best be made in the words of the most outstanding and respected student of the budget process:

[N]either Congress nor the President can effectively budget if most spending decisions are made outside the budget process. . . . [T]he fact that three-quarters of total expenditures are deemed to be uncontrollable [entitlements provided by law, "off-budget" commitments in loans and loan guarantees, etc.] means that the amounts cannot be determined through budget decisions alone but can be controlled through other actions such as legislative changes in existing laws. In effect, budgeting is subordinate to other resource allocation processes which lack its routines and sensitivity to the relationship between claims on the budget and available resources. . . . As a result, while the Government's control of the "administrative budget" is adequate, its control of the political budget is not. . . . *Tinkering with the machinery of budgeting will not solve the problem of control nor will it restore the process to the status it once had.* Budgeting is not designed to cope with the issues it now faces. The problem is not solely one of budgeting, but goes to the heart of governance. . . . When the federal government effectively governs, it will again have the capacity to budget.*

Presidential Power: If Building It Up Won't Work Try Building It Down

America approaches the end of the twentieth century with an enormous bureaucratized government, a plebiscitary presidency, and apparent faith that the latter can impose on the former an accountability sufficient to meet the rigorous test of democratic theory. Anyone who really shares this faith is living under a happy state of delusion. Anyone who does not believe and argues it nevertheless is engaging in one of Plato's Noble Lies; that is to say, the leaders do not believe it but believe it is in the public interest that the rest of us believe it. Then there are others who don't believe it but would like to make it the truth by giving the president more and more help. Presidents have themselves tried nearly everything to build for themselves a true capacity to govern. Congress, with few exceptions, has cooperated. The Supreme Court . . . has cooperated. The public seems willing to cooperate in making truth out of the noble lie by investing more and more power in the presidency. The intellectuals, perhaps most of all, have cooperated. If that's not enough, then it's possible nothing is enough.

Since building up the presidency has not met the problem of presidential capacity to govern, the time has come to consider building it down. Building down goes against the mentality of American capitalism, whose primary measure of success is buildups. Buildups are so important to American corporate managers that they fake them if necessary, through anything from useless mergers to misrepresentation of profits. Very few leaders have tried to succeed by making a virtue of building down. There was Bismarck, who perceived greater strength in a "smaller Germany." There may be a case or two of weekly magazines whose publishers have sought to strengthen their position by abandoning the struggle for a maximum mass subscription in favor of a smaller and more select but stable readership. But most leaders, in commerce and government, are guilty of what Barry Goldwater popularized in the 1960s, "growthmanship." In many circumstances, building up is an illusory solution, or, at best, a short-term gain.

The most constructive approach to building down the presidency would

---

*Allen Schick, "The Budget as an Instrument of Presidential Policy,"—an unpublished paper. A longer version of this paper, "How the Budget was Won and Lost," can be found in Norman Ornstein, ed., *President and Congress: Assessing Reagan's First Year*, (Washington, D.C.: American Enterprise Institute, 1982), pp 25–26.

be the strengthening of political parties. If party organizations returned to the center of presidential selection, they would build down the presidency by making collective responsibility a natural outcome of the selection process rather than an alien intruder. Real parties build down the presidency in constructive ways by making real cabinets possible. The present selection process and the present relationship between the president and public opinion produced the star symbol that renders a president's sharing power almost inconceivable. The selection process with parties involved makes the star system itself hard to conceive of.

A three-party system comes into the picture in at least two ways. First, if a two-party system is indeed an anachronism in modern programmatic governments, a three-party system could be the most reasonable way to make real parties possible. Second, a three-party system might build down the presidency by making it more of a parliamentary office. This development would constitute something of a return to the original intent of the Founders' design, a selection process culminating in the House of Representatives. The French improved upon their system by mixing theirs with ours to create the Fifth Republic. It is time we consider mixing ours with theirs. The Fifth Republic established a better balance than we have by successfully imposing an independently elected president upon a strong parliament, giving the parliament the leadership lacking in the Fourth Republic but keeping the popularly elected president tied closely to it.

The crying need to impose parliamentary responsibility in our independently elected president can be accomplished without formally amending the Constitution. Just as the two-party system transformed the presidential selection system and thereby the presidency, so would a three-party or multiparty system transform the presidency, by bringing Congress back into the selection process. This transformation could, in addition, give Congress incentive to confront the real problems of the presidency. Although I admit that is unlikely, the probability could be improved as more of its members came to realize that Congress's survival as an institution may depend upon depriving the presidency of its claim to represent the Great American Majority. The presidency must be turned into a more parliamentary office.

Presidents who are products of the present system are also unlikely to try to change it—unless they come to recognize its inherent pathologies. The first president to recognize these pathologies will want to build down the presidency, and his or her legacy will be profound and lasting. A president who recognizes the pathology of the plebiscitary presidency will demand changes that will ward off failure and encourage shared responsibility. At a minimum, a rational president would veto congressional enactments delegating powers so broad and so vague that expectations cannot be met. This step in itself would build down the presidency in a very special way: It would incorporate more of Congress into the presidency because the clearer the intentions and the criteria of performance written into a statute, the more responsibility for its outcomes would be shared by the majority in Congress responsible for its passage. Such a way of building down alone would not produce a third party, but it would make the presidency more parliamentary, and thus more accommodating to strong parties and to three parties or more. Put this way, the prospect does not seem so unrealistic. To accomplish it, the president must simply make an analysis of the situation. A president must simply change his point of view. . . .

On one point at least there is strong agreement between my point of view and that of Ronald Reagan: his observation that where once government was part of the solution it is now part of the problem. Since I have been arguing the same thing at least since 1969, I celebrate Reagan's recognition of the truth and regret the fact he did not actually believe it. He embraced big government and embraced, nay, enlarged the plebiscitary presidency more than most of his predecessors. Why do all recent presidents and important presidential aspirants look back with such admiration to Harry Truman, a man of such ordinary character and talents? I think they do so because Truman was the last president who was made bigger by the office he occupied. This is not to say that recent presidents have made more mistakes than presidents of the past. It is to say that they have been diminished by having to achieve so much more than past presidents and by having to use so much more deception to compensate for their failures. Modern presidents blame their failures on everything but the presidency, when the fault is the presidency more than anything else. It is there that successful coping must begin, with a change of attitude toward the plebiscitary presidency that will enable presidents and presidential candidates to confront the contradictions in the modern presidency rather than by embracing the office as it is. Real reform in American presidential government will not come until there is real change in the points of view of powerful people. As in psychoanalysis, so in politics, coping is a solution, and it will be found not in techniques but in awareness of the nature of the problem. Techniques will follow.

BUREAUCRACY IN A DEMOCRACY

See text p. 161

All agencies, regardless of their fundamental nature have a vested interest in assuring their continued existence. Since 1989, unprecedented changes in the international political situation have called into question the traditional functions of American external security agencies like the CIA. During the Cold War, the CIA had little trouble justifying its existence; indeed, because most of its activities were secret for reasons of national security, it was easier for the CIA to establish its credentials than other agencies whose work product was on public display. Upsets in the global political order have altered that situation considerably. After a long confirmation hearing, Robert Gates was confirmed as Bush's director of the CIA in November 1991. In the following article, written just as the nomination hearings got underway in the Spring of 1991, political commentator Patrick Tyler discussed the task that Gates would have defining the CIA's role in a post–Cold War world.

Patrick E. Tyler
"The Task: Slip Spies into the New World Order"*

If confirmed by the Senate as the Director of Central Intelligence, Robert M. Gates may well take the United States intelligence "community" through its most important transition since President Harry Truman set the structure for America's bureaucracy of spies in 1947.

Despite the best efforts by the departing director, William H. Webster, to define a new role for the spy agencies he has supervised since the death of William J. Casey in 1987, the farflung American intelligence apparatus remains in search of enemies and threats to justify not just its $30 billion budget, but its very existence.

Saddam Hussein and the Persian Gulf war provided a respite from the "What-are-we-about?" debate that has seized the nation's intelligence agencies since the Berlin wall came down. But President Bush's nomination of Mr. Gates last week abruptly returned the spotlight to the intelligence agenda, which is anything but in order.

Both the House and Senate oversight committees are warning that if the new C.I.A. director does not bring discipline to intelligence spending and cut duplication between military and civilian agencies, they will force changes by legislation. Mr. Gates is viewed as a forceful bureaucrat with C.I.A. and White House training who will seek to pre-empt the intelligence committees by making his own changes. But any major restructuring will meet formidable institutional resistance.

"My concern about the new director," said the House Intelligence Committee chairman, Dave McCurdy, "is that he be willing to take on the bureaucracy and the culture in order to bring about the necessary changes and have a much broader focus for intelligence."

One of the changes both committees are considering could strip away the broad mandate the C.I.A. head currently has to direct the entire intelligence community, leaving him to run only his agency, and create a director of national intelligence to be the President's intelligence czar.

Aside from the C.I.A., the "community" includes the National Reconnaissance Office, which is in charge of imagery satellites; the National Security Agency, which is in charge of signal interception; the Defense Intelligence Agency, the Pentagon's analytical arm, and an assortment of military intelligence services.

Whatever changes are wrought by Mr. Gates or the oversight committees, the C.I.A. and its sister agencies appear to be headed for a period of budgetary decline. "There are actually greater requirements for sophisticated intelligence than ever before," said Mr. McCurdy, "but they are going to have to be accomplished with fewer resources."

Shrinking Threats

In the same pattern as the Pentagon's $300 billion budget, more than half of the dollars spent for intelligence collection and analysis over the last four decades have been targeted at the Soviet Union and its Warsaw Pact allies. With that threat gone, American intelligence czars have yet to answer the questions about what they are going to do in the next century.

To be sure, there will be drug trafficking to combat, terrorism to counter and third world brush-fire wars to monitor, but these problems pale against the overarching military threat the Soviet Union once posed—although some monitoring of Soviet strategic and conventional forces will be necessary for years to come.

With a fleet of high-technology reconnaissance satellites, scores of aircraft, submarines, underwater sensors, mountaintop listening posts, legions of spies and analysts, the intelligence agencies live in an insular and well-funded world, issuing reports on worldwide trends and events, but driven less and less by the engines of East-West competition.

Many experts believe the problems of the future, such as economic collapse in the third world, ethnic and regional conflict, environmental degradation and population control, will be readily apparent. The challenge will be more to understand what is visible than to ferret out what is hidden.

Today, and increasingly in the future, large parts of the multibillion dollar intelligence programs are destined to suffer the crisis of justification that has befallen the B-2 Stealth Bomber, a weapon built to penetrate Soviet air space during nuclear war but now seeking a new mission in a safer world.

An intelligence parallel is the National Security Agency, with 27,000 employees and an annual budget of $4 billion. Behind the high security fences at its headquarters in Ft. Meade, Md., one of N.S.A.'s largest single activities is collating, interpreting and breaking the codes of Soviet communications, radar signals, telemetry and computer data intercepted by $1 billion-plus satellites or by squadrons of spy planes. Billions of dollars have been spent for the banks of supercomputers the agency uses to run programs that decode what Soviet political leaders and military commanders are saying to each other.

Is this agency ripe for cutting? "Yes," said Bobby Ray Inman, a former N.S.A. director and now a member of the President's intelligence advisory board.

"But before you start reorganizing, you need to decide what you want to know about the outside world and you need to look ten years out and not five," he said. "We will have almost no concerns about military activity in Eastern Europe, but we will be vastly more interested in internal stability, economic and political developments. It's not that we are going to be doing vastly less, but we're going to be doing it in the open."

One former intelligence officer observed that more could be learned today about the implosion of the Soviet empire by openly sending American cultural attaches to each of the Soviet Republics than by recruiting networks of spies to dig out secret data.

"I think American intelligence needs to have a better feel for the societies in which they operate overseas," said Graham Fuller, a former Middle East analyst for the C.I.A. "It isn't just the collection of secrets that helps the agency predict events, it's getting our fingers on the pulse of society. That's not secret, it's just hard to find out."

For all the billions of dollars sunk into intelligence systems in the last decade, the intelligence community has a mixed record on spotting trouble. In the national security review Mr. Bush conducted in early 1989, C.I.A. analysts predicted: "War weary Iraq will pose a military threat to small neighboring states during this period, but will be reluctant to engage in foreign military adventures. It is more likely to resort to diplomacy and subversion to achieve its goals." By March 1990, the agency was saying that the Iraqi leader might undertake a new military campaign in the region after three more years of recuperation from its war with Iran.

Even Mr. Gates, who built his reputation as a C.I.A. analyst with well-grounded predictive powers, was confidently forecasting in January 1989 that the Afghan leader, Najibullah, would not last through the summer after the Soviet army's pullout. Yet Najibullah still dominates Kabul two years later and has confounded American policy in Afghanistan.

These and other examples demonstrate that the intelligence business is a very expensive game of informed assessments and predictions in which truth is often the most elusive product. The question is, said the Senate Intelligence Committee chairman, David Boren, in recent hearings, how much should the United States pay for it?

As Mr. Gates heads for what may be a grueling series of confirmation hearings, he will have to be concerned not just about the price, but how, in a rapidly changing world, to find the product.

See text p. 163

If the key activity of regulatory agencies during the 1980s was deregulation, the watchword of the 1990s is likely to be reregulation. Despite perennial complaints about government interference in the free operation of the market, regulation has often facilitated business, especially at the federal level, where it has provided a uniform set of standards that allow companies to operate in several different states at the same time. In the wake of declining federal regulatory programs, many states have stepped in to regulate commerce on a local level, creating a confusing patchwork of standards that businesses are finding difficult to work with—a consequence of the federalist nature of the American system discussed in Chapter 3. In a February 1991 article, commentator John Holusha points out that the 1990s may be marked by increasing requests for "the good old days of . . . federal control."

John Holusha
"Some Corporations Plead for the Firm Hand of Uncle Sam"*

The pace of regulatory activity in Washington slowed sharply after President Ronald Reagan promised to get big government off the back of industry in the 1980s. Budgets were cut and top officials emphasized a free market approach. But now, faced with a patchwork of conflicting regulations at the state level, a broad coalition of companies that produce and sell consumer products is deciding that maybe uniform Federal regulations wouldn't be such a bad thing after all. In some cases, companies are actually going to Washington and asking for a return to the good old days of broader Federal control.

"It may be that, after the fact, nationwide marketers are becoming opposed to the trend and are moving to stem the onrush to deregulation," said Susan Edelman, a professor at the Columbia University Business School.

For those who have felt that in many cases deregulation went too far, the idea of executives asking for regulation is a welcome twist.

"With environmental issues, it is not clear that the invisible hand will optimize," said John Meyer, a professor at the Kennedy School of Government at Harvard University. "There are too many external factors that have high public costs. So it would appear that the benefits of government action would exceed the costs."

States are increasingly moving to fill the void left by the Federal Government by imposing their own regulations on packaging, hazardous waste, automotive emissions and other environmentally related activities. With no sign that the Federal Government was interested in decreeing when a company can claim that a product is "recyclable" or "recycled"—designations that consumer products manufacturers want to be able to use on their packages because surveys have shown that buyers feel better about products that appear to be environmentally sound—New York, Rhode Island and California have enacted their own conflicting rules. Other states are considering their own measures.

Executives for companies like Proctor & Gamble and Lever Brothers, which manufacture products in large centralized factories and distribute them across the country, say that contradictory state laws can be a nightmare. For example, California requires that 10 percent of a product consist of recovered material before it can be labeled "recycled." In New York, the requirement varies from product to product; paper towels need 40 percent recycled content, while for aluminum packaging the requirement is 15 percent. Some industry officials say the companies might reluctantly drop the environmental claims rather than try to meet different requirements in different states.

"The states moved into a vacuum," said Robert M. Viney, a environmental marketing specialist at Proctor & Gamble. "There were no Federal standards or guidelines for labeling."

Looking to Washington

Many manufacturers fear they will be victimized by politically ambitious state officials seeking to exploit the environmental issue. Last year several state attorneys general accused a subsidiary of Mobil Oil of false advertising when it labeled its Hefty plastic trash bags "degradable." The company has agreed to remove the claim. Last November, 10 attorneys general, 7 of them Democrats, appeared to be trying to seize control of the labeling issue when they issued a report of "recommendations for responsible environmental advertising."

Hoping that the Republican Bush Administration would give them standards that were not only uniform but more lenient, Proctor & Gamble, Lever Brothers, Kraft Foods and a number of trade associations, including the National Retail Federation, the Grocery Manufacturers Association and the Food Marketing Institute, asked the Federal Trade Commission on Feb. 14 to issue guidelines regulating the use of environmental claims. Officials of the agency have indicated they are receptive to such an approach.

Officials of some of the companies involved concede that it is unusual for them to seek direction from Washington. "This is an anomaly," said Melinda Sweet, the director of environmental affairs for Lever Brothers. "Normally we would shout and fight."

But she said many of the same companies and associations may be back in Washington later this year if states start imposing limits on packaging, requiring, for example, that it contain a certain percentage of recycled material. This, too, is an issue that Federal regulators have never addressed.

Fighting Back

"Modifying package designs state by state would be impractical and uneconomical," Ms. Sweet said. "Distribution would be impossible." Since the Resource Conservation and Recovery Act, which deals with solid waste, is due for reauthorization this year, it could become the vehicle for attempts to pre-empt state actions.

Packaging manufacturers and consumer goods companies have good reason to be worried about state action. Legislators in Maine last year voted to ban single-serving juice boxes made with layers of plastic, aluminum and paper on the ground that they are difficult to recycle.

Model legislation developed by the Coalition of Northeast Governors and adopted by eight states, which would limit the amount of heavy metals in printing inks, is on its way to becoming a national standard. The coalition has been working on developing rules to make packaging more recyclable, although the process has been slowed recently by infighting between environmental groups and state officials.

Some industry representatives say the Reagan Administration's reluctance to do anything that smacked of regulation is the reason for the unwanted upsurge in activity by the states. "You have a maturing environmental movement that was blocked in Washington, so they went to the states," said Jeffrey Nedelman, a vice president of Grocery Manufacturers of America. "The Reagan Administration stiff-armed them for eight years."

Susan Birmingham, a lobbyist for the United States Public Interest Research Group, an umbrella organization of state environmental and consumer groups, said that ideally the Federal Government should take a leadership role. "But the political reality is that you have to be successful at the state level before you can start persuading Congress," she said. "We have much more room to maneuver in the states."

CHAPTER 7

The Federal Judiciary: Least Dangerous Branch or Imperial Judiciary?

JUDICIAL REVIEW

See text p. 177

The power of judicial review—the authority of the federal courts to determine the constitutionality of state and federal legislative acts—was established early in the nation's history in the case of Marbury v. Madison (1803). While the doctrine of judicial review is now firmly entrenched in the American judicial process, the outcome of Marbury was by no means a sure thing. The doctrine had been outlined in The Federalist No. 78, and had been relied upon implicitly in earlier, lower federal court cases, but there were certainly sentiments among some of the Founders to suggest that only Congress ought to be able to judge the constitutionality of its acts.

Marbury v. *Madison* (1803)[*] ✻ *Exam*

[The facts leading up to the decision in Marbury *v.* Madison *tell an intensely political story. Efforts to reform the federal judiciary had been ongoing with the Federalist administration of President Adams. Following the defeat of the Federalist party in 1800, and the election of Thomas Jefferson as president, the Federalist Congress passed an act reforming the judiciary. The act gave outgoing President Adams authority to appoint several Federalist justices of the peace before Jefferson's term as president began. This would have enabled the Federalist party to retain a large measure of power.*

Marbury was appointed to be a justice of the peace by President Adams, but his commission, signed by the president and sealed by the secretary of state, without which he could not assume office, was not delivered to him before President Jefferson took office March 4, 1803. Jefferson refused to order James Madison, his secretary of state, to deliver the commission. Marbury, in turn, filed an action in the U.S. Supreme Court seeking an order—called a writ of mandamus—directing the secretary of state to compel the delivery of the commission.

The Constitution grants the Supreme Court original jurisdiction in only a limited number of cases—those involving ambassadors, public ministers, and those in which a state is a party; in the remaining cases, the Court has authority only as an appellate court. When it acts according to its original jurisdiction, the Court exercises initial authority over a controversy, just like a trial court, as distinguished from the more limited authority it exercises when a case is presented as an appeal from a lower court's decision.

[*]Marbury v. Madison, 5 U.S. 137, 1803.

In 1789, Congress passed legislation setting up the federal courts, called the Judiciary Act of 1789. That legislation gave the Supreme Court the original authority to "issue writs of mandamus in cases warranted by the principles and usage of law. . . ." Thus, the ultimate question in Marbury v. Madison *was whether Congress could, by statute, enlarge the original jurisdiction of the Court.*

The Court first considered whether Marbury's appointment was complete—and therefore irrevocable—before Jefferson took office. Under the law, the appointment was deemed complete when the president signed the commission and the secretary of state sealed it; the appointment was a completed fact at that time, and was not dependent upon delivery. Therefore, the Court found that Marbury was entitled to his commission. The Court then decided that by witholding the commission, Secretary of State Madison was violating Marbury's legal rights. The remaining question was whether the Supreme Court could issue an order compelling the delivery of the commission.]

CHIEF JUSTICE MARSHALL delivered the opinion of the Court.

. . . It is, then, the opinion of the Court,

1st. That by signing the commission of Mr. Marbury, the President of the United States appointed him a justice of peace for the county of Washington, in the District of Columbia; and that the seal of the United States, affixed thereto by the Secretary of State, is conclusive testimony of the verity of the signature, and of the completion of the appointment, and that the appointment conferred on him a legal right to the office for the space of five years.

2d. That, having this legal title to the office, he has a consequent right to the commission; a refusal to deliver which is a plain violation of that right, for which the laws of his country afford him a remedy.

It remains to be inquired whether,

3d. He is entitled to the remedy for which he applies. This depends on,

1st. The nature of the writ applied for; and,

2d. The power of this court. . . .

This . . . is a plain case for a mandamus, either to deliver the commission, or a copy of it from the record; and it only remains to be inquired,

Whether it can issue from this court.

The act to establish the judicial courts of the United States authorizes the Supreme Court "to issue writs of mandamus in cases warranted by the principles and usages of law, to any courts appointed, or persons holding office, under the authority of the United States."

The Secretary of State, being a person holding an office under the authority of the United States, is precisely within the letter of the description, and if this court is not authorized to issue a writ of mandamus to such an officer, it must be because the law is unconstitutional, and therefore absolutely incapable of conferring the authority, and assigning the duties which its words purport to confer and assign.

The constitution vests the whole judicial power of the United States in one Supreme Court, and such inferior courts as congress shall, from time to time, ordain and establish. This power is expressly extended to all cases arising under the laws of the United States; and, consequently, in some form, may be exercised over the present case; because the right claimed is given by a law of the United States.

In the distribution of this power it is declared that "the Supreme Court shall have original jurisdiction in all cases affecting ambassadors, other public ministers and consuls, and those in which a state shall be a party. In all other cases, the Supreme Court shall have appellate jurisdiction." . . .

To enable this court, then, to issue a mandamus, it must be shown to be an exercise of appellate jurisdiction, or to be necessary to enable them to exercise appellate jurisdiction. . . .

It is the essential criterion of appellate jurisdiction, that it revises and corrects the proceedings in a cause already instituted, and does not create that cause. . . . [Y]et to issue such a writ to an officer for the delivery of a paper, is in effect the same as to sustain an original action for that paper, and, therefore, seems not to belong to appellate, but to original jurisdiction.

The authority, therefore, given to the Supreme Court, by the act establishing the judicial courts of the United States, to issue writs of mandamus to public officers, appears not to be warranted by the constitution; and it becomes necessary to inquire whether a jurisdiction so conferred can be exercised.

The question, whether an act, repugnant to the constitution, can become the law of the land, is a question deeply interesting to the United States; but, happily, not of an intricacy proportioned to its interest. It seems only necessary to recognize certain principles, supposed to have been long and well established, to decide it.

That the people have an original right to establish, for their future government, such principles, as, in their opinion, shall most conduce to their own happiness is the basis on which the whole American fabric has been erected. The exercise of this original right is a very great exertion; nor can it, nor ought it, to be frequently repeated. The principles, therefore, so established, are deemed fundamental. And as the authority from which they proceed is supreme, and can seldom act, they are designed to be permanent.

This original and supreme will organizes the government, and assigns to different departments their respective powers. It may either stop here, or establish certain limits not to be transcended by those departments.

The government of the United States is of the latter description. The powers of the legislature are defined and limited; and that those limits may not be mistaken, or forgotten, the constitution is written. To what purpose are powers limited, and to what purpose is that limitation committed to writing, if these limits may, at any time, be passed by those intended to be restrained? The distinction between a government with limited and unlimited powers is abolished, if those limits do not confine the persons on whom they are imposed, and if acts prohibited and acts allowed, are of equal obligation. It is a proposition too plain to be contested, that the constitution controls any legislative act repugnant to it; or, that the legislature may alter the constitution by an ordinary act.

Between these alternatives there is no middle ground. The constitution is either a superior paramount law, unchangeable by ordinary means, or it is on a level with ordinary legislative acts, and, like other acts, is alterable when the legislature shall please to alter it.

If the former part of the alternative be true, then a legislative act contrary to the constitution is not law: if the latter part be true, then written constitutions are absurd attempts, on the part of the people, to limit a power in its own nature illimitable.

Certainly all those who have framed written constitutions contemplate them as forming the fundamental and paramount law of the nation, and, consequently, the theory of every such government must be, that an act of the legislature, repugnant to the constitution, is void.

This theory is essentially attached to a written constitution, and, is consequently, to be considered, by this court, as one of the fundamental principles of our society. It is not therefore to be lost sight of in the further consideration of this subject.

If an act of the legislature, repugnant to the constitution, is void, does it, notwithstanding its invalidity, bind the courts, and oblige them to give it effect? Or, in other words, though it be not law, does it constitute a rule as operative as if it was a law? This would be to overthrow in fact what was established in theory; and would seem, at first view, an absurdity too gross to be insisted on. . . .

It is emphatically the province and duty of the judicial department to say what the law is. Those who apply the rule to particular cases, must of necessity expound and interpret that rule. If two laws conflict with each other, the courts must decide on the operation of each.

So if a law be in opposition to the constitution; if both the law and the constitution apply to a particular case, so that the court must either decide that case conformably to the law, disregarding the constitution; or conformably to the constitution, disregarding the law; the court must determine which of these conflicting rules governs the case. This is of the very essence of judicial duty.

If, then, the courts are to regard the constitution, and the constitution is superior to any ordinary act of the legislature, the constitution, and not such ordinary act, must govern the case to which they both apply.

Those, then, who controvert the principle that the constitution is to be considered, in court, as a paramount law, are reduced to the necessity of maintaining that courts must close their eyes on the constitution, and see only the law.

This doctrine would subvert the very foundation of all written constitutions. It would declare that an act which, according to the principles and theory of our government, is entirely void, is yet, in practice, completely obligatory. It would declare that if the legislature shall do what is expressly forbidden, such act, notwithstanding the express prohibition, is in reality effectual. It would be given to the legislature a practical and real omnipotence, with the same breath which professes to restrict their powers within narrow limits. It is prescribing limits, and declaring that those limits may be passed at pleasure.

That it thus reduces to nothing what we have deemed the greatest improvement on political institutions, a written constitution, would of itself be sufficient, in America, where written constitutions have been viewed with so much reverence, for rejecting the construction. But the peculiar expressions of the constitution of the United States furnish additional arguments in favour of its rejection.

The judicial power of the United States is extended to all cases arising under the constitution.

Could it be the intention of those who gave this power, to say that in using it the constitution should not be looked into? That a case arising under the constitution should be decided without examining the instrument under which it arises?

This is too extravagant to be maintained.

In some cases, then, the constitution must be looked into by the judges.

. . . [I]t is apparent, that the framers of the constitution contemplated that instrument as a rule for the government of courts, as well as of the legislature.

Why otherwise does it direct the judges to take an oath to support it? This oath certainly applies in an especial manner, to their conduct in their official character. How immoral to impose it on them, if they were to be used as the instruments, and the knowing instruments, for violating what they swear to support!

The oath of office, too, imposed by the legislature, is completely demonstrative of the legislative opinion on this subject. . . .

Why does a judge swear to discharge his duties agreeably to the constitution of the United States, if that constitution forms no rule for his government? if it is closed upon him, and cannot be inspected by him?

If such be the real state of things, this is worse than solemn mockery. To prescribe, or to take this oath, becomes equally a crime.

It is also not entirely unworthy of observation, that in declaring what shall be the supreme law of the land, the constitution itself is first mentioned; and not the laws of the United States generally, but those only which shall be made in pursuance of the constitution, have that rank.

Thus, the particular phraseology of the constitution of the United States confirms and strengthens the principle, supposed to be essential to all written constitutions, that a law repugnant to the constitution is void; and that courts, as well as other departments, are bound by that instrument.

See text p. 180

In the mid-1980s, the composition of the federal judiciary began to change dramatically as the Reagan administration's appointment of new judges at all levels in the federal courts began to take hold, generating considerable discussion over the nature and functions of judicial interpretation of the Constitution. Eventually, this debate evolved into what is known as the activist/original intent debate, with conservatives such as Edwin Meese, President Reagan's attorney general, arguing that in reviewing legislation, *courts should look for guidance by seeking the "original intent" of the Constitution's framers, while more liberal actors, like former Justice William Brennan, argued that the courts had to respond to changing times and act with an understanding of contemporary concerns.*

In the following article from a 1987 issue of the New York Times, *Harvard law professor Laurence Tribe reflects on the political significance of judicial review, with reference to the "original intent" controversy, and makes a strong case for the preservation of an independent judiciary with broad powers of judicial review.*

Lawrence H. Tribe
"The Final Say"*

ARTICLE III: Section 2. The judicial Power shall extend to all case. . . .

Not long ago, a New York Times/CBS News Poll showed that nearly a third of the American people surveyed opposed judicial review, the process by which the lower Federal courts and, ultimately, the Supreme Court of the United States can pass judgment on constitutional challenges to legislative and executive actions. Many Americans, it seems, prefer that the executive and legislative branches check and balance themselves. In the same poll, only 16 percent of the public favored life tenure for Supreme Court justices. Even when life tenure was explained as providing judges with independence from political pressures, only 35 percent favored it.

The public's distaste for the authority of the Federal judiciary to decide the constitutionality of governmental actions has found a voice in, of all people, the Attorney General of the United States. Last fall, Edwin Meese 3d issued a surprisingly casual invitation to government officials throughout the country to disregard Supreme Court decisions on constitutional matters in cases to which they were not parties. His reasoning: the Court's views are not to be confused with the Constitution itself.

Certainly, there are contexts in which the Constitution's own structure gives Congress or the President or the states the last word in constitutional debate. For example, if a President vetoes a bill because he believes it to be unconstitutional, the Supreme Court cannot reach out to overrule that veto should it disagree with the President's constitutional analysis.

Nor can the Court "correct" the Senate's rejection of a President's Supreme Court nominee whose views of the Constitution it deems dangerous. The controversy surrounding the nomination of Robert H. Bork to the Supreme Court confirms that the power of the Senate to give "advice and consent" on Presidential appointments remains a potent political influence on the power and independence of the judiciary.

But outside these special spheres, constitutional chaos would ensue— and the peculiar significance of the Constitution in our public life would be at an end—if every Federal agency, every school district, every city council felt free to act on its own constitutional theory unless and until used by its latest victim and brought into line by the Supreme Court.

Our society would be wholly unworkable if the meaning of the legal documents by which we regulate our lives and conduct our affairs—contracts, deeds, wills, statutes, the Constitution itself—were to be determined by each of us according to individual interests and opinions. The meaning of a legal document in any particular context is ultimately—and necessarily—a judicial question. So it is that Article III of the Constitution provides that "the judicial power of the United States shall be vested in one Supreme Court and in such inferior courts as the Congress may . . . establish."

Well aware of the gravity of such questions of legal interpretation, especially with respect to a nation's fundamental charter, the framers elevated the judiciary—heretofore the captive creature of monarchs, chancellors and parliaments—to the status of an independent and equal third branch of government.

The decision of the Framers to place their faith—and the Constitution—in the hands of an independent judiciary was not predicated on the assumption that the Supreme Court would always reach a "correct" reading of that document. Certainly, the Court's infamous decisions affirming racial separation if the facilities—schools and restrooms—were "equal," or the ones handed down after the attack on Pearl Harbor allowing Americans of Japanese descent to be herded into detention camps without proof of wrongdoing, do not strike us today as correct. The importance of the Court was, instead, well summarized in Justice Robert Jackson's mildly cynical assessment: "We are not final because we are infallible, but we are infallible only because we are final."

The absolute finality of Court decisions—barring a constitutional amendment or subsequent reversal by the Court itself—does more than give gravity to that body's pronouncements on constitutional matters; it makes constitutional arguments and determinations count, in a way that they would not count if each government official were bound only by that person's own opinion of the Constitution's meaning.

Yet the authority of the Supreme Court to exert such influence over the country as a whole, and even its authority to make the parties before it—Richard M. Nixon in the famous Watergate Tapes case, for example—abide by its reading of the Constitution are not spelled out anywhere in the document.

Decades of scholarly debate have left little doubt about the reason the Constitution was silent on the issue of judicial review. The framers said nothing about it simply because they took it for granted. They were, after all, creating neither a pure nor even a representative democracy, but a constitutional democracy.

"We the people" who "ordain and establish this Constitution" were not to be confused with the popular majority of any given historical moment, not even the historical moment of the founders' generation, when—as Justice Thurgood Marshall stressed in a speech last May—only a handful of propertied white males were eligible to participate in governance. Without lodging power in an independent judiciary to enforce "the people's" enduring Constitution against those who happen to wield power at any given moment, the document would in all likelihood be reduced to a dead letter—a matter for idle talk, signifying little or nothing of operational moment.

Yet the very independence of the Federal judiciary that makes it possible for it to perform this unique function exposes it to attack as elitist, undemocratic and counter-majoritarian, a form of government without the consent of the governed.

Such an attack is not easily dismissed. But it also does not provide a guide to how judges should decide constitutional questions. It is as inconclusive as the doctrine of "original intent" so warmly embraced by legal conservatives.

As Justice Antonin Scalia observed in an opinion last June, discovering the subjective intentions even of the handful of lawmakers who enacted a relatively recent statute "is, to be honest, almost always an impossible task." Joined by Chief Justice William H. Rehnquist, Justice Scalia conceded that searching for the "sole purpose of even a single legislator" is probably searching "for something that does not exist." When one turns to the Constitution and its amendments, ratified by state conventions or legislatures containing more than 1,600 members, the search is even more confounding.

In any event, it is the Constitution's sometimes deliberately general text, and not the unenacted thoughts of those who drafted or approved it, that binds future generations. The fact that many of the legislators who ratified the 14th Amendment in 1868 believed black and white children should be segregated by law does not discredit subsequent interpretations of the equal-protection clause.

Neither "original intent" nor the virtues of governing according to the consent of the governed leads to a useful general formula for how to approach difficult constitutional cases.

Consider perhaps the hardest case of modern times: *Roe* v. *Wade,* the Supreme Court's often reaffirmed but still controversial decision in 1973 affirming a woman's right to an abortion. If the Supreme Court's ruling is problematic because the Constitution was unclear on the subject, leaving the matter in local hands would hardly be less so. After all, may either women or the unborn be said to have "consented" to a regime under which the fates of both would be disposed of by local majorities?

"The very purpose of a Bill of Rights," Justice Jackson wrote when the Supreme Court struck down the compulsory flag salute in 1943, "was to withdraw certain subjects from the vicissitudes of political controversy, to place them beyond the reach of majorities and officials and to establish them as legal principles to be applied by the courts." We might amend the observation by adding: the very purpose of a Constitution is to place certain principles, both of individual liberty and of government structure, beyond the reach of contemporary majorities—and of those accountable to them.

Judicial review's most vital role has been to evaluate both traditional and emerging political practices in terms of ideals expressed in the Constitution, thereby insuring that crucial controversies over what kind of nation we are—and would become—are ultimately reconciled with the fundamental principles of the nation.

The Supreme Court's challenge to the social-welfare state in the first third of this century—in decisions striking down minimum-wage laws, child-labor laws and the like—reflected a genuine tension between the Constitution's textual protections of contract and property rights, and newer imperatives favoring governmental activism in regulating the economy and redistributing wealth. After the Court abruptly changed course in 1937, that tension was resolved in favor of an active role for government. But the reversal in no way proves that judicial review as an institution ill-served the nation. If the Court's earlier review of activist legislation seemed to impede social and economic progress, the later review was the vehicle through which social-welfare legislation finally established its legitimacy.

So too, *Roe* v. *Wade*'s challenge to the entrenched legal tradition denying women sexual and reproductive freedom reflects a profound tension between longstanding rules governing sexuality and reproduction, on the one hand, and the Constitution's guarantees of liberty and equality, on the other. Whether history ultimately deems the Supreme Court's protection of a woman's right to choose to be wisdom or folly, just or unjust, it is beyond cavil that such a profound issue must be resolved in terms of the principles by which we have constituted ourselves as a nation.

What counts most in assessing the value of an independent judiciary reviewing government actions for consistency with the Constitution is not which challenges succeed and which fail. What counts most is how an independent judiciary, in making such challenges possible, compels political discourse to address issues of power in the language of constitutional principles that connects our past to our aspirations.

In the face of polls indicating public disfavor for an independent judiciary, one wonders whether people would continue to hold these views after thinking long and hard about the sort of country we would have if the Constitution's interpretation and enforcement were indeed entrusted to a process more closely linked to electoral politics.

Only a decade ago, the Supreme Court overturned a jail sentence imposed on a grandmother for the "crime" of violating her neighborhood's statutory ideal of the nuclear family because she raised grandchildren who were cousins rather than brothers. Would people really want judges so "restrained" by popular will that citizens could be prosecuted for such "offenses"? Would they really want judges so lacking in independence that a government agency could put highways through their backyards without paying them just compensation? I hope not.

It would be sad indeed if our historic commitment to constitutionalism, weakened by the Reagan Administration's assaults on the Supreme Court and its work, had so eroded that the Constitution's principle of judicial independence were replaced with political buzzwords like "judicial restraint" and "original intent." That would make the Constitution's bicentennial less a birthday than a wake.

INFLUENCES ON SUPREME COURT DECISIONS

See text p. 189

One of the means by which the Supreme Court affects its case flow and establishes its political objectives is by indicating what kinds of claims it is willing to hear. For example, the Rehnquist Court can be expected to grant greater deference (honor) to state and national legislative enactments than was granted by the Warren and Burger Courts; that deference, especially to generally conservative state legislative schemes, will noticeably affect the direction of constitutional legal development. It may also be more or less restrictive in defining what constitutes state action, which will in turn affect whether Constitutional guarantees restrict those actions, as in the following case.

The Supreme Court's 1989 decision in DeShaney v. Winnebago County Department of Social Services *was a surprise to many observers of the Court. In deciding that Wisconsin could not be liable for failing to protect a child from abuse by his parent, the Court applied a definition of state action that was at odds with the expansive definition that had been accorded the concept of state action in previous years. In retrospect, the decision has since proved to be merely one of the first of a new wave of Supreme Court decisions attempting to limit the reach of the due process clause of the Constitution.*

DeShaney v. Winnebago County Department of Social Services (1989)*

[Joshua DeShaney was four-years-old when he was beaten so severely by his father that he suffered irreparable brain damage and will have to spend the remainder of his life in an institution. In the year preceding the final incident of abuse, the Winnebago County Department of Social Services had investigated numerous complaints against Joshua's father. Joshua had been admitted to the local hospital for injuries at least once, and had visited the emergency room again with suspicious injuries; a caseworker had several times visited Joshua's home and noted injuries on the child's head, but no action was taken to remove Joshua from his father's custody.

After Joshua incurred the life-threatening injuries that rendered him permanently damaged, his mother sued the Department of Social Services, claiming that their failure to protect Joshua from his father's violence violated the due process clause of the Fourteenth Amendment. The district and circuit courts denied the claim.]

CHIEF JUSTICE REHNQUIST writing for the majority.

The Due Process Clause of the Fourteenth Amendment provides that "[n]o State shall . . . deprive any person of life, liberty, or property, without due process of law." Petitioners contend that the State deprived Joshua of his liberty interest in "free[dom] from . . . unjustified intrusions on personal security," see Ingraham v. Wright by failing to provide him with adequate protection against his father's violence. The claim is one invoking the sub-

---

*DeShaney v. Winnebago County Department of Social Services, 488 U.S. 189, 1989.

stantive rather than procedural component of the Due Process Clause; petitioners do not claim that the State denied Joshua protection without according him appropriate procedural safeguards, but that it was categorically obligated to protect him in these circumstances.

But nothing in the language of the Due Process Clause itself requires the State to protect the life, liberty, and property of its citizens against invasion by private actors. The Clause is phrased as a limitation on the State's power to act, not as a guarantee of certain minimal levels of safety and security. It forbids the State itself to deprive individuals of life, liberty, or property without "due process of law," but its language cannot fairly be extended to impose an affirmative obligation on the State to ensure that those interests do not come to harm through other means. Nor does history support such an expansive reading of the constitutional text. Like its counterpart in the Fifth Amendment, the Due Process Clause of the Fourteenth Amendment was intended to prevent government "from abusing [its] power, or employing it as an instrument of oppression." Its purpose was to protect the people from the State, not to ensure that the State protected them from each other. The Framers were content to leave the extent of governmental obligation in the latter area to the democratic political processes.

Consistent with these principles, our cases have recognized that the Due Process Clauses generally confer no affirmative right to governmental aid, even where such aid may be necessary to secure life, liberty, or property interests of which the government itself may not deprive the individual. . . .

Petitioners contend, however, that even if the Due Process Clause imposes no affirmative obligation on the State to provide the general public with adequate protective services, such a duty may arise out of certain "special relationships" created or assumed by the State with respect to particular individuals. Petitioners argue that such a "special relationship" existed here because the State knew that Joshua faced a special danger of abuse at his father's hands, and specifically proclaimed, by word and by deed, its intention to protect him against that danger. Having actually undertaken to protect Joshua from this danger—which petitioners concede the State played no part in creating—the State acquired an affirmative "duty," enforceable through the Due Process Clause, to do so in a reasonably competent fashion. Its failure to discharge that duty, so the argument goes, was an abuse of governmental power that so "shocks the conscience," Rochin v. California, as to constitute a substantive due process violation.

We reject this argument. It is true that in certain limited circumstances the Constitution imposes upon the State affirmative duties of care and protection with respect to particular individuals. In Estelle v. Gamble, we recognized that the Eighth Amendment's prohibition against cruel and unusual punishment [requires] the State to provide adequate medical care to incarcerated prisoners. We reasoned that because the prisoner is unable " 'by reason of the deprivation of his liberty [to] care for himself,' " it is only " 'just' " that the State be required to care for him.

In Youngberg v. Romeo, we extended this analysis beyond the Eighth

Amendment setting, holding that the substantive component of the Fourteenth Amendment's Due Process Clause requires the State to provide involuntarily committed mental patients with such services as are necessary to ensure their "reasonable safety" from themselves and others.

But these cases afford petitioners no help. Taken together, they stand only for the proposition that when the State takes a person into its custody and holds him there against his will, the Constitution imposes upon it a corresponding duty to assume some responsibility for his safety and general well-being. The rationale for this principle is simple enough: when the State by the affirmative exercise of its power so restrains an individual's liberty that it renders him unable to care for himself, and at the same time fails to provide for his basic human needs—e.g., food, clothing, shelter, medical care, and reasonable safety—it transgresses the substantive limits on state action set by the Eighth Amendment and the Due Process Clause. The affirmative duty to protect arises not from the State's knowledge of the individual's predicament or from its expressions of intent to help him, but from the limitation which it has imposed on his freedom to act on his own behalf. In the substantive due process analysis, it is the State's affirmative act of restraining the individual's freedom to act on his own behalf—through incarceration, institutionalization, or other similar restraint of personal liberty—which is the "deprivation of liberty" triggering the protections of the Due Process Clause, not its failure to act to protect his liberty interests against harms inflicted by other means.

The Estelle-Youngberg analysis simply has no applicability in the present case. Petitioners concede that the harms Joshua suffered did not occur while he was in the State's custody, but while he was in the custody of his natural father, who was in no sense a state actor. While the State may have been aware of the dangers that Joshua faced in the free world, it played no part in their creation, nor did it do anything to render him any more vulnerable to them. That the State once took temporary custody of Joshua does not alter the analysis, for when it returned him to his father's custody, it placed him in no worse position than that in which he would have been had it not acted at all; the State does not become the permanent guarantor of an individual's safety by having once offered him shelter. Under these circumstances, the State had no constitutional duty to protect Joshua. Affirmed.

JUSTICE BRENNAN, with whom JUSTICE MARSHALL and JUSTICE BLACKMUN join, dissenting.

"The most that can be said of the state functionaries in this case," the Court today concludes, "is that they stood by and did nothing when suspicious circumstances dictated a more active role for them." Because I believe that this description of respondents' conduct tells only part of the story and that, accordingly, the Constitution itself "dictated a more active role" for respondents in the circumstances presented here, I cannot agree that respondents had no constitutional duty to help Joshua DeShaney. . . .

I would begin from the opposite direction. I would focus first on the action that Wisconsin *has* taken with respect to Joshua and children like him, rather than on the actions that the State failed to take. . . .

[It] simply belies reality [to] contend that the State "stood by and did nothing" with respect to Joshua. Through its child-protection program, the State actively intervened in Joshua's life and, by virtue of this intervention, acquired ever more certain knowledge that Joshua was in grave danger. These circumstances, in my view, plant this case solidly within the tradition of cases like Youngberg and Estelle.

[As] the Court today reminds us, "the Due Process Clause of the Fourteenth Amendment was intended to prevent government 'from abusing [its] power, or employing it as an instrument of oppression.' " My disagreement with the Court arises from its failure to see that inaction can be every bit as abusive of power as action, that oppression can result when a State undertakes a vital duty and then ignores it. Today's opinion construes the Due Process Clause to permit a State to displace private sources of protection and then, at the critical moment, to shrug its shoulders and turn away from the harm that it has promised to try to prevent. Because I cannot agree that our Constitution is indifferent to such indifference, I respectfully dissent.

JUSTICE BLACKMUN, dissenting.

Today, the Court purports to be the dispassionate oracle of the law, unmoved by "natural sympathy." But, in this pretense, the Court itself retreats into a sterile formalism which prevents it from recognizing either the facts of the case before it or the legal norms that should apply to those facts. As Justice Brennan demonstrates, the facts here involve not mere passivity, but active state intervention in the life of Joshua DeShaney—intervention that triggered a fundamental duty to aid the boy once the State learned of the severe danger to which he was exposed.

The Court fails to recognize this duty because it attempts to draw a sharp and rigid line between action and inaction. But such formalistic reasoning has no place in the interpretation of the broad and stirring clauses of the Fourteenth Amendment. . . .

Like the antebellum judges who denied relief to fugitive slaves, the Court today claims that its decision, however harsh, is compelled by existing legal doctrine. On the contrary, the question presented by this case is an open one, and our Fourteenth Amendment precedents may be read more broadly or narrowly depending upon how one chooses to read them. Faced with the choice, I would adopt a "sympathetic" reading, one which comports with dictates of fundamental justice and recognizes that compassion need not be exiled from the province of judging.

Poor Joshua! Victim of repeated attacks by an irresponsible, bullying, cowardly, and intemperate father, and abandoned by respondents who placed him in a dangerous predicament and who knew or learned what was going on, and yet did essentially nothing except, as the Court revealingly observes, "dutifully recorded these incidents in [their] files." It is a sad commentary upon American life, and constitutional principles—so full of late of patriotic fervor and proud proclamations about "liberty and justice for all," that this child, Joshua DeShaney, now is assigned to live out the remainder of his life profoundly retarded. Joshua and his mother, as petitioners here, deserve—but now are denied by this Court—the opportunity to have the facts of their case considered in the light of the constitutional protection that 42 U.S.C. § 1983 is meant to provide.

JUDICIAL POWER AND POLITICS

See text p. 193

President George Bush has continued the efforts of his predecessor, Ronald Reagan, to appoint conservative jurists to the lower federal courts and the U.S. Supreme Court. These efforts have been resisted by Democrats who have feared that a more conservative judiciary would reverse liberal gains in such areas as abortion and affirmative action. As discussed in the text, the Supreme Court has already made a number of decisions that limit the scope of affirmative action programs and allow more state regulation of access to abortion. As a result, Senate Democrats have fought bitterly against Republican presidents' Supreme Court nominees. The Democrats were able to defeat Ronald Reagan's efforts to appoint conservatives Robert Bork and Douglas Ginsberg to the high court. President George Bush, however, succeeded in securing Senate approval for conservative Justice David Souter. In October 1991, after one of the most bitter struggles in recent American political history, Bush was able to place Judge Clarence Thomas on the Supreme Court. Thomas, a black conservative and former head of the Equal Opportunity Employment Commission (EEOC) was bitterly opposed by civil rights and feminist groups. During his lengthy confirmation hearings, Thomas refused to discuss his views on abortion, particularly refusing to indicate how he viewed the Supreme Court's landmark decision in the case of Roe v. Wade. *The day before the Senate was to vote on his confirmation, with a favorable vote likely, opponents of the nomination leaked to the press an affidavit in which a University of Oklahoma law professor, Anita Hill, alleged that Thomas had sexually harrassed her when she worked for him at the EEOC and, previously, at the Department of Education. This allegation resulted in days of dramatic, nationally televised Senate hearings which failed to reach a definitive conclusion. Thomas was subsequently confirmed by the full Senate by a vote of 52–48.*

During the hearings, Republican Senator Orin Hatch of Utah read into the record an October 10, 1991, column by Washington Post *reporter, Juan Williams. In this column Williams, who is himself black, describes the intensity of the last-ditch effort to defeat Thomas—an effort he characterizes as a smear campaign. Ironically, after the publication of his column, Williams, too, was charged with sexual harrassment and subsequently admitted to having sexually harrassed several* Post *employees.*

Juan Williams
"Open Season on Clarence Thomas"*

The phone calls came throughout September. Did Clarence Thomas ever take money from the South African government? Was he under orders from the Reagan White House when he criticized civil rights leaders? Did he beat his first wife? Did I know anything about expense account charges he filed for out-of-town speeches? Did he say that women don't want equal pay for equal work? And finally, one exasperated voice said: "Have you got anything on your tapes we can use to stop Thomas."

The calls came from staff members working for Democrats on the Senate Judiciary Committee. They were calling me because several ariticles written about Thomas have carried my byline. When I was working as a White House correspondent in the early '80s, I had gotten to know Thomas as a news source and later wrote a long profile of him.

The desperate search for ammunition to shoot down Thomas has turned the 102 days since President Bush nominated him for a seat on the Supreme Court into a liberal's nightmare. Here is indiscriminate, mean-spirited mudslinging supported by the so-called champions of fairness: liberal politicians, unions, civil rights groups and women's organizations. They have been mindlessly led into mob action against one man by the Leadership Conference on Civil Rights. Moderate and liberal senators, operating in the proud tradition of men such as Hubert Humphrey and Robert Kennedy, have allowed themselves to become sponsors of smear tactics that have historically been associated with the gutter politics of a Lee Atwater or crazed right-wing self-promoters like Sen. Joseph McCarthy.

During the hearings on his nomination Thomas was subjected to a glaring double standard. When he did not answer questions that former nominees David Souter and Anthony Kennedy did not answer, he was pilloried for his evasiveness. One opponent testified that her basis for opposing him was his lack of judicial experience. She did not know that Supreme Court justices such as liberal icons Earl Warren and Felix Frankfurter, as well as current Chief Justice William Rehnquist, had no judicial experience before taking a seat on the high court.

Even the final vote of the Senate Judiciary Committee on whether to recommend Thomas for confirmation turned into a shameless assault on Thomas by the leading lights of progressive Democratic politics. For example, in an incredibly bizarre act, Chairman Joseph Biden stood up after a full slate of testimony and said Thomas would make a "solid justice," but then voted against him anyway.

At the time of the vote, two of the committee's Democrats later explained to me, the members of the Judiciary Committee figured it would make no difference, since Thomas had the votes to gain confirmation from

---

the full Senate. So, they decided, why not play along with the angry roar coming from the Leadership Conference? "Thomas will win, and the vote will embarrass Bush and leave [the Leadership Conference] feeling that they were heard," explained one senator on the committee.

Now the Senate has extended its attacks on fairness, decency and its own good name by averting its eyes while someone in a position to leak has corrupted the entire hearing process by releasing a sealed affidavit containing an allegation that had been investigated by the FBI, reviewed by Thomas's opponents and supporters on the Senate committee and put aside as inconclusive and insufficient to warrant further investigation or stop the committee's final vote.

But that fair process and the intense questioning Thomas faced in front of the committee for over a week were not enough for members of the staffs of Sens. Edward M. Kennedy and Howard Metzenbaum. In addition to calls to me and to people at the Equal Employment Opportunity Commission, they were pressing a former EEOC employee, University of Oklahoma law professor Anita Hill, for negative information about Thomas. Thomas had hired Hill for two jobs in Washington.

Hill said the Senate staffers who called her were specifically interested in talking about rumors involving sexual harassment. She had no credible evidence of Thomas's involvement in any sexual harassment, but she was prompted to say he had asked her out and mentioned pornographic movies to her. She rejected him as a jerk, but said she never felt her job was threatened by him, he never touched her, and she followed him to subsequent jobs and even had him write references for her.

Hill never filed any complaint against Thomas; she never mentioned the problem to reporters for The Post during extensive interviews this summer after the nomination, and even in her statement to the FBI never charged Thomas with sexual harassment but "talked about [his] behavior."

Sen. Paul Simon, an all-out opponent of Thomas, has said there is no "evidence that her turning him down in any way harmed her and he later recommended her for a job [as a law professor]." Hill did say that because Thomas was her boss, she felt "the pressure was such that I was going to have to submit . . . in order to continue getting good assignments." But by her own account she never did submit and continued to get first-rate assignments.

The bottom line, then, is that Senate staffers have found their speck of mud to fling at Clarence Thomas in an alleged sexual conversation between two adults. This is not the Senate Judiciary Committee finding out that Hugo Black had once been in the Ku Klux Klan (he had, and was nonetheless confirmed). This is not the Judiciary Committee finding that the nominee is an ideologue incapable of bringing a fair and open mind to the deliberations of the court. This slimy exercise orchestrated in the form of leaks of an affidavit to the Leadership Conference on Civil Rights is an abuse of the Senate confirmation process, an abuse of Senate rules and an unforgivable abuse of a human being named Clarence Thomas.

Further damaging is the blood-in-the-water response from reputable news operations, notably National Public Radio. They have magnified every question about Thomas into an indictment and sacrificed journalistic balance and integrity for a place in the mob. The New York Times ran a front-page article about "Sexism and the Senate" that gave space to complaints that only two of the 100 members of the Senate are female. The article, in an amazing leap of illogic, concluded that if a woman had been on the Judiciary Committee, more attention would have been given to Professor Hill's report. But attention was given to what she said. A full investigation took place. Why would a woman senator not have reached the conclusion that what took place did not rise to the level necessary to delay the vote on Thomas in the committee or to deny him confirmation?

To listen to or read some news reports on Thomas over the past month is to discover a monster of a man, totally unlike the human being full of sincerity, confusion, and struggles whom I saw as a reporter who watched him for some 10 years. He has been conveniently transformed into a monster about whom it is fair to say anything, to whom it is fair to do anything. President Bush may be packing the court with conservatives, but that is another argument, larger than Clarence Thomas. In pursuit of abuses by a conservative president the liberals have become the abusive monsters.

Sen. Charles E. Grassley said on the Senate floor Tuesday that the smears heaped on Thomas amounted to the "worse treatment of a nominee I've seen in 11 years in the Senate." Sen. Dennis DeConcini said it "is inconceivable, it is unfair and I can't imagine anything more unfair to the man." And Sen. Orrin G. Hatch described the entire week's performance as a "last-ditch attempt to smear the judge."

Sadly, that's right.

CHAPTER 8

Public Opinion and the Media

SHAPING PUBLIC OPINION

See text p. 206

> *As opportunities expand for getting public opinion before public officials, so do the opportunities for manipulating that opinion. The nature of the opinion poll—the way that it tames or domesticates public opinion—has allowed modern governments to transform public opinion from a tool for objecting to governmental actions into something that can be manipulated to generate support for state policies.*

Benjamin Ginsberg
"How Polling Transforms Public Opinion"*

The "will of the people" has become the ultimate standard against which the conduct of contemporary governments is measured. In the democracies, especially in the United States, both the value of governmental programs and the virtue of public officials are typically judged by the extent of their popularity. . . .

Much of the prominence of opinion polling as a civic institution derives from the significance that present-day political ideologies ascribe to the will of the people. Polls purport to provide reliable, scientifically derived information about the public's desires, fears and beliefs, and so to give concrete expression to the conception of a popular will. The availability of accurate information certainly is no guarantee that governments will actually pay heed to popular opinions. Yet, it has always been the belief of many students and practitioners of survey research that an accurate picture of the public's views might at least increase the chance that governments' actions would be informed by and responsive to popular sentiment.

Unfortunately, however, polls do more than simply measure and record the natural or spontaneous manifestation of popular belief. The data reported by opinion polls are actually the product of an interplay between opinion and the survey instrument. As they measure, the polls interact with opinion, producing changes in the character and identity of the views receiv-

*Benjamin Ginsberg, "How Polling Transforms Public Opinion," in Michael Margolis and Gary Mauser, *Manipulating Public Opinion* (New York: HarperCollins, 19XX). Reprinted with permission.

ing public expression. The changes induced by polling, in turn, have the most profound implications for the relationship between public opinion and government. In essence, polling has contributed to the domestication of opinion by helping to transform opinion from a politically potent, often disruptive, force into a more docile, plebiscitary phenomenon.

Publicizing Opinion

Over the past several decades, polling has generally come to be seen as the most accurate and reliable means of gauging the public's sentiments. Indeed, poll results and public opinion are terms that are used almost synonymously. But, despite this general tendency to equate public opinion with survey results, polling is obviously not the only possible source of knowledge about the public's attitudes.

[A] presumption in favor of the polls . . . [however] stems from both the scientific and representative character of opinion polling. Survey research is modeled after the methodology of the natural sciences and at least conveys an impression of technical sophistication and scientific objectivity. Occasional press accounts of deliberate bias and distortion of survey findings only partially undermine this impression.

At the same time, the polls can claim to offer a more representative view of popular sentiment than any alternative source of information is likely to provide. Group spokespersons sometimes speak only for themselves. The distribution of opinion reflected by letters to newspapers and public officials is notoriously biased. Demonstrators and rioters, however sincere, are seldom more than a tiny and unrepresentative segment of the populace. The polls, by contrast, at least attempt to take equal account of all relevant individuals. And, indeed, by offering a representative view of public opinion the polls have often served as antidotes for false spokespersons, correctives for mistaken politicians, and guides to popular concerns that might never have been mentioned by the individuals writing letters to legislators and newspaper editors.

Nevertheless, polling does more than offer a scientifically derived and representative account of popular sentiment. The substitution of polling for other means of gauging the public's views also has the effect of changing several of the key characteristics of public opinion. Critics of survey research have often noted that polling can affect both the beliefs of individuals asked to respond to survey questions and the attitudes of those who subsequently read a survey's results. However, the most important effect of the polls is not a result of their capacity to change individuals' beliefs. The major impact of polling is, rather, on the cumulation and translation of individuals' private beliefs into collective public opinion. Four fundamental changes in the character of public opinion can be traced to the introduction of survey research.

Changing the Character of Public Opinion

First, polling alters both what is expressed and what is perceived as the opinion of the mass public by transforming public opinion from a voluntary to an externally subsidized matter. Second, polling modifies the manner in which opinion is publicly presented by transforming public opinion from a behavioral to an attitudinal phenomenon. Third, polling changes the origin of information about public beliefs by transforming public opinion from a property of groups to an attribute of individuals. Finally, polling partially removes individuals' control over the subject matter of their own public expressions of opinion by transforming public opinion from a spontaneous assertion to a constrained response.

Individually and collectively, these transformations have profound consequences for the character of public opinion and, more important, for the relationship of opinion to government and policy. To the extent that polling displaces alternative modes of gauging popular sentiment, these four transformations contribute markedly to the domestication or pacification of public opinion. Polling renders public opinion less dangerous, less disruptive, more permissive and, in some instances, more amenable to governmental control.

Polling does not make public opinion politically impotent. Nor, as the recent failure of the Reagan administration's efforts to "disinform" the American public on the government's policies toward Iran and Central America indicate, does the availability of polling guarantee that governments will be able to successfully manipulate public beliefs for an indefinite length of time. Nevertheless, polling helps to diminish the danger that public opinion poses to those in power and helps to increase the potential for government management of mass beliefs.

From Voluntarism to Subsidy

In the absence of polling, the cost and effort required to organize and publicly communicate an opinion are normally borne by one or more of the individuals holding the opinion. . . . The polls, by contrast, organize and publicize opinion without necessitating any initiative or action on the part of individuals. . . .

This displacement of costs from the opinion-holder to the polling agency has important consequences for the character of the opinions likely to receive public expression. In general, the willingness of individuals to bear the costs of publicly asserting their views is closely tied to the intensity with which they hold those views. . . . So long as the costs of asserting opinions are borne by opinion-holders themselves, those with relatively extreme viewpoints are also disproportionately likely to bring their views to the public forum.

The polls weaken this relationship between the public expression of opinion and the intensity or extremity of opinion. The assertion of an opinion through a poll requires little effort on the part of the opinion-holder. As a result, the beliefs of those who care relatively little or even hardly at all, are as likely to be publicized as the opinions of those who care a great deal about the matter in question. Similarly, individuals with moderate viewpoints are as likely as those taking extreme positions to publicly communicate their opinions through a survey. The upshot is that the distribution of public opinion reported by the polls generally differs considerably from the distribution that emerges from forms of public communication initiated by citizens. . . .

This difference between polled and voluntarily expressed opinion can have important implications for the degree of influence or constraint that public opinion is likely to impose upon administrators and policymakers. The polls, in effect, submerge individuals with strongly held views in a more apathetic mass public. The data reported by the polls are likely to suggest to public officials that they are working in a more permissive climate of opinion than might have been thought on the basis of alternative indicators of the popular mood. A government wishing to maintain some semblance of responsiveness to public opinion would typically find it less difficult to comply with the preferences reported by the polls than to obey the opinion that might be inferred from letters, strikes, or protests. Indeed, relative to these other modes of public expression, polled opinion could be characterized as a collective statement of permission.

Certainly, even in the era of polling, voluntary expressions of public opinion can still count heavily. In recent years, for example, members of Congress were impressed by calls, letters, and telegrams from constituents—and threats from contributors—regarding President Reagan's various tax reform proposals. Of course, groups like the National Rifle Association are masters of the use of this type of opinion campaign. Nevertheless, contradiction by the polls tends to reduce the weight and credibility of other sources of public opinion. This effect of polling can actually help governments to resist the pressure of constituent opinion. Constituency polls, for example, are often used by legislators as a basis for resisting the demands of political activists and pressure groups in their districts.

Polling is especially useful when voluntary expressions of public opinion indicate severe opposition to a government and its programs. The relatively permissive character of polled opinion can allow a government faced with demonstrations, protests, and other manifestations of public hostility a basis for the claim that its policies are compatible with true public opinion and opposed only by an unrepresentative group of activist malcontents. A notable contemporary illustration of this role of the polls is the case of the "silent majority" on whose behalf Richard Nixon claimed to govern. The notion of a silent majority was the Nixon administration's answer to the protestors, who demanded major changes in American foreign and domestic policies. Administration spokespersons frequently cited poll data, often drawing upon Scammon and Wattenberg's influential treatise, *The Real Majority* (1970) to question the popular standing of the activist opposition. According to the administration's interpretation, its activist opponents did not represent the views of the vast majority of "silent" Americans who could be found in the polls but not on picket lines, marches, or in civil disturbances. . . .

From Behavior to Attitude

Prior to the advent of polling, public opinion could often only be inferred from political behavior. Before the availability of voter survey data, for example, analysts typically sought to deduce electoral opinion from voting patterns, attributing candidates' electoral fortunes to whatever characteristics of the public mood could be derived from election returns. Often, population movements served as the bases for conclusions about public preferences. Even in recent years, the movement of white urbanites to the metropolitan fringe, dubbed "white flight," has been seen as a key indicator of white attitudes toward racial integration. Particularly, however, where the least articulate segments of the populace were concerned, governments often had little or no knowledge of the public's mood until opinion manifested itself in some form of behavior. Generally, this meant violent or disruptive activity. . . .

From Assertion to Response

In the absence of polling, individuals typically choose for themselves the subjects of any public assertions they might care to make. Those persons or groups willing to expend the funds, effort, or time needed to acquire a public platform, normally also select the agenda or topics on which their views will be aired. The individual writing an angry letter to a newspaper or legislator generally singles out the object of his or her scorn. The organizers of a protest march typically define the aim of their own wrath. Presumably, 19th-century mobs of "illuminators" determined of their own accord the matters on which the larger public would be enlightened.

   The introduction of opinion surveys certainly did not foreclose individuals' opportunities to proffer opinions on topics of their own choosing. Indeed, in the United States, a multitude of organizations, groups, and individuals are continually stepping forward to present the most extraordinary notions. Nevertheless, the polls elicit subjects' views on questions which have been selected by an external agency—the survey's sponsors—rather than by the respondents themselves. Polling thus erodes individuals' control over the agenda of their own expressions of opinion. With the use of surveys, publicly expressed opinion becomes less clearly an assertion of individuals' own concerns and more nearly a response to the interests of others.

   The most obvious problem stemming from this change is that polling can create a misleading picture of the agenda of public concerns. The matters which appear significant to the agencies sponsoring polls may be quite different from the concerns of the general public. Discrepancies between the polls' agenda and the general public's interests were especially acute during the political and social turmoil of the late 1960s and early 1970s. Though, as we saw, polling was used by the government during this period to help curb disorder, the major commercial polls took little interest in the issues which aroused so much public concern. The year 1970, for example, was marked by racial strife and antiwar protest in the United States. Yet, the 1970 national Gallup Poll devoted only 5 percent of its questions to American policy in Vietnam and only 2 of 162 questions to domestic race relations.

But, whatever the particular changes polling may help to produce in the focus of public discourse, the broader problem is that polling fundamentally alters the character of the public agenda of opinion. So long as groups and individuals typically present their opinions on topics of their own choosing, the agenda of opinion is likely to consist of citizens' own needs, hopes, and aspirations. A large fraction of the opinion which is publicly expressed will involve demands and concerns that groups and individuals wish to bring to the attention of the government. Opinions elicited by the polls, on the other hand, mainly concern matters of interest to government, business, or other poll sponsors. Typically, poll questions have as their ultimate purpose some form of exhortation. Businesses poll to help persuade customers to purchase their wares. Candidates poll as part of the process of convincing voters to support them. Governments poll as part of the process of inducing citizens to obey. Sometimes several of these purposes are combined. In 1971, for example, the White House Domestic Council sponsored a poll dealing with a host of social issues designed both to assist the administration with policy planning and to boost the president's reelection efforts.

In essence, rather than offer governments the opinions that citizens want them to learn, the polls tell governments—or other sponsors—what they would like to learn about citizens' opinions. The end result is to change the public expression of opinion from an assertion of demand to a step in the process of persuasion.

Making Opinion Safer for Government

Taken together, the changes produced by polling contribute to the transformation of public opinion from an unpredictable, extreme, and often dangerous force into a more docile expression of public sentiment. Opinion stated through the polls imposes less pressure and makes fewer demands upon government than would more spontaneous or natural assertions of popular sentiment. Though opinion may be expressed more democratically via the polls than through alternative means, polling can give public opinion a plebiscitary character—robbing opinion of precisely those features that might maximize its impact upon government and policy. . . .

Government: From Adversary to Manager of Opinion

Because it domesticates public opinion, polling has contributed to one of the 20th century's major political transformations—the shift from an adversarial to a managerial relationship between government and popular opinion. . . .

On a day-to-day basis, the 20th-century state depends upon considerable support, cooperation, and sacrifice from its citizens in forms ranging from military service and large tax payments, through popular adherence to a multitude of rules and regulations. The scope and technical complexity of the modern state's activities, moreover, render governmental administration extremely sensitive to popular opposition. In the short term, opposition can often be forcibly quelled and a populace forcibly compelled to obey its rulers' edicts, pay taxes, and serve in the military. But, over long periods, even many of those governments commanding both the requisite armed might and appropriate lack of scruples have come to appreciate the wisdom of the Napoleonic dictum that one "may do anything with a bayonet but sit on it." By cultivating favorable public opinion, present-day rulers hope to persuade their citizens to voluntarily obey, support, and make whatever sacrifices are needed to further the state's goals. In the 20th century, management of public opinion has become a routine public function in the democracies as well as in the dictatorships. Typically, the censor has been supplanted, or at least joined, by the public relations officer as the governmental functionary most responsible for dealing with public opinion. . . .

Polling is the spearhead of this vast opinion-management apparatus. Opinion surveys provide governments with more or less reliable information about current popular sentiment, offer a guide to the character of the public relations efforts that might usefully be made, and serve as means of measuring the effect of "information programs" upon a target population. Though it cannot guarantee success, polling allows governments a better opportunity to anticipate, regulate, and manipulate popular attitudes. Ironically, some of its early students believed that polling would open the way for "government by opinion." Instead, polling has mainly helped to promote the governance of opinion.

THE MEDIA

See text p. 209

The Persian Gulf conflict in 1991 was a real media "event." Round-the-clock news coverage kept viewers glued to their television sets; even Saddam Hussein was reported to have watched events unfold on the Cable News Network. But despite the media blitz, war coverage was highly managed by the Pentagon, whose actions have since been subject to a great deal of criticism as an effort to shield the government's operations from inquiry. Military officials seemed to be openly hostile to the news media; distrust of the media had been candidly disclosed by Major General Patrick H. Brady of the Sixth Army in an article written for Army *magazine only a few months before the war, when he observed: "Some look on the news as just a four-letter word, but I believe it is more useful to look at it as a C-letter word: chaos, confusion, contradiction, crime, corruption, color, catastrophe. It does not hurt if you add some S's—sex, sensationalism, state secrets."*

At the center of the dispute during the Gulf War was the Pentagon's decision to require all reporters to have a military escort at all times, as well as its decision to allow only a limited number of reporters to accompany troops; these in turn were obligated to share or pool their reports with other journalists. Both actions, according to reporters, limited the kind of news reported and its accuracy by constraining the sources to which journalists could look to generate their stories.

Jason DeParle
"After the War"*

The American military operation in the Persian Gulf was still in its frantic, tentative youth on August 14, 1990, when Captain Ron Wildermuth of the Navy sat in his office at United States Central Command headquarters in Tampa, Florida, and sent a classified message flashing across military computers on three continents.

As General H. Norman Schwarzkopf's chief aide for public affairs, Captain Wildermuth had spent days drafting the message, a 10-page document known as Annex Foxtrot, which laid out a blueprint for the operation's public information policy. The movement of troops, weapons and materiel was to become the largest since the humiliating—and televised—Vietnam War defeat. And in the officer's mind, one point bore repetition.

"News media representatives," he wrote, "will be escorted at all times. Repeat, at all times."

The drafting of Annex Foxtrot was one step in a long march of decisions that, by war's end, left the Government with a dramatically changed policy on press coverage of military operations.

The Gulf War marked this century's first major conflict where the policy was to confine reporters to escorted pools that sharply curtailed when and how they could talk to troops. And within months, Americans were receiving news accompanied by words that had not been connected with combat accounts for nearly 50 years: "Reports reviewed by military censors."

The policy began with a decision by the Administration's most senior officials, including President Bush, to manage the information flow in a way that supported the operation's political goals and avoided the perceived mistakes of Vietnam.

But the elaboration of this approach took place incrementally, with the main oversight responsibility delegated to Defense Secretary Dick Cheney, whose press policy during the Panama invasion had been faulted by an official Pentagon inquiry for its "excessive concern for secrecy."

And Mr. Cheney, in turn, left many decisions in the hands of field commanders, many of whom had left Vietnam deeply suspicious of reporters, who were relatively free to cover American forces in action.

While critics of the policy have argued that the restrictions on independent reporting were intended to produce a sanitized view of the war, top officials have said they were necessary to prevent security lapses in a new era of instant communications.

"It isn't like World War II, when George Patton would sit around in his tent with six or seven reporters and muse," with the results "transcribed and reviewed" for eventual release, said General Colin L. Powell, the Chairman of the Joint Chiefs of Staff.

If a commander "in Desert Shield sat around in his tent and mused with a few CNN guys and pool guys and other guys, it's in 105 capitals a minute later," General Powell said.

Cheney's Central Role

Dozens of interviews with civilian and military officials and a review of major planning documents disclose the following points:

- The White House, while delegating most decisions to Mr. Cheney, closely monitored some details. Mr. Bush watched virtually every briefing, while his aides urged that certain officers be swept from television screens and promoted Lieutenant General Thomas W. Kelly as a briefer with star potential. The Pentagon, once it realized the power of televised briefings, set up daily rehearsal sessions for General Kelly, and happened onto a system for learning the questions that reporters would throw at him.

- The military, assuming that correspondents from the small-town press would write sympathetic articles, provided free transportation to Saudi Arabia and special access to servicemen and women from their areas. Aides also analyzed articles written by other reporters to determine their interests and to screen out interview requests from those likely to focus on mistakes by the military.

- Pentagon officials decided early in the operation to radically change the purpose of press pools, taking what had been set up as a temporary device to get reporters to a combat zone and turning it into the sole means of combat coverage. Despite that decision, Mr. Cheney's spokesman, Peter Williams, held a series of autumn meetings with news executives that encouraged them to believe that traditional independent reporting would follow.

- White House officials, in the face of criticism, wavered at one point but dropped the idea of easing press restrictions after a "Saturday Night Live" sketch lampooning the press convinced them and the President that the public was on their side.

Striding into his press secretary's office during an interview about war coverage last month, Mr. Bush stamped the policy with his own seal of approval.

"I think that the American people stand behind us," he said. "I think they felt they got a lot of information about this war."

Public opinion polls have shown overwhelming majorities backing the military over the press.

In separate interviews, Mr. Cheney and John H. Sununu, the White House chief of staff, called the policy a model for the future. The only time information was withheld, Mr. Sununu said, was when it would compromise military security. "There was never an effort not to give information out," he said. "There was never an effort not to focus on things."

And Mr. Cheney, the policy's chief architect, said, "there was better coverage, more extensive coverage, more elaborate coverage, greater knowledge on the part of the American people, about this war, as it unfolded, than any other war in history." But few journalists agree.

"I'm not sure the public's interest is served by seeing what seems to have been such a painless war, when 50,000 to 100,000 people may have died on the other side," said Ted Koppel, host of the ABC News program "Nightline."

"Obviously this was done so they could maintain the closest possible control over public opinion, to increase support for the war."

Guiding Principles
No Accidents In This Campaign

Early in the troop buildup, the President and the group of top advisers discussed past military endeavors in which they felt press policy was handled poorly, including Vietnam, Panama and the May 1975 seizure of the American merchant ship Mayaguez off Cambodia. The group instructed Mr. Cheney, one of its members, to take charge.

"Nobody dwelled on it," one official at the meeting said. "The sense was, 'Set it up over there, pay attention to it—don't have things happen by accident, take control of it.' "

In an interview, Mr. Cheney said he was guided by two overarching principles. One was that military needs had to take precedence over journalistic rights, and so the "lore" of past practice needed to be disregarded.

Another was to guard Government credibility. "There was ample precedent that one of the really great ways to screw up an operation—certainly was one of the lessons learned in Southeast Asia—is don't get out there making claims you can't back up," Mr. Cheney said.

Indeed, one of the reasons that the Government lost public support for the conflict in Vietnam was the much-discussed credibility gap, attributed to the Johnson Administration's failure to be candid with the public about its policy.

Mistakes of Vietnam

President Lyndon B. Johnson for a time tried to hide the extent of the American military buildup and repeatedly cast an optimistic gloss on the military effort and on the ability of the South Vietnamese to govern in the face of on-the-scene reporting showing the opposite. . . .

While Mr. Cheney and other leaders were explicit in saying they were shaped by the lessons of Vietnam, General Powell said, "I never gave it the first thought."

Calling Vietnam references "a cheap shot," General Powell said that whenever reporters were unhappy, "you take out your little branding iron with the 'V' and heat it up and burn it into our foreheads."

Emphasizing that he was just a captain in Vietnam, General Powell said that his experiences as a top commander or national security adviser during the 1983 bombing of the United States Marines barracks in Beirut and in Grenada and Panama taught him much more about "how we had to handle the information."

General Powell did say that one of his top priorities in training commanders has been to make "them understand the proper role of media." While some have pointed to such training to argue that the military has grown more skilled at manipulating the press, General Powell said, "I spin it differently."

"Sure, you want to see if you can get the press to support the goals, but that's not why you work with the press," he said. "You work with the press because it is your obligation."

Correspondents' Imperative

When he arrived in Saudi Arabia, Captain Wildermuth, the Schwarzkopf aide, compiled a list of ground rules that journalists were required to sign in exchange for credentials. From the correspondents' standpoint, the trouble began with these words: "You MUST remain with your military escort at all times."

Captain Wildermuth said he added that provision on his own. "You needed an escort to provide a liaison with the units," he said. "That military guy speaks military. It's just smart." For that reason, he said, escorts were a standard part of press pools.

But critics say this decision fundamentally changed coverage of military operations, by transforming escorts into a permanent part of the news-gathering process.

Fred S. Hoffman, a former Pentagon spokesman who helped design the pool system in the mid-1980's, said the new rule was "far more restrictive than anything we'd ever tried to do."

Captain Wildermuth said he did not directly consult General Schwarzkopf about the rules. But, he added, he was careful to make them reflect the commander's general philosophy.

Rules at Work
Better Treatment for Local Press

Without the independent movement they had in Vietnam, reporters covering the buildup last fall said they were rarely able to talk to the troops. The escorted visits were conducted infrequently and typically lasted one night.

Public affairs officials said the presence of reporters would distract units from their war preparations. . . .

On the one occasion the Pentagon suggested giving the major news organizations more time in the field, General Schwarzkopf vetoed the suggestion. That was in October, after planners sent to Saudi Arabia by Mr. Williams, Mr. Cheney's spokesman, recommended sending four six-member pools to the front lines and treating reporters as "de facto members of the units." The first pools were not in place until January 14, three days before the start of the air war.

While lack of access to troops brought one set of reporters' complaints, the conduct of escorts brought another. The escorts helped choose whom reporters could talk to. Some hovered over interviews and others stepped in front of cameras to interrupt ones they did not like.

Mr. Williams has described such incidents as isolated, involving inexperienced officers. "That's not the way it's supposed to work," he told a Congressional committee in February.

But others argue that leaders set a restrictive tone by design. After [the *New York Times*] quoted a private criticizing President Bush, General Schwarzkopf called the enlisted man's commanding general, asking for an explanation.

Aides to General Schwarzkopf said they screened requests for interviews by researching the reporter's past articles "to be aware of what the person's interests were," as one said, adding that such research is standard peacetime procedure. . . .

Pool Coverage:
Some Assumptions and the Deception

The autumn skirmishes between reporters and escorts were followed by perhaps the most important information-policy decision of the war: the order to limit battle coverage to officially sanctioned pools.

"There's a huge gaggle of reporters out there, and the press has absolutely no capacity to police itself," Mr. Cheney said in the interview. "There was no way we were ever going to put 100 percent of the reporters who wanted to go cover the war out with the troops."

But the decision to confine reporting to official pools represented a departure not only from Vietnam, but also from World War II, where reporters had generally been given wide access to combat action and to commanders, with their dispatches reviewed by military censors for security violations.

It was also a departure from the pool system conceived after the 1983 invasion of Grenada, which led to reporters' protests at being left behind. Pool members were to accompany troops into combat on a moment's notice, sharing their reports, then quickly dissolving as soon as other reporters could arrive. Then, independent, or "unilateral" coverage would follow.

But Mr. Cheney scrapped the system in Panama by delaying the pool's departure when United States forces invaded in 1989. He later said he feared security breaches; the inquiry commissioned by the Pentagon found that fear "excessive."

'Don't Worry,' Spokesman Says

A group of news executives that met with Mr. Williams in the fall to discuss visas says he reassured them that any pool coverage of actual combat would be short-lived.

"It was, 'Don't worry about it, boys, we understand your concerns— we're going to have unilateral coverage,' " said George Watson, Washington bureau chief of ABC News.

But by his own account, Mr. Williams left the last of those meetings, on November 28, and briefed Mr. Cheney and General Powell on precisely the opposite approach—a plan to make pools the sole means of combat coverage, which they accepted. On December 14, Mr. Williams made that plan public.

"Obviously we didn't make it as clear as we should have," Mr. Williams said of the news executives' angry reaction. "But fully a month before the war started, we submitted a draft to them."

After making only minor modifications, he issued a final order imposing pools on January 15, less than 48 hours before the start of the air war.

The journalists involved in the meetings have been accused by colleagues—and some have accused themselves—of failing to exercise sufficient vigilance.

But Mr. Williams says that while the journalists may have felt they were in a negotiation, he never considered them equal partners.

"This was not a decision made by a committee," he said. "They bear no responsibility for the decision."

See text p. 210

Because the media have enormous power to shape public perception of issues and public opinion generally, it is especially important to ensure that a wide variety of opinions and issues find their way into the national agenda. In the following article, journalist David Shaw talks about the homogeneity in the news that results as larger and larger numbers of reporters cover the same limited number of events. Moreover, changes in technology—particularly the increased reliance on television as the primary source of news coverage—has changed both the nature and the content of the news. Shaw argues that these changes have influenced the public agenda in ways that do not encourage thoughtful public understanding.

David Shaw
"Washington's Influential Sources: Opinion Leaders Dictate the Conventional Wisdom"*

Former Senator Eugene McCarthy once likened reporters to blackbirds on a telephone wire—when one lands, they all land, he said; when one takes off, they all take off.

Nowhere is this phenomenon more pervasive than in Washington, where McCarthy served in Congress for twenty-two years.

"Washington is more susceptible to pack journalism than any place I've been," says John Balzar, a political writer for the Los Angeles Times. "I've watched reporters go through the agonies of hell because their stories differed slightly from their colleagues'."

New York is the media capital of the United States—headquarters for the *New York Times,* the *Wall Street Journal, Time, Newsweek,* the Associated Press, NBC, CBS, ABC and virtually all the major book and opinion magazine publishers. To some degree, journalistic consensus—conventional wisdom—on any given issue can be said to develop simply because many top decision-makers for these organizations see each other socially, have friends and ideas in common, are exposed to the same stimuli daily and—surprise—arrive at similar conclusions.

But reporters and commentators are more likely than editors and publishers to form the conventional wisdom, and in terms of public policy issues, most of the truly influential reporters and commentators are in Washington.

News organizations continue to send many of their best people to Washington. The number of journalists there has almost doubled in the last decade. Should not this concentration of talent and competition—unparalleled anywhere else in the country—produce cutting-edge journalism, with 4,000 ego-driven reporters all eager to be best, first, different from their colleagues?

"It seems paradoxical to say that competition produces uniformity, rather than diversity," says Howell Raines, Washington bureau chief of the *New York Times,* but that's exactly what often happens in Washington. . . .

A Company Town

[D]iversity and originality are not indigenous to Washington journalism, even under the best circumstances. Washington is a most insular city, a company town, with the United States government as The Company; as Raines says, most Washington journalists are "drinking from a pretty small pool of news."

---

*David Shaw, "Washington's Influential Sources," *Los Angeles Times* (August 26, 1989). Copyright © 1989 The Los Angeles Times. Reprinted with permission.

Unlike Paris or London, which are not just government capitals but financial, cultural and communications capitals, Washington is purely a government capital; news coverage and commentary there generally move within a narrower range than in the other, more cosmopolitan capitals. When you have journalists with a great deal in common covering news within relatively narrow parameters, the likelihood of conformity—the pressure to conform—can be great.

"I don't think a reporter . . . wants to be off . . . from where the *New York Times* and the *Wall Street Journal* and the *Washington Post* are," Novak says. "I don't think he has that much faith in his own opinion or . . . that much desire to swim . . . upstream."

The compulsion toward consensus in Washington is exacerbated by an insidious "inside-the-beltway" mentality, one of the most important corollaries of which is that people beyond the freeway that encircles Washington are seen as somehow inferior to those within the charmed circle.

As top journalists have become more and more a part of the Establishment—making big salaries and sharing priorities and friends with those they cover—they have also come to share the conventional wisdom of those they cover.

Dismiss Outlanders

Thus, the conventional wisdom in Washington, among politicians and journalists alike in 1981, was that outlander Ronald Reagan, the Hollywood actor turned governor of California, could not possibly know enough about the congressional levers of power to push his tax reform bill into law. More recently, conventional wisdom held that outlander Sununu could not possibly master the sophisticated bureaucratic infighting necessary to be a successful chief of staff for President Bush.

Sununu was perceived in Washington as "a jack-leg governor from a horse's ass state; how could he play with us in the big leagues?" says Benjamin C. Bradlee, executive editor of the *Washington Post.* . . .

Washington journalism is, of course, largely political journalism; the line between campaigning and governing seems increasingly vague in an era when the media begins handicapping the next race almost before the winner of the last race has taken office. Perhaps it is no wonder then that there is so much consensus journalism coming out of the capital, a great deal of which ultimately proves wrong; after all, the most striking examples of consensus journalism—and of consensus journalism gone awry—come every four years, during presidential election campaigns, and they are often written by the same people who cover Washington between elections.

Peters, of the *Washington Monthly*, feels particularly strongly about the unhealthy nexus between campaign coverage and Washington coverage.

Respected Voice

A former state legislator and Peace Corps executive, Peters has run the *Washington Monthly* since 1969, and in that time, it has become both a respected voice for neo-liberalism and a training ground for talented young journalists who have gone on to the *New Yorker,* the *Washington Post, Harper's* and *The Atlantic Monthly.*

Peters says that even journalists who come to Washington determined to establish their own individuality "learn quickly to take on the values of the community . . . the group instinct," in part because so many of them have spent time on the campaign trail, where "they travel together . . . (and) get very anxious about deviating any from the opinion of the group. They are very concerned about finding out what group consensus is developing. They build a habit of thinking in terms of a herd." . . .

Campaign reporters [especially] operate in an echo chamber whose resonance has increased so much in recent years that they sometimes seem deaf to any voices but one another's. Their words are played back instantly and incessantly via the networks, the national daily newspapers, Cable News Network and Hot Line, a computerized service developed in 1988 to provide journalists with extracts from newspaper and television stories and commentaries throughout the nation every day.

"Every reporter everywhere in the country, as long as he had a laptop computer with a modem, could download the conventional wisdom at 8 A.M. for the day in the most incredible microdetail," says Michael Kinsley, editor of *The New Republic.* "There was no chance that anyone would react independently to the day's events."

Fortunately, not all political reporters and Washington correspondents are journalistic myna birds. A few actually have original thoughts.

The most influential Washington journalist today is probably David Broder of the *Washington Post,* and the most original thinker may be William Safire of the *New York Times.*

Broder is both an excellent reporter and a respected commentator whose influence is especially strong during political campaigns. Broder analyzes the results of each primary instantly, in time for the next morning's *Post,* in a way that establishes "the betting line on politics," says syndicated columnist Charles Krauthammer. "He's fantastically quick. . . . He comes up with his own idea and within four minutes, everybody accepts it, it's repeated by everybody, and it's now conventional wisdom.

"Broder's influence is such that he helps to set up the game even before it starts," Krauthammer says.

'He's Not Predictable'

Safire is influential in setting the conventional wisdom in part because he, too, is a good reporter with excellent sources but also because, unlike most columnists, he's not predictable; he sometimes criticizes his friends and differs with his ideological soul mates. Safire is a congenital contrarian; he delights in staking out positions counter to the conventional wisdom, thus establishing a new conventional wisdom for others to emulate.

But Broder and Safire are exceptions in more ways than one. They are not just original voices in a largely copycat chorus; they are print journalists in a television era.

. . . [E]xcept for Safire, Broder and very few others, it is increasingly television that drives the journalistic consensus today, especially on Washington-based public affairs stories.

There are now more than twenty public affairs talk and interview shows on television, and their proliferation, combined with the decline of the Washington columnist, "can't help . . . diminish the quality of conventional wisdom" and the public discourse that ensues, says Robert Merry, managing editor of *Congressional Quarterly*.

"There's a show-biz imperative to spout off," Merry says. "You don't survive on these shows if your aim is to . . . dig deep into the complexities of Washington happenings and emerge with wisdom. . . . You survive on these shows by being quick—provocative."

Merry is far from alone in this lament.

The Washington-based TV talk shows are "the most insidious, the most destructive (force) to independent thinking," says Hodding Carter III, former assistant secretary of state for public affairs and now president of MainStream Television Production Co.

"The best of the shows put a premium on essentially superficial reactions," Carter argues. "Insight and any depth of analysis, any nuance, is completely gone."

No one is suggesting that Lippmann and his fellow print pundits were unfailingly enlightened in their analyses. Lippmann, after all, dismissed candidate Franklin D. Roosevelt as "an amiable boy scout . . . without any important qualifications" for the presidency, and he praised Hitler as "the authentic voice of a genuinely civilized people."

But Lippmann's mistakes—as egregious as they were—did not derive from theatricality or superficiality. He read and thought and wrote; he didn't just pop off.

Participants in some Washington TV talk shows are encouraged to make thumbs-up/thumbs-down judgments and to give 1-to-10 ratings or A-to-F grades on complex issues and personalities. Since many of the participants also write newspaper and magazine columns, critics worry that these superficial practices spill over into their work in those forums as well, further trivializing both the conventional wisdom and the general political dialogue.

James Fallows, writing in the *New York Review of Books* three years ago, complained that the pundits who participate in talk shows "drum the subtlety and complication out of public issues and encourage journalists to think as predictably as politicians." . . .

Significant Role

The morning and evening news shows play a significant role, too—in part because television, even more than newspapers, focuses on institutions, largely Washington-based government institutions. . . .

Most broadcast news comes from "commercially oriented, mass market agencies which don't go very far out of the mainstream," [David] Broder contends. And yet, "Voices on television have a reach which most of us on the print side don't have, and they have an impact."

This combination of reach, impact and mainstream predictability make television a potent force in shaping the journalistic consensus—all the more so because the very nature of television requires brevity.

"Television has created a compulsion to judgment," says Bradlee of the *Washington Post.* "It takes too long to tell everybody what happened. . . . You've got to tell them 'this is good' or 'this is bad' and therefore you've got to be judgmental."

"Good or bad" leaves little room for gradations, and it yields instant conventional wisdom.

"Anchors . . . have an imperative to truncate ideas down to something they can communicate in the fewest possible seconds to introduce a story . . . (that) is itself not usually able to have nuance," says John Buckley, communications director for the National Republican Congressional Committee. "By so doing, there is an extraordinary role of setting conventional wisdom. The luxury of a print reporter . . . getting in different ideas, showing nuance and . . . alternative positions to the conventional wisdom isn't there."

Moreover, Buckley says, "The interdependence between print reporters and television is greater than it ever has been before in that more print news organizations' conventional wisdom is set by what was on television the night before and not . . . the other way around . . . as it used to be."

Dan Rather makes the point even more strongly. Increasingly, he says, print journalists "cover events by watching television, and that means that everybody sees and hears a lot of the same thing in a lot of the same ways."

In a sense, there is a circular, self-perpetuating quality to the development of conventional wisdom in the media, and not only in the recycling of Sunday talk shows in Monday newspapers. The print media is still a major agenda-setter, whether through the columns of Broder and Safire, the front pages and editorial pages of the *New York Times, Washington Post* and *Wall Street Journal* or the covers of *Time* and *Newsweek.* But television increasingly acts as a megaphone, broadcasting the conventional wisdom back to its vast audience—which includes other print journalists. . . .

See text p. 210

Recent events underline the question of media power and responsibility. In November 1991, former Klu Klux Klan leader and neo-Nazi David Duke was defeated in the

Louisiana gubernatorial election. During the course of his campaign, Duke was able to obtain national publicity despite his unsavory past. Although Duke frequently referred to his former activities as "youthful indescretions," many observers feared that he was simply manipulating the media and hiding his true beliefs. Duke ultimately won only 39 percent of the overall Louisiana vote, but nearly 55 percent of the state's white voters supported him—despite his record of racism and anti-semitism. One major question raised by the Duke candidacy is the role of the national media in local elections. Some analysts and media executives assert that the media were instrumental in bringing Duke's record to light. Other analysts, however, argue that an uncritical and credulous broadcast media permitted a dangerous extremist to obtain national publicity while hiding the most sordid elements of his record. In other words, did the media behave responsibly? Did they use their power wisely? The following article, by Peter Applebome of the New York Times examines these questions.

Peter Applebome
"On the Past and Future of a Politician: Was Duke Made for TV, or Made by It?"*

"Take it from someone who has spent most of his adult life working in this medium," said Ted Koppel at the beginning of the ABC News program "Nightline" on Friday night. "Television and David Duke were made for each other."

The words, coming as Mr. Duke got a half-hour of free time on the eve of the election for Louisiana governor, may be truer than he meant them to be. Despite his railing against "the liberal media," Mr. Duke's evolution from a lifetime at the fringes of racial politics to a new life as an aspiring national politician is largely the result of his symbiotic relationship with broadcast journalism. And, some analysts say, his future in politics may depend in good measure on how television continues to treat him.

Former Gov. Edwin W. Edwards was the landslide winner over Mr. Duke, a State Representative, in the runoff on Saturday. But on the Sunday talk shows, and on the Monday night news, where Mr. Duke appeared live with Dan Rather on the CBS News, the focus was still on Mr. Duke, who announced on Monday that he was forming an exploratory committee to consider a race for President.

The Ability to Articulate

Even critics say Mr. Duke's national visibility reflects his ability to articulate gut-level issues that resonate with many white voters. But many say it also reflects television's infatuation with his telegenic looks and bizarre personal

---

story, the eagerness of unprepared television interviewers to give him air time without the presence of critics who can refute his points or correct his errors, and their acceptance of Mr. Duke's own conditions for going on the air.

"If David Duke has one unique quality, he's the consummate master of broadcast media," said Lance Hill, executive director of the Louisiana Coalition Against Racism and Nazism. "He doesn't look good in print, but he triumphs on television. He's such an exotic story that broadcast media can't resist him, but they're playing a dangerous game. They think they're using him for ratings, but he's using them to advance his political agenda."

Mr. Duke sees it differently. "Broadcast is always better," he said today. "One-on-one interviews is the very best type, because then there's not any editing. The power to edit is an awesome weapon. You can make a sinner into a saint or a saint into a sinner."

By any measure, Mr. Duke's visibility breaks all laws of conventional logic and politics. A racial extremist who in seven campaigns for public office has won only a State Representative's seat in an all-white district, he is by any traditional measurement the smallest of minnows in the political sea.

"I think the national media have, in fact, created David Duke," Mr. Edwards said Sunday.

'A Certain Priesthood'

And some television figures say it is hypocritical of print journalists to single out television. "There's a certain priesthood, especially among the print guys, that somehow you're the news, and we're not," Phil Donahue, host of a nationally syndicated interview show, said in an interview today. "I gave him less coverage than The New York Times did. Anyway, I think David Duke ought to get more coverage, not less. Give people more light, and they'll find their own way, as they obviously did in Louisiana."

But many observers say that television, where Mr. Duke makes his patented pitches to white votes and gives out his address to potential supporters, has been the most sympathetic medium. "He appears on TV with almost numbing regularity," said Arnold Hirsch, a history professor at the University of New Orleans. "He has become the Robert Redford of hate."

The race for governor allowed him to take his message to the nation on shows like the Cable News Network's "Larry King Live," "Donahue" and "Nightline."

What Kind of Attention?

Mr. Hill does not criticize the amount of attention given to Mr. Duke, but he does criticize the way much of it was done. Many interviewers, he said, were simply unprepared. Thus, he said, they allowed Mr. Duke to profess contrition for youthful flirtations with extremism but did not rebut him with examples of the same behavior in his recent past, or statements in which Mr. Duke said his plan was to cloak an extremist agenda in mainstream rhetoric.

After Mr. Duke's appearance on Larry King, James Gill in The New Orleans Times-Picayune called the show "indistinguishable from a campaign commercial" and said it consisted of "a solid hour of largely uninterrupted propaganda and uncontradicted lies."

To which Mr. King said: "If a guy is going on television tonight and his desire is to fool you, and whenever you ask him about the past, his answer will be, 'I've changed,' there's only so much you can do."

But Mr. Hill, who says Mr. Duke has not strayed from the extremist views that have characterized most of his career, said Mr. Duke's ability to reinvent himself and his propensity for distortion require a higher standard of preparedness than most television interviewers have shown.

"He is the only political figure in the 20th century who has attempted this kind of political masquerade that I know of, from the left or the right," Mr. Hill said. "Television is a perfect medium for a dissembler like Duke. He will evade. He will lie. He will do whatever he needs to do to get through those 30 minutes."

Did Interviewers Fold?

Mr. Hill said he was also concerned about preconditions to which some interviewers agreed.

On Mr. Donahue's program, for instance, Mr. Duke required that no footage be shown of him in Ku Klux Klan regalia, and that there be no broadcasting of printed quotes from past interviews that might conflict with his newer positions.

Tyler Bridges, a reporter with The Times-Picayune who covered Mr. Duke, said that he himself was invited to appear on "Nightline" but then was told that the invitation was canceled because Mr. Duke would not appear with him. Mr. Duke said he did not want to be on the program with a reporter whom he considers adversarial, but that he was not aware what specific provisions his staff made with "Nightline." Program officials said Mr. Bridges and others were contacted about the possibility of appearing, but that no firm offer was made.

Whatever the case, after Mr. Edwards declined to appear, Mr. Duke was interviewed alone on "Nightline," perhaps the nation's most prestigious interview program, on election eve.

"I think it's a gross misuse of discretionary authority on the part of a national television show to put a candidate on the night before the election and give him a half-hour of free time," said Joe Walker, a local poll taker. "It's outrageous.

Some, like Mr. King, say it is hard to argue that Mr. Duke used television very well. "David Duke got all this exposure and 39 percent of the vote," he said.

Tom Bettag, executive producer of "Nightline," said that whether or not Mr. Duke was the right messenger he had a message that people were responding to, and that it was foolish to blame television for his appeal.

"Television is a part of the reality of life," he said, "and it all goes into the mix, as there was a time when Roosevelt thrilled the nation with speeches on radio. That's not an artificial part of life. That's the way we communicate with each other."

MEASURING PUBLIC OPINION

See text p. 222

Despite the sophistication of contemporary public opinion measurements, the data generated still has limitations. As the text points out, the two primary problems with polling data are the illusion of central tendency and the illusion of salience. The illusion of central tendency occurred during the public opinion polls on the Gulf War, as journalist Jon Margolis points out in the following article.

Jon Margolis
"Insufficient Data: It's Not that Polls Are Wrong, They're Just Highly Inadequate"*

If so many agree, why are so few happy?

Just about the whole country supports President Bush and his decision to go to war in the Persian Gulf.

But because of that decision people say they can't sleep, can't pay attention to their work or their studies, can't even read a book or enjoy their favorite television shows.

How do we know this? From the polls. Several of them report that about 80 percent of the people—that's as close to consensus as this contentious country ever gets—approves of the president and the war he has chosen. One respected poll—by *Times Mirror*—last week documented the feeling of unease and discomfort that is palpable on the streets.

All of which reveals two realities, one about the public and one about public opinion polls. The reality about the public is that it is always more complex than the polls say it is. The reality about polls is that they are almost always less complex than they ought to be.

This does not mean polls are wrong. Polls are almost never wrong. It's just that they are usually inadequate.

"Polls have the same limitations as politicians and newspaper reporters," said David Axelrod, a Chicago political consultant who has seen his candidates rise and fall in public opinion surveys. "They tend to reflect the passions and sentiments of the moment."

Axelrod was being polite. Had he been blunt he would have said that like politicians and reporters, polls are often simplistic. Or maybe even simple-minded.

There is a connection here. It is the simplistic (simple-minded?) reporter or editor who uses the poll finding as though it were not merely a fact, which it is, but a meaningful fact, which it may not be.

The poll result is more than just a fact. It is an objective, even a scientific, fact. It comes in computer printouts. Being a fact, it is merely reported, not put in context. Once reported, it becomes part of the body of knowledge, however misleading, on which further analysis is based.

"Polls don't measure the psychology of people," said Peter Hart, one of the country's most successful and respected pollsters. "People respond to polls in quantitative ways. They're given a choice of whether they prefer a, b, c or do, and if it's a media poll it's usually just a or b. That doesn't get to the complex person underneath the answer. Polling doesn't get to the fears, concerns or apprehensions people have."

A poll, in other words, is not only somewhat simplistic itself, but treats its subjects (the respondents) as though they were simplistic, as though they were computers with two positions—yes or no, on or off—rather than human beings with all their confusions and uncertainties.

Unlike computers, people rarely have simple yes or no, likes and dislikes. Asked whether they like blue shirts, anchovies, college basketball, "Murphy Brown," or mystery novels, most people probably would say, "That depends." On the time of day, the place, their mood, who else was around, what else was going on.

"Polls assume that all opinion is equal," Hart said. "In reality, some opinion is more equal than others. In this case (the war) some people are very committed in their support, others are marginal and likely to change their minds."

"The approval rating (of Bush) doesn't tell you everything you need to know," said Lee Miringoff, director of the Marist Poll in Poughkeepsie, N.Y. "The answer depends on what you ask and the order you ask it. Sometimes the interpretation is more to the art side than a science."

Pollsters know this, and they do have ways of probing beneath the surface of public opinion. "But it's not done often because it's very expensive," said Nelson Polsby, the director of the the University of California's Institute of Governmental Studies. "The public opinion survey is much more sophisticated than it used to be. You can use focus groups, which do get into the context of events."

So far, none of the polls about public reaction to the war have used the focus group, usually about 12 randomly selected people who spend a couple of hours answering questions from a pollster and sometimes conversing with each other.

Hart, who uses focus groups, said even this technique and other sophisticated methods which try to pierce the surface of popular opinion have their limits.

"It's very tough to measure the psychology without the event," Hart said.

"You can measure apprehension, which gives you some sense of what people will feel. But you can not feel what you have not felt. Until something really happens, you don't know how you'll feel about it."

What has happened is that war has broken out, and whatever they thought or felt before the shooting started, the American people know how they feel about it now: they want to win it as quickly as possible with as few American casualties as possible.

Because they support the war and the troops fighting it, they also support the president, because, once war starts, the president, any president, becomes a symbol of the country.

"Like a monarch," wrote political scientist Peter Schwartz, "the modern president mystically embodies and represents the nation."

That might be a bit overstated, but the history of polls shows that presidential popularity goes up when the shooting starts.

"Right now, the president's approval has to do with the feeling people have about the troops over there," Miringoff said. And Polsby explained that "rally around the flag is the cliché we use to talk about how presidential popularity increases in foreign confrontations, whether they are fiascos or successes."

George Edwards, a political scientist at Texas A&M and co-author of the book *Presidential Approval,* said there are a few small exceptions to this rule. The 1983 invasion of Grenada didn't do much for Ronald Reagan's already high ratings, and by the time Jimmy Carter authorized the unsuccessful "Desert One" rescue mission to Iran in 1980, public confidence in him had already fallen so far that his poll rating did not improve, although perhaps it would have had the mission been a success.

Bush's high standing now means he still has the public's confidence. It does not mean that he will keep it.

"What's the decay rate likely to be?" Polsby said. "It will start under one set of conditions—criticism from opinion leaders hinged in part on an unwillingness to pay costs in human lives."

Some think that the public will accept even that cost if the war seems to be going well. But if casualties increase and the battle seems stalemated, both Bush and the war are likely to become very unpopular very quickly.

"The day before we went to war there was an almost perfect split," over the wisdom of war, Edwards said. That disagreement has not disappeared so much as it has been submerged by a tide of caring about the country and its soldiers.

The long-range lesson, after the war is over, is that polls should be viewed as useful but limited tools, easily misunderstood and subject to change.

The short range lesson is that the poll results on the war mean only that the American people are patriotic and hopeful. If their hopes are fulfilled they will be patriotic and confident. If their hopes are dashed, they will be patriotic and angry. This finding has a margin of error of plus-or-minus zero.

CHAPTER 9

Elections

POLITICAL PARTICIPATION

See text p. 227

    As U.S. citizens, most Americans are aware that they have an "obligation" to participate knowingly in democratic processes, particularly that they ought to be informed about major issues of public policy and that they ought to vote intelligently in light of that knowledge. Yet studies of citizen participation and knowledge reveal that ideals of an informed electorate are appallingly inaccurate: most people participate only minimally and on limited information.

    The reading for this section suggests that concerns about low voter participation may be overstated. The fact that most citizens do not meet the democratic ideal when it comes to voter participation is no reason to despair; different levels of participation contribute to the smooth functioning of the democratic system as a whole. In 1990, Richard Harwood, a writer for the Washington Post, *addressed this problem just before the elections. Harwood argues that the level of complexity in modern politics suggests that perhaps one of the strengths of the system itself is that there is no such thing as public opinion that voting can measure or reflect.*

Richard Harwood
"Do We Really Have to Vote? Don't Panic—Low Turnout Isn't the End of Democracy"*

As I set forth on the morning of Sept. 11, [1990] a neighbor called out to remind me to vote. "Vote for what?" I asked. It was, she informed me, primary election day in Montgomery County, where I have lived for almost 30 years.

    I had forgotten and wanted to say, "Frankly, my dear, I don't give a damn." But that would have gotten me in trouble. She is a friend and a precinct boss, the Jiminy Cricket of the neighborhood who is always pointing us to our civic responsibilities.

    She was aware that with one or two exceptions I never know any of the local candidates, that I have no interest whatever in the register of wills or such ballot issues as the method for electing members of the Democratic Party Executive Committee and that however it turns out, my taxes are going up faster than the high rises in Bethesda. She generously handed me a sample ballot with check marks by the names of the goo-goos. I stuck it in my pocket, drove off to the polls, punched the cards according to her instructions and asked myself, "Why in the hell am I doing this?"

A week from Tuesday, the whole nation will ask itself the same question; and the next day we will begin our binennial rite of self-reproach over "low voter turnout." But maybe we shouldn't be quite so concerned.

Life is a very complicated proposition in these last throes of the 20th century, so complicated that we have learned to deal with it through endless divisions of labor. We no longer deliver our own babies, bury our dead, grow the food we eat or build our homes. We hire people to do those things and a thousand other tasks that separate us from self-sufficiency. The car mechanic, the brain surgeon, the weaver, the plumber, the computer doctor: We are dependent on them all because the things they do are either beyond our capacities or too time-consuming.

That is the truth about politics and government in America today, and it has made the idea of "self-government" absurd. The governmental apparatus that has been created for us is the largest and, in many ways, one of the least accessible institutions in human history. Even the numbers we use to describe it are beyond the comprehension of all but a few: It consumes trillions of dollars, a third of our gross national product. (What is a trillion?) It directly employs nearly 20 million people, more than all the manufacturing enterprises in the United States. The variety of activities in which they engage is beyond our grasp.

How do I, John Q. Citizen, govern this monster? How do I make "informed" decisions? Do I need a B-2? What is a "throw-weight" and what should I think about it? Why haven't policies A, B, C, D, E and F eliminated "welfare dependency" and created a self-sufficient post-welfare class? What really is wrong with our system of education? Why did the S & Ls fail? Why are fewer deliveries and short pants the only change in the Postal Service during my lifetime? What and who do PACs buy with their money? Who writes the laws? Who fixes the potholes in Interstate 95?

As a people of genius, we have devised by default or design (it doesn't matter) a solution to these problems of bigness and complexity: a division of labor. Since we can no longer govern ourselves even in the abstract sense, we have created a professional class of people to perform that function. They relieve us of the need to pretend we understand what Leviathan is all about.

This class includes the politicians whose names and faces flit across our consciousness and our television screens from time to time. We grant them, mostly by passive acquiescence, lifetime tenure—just as we grant, through civil-service protections, lifetime tenure to those faceless men and women in the bureaucracies who govern in fact, if not in theory. Ronald Reagan was going to dismantle all that, he and his enemies claimed. But it was beyond his control, as it is ours.

The governing class includes as well the thousands of lobbies, lawyers, associations and "public-interest" busybodies who swarm around these governmental institutions and manipulate them in various ways in our name.

Finally, the governing class includes the "media" which, like the tick birds on the rhino, ride along on the beast under the illusion that it responds to their direction.

As for the "sovereign citizen" from whom all just powers are derived, he is, as most of us are, best described by Walter Lippmann. We resemble, he said, "the deaf spectator in the back row, who ought to keep his mind on the mystery off there, but cannot quite manage to keep awake. He knows he is somehow affected by what is going on; rules and regulations continually, taxes annually, and wars occasionally remind him that he is being swept along by great drifts of circumstance. Yet these public affairs are in no convincing way his affairs. They are for the most part invisible." We are not merely deaf and half-asleep. A great many of us are hollow logs so far as public affairs are concerned. We have no opinions of any kind on many of the great issues of the day and those we have are often worthless.

Richard Morin, *The Post's* polling director, published an article earlier this year on the "Ignorant '80s." Nearly half of our people, he reported, do not know if the United States and the Soviet Union were allies or enemies in World War II. A third don't know what the Holocaust was. Millions don't know whether we supported North or South Vietnam in the late unpleasantness or whether we were for or against the Sandinistas in Nicaragua. A majority can identify Judge Wapner of "The People's Court," but fewer than 10 percent can name the chief justice of the United States. Half of us can't name our congressman and my guess is that 90 percent cannot name their state senator or representative on pain of death or dismemberment.

"Boobus Americanus," H.L. Mencken called us, and in terms of our civic roles he was right. Millions of us are not merely politically illiterate, we are functionally illiterate as well. The American Newspaper Publishers Association, fearful that the readers among us are vanishing, estimates that 27 million Americans read below the fifth-grade level and that 60 to 65 million read below the ninth-grade level. By comparison, you need approximately a 12th-grade education to read the Outlook section with a modest degree of comprehension.

This is the raw material of the American electorate which hand-wringing reformers fear is growing "alienated," "apathetic" and otherwise disabled from performing the tasks of citizenship. I have preached that sermon myself based on the relatively low voter turnouts of recent years. Curtis Gans, an expert on that subject, used a graphic description for the results of the 1986 off-year elections: Republicans 17 percent, Democrats 19 percent, non-voters 67 percent. That is about what we should expect next week. Is it possible that those voting minorities have evolved through some inexplicable sociological process into a "professional" voting class that serves, like the warrior class in many societies, a specific and useful function? Perhaps we should regard them as our surrogates, specialists who know that the wills register is not some guy in the Orioles bullpen and who provide that element of informed and semi-informed consent which our democratic system requires.

That is an undemocratic notion but it is essentially the theory on which our nation was founded. It denied that there is any law of God or nature ordaining that larger and larger turnouts of increasingly uninformed and uninterested citizens save or strengthen our democracy. Is there reason to accept the contrary argument that the "public," voting en masse, intrinsically or mystically brings to the political process some form of moral enrichment and uplift? Or is this uninvolved "public" cynically regarded as an inert and pliable mob available for "delivery" to the highest bidder or to the most skillful manipulators?

For many years, Lippmann wrote, we hung our belief in the dignity of man "on the very precarious assumption that he would exhibit that dignity instinctively in wise laws and good government. Voters did not do that, and so the democrat was forever being made to look a little silly by tough-minded men. But if instead of hanging human dignity on that one assumption about self-government, you insist that man's dignity requires a standard of living in which his capacities are properly exercised, the whole problem changes.

"The criteria which you then apply to government are whether it is producing a certain minimum of health, of decent housing, of material necessities, of education, of freedom, of pleasures, of beauty, not whether at the sacrifice of all these things it vibrates to the self-centered opinions that happen to be floating around in men's minds." The "public" as in "public opinion" and the "public will" and "public consent" may, in fact, be a figment of our imagination. Jay Rosen of New York University, like Lippmann before him, propounded that subversive idea a couple of years ago: "Suppose that the real problem is not with the polls, but with the assumption that there is something out there to measure. . . . The press, the pollsters, academics who study the polls and everyone else who refers to the public as a living, thinking, speaking thing help paper over the doubts that might otherwise exist about what a public is and whether it exists. The most convenient assumption is that the public is "out there" following the issues, forming opinions and expressing its will. . . . [But] on some issues, at least, there is no functioning public realm in America—no national forum in which leaders can talk seriously about problems they themselves see as serious."

James Carey of the University of Illinois put it in starker terms: "Despite the fact that the public is regularly invoked as the final justification for the press, the simple fact is that the public has disappeared. There is no public out there. . . . In professional circles talk about the public continues, but no one knows what they are talking about."

That is true of the voter turnout issue. We talk about it constantly, form commissions, organize conferences, produce monographs, pamphlets and books. But none of us knows what we are talking about or whether there is a real problem "out there" or whether it has or needs a solution.

If they held an election and nobody came, that would be cause for concern. But we are not at that point and there is no reason to assume it will ever be reached. Our democracy limps along. My neighbor will remind me to vote, and I will cast the ballot for her choice for register of wills. Whether I have enriched the democratic process, I leave to the next study commission.

REGULATING THE ELECTORAL PROCESS

See text p. 230–35

As the text notes, the government can control the electorate to some extent by constraining the composition of that voting constituency itself. In the United States, the history of electoral composition has been a history of expanding the franchise, although it has been a slow and painful process, especially for people of color.

When Congress passed the Voting Rights Act of 1965, it intended to sweep away many of the impediments meant to restrict voting by blacks in the South. But southern states continued to be recalcitrant. One favorite device for limiting electoral participation involved the imposition of a poll tax, or a fee that had to be paid if the voter wanted to cast a vote. The poll tax was declared unconstitutional in the 1966.

Gerrymandering electoral districts to dilute or strengthen the power of selected voting blocs has a long tradition in this country. For many years, the Supreme Court refused to consider the constitutionality of such legislative districting on the ground that determining the composition of a legislative district was outside of its authority since the question was of such a political nature. In 1962, however, the Court finally ruled on the issue, holding in Baker v. Carr that legislative districting schemes that unduly diluted the vote of particular groups could be declared a violation of the "Equal Protection clause" of the Fourteenth Amendment. Subsequently, in Reynolds v. Sims, the Court declared that voters have a right to "an equally effective voice in the election of members of his state legislature," establishing what has since become known as the principle of "one man, one vote."

These cases, however, did not settle, by any means, the particulars of legislative districting schemes. In fact, the process of redistricting is a complex phenomenon. The following two articles, by Thomas Edsall and Barbara Vobejda, discuss recent problems created by redistricting. The first describes the impact of redistricting on traditional voting blocs in Texas; the second exposes some of the actual methods that most legislatures use to come up with districting plans.

Thomas B. Edsall
"In Texas, New Lines and Ethnic Ambition Divide the Party"*

Democratic Rep. Martin Frost of Texas is afraid he may be a victim of the congressional redistricting process now underway in state legislatures across America. "The endangered species in Texas may be the white urban Democrat," says one of his colleagues—and Frost is one of them.

A seven-term incumbent who represents part of Dallas and adjoining suburbs and, ironically, is chairman of Impact 2000, the national organization seeking to protect Democratic interest in House redistricting, Frost finds himself caught betweeen two powerful forces: blacks and Hispanics newly empowered under the Voting Rights Act and demanding districts that will elect some of their own, and Republicans ready to exploit the strength they have accumulated over the past decade in burgeoning suburban areas.

"What you have is a suburban doughnut ring that is predominately Republican and an inner core that is minority Democrat—black and Hispanic," says George Strake, former chairman of the Texas Republican Party, who could not be more pleased with the situation.

If every effort possible is made to ensure the election of blacks and Hispanics by creating districts dominated by minority voters, he says, the outlying districts by necessity must be more solidly white, and consequently more Republican.

"The net loser in that deal," he says, "is the Anglo Democrat."

. . . Texas, is a case study of the nationwide struggle the Democratic Party faces in preserving its traditional urban stronghold in the faces in preserving its traditional urban stronghold in the face of shifting demographics and an increasingly hostile political environment.

In metropolitan areas as diverse as Los Angeles, Chicago, Detroit, Cleveland and New York, other incumbents . . . also are likely to be affected. Their vulnerability is but one of the ways congressional redistricting will force a shift in the balance of political power of the 1980s to reflect the migration of people between states and within them.

That shift will reflect the continuing decline of once-powerful northern cities and the continuing movement of people and power away from the Northeast and Midwest to the South and West. It will strengthen the political representation of Hispanics, who are now a powerful force not only in the Southwest but in cities such as Chicago and New York.

And it will further empower the suburbs, which in 1992, for the first time in the nation's history, will cast a majority of votes in a presidential race. . . .

In the politics of redistricting, [adding new seats based on population gains is] the easy part. The hard part—and the source of the coming warfare—is that these new seats must be carved out of old ones, sharply increasing the likelihood that incumbents will be forced out of power.

In Dallas the state legislature is sure to create a new district that will elect a black lawmaker, while forcing Frost to run in a newly redrawn district farther out in the Republican suburbs.

As Frost struggles to persuade legislators to draw him the most favorable district possible, he is running into a deeply held resentment that dates back 10 years. A number of black political leaders in Dallas believe that Frost benefited from court decisions in 1981 that, in their view, prevented the creation of a majority black district at that time.

One of those leaders, Democratic state Sen. Eddie Bernice Johnson, chairman of the Senate's special congressional redistricting subcommittee, now controls Frost's chances of survival.

Johnson is determined this time to create a new black district and, this time, she can do it, thanks in part to changes in the Voting Rights Act.

Under amendments to the act in 1982 and Supreme Court rulings since then, legislatures drawing district lines in areas with histories of racially polarized voting are effectively required to create districts giving blacks and Hispanics voting majorities whenever reasonably possible.

Johnson is not without self-interest in the process. She intends to run for Congress herself in the new district. To create it, she is prepared not only to reduce the black and Hispanic (and therefore reliably Democratic) vote in Frost's . . . district to a minimum, but to take from [it] some of the few remaining white voters in the region whose loyalty to the Democratic Party remains firm.

"Basically, the argument at this point is over the Democratic white areas," Frost says, noting that the competing plans he and Johnson have backed have "very little difference in terms of the black and brown areas."

In his struggle to get those white areas in his new district, Frost lacks support not only from Johnson but also from some other key members of the legislature. The chairman of the legislature's black caucus, Democratic Rep. Fred Blair, has gone out of his way to make it clear that Frost's political survival is not his top priority.

"I'd love to see Frost remain in Congress," he says, adding quickly: "But the African American community has been denied. . . . I have to make sure we are represented in Congress from Dallas."

Ultimately, this pressure from the black community dovetails with the goals of the Republican Party, which is eager to convert the gains it has made in the state in recent years to more than the eight House seats it now holds.

In the district Johnson has proposed for herself, Democratic presidential nominee Michael S. Dukakis, who lost Texas with 44 percent of the vote in 1988, got 67 percent.

In contrast, in the district she has proposed for Frost, Dukakis lost by the same margin as he did statewide . . . according to figures supplied by GOP strategists.

Underlying the difficulties facing Frost . . . is the nosediving support for the Democratic Party among white Texans.

Among all Texas voters, partisan allegiance over the years has shifted from an awesome 66 percent Democratic voter identification and 6 percent Republican (with the rest independent or undecided) in 1952, to 57 and 14 in 1972, to 39 and 23 in 1983, to virtual parity now. This movement has been driven almost entirely by white voters, who now favor the GOP by a decisive edge.

Over the past decade, the Texas Hispanic population has grown by 1.35 million, while the number of blacks in the state has increased by 280,000. Most of the 1.1 million population growth in non-Hispanic whites is Republican.

The outcome of the struggle over the Texas seats will be critical in the determination of which party comes out the winner in the huge transfer of power involved in the decennial redrawing of congressional districts.

Because they hold both the governorship and legislative majorities in Texas and Florida, which will gain four House seats, Democrats are counting on full control of the process in those states to blunt growing Republican strength and to counter what are almost guaranteed GOP gains in California.

But as the Texas legislature wrestles with redistricting, many white Democrats are discomfited by the strong language used by minority groups in describing what they want out of the process. . . .

. . . In Dallas, the Rev. S.M. Wright, president of the International Ministerial Alliance said, "I know one thing: We [blacks] are going to have a black district in this area," he says. "I would hope our [white] Democratic congressmen can be spared, but we have suffered too long, doing all the giving. Now, it's our time to receive."

These assertions are music to the ears of Fred Meyer, chairman of the Texas Republican Party.

"Three communities have been treated alike by the [white] Democrats: African Americans, Hispanics and Republicans. Our interests are all maximized at the same time," he says.

He and other Republicans are calculating that the commonality of redistricting interest among these groups will end up making Frost . . . vulnerable.

"When push comes to shove, their [black and Hispanic] interest is more with us because we will guarantee them the best, most solid minority districts. We will build our plan around them [minorities]," declares Republican Rep. Joe Barton of Texas.

Some federal courts have used the goal of achieving 65 percent black majority districts to assure election of a black candidate, and even higher percentages could be needed for Hispanics, whose turnout rates generally are very low.

That requirement would leave even fewer minority voters who could be included in adjoining districts where white Democrats were in trouble.

Despite these daunting prospects, Democratic strategists hope the Texas legislature will adopt a plan that accomplishes three key goals: assuring the safety of all 19 Democratic incumbents; creating three new congressional districts designed to be won by Democratic blacks or Hispanics; and holding the Republicans to their eight seats in the new 30-member delegation.

No one knows for sure when Johnson's committee will come up with its recommendations and a plan will be adopted, but for the moment, the prospects for Democratic internecine conflict appear high. Johnson has told reporters in Austin that her black constituents "want a district at all costs, regardless of who it hurts."

Barbara Vobejda
"Apportionment Formulas Make and Break Districts"*

It ends in the most human of dramas: candidate pitted against candidate, fighting to represent a chunk of territory carved out as a political district.

It begins with a mind-numbing mathematical process understood by few, even in the political circles where careers are made and broken by the numbers.

Now the esoteric number-crunching used every 10 years to distribute House seats among the states is emerging as a point of controversy.

Massachusetts and Montana, both of which lost congressional seats in the 1990 reapportionment, have filed federal lawsuits challenging the Census Bureau's 50-year-old method of apportionment.

And as the legal challenges grind through the system, lawyers and policy-makers and politicians who have paid little attention to the minutiae of apportionment formulas are being forced to tackle the daunting mathematics at the heart of the process.

"A lot of people who thought they had given up on fractions when they graduated from the sixth grade," says Democratic Rep. Chester G. Atkins of Massachusetts, "are going to get back into a deep and intense understanding of fractions."

It is not a new problem: For 200 years the challenge of distributing House seats simply and fairly has frustrated mathematicians and politicians. The first presidential veto was exercised in 1791 when George Washington rejected Alexander Hamilton's apportionment method in favor of one proposed by Thomas Jefferson.

Since then, several methods have been tested and used, all with their supporters and detractors.

The current method—known as the Method of Equal Proportions—has been in place with relatively little controversy since 1940. But the loss of congressional seats has prompted state leaders and politicians in Massachusetts and Montana to haul out their calculators and pore over dusty studies of the current method and its alternatives.

To those whose political futures are at risk, there are crystal-clear implications to the complicated math.

Apportionment—the process of distributing the 435 House seats among the 50 states—takes place once a decade after the national census. That process leads to the second critical step of redistricting, when state legislatures redraw the boundaries for congressional and state legislative districts.

In Massachusetts, the 1990 apportionment means that the state's 11 existing congressional districts must be reconfigured into 10. And that, of course, means uncertain futures for Atkins and his fellow incumbents, who may be forced to run against each other in a redesigned district.

It is that jarring political reality that brings to life the otherwise abstract process of apportionment, which, according to Atkins, is taken for granted by most members of Congress.

"I've never heard anybody talk about the difference between the major fractions and the proportional method," he says.

Those terms are central to the claim by Massachusetts Attorney General Scott Harshbarger that the 1990 apportionment "is invalid on several legal grounds." The current Method of Equal Proportions, says Harshbarger, is biased against the more populous states, including Massachusetts.

The state advocates that Congress adopt an alternative process, first proposed in 1832 by Daniel Webster and known as the Method of Major Fractions, because it is not biased against either large or small states. Montana is advocating either of two other apportionment methods.

The stakes are high in the suits, which are awaiting hearings in federal courts in Boston and Helena, Mont.: If a federal judge ordered the Census Bureau to adopt an alternative apportionment method, a handful of congressional seats could shift among the states.

Massachusetts also is challenging a decision by the Census Bureau to include for only the second time in history in the population totals federal employees and their families stationed overseas (the first was in 1970 during the Vietnam War). If those persons had not been included, Massachusetts would have retained its 11th seat.

Montana raises another issue, arguing that House seats should not be distributed automatically, without congressional attention. Because the 1990 apportionment leaves the state with a very large, single district, it diminishes the voting power of Montana voters, according to the suit.

"If that is going to happen, Congress has to vote on that," says Beth Baker, an assistant attorney general in Montana.

Dividing up the 435 seats in the House would seem straightforward. But it is not, for several reasons: First, each state must receive at least one seat, regardless of how small its population. Second, House districts cannot cross state lines. And finally, the size of the House is fixed at 435 seats.

As a result, the process is riddled with complexities.

In theory, it can be done this way: Divide the nation's population by the number of available seats, 435, to yield an "ideal district size." (The ideal district size is adjusted for the different methods of apportionment to yield exactly 435 seats).

To determine how many seats should go to each state, divide the "ideal district" figure into each state's population. The result will be a whole number and a fraction.

The difference between the several methods of apportionment is the "rounding point" used in each—the point at which that fraction should be rounded up, giving the state an additional seat, or rounded down.

Massachusetts argues that the Method of Major Fractions, which rounds up to a new seat at the arithmetical mean, or 0.5, would be more fair than the Method of Equal Proportions, which rounds up at the "geometric mean" between the two numbers. The geometric mean is calculated by multiplying the two numbers and taking the square root of the product.

Because the geometric mean grows larger as the number of House seats grows, it is increasingly difficult for larger states to win additional seats.

Such mathematical idiosyncracies have plagued all of the various apportionment formulas. After President Washington's veto of Hamilton's method, Jefferson's method was used until 1830. Webster's proposal, the Method of Major Fractions, was used in 1840. A version of the Hamilton method was adopted in the latter half of the 19th century, to be replaced again by Webster's method until the current formula was adopted.

David C. Huckabee, an analyst at the Congressional Research Service, reported in a 1988 document that the Method of Equal Proportions yields the most equitable distribution of congressional seats on a proportional basis. For example, Massachusetts wins 10 seats and Oklahoma wins 6 seats under this method. That gives Massachusetts 1.6586 representatives per million inhabitants, compared with Oklahoma's figure of 1.9002. Under the Method of Equal Proportions, seats are distributed in such a way as to minimize the percentage difference between those two figures.

By comparison, the Method of Major Fractions produces the most equitable distribution when representation is compared on an absolute, rather than proportional, basis. Under this method, Massachusetts would win 11 seats and Oklahoma would win 5. The goal is to minimize the absolute difference in representation between the two states—calculated by subtracting the number of representatives per million inhabitants in Oklahoma from the figure for Massachusetts.

In an analysis of past apportionments, H.P. Young, an economist at the University of Maryland's school of public policy and a coauthor of a book on apportionment, found that, under the Method of Equal Proportions, small states fare better—receiving a 3.5 percent advantage—in terms of the number of congressional seats per million residents.

"We're supposed to have proportionality," Young says. "What's going on here? This is not the intent of the Constitution."

A 1929 report by the National Academy of Sciences, however, concluded that the method "occupies a mathematically neutral position" with respect to population size.

Young disputes those findings and advocates the Major Fractions method as the only alternative that eliminates a systematic advantage to either small or large states.

It is "the fairest method among all reasonable methods," he says, "and it has a strong historical weight behind it."

While Census Bureau officials are aware of such arguments, they say they have no intention of changing the practice unless instructed to do so by Congress or the courts. Robert Speaker, a branch chief in the bureau's population division, says the bureau "basically takes no position on what method is used. . . . Congress can decide to do it any way it wants."

ELECTORAL REALIGNMENTS

See text p. 244

For over ten years, political observers have attempted to determine whether the conservative electoral coalition headed by Ronald Reagan has in fact generated a permanent swing to the right. In the following article, political commentator James Barnes discusses some of the changes in Washington that occurred during the Reagan years that suggested a long-term move to the right in the Washington community itself. Despite these noticeable changes, however, Barnes suggests that the Democrats have not been permanently displaced, and any conclusions about whether these changes signal a more broadly based critical realignment are at best premature.

James A. Barnes
"Changing Company Town"*

. . . Washington, the ultimate company town, is changing. Ideologically, it has gradually been shifting to the right, driven by the conservative ideas and conservative idealists that Reagan brought to Washington eight years ago. And Reagan's failure to disperse elements of the Washington power structure has, ironically, probably provided opportunities for Reaganites to become part of that power structure.

At the same time, though, conservatism, having established a Washington beachhead in the past eight years, faces some evolutionary challenges as well.

Reagan's drive to the White House took 12 years, from the time he first ran for the Republican presidential nomination in 1968 as the ideological disciple of Barry Goldwater to his election in 1980. But it took another eight years until conservatism was finally accepted, or at least respected, in Washington. The conservative movement, characterized in the 1960s as a collection of crackpot ideas hopelessly out of step with the rest of the country, became in the 1970s a credible theoretical basis for critiquing liberal programs. But it is really only now, with the conclusion of Reagan's successful presidency, that it has attained the status of a practical governing philosophy.

If not for Reagan, conservatism might not be getting a respectable hearing today. Reagan in 1980 was able to meld public policy proposals such as the earlier Kemp-Roth tax cut plan into a successful political movement that created an electoral mandate for turning some of these ideas into law.

Reagan's impact has been felt on both sides of the partisan aisle. Rep. Dan Glickman, D-Kan., said, "We haven't gone as far as his rhetoric did, but I think that attitudinally, Members of Congress view the federal establishment a little more like Reagan does now than we did eight years ago." And Rep. Olympia J. Snowe, R-Maine, observed that "over all, the Republican

---

*James A. Barnes, "Changing Company Town," *National Journal* (February 4, 1989). Reprinted with permission.

Party has become more conservative." Democrats, in the wake of their third successive presidential election defeat, are grappling with how to improve their image on crime and defense issues. Republicans who doubted the logic of supply-side economics are now professing their conversion.

And both Glickman and Snowe agreed that Reagan's articulation of traditional social values—family, community and religion—now frames some of the debate over public policy issues. A clear example of this was the welfare reform bill passed by a bipartisan majority last year that embraced the concept that welfare programs should encourage work rather than dependency and that absent fathers should bear more responsibility for their children. . . .

There might be a lesson for hard-line conservatives in the liberal experience of the past two decades. Cohen thinks that a major reason for liberal activists' declining effectiveness has been their tendency not to appreciate their own success. Instead of proclaiming victory after achieving perhaps 80–90 per cent of a legislative goal, he said, liberals once viewed this kind of result as "only half a loaf."

Cohen said liberals' failure to consolidate their gains, along with the ever-higher expectations created for liberal programs during the 1960s, led to counterproductive and dogmatic approaches to issues. "We had some very real successes," he said. "People had been lifted out of poverty. That's very different from saying, 'We are still an imperfect society that is unjust and unfair.' We should have embraced them [the successes], and we wouldn't have lost our ability to be credible critics of society." . . .

Bench Strength

When Reagan came to Washington in 1981, he brought with him many conservative activists who probably would not have been recruited for government jobs by a moderate Republican President. He gave them the chance to play in the big leagues, run a Cabinet subdivision or at least get their feet wet as an agency deputy counsel, gaining invaluable experience for future service. Even if 1988's election results had swept them out of power, they would have been able to return with the next Republican tide, their government service credentials in hand.

But Bush won the election, and the flip side of this process is becoming painfully clear to Democrats: They are being decredentialed. "The Republicans have a hell of a front bench and, increasingly, we don't," Sen. Daniel Patrick Moynihan, D-N.Y., lamented. "A generation of people who have had a career like Dick Darman has been missed." His reference was to Bush's budget director, Richard G. Darman, who held important jobs in the Nixon, Ford and Reagan Administrations.

The revolving door has stopped turning for many Democratic and liberal activists, who hadn't gone more than eight years without a kindred President since the 1920s. "You had liberals going in and out of government, people coming in as deputy assistant secretary, lots of them who were going to become the next Clark Cliffords and so forth," Heritage's Pines said of those who had worked in Democratic Administrations. "The career ladder has been pulled out from under them," he said with relish.

If Bush wins reelection in 1992, "it means disenfranchising an entire generation, not giving them the opportunity to serve," said Stuart E. Eizenstat, who was the chief domestic policy adviser in Jimmy Carter's White House after having served in a lesser post in the Johnson Administration. Eizenstat, now practicing law at the Washington office of Powell, Goldstein, Frazer & Murphy, an Atlanta law firm, added, "By the time Democrats get back into power, the people who served in the Johnson Administration will be in their 70s and the people in the Carter Administration will be in their 50s."

In that case, Democrats would be at least a little rusty at pulling the levers of power, which have changed considerably since they were at the helm during the Great Society and even since the more recent Carter era. Democrats could also have recruitment problems. Why uproot yourself and your family when there could be long gaps in your executive branch career? "It does discourage your younger people from coming to Washington," Eizenstat said. "They will say, 'I might as well stay at my university.' "

The stereotype of federal officeholders was that after they finished their work in Washington, voluntarily or otherwise, Republicans returned to their homes in the hinterlands and Democrats flocked to Connecticut Avenue and K Street, the prime nesting place for Washington's legal and lobbying community. Pines and some other conservatives maintain that it is still very hard for a Republican Administration to enlist political appointees from the ranks of business middle management because these executives fear that restrictive ethics laws would make it hard for them to return to private-sector careers; and philosophically, they aren't inclined to stay in a government town. . . .

But regardless of which party controls the White House, there is a need for conservative troops-in-waiting. Had Democratic presidential nominee Michael S. Dukakis won the 1988 election, the conservative movement would have faced wholesale resettlement problems, complicated by the tendency of conservatives to want to return home. Pines said that conservative leaders in Washington had discussed through late September how important it was not to abandon Washington to "Harvard left-wingers. The lesson we learned from liberals in '80 and '84 is, you can't go home. And if you hang on to your turf and fight, you are pushed back [only] inch by inch, and you can significantly keep much of what you have."

With Bush's victory, conservative thinkers have incentives to stay in Washington, if for nothing more than to provide some intellectual mettle for the new Administration. They might also be able to marshal public and elite opinion for Administration causes. Many of Robert H. Bork's allies contend that a reason his nomination to the Supreme Court failed was the sophisticated lobbying efforts of liberal interest groups. Their leaders were more effective than Bork's supporters, both in and out of the White House, in framing the intellectual arguments against the nomination.

"As conservatives stay in this town, the battle lines will be drawn more evenly on that next time, and maybe with people with as good skills," said Terry Eastland, who was the Justice Department's spokesman during the Bork Battle and is now a resident scholar at the National Legal Center for the Public Interest, which produces studies on legal issues of interest to business.

But even conservatives wonder how many members of the corps that is now leaving the executive branch have been well prepared and would want to stay on in Washington. Pines said that Reagan missed a tremendous opportunity in this regard. "To my knowledge," he said, "Reagan did not sit down with his top advisers in January of 1981 and say, 'Let's devise a strategy for creating conservative cadres and make them the governing majority, or make the governing elite in Washington more conservative.'" Had the former President made that a goal, the Heritage official suggested, he would have succeeded.

But the conversion of the pragmatists, certainly in the short run, offsets the shortage of conservative troops and is an indicator that conservative ideas are on the ascendency, at least within the ranks of the Republican Party. Secretary of State James A. Baker III has confessed his initial agnosticism on supply-side economics theory by joking that while he once considered it "voodoo economics," he now describes it as "can-do" economics. "A revolution of ideas is successful," Quayle adviser Kristol said, "precisely when people who are not revolutionaries adopt the thinking."

Conservatives hope that just as President Franklin D. Roosevelt's New Deal domestic agenda was continued in President Truman's Fair Deal, and the goals of President Kennedy's New Frontier were brought to fruition by President Johnson's Great Society, the conservative agenda adopted by Reagan will be nurtured by Bush. In each case, they note, the vice presidential successor was not initially an advocate of his predecessor's ideas.

Temperament

Given Bush's Cabinet's pragmatic coloration and his demeanor since Election Day, the Washington establishment seems to be less coiled and ready to react than it was during the past eight years. "I think there was somewhat of an unease during the Reagan era, because I think people were uncomfortable with the President's attitude toward the Washington community," said former Carter adviser Anne Wexler, chairwoman of Wexler, Reynolds, Fuller, Harrison & Schule Inc., a government relations firm in Washington. Wexler noted approvingly that such Bush White House appointees as national security adviser Brent Scowcroft and economic and domestic policy assistant Roger B. Porter were both "old hands, . . . folks who will know whom to turn to on the outside for good advise."

"The confrontational mode will be abjured," said superlawyer Leonard Garment, an adviser to Presidents Nixon and Ford who practices at the Washington law firm of Dickstein, Shapiro & Morin. And, Eastland predicted, conservatives who prosper in the Washington community "will, for better or worse, learn certain rules of the game, . . . civility and treatment of each other, . . . certain rules of comity."

With elections always around the corner, that may not last long. Eizenstat said that the 1988 election, which postponed for at least another four years a Democratic restoration at the White House, "if anything will increase the hunger to get back in."

Michael J. Horowitz, counsel at the Office of Management and Budget from 1981–85 and now with the Washington law firm of Myerson & Kuhn, also detected an undercurrent of restlessness among Democrats, an anxiety about when they might return to federal service. That state of mind might not be conducive to bipartisanship. "This level of frustration is increasing from having their nose on the window, and that is troublesome," he said.

Despite their prolonged exile, Democrats remain a formidable force in the Washington community, although their latest defeat at the polls has tempered their insularity. "Ronald Reagan will have changed this town in the best sense," Horowitz said. "Neither party will be on God's side." . . .

CHAPTER 10

Political Parties

THE TWO-PARTY SYSTEM IN AMERICA

See text p. 259

Political parties in America, as the text points out, have always been weaker than their European counterparts. One of the oddities of the American political system that has fascinated political scientists for decades is the absence of a strong left-wing political party: Americans have no equivalent to Britain's Labor Party or Germany's Social Democratic Party, for example.

The lack of political parties divided along strong philosophical lines was one of the subjects that struck Alexis de Tocqueville, a French citizen who travelled throughout the United States in the early nineteenth century, whose insights into the advantages and disadvantages of the American democratic system were uncannily shrewd. In the essay that follows, Tocqueville speculated on the nature of the American party system. While the party system of the 1820s and 1830s might be considered strong by today's standards, it did not, according to Tocqueville, bring to the fore great issues of principle such as those that had been the subject of the debates between the Republicans and the Federalists at the time of the founding. In Tocqueville's eyes, American parties dallied on small issues—they took their direction not from principles but from material interests. Parties were formed not to contest the basic foundations of government, but are when a politician "see[s] what his own interest is and who have analogous interests which can be grouped around his own."

Alexis de Tocqueville
"Parties in the United States"*

. . . When there are differences between the citizens concerning matters of equal importance to all parts of the country, such for instance as the general principles of government, then what I really call parties take shape.

Parties are an evil inherent in free governments, but they do not always have the same character and the same instincts.

There are times when nations are tormented by such great ills that the idea of a total change in their political constitution comes into their minds.

---

*Alexis de Tocqueville, "Parties in the United States," from *Democracy in America,* ed. J. P. Mayer and Max Lerner, tr. G. Lawrence. English translation copyright © 1965 by Harper & Row, Publishers, Inc. Reprinted by permission of HarperCollins Publishers.

There are other times when the disease is deeper still and the whole social fabric is compromised. That is the time of great revolutions and of great parties.

Between these centuries of disorder and of misery there are others in which societies rest and the human race seems to take breath. That is in truth only apparently so: time does not halt its progress for peoples any more than for men. . . .

[T]here are times when the changes taking place in the political constitution and social structure of peoples are so slow and imperceptible that men think they have reached a final state; then the human spirit believes itself firmly settled on certain fundamentals and does not seek to look beyond a fixed horizon.

That is the time for intrigues and small parties.

What I call great political parties are those more attached to principles than to consequences, to generalities rather than to particular cases, to ideas rather than to personalities. Such parties generally have nobler features, more generous passions, more real convictions, and a bolder and more open look than others. Private interest, which always plays the greatest part in political passions, is there more skillfully concealed beneath the veil of public interest; sometimes it even passes unobserved by those whom it prompts and stirs to action.

On the other hand, small parties are generally without political faith. As they are not elevated and sustained by lofty purposes, the selfishness of their character is openly displayed in all their actions. They glow with a factitious zeal; their language is violent, but their progress is timid and uncertain. The means they employ are as disreputable as the aim sought. That is why, when a time of calm succeeds a great revolution, great men seem to disappear suddenly and minds withdraw into themselves.

Great parties convulse society; small ones agitate it; the former rend and the latter corrupt it; the first may sometimes save it by overthrowing it, but the second always create unprofitable trouble.

America has had great parties; now they no longer exist. This has been a great gain in happiness but not in morality.

When the War of Independence came to an end and a new government had to be established, the nation was divided between two opinions. Those opinions were as old as the world itself and are found under different forms and with various names in all free societies. One party wanted to restrict popular power and the other to extend it indefinitely.

With the Americans the struggle between these two opinions never took on the violent character that has often marked it elsewhere. In America the two parties agreed on the most essential points. Neither of the two had, to succeed, to destroy an ancient order or to overthrow the whole of a social structure. Consequently, in neither case did the private existence of a great number of people depend on the triumph of its principles. But immaterial interests of the first importance, such as love of equality and of independence, were affected. That was enough to rouse violent passions.

The party which wished to restrict popular power sought especially to have its ideas applied in the federal Constitution, from which it gained the name of Federal.

The other, which claimed to be the exclusive lover of liberty, called itself Republican.

America is the land of democracy. Consequently, the Federalists were always in a minority, but they included almost all the great men thrown up by the War of Independence, and their moral authority was very far-reaching. Moreover, circumstances favored them. The ruin of the first Confederation made the people afraid of falling into anarchy, and the Federalists profited from this passing tendency. For ten or twelve years they directed affairs and were able to apply some but not all of their principles, for the current running in the opposite direction became daily stronger and they could not fight against it. . . .

There had always been something artificial in the means and temporary in the resources which maintained the Federalists; it was the virtues and talents of their leaders, combined with lucky circumstances, which had brought them to power. When the Republicans came in turn to power, the opposing party seemed to be engulfed by a sudden flood. A huge majority declared against it, and suddenly finding itself so small a minority, it at once fell into despair. Thenceforth the Republican, or Democratic, party has gone on from strength to strength and taken possession of the whole of society.

The Federalists, feeling themselves defeated, without resources, and isolated within the nation, divided up; some of them joined the victors; the others lowered their flag and changed their name. For many years now they have entirely ceased to exist as a party.

The period of Federalist power was, in my view, one of the luckiest circumstances attending the birth of the great American Union. The Federalists struggled against the irresistible tendency of their age and country. Whatever the virtues or defects of their theories, they had the disadvantage of being inapplicable in their entirety to the society they wished to control, so what happened under Jefferson would have come about sooner or later. But their rule at least gave the new republic time to settle down and afterwards to face without ill consequences the rapid development of the very doctrines they had opposed. Moreover, in the end many of their principles were introduced under their adversaries' slogans, and the still-extant federal Constitution is a lasting memorial to their patriotism and wisdom.

Thus today there is no sign of great political parties in the United States. There are many parties threatening the future of the Union, but none which seem to attack the actual form of government and the general course of society. The parties that threaten the Union rely not on principles but on material interests. In so vast a land these interests make the provinces into rival nations rather than parties. Thus recently we have seen the North contending for tariffs and the South taking up arms for free trade, simply because the North is industrial and the South agricultural, so that restrictions would profit the former and harm the latter.

Lacking great parties, the United States is creeping with small ones and public opinion is broken up ad infinitum about questions of detail. It is impossible to imagine the trouble they take to create parties; it is not an easy matter now. In the United States there is no religious hatred because religion is universally respected and no sect is predominant; there is no class hatred because the people is everything, and nobody dares to struggle against it; and finally, there is no public distress to exploit because the physical state of the country offers such an immense scope to industry that man has only to be left to himself to work marvels. Nevertheless, the ambitious are bound to create parties, for it is difficult to turn the man in power out simply for the reason that one would like to take his place. Hence all the skill of politicians consists in forming parties; in the United States a politician first tries to see what his own interest is and who have analogous interests which can be grouped around his own; he is next concerned to discover whether by chance there may not be somewhere in the world a doctrine or a principle that could conveniently be placed at the head of the new association to give it the right to put itself forward and circulate freely. It is like the royal imprimatur which our ancestors printed on the first page of their works and incorporated into the book even though it was no part of it.

This done, the new power is introduced into the political world.

To a foreigner almost all the Americans' domestic quarrels seem at the first glance either incomprehensible or puerile, and one does not know whether to pity a people that takes such wretched trifles seriously or to envy the luck enabling it to do so.

But when one comes to study carefully the secret instincts governing American factions, one easily finds out that most of them are more or less connected with one or other of the two great parties which have divided mankind since free societies came into existence. As one comes to penetrate deeper into the intimate thought of these parties, one sees that some parties are working to restrict the use of public power and the others to extend it.

I am certainly not saying that American parties always have as their open or even their concealed aim to make aristocracy or democracy prevail in the country. I am saying that aristocratic or democratic passions can easily be found at the bottom of all parties and that though they may slip out of sight there, they are, as it were, the nerve and soul of the matter.

See text p. 263

International events have a significant impact on the domestic fate of the Democratic and Republican parties. Success—especially presidential success—in the international arena is likely to increase the fortunes of whatever party enjoyed the victory. President Bush's actions in the Gulf War were extremely effective in boosting both his own popularity and support for the Republican party generally. In the following piece, Professors Benjamin Ginsberg and Martin Shefter discuss the likelihood that the Republi-

cans can convert their perceived success in the international arena into a decisive victory on the domestic front.

Benjamin Ginsberg and Martin Shefter
Will the Republicans Win the Peace? *

There is widespread agreement that the Bush administration's handling of the Persian Gulf Crisis was masterful. The president assembled an unprecedented international coalition, neutralized the Soviet Union, and launched a military campaign that routed the Iraqis with minimal loss of American life.

GOP strategists hope to convert George Bush's diplomatic and military triumph over Iraq into a victory over the Republicans' domestic political opponents. The party's national chairman, Clayton Yeutter, has already served notice that the GOP plans to make the Democrats' collective lack of resolve in the face of the Iraqi invasion of Kuwait a major theme of the 1992 presidential and congressional campaigns. Senator Phil Gramm, chairman of the National Republican Senatorial Campaign Committee, recently predicted that Bush's overwhelming popularity would help sweep many Republican senatorial and congressional candidates to victory in 1992.

Barring some unforeseen disaster, George Bush's own reelection in 1992 seems assured. But the success of the president's foreign policy and Bush's impressive popularity are unlikely to translate into a broader victory for the Republican party. Indeed, in some respects the Democrats are as well positioned to win the peace as the Republicans were to win the war.

From the early phases of President Bush's decision to respond militarily to Iraq's invasion of Kuwait, the conflict in the Persian Gulf has involved a struggle not only between the United States and Iraq, but also between two segments of the American governmental system. These are the Democratic welfare state organized around Congress, and the Republican national security state controlled by the White House.

Since the 1960s, Democrats have secured the enactment of numerous social and regulatory programs. The bureaucracies that administer these programs are linked by grants-in-aid to public agencies and nonprofit organizations at the state and local levels. This complex is tied to Democrats in Congress, who affirm the worth of federal social and regulatory programs and defend the authority and budgets of the agencies responsible for their administration.

Domestic programs and agencies tie the Democrats to constituency groups throughout the nation and give them an enormous advantage in congressional elections. One reason that Democrats dominate Congress is that they can draw upon the support of thousands of individuals who are

Will the Republicans Win the Peace? Reprinted courtesy of Benjamin Ginsberg and Martin Shefter.

affiliated with local governments and nonprofit organizations and who are prepared to work for candidates committed to domestic programs and expenditures. Such troops on the ground are a more effective weapon than televised attack ads in congressional campaigns. A central reason why the Democrats are so heavily committed to high levels of domestic spending is that expenditures on social programs support the agencies and organizations that comprise the party's political infrastructure.

The Republicans, for their part, have established an institutional base for themselves in the national security apparatus. This is a major reason why the Reagan administration greatly expanded defense spending while attempting to slow the flow of funds to the domestic agencies linked to its opponents. The Democrats responded to this assault by conducting highly publicized investigations of military procurement scandals, charging that billions of dollars were spent on such things as outrageously overpriced coffee pots and toilet seats rather than for the purchase of useful weapons. They also charged that many complex weapons systems—anti-missile defenses, the stealth fighter, the Apache helicopter and the M1A1 tank, among others—would not work effectively on the battlefield. The grounding of the two parties in different segments of the American state apparatus is a major reason why many congressional Democrats were reflexively opposed to the use of American military forces in the Persian Gulf. From the Democrats' perspective, policies that enhance the importance and prestige of the military also serve the interests of their Republican opponents.

In the Persian Gulf War, the U.S. military routed Iraq. On the domestic front, however, the outcome of the battle between the Republican national security state and the Democratic welfare state is still uncertain. Of course, Republicans will remind voters that all but a few Democrats opposed the president's firm stand against the Iraqis. This will reinforce voters' already substantial doubts that the Democrats can be relied upon to defend the nation's security interests against foreign foes. Republican House Minority Leader Robert Michel said immediately after the war that if critics of defense spending "had their way, Saddam Hussein would be astride the Middle East like a conqueror." Such rhetoric will help ensure that the presidency will remain in Republican hands. Moreover, that the high-tech weapons so frequently assailed by congressional Democrats did in fact work will make it harder for them to mount successful attacks on military spending. But, this may be about the limit of Republican success.

Many congressional Democrats, to be sure, will be embarrassed in 1992, by a campaign which contrasts their opposition to the use of military force with the president's firm stand. One can imagine the Republican TV commercials juxtaposing Democratic calls to give economic sanctions a year or two to work with film clips of jubilant Kuwaiti citizens embracing the American troops who liberated their country. However, few Democrats, at least in the House, will be defeated by this tactic. The entrenchment of the Democrats in the domestic state has enabled that party's congressmen to establish links with such an extensive array of interests that they are all but impossible to dislodge.

Republican efforts to use the Persian Gulf issue, moreover, will be countered by the Democrats. First, liberal commentators will continue to denounce such a Republican tactic as an effort to exploit the sacrifice and bravery of American troops for narrow partisan advantage—an effort to question the patriotism of the opposition party that, it will be said again and again, smacks of McCarthyism. Second, Democrats will continue to point to the history of dealings between the Bush administration and Saddam Hussein's regime, arguing that the growth of Iraqi military power and the invasion of Kuwait were the fault of the Republicans in the first place. Democrats are already charging that a number of prominent Republicans, including Phil Gramm and Clayton Yeutter, advocated cooperation with Iraq as recently as last summer.

The Democrats, furthermore, will not wait until 1992 to launch a political offensive of their own. Unlike the Iraqis, they have the capacity to emerge from their congressional and bureaucratic bunkers inside the Beltway and, despite a month of heavy bombing, wage a successful flanking campaign against the Republicans. Democrats will endeavor to use the successful military effort itself as a justification for increases in spending on the domestic social programs that are the party's life blood. To this end, they have already begun to argue that a grateful nation must now pay its debt to its brave soldiers, their families, and the communities from which they were drawn. Congresswoman Pat Schroeder, for example, who made her name attacking most known U.S. weapons systems, has already pointed out that America lags behind all of its European coalition partners in the provision of social services to its military personnel and veterans.

Bolstering congressional efforts in this area, the brigades of mental health professionals, social service providers, and tort lawyers linked to the Democratic party will hasten to offer their services to veterans and their families. These forces are extremely resourceful and can often identify hitherto unsuspected psychological and medical problems requiring new federal spending programs. In the wake of the Vietnam War, for example, coalitions of helping professionals and political activists had little difficulty persuading Congress that the federal government should spend hundreds of millions of dollars for the treatment of "post-traumatic stress disorder," a consequence of combat that had somehow been overlooked during the previous millenia of organized warfare. To help defend these programs, the Democrats also created liberal Vietnam veterans groups that, unlike traditional veterans' organizations, portrayed soldiers not as heroes but as victims of the government they had served.

Can the Republicans win the peace? Probably not. More than a century ago, in the aftermath of the Civil War, the GOP recognized that successful efforts to make lasting political use of military victory depended upon establishing institutions that provided significant constituencies with a continuing reason to support the politicians who fought and won the war. This is most easily done through programs that supplement patriotic appeals with material rewards. The party created an extensive pension system for former soldiers and their dependents that was linked to the Grand Army of the

Republic, a veterans organization given quasi-official recognition. This apparatus served as a major element of the Republican party's political machine and gave millions of Americans a material stake in the GOP's victory that supplemented the patriotic appeals made by Republican politicians in their "bloody shirt" campaigns. The Veterans Administration and the American Legion served the political interests of the bipartisan Cold-War coalition in a similar fashion following the Second World War.

Benefit programs, patriotic organizations, government bureaucracies—these are the sorts of building blocks that would be needed to construct a Republican party with the organizational capacity to mount a serious bid for control of Congress. It is difficult, however, to see today's GOP following the example of its forebears. Many contemporary Republicans are more concerned with protecting their upper-income and business constituents from the unpleasant necessity of having to pay taxes than with strengthening their party's organizational infrastructure. But even assuming that Republicans sought to do this, there is little chance that a Democratic Congress would allow the Republicans to construct a domestic political machine to rival their own. Congress would sooner participate in the rebuilding of Iraq.

Many commentators have noted that George Bush's handling of the Persian Gulf Crisis parallels the performance of the marshal played by Gary Cooper in the movie, *High Noon.* Like Cooper, Bush refrained from unnecessary palaver, ignored the timid townsfolk who argued against confrontation, and resolutely did what had to be done. But it is worth remembering that after the showdown, Cooper's term expired and he moved on. His timorous neighbors, emerging from the safety of their hiding places, then resumed control of the town.

THE FUNCTIONS OF THE PARTIES

See text p. 264

This section of the text discusses the very important but in some ways mechanical functions of the parties: nominating candidates and getting out the vote are critically important to the operation of the American electoral system. Parties have also served another important function: they have provided a focal point for assigning responsibility for various governmental actions. In the following article, which relates to both this section of the text and the following section dealing with the decline of party organizations, political scientist Morris Fiorina discusses the role that the parties have traditionally played in enhancing accountability in the political arena, as well as the effects that the decline of the parties has had on that important function.

Morris P. Fiorina
"The Decline of Collective Responsibility in American Politics"*

Though the Founding Fathers believed in the necessity of establishing a genuinely national government, they took great pains to design one that could not lightly do things *to* its citizens; what government might do *for* its citizens was to be limited to the functions of what we know now as the "watchman state." . . .

Given the historical record faced by the Founders, their emphasis on constraining government is understandable. But we face a later historical record, one that shows two hundred years of increasing demands for government to act positively. Moreover, developments unforeseen by the Founders increasingly raise the likelihood that the uncoordinated actions of individuals and groups will inflict serious damage on the nation as a whole. The by-products of the industrial and technological revolutions impose physical risks not only on us, but on future generations as well. Resource shortages and international cartels raise the spectre of economic ruin. And the simple proliferation of special interests with their intense, particularistic demands threatens to render us politically incapable of taking actions that might either advance the state of society or prevent foreseeable deteriorations in that state. None of this is to suggest that we should forget about what government can do *to* us—the contemporary concern with the proper scope and methods of government intervention in the social and economic orders is long overdue. But the modern age demands as well that we worry about our ability to make government work *for* us. The problem is that we are gradually losing that ability, and a principal reason for this loss is the steady erosion of *responsibility* in American politics. . . .

Unfortunately, the importance of responsibility in a democracy is matched by the difficulty of attaining it. In an autocracy, individual responsibility suffices; the location of power in a single individual locates responsibility in that individual as well. But individual responsibility is insufficient whenever more than one person shares governmental authority. We can hold a particular congressman individually responsible for a personal transgression such as bribe-taking. We can even hold a president individually responsible for military moves where he presents Congress and the citizenry with a *fait accompli.* But on most national issues individual responsibility is difficult to assess. If one were to go to Washington, randomly accost a Democratic congressman, and berate him about a 20-percent rate of inflation, imagine the response. More than likely it would run, "Don't blame me. If 'they' had done what I've advocated for *x* years, things would be fine

*Morris P. Fiorina, "The Decline of Collective Responsibility in American Politics," reprinted by permission of *Daedalus,* Journal of the American Academy of Arts and Sciences, from the issue entitled, "The End of Consensus?" Summer 1980, Vol. 109/3.

today." And if one were to walk over to the White House and similarly confront President Carter, he would respond as he already has, by blaming Arabs, free-spending congressmen, special interests, and, of course, us.

American institutional structure makes this kind of game-playing all too easy. In order to overcome it we must lay the credit or blame for national conditions on all those who had any hand in bringing them about: some form of *collective responsibility* is essential.

The only way collective responsibility has ever existed, and can exist given our institutions, is through the agency of the political party; in American politics, responsibility requires cohesive parties. This is an old claim to be sure, but its age does not detract from its present relevance. In fact, the continuing decline in public esteem for the parties and continuing efforts to "reform" them out of the political process suggest that old arguments for party responsibility have not been made often enough or, at least, convincingly enough, so I will make these arguments once again in this essay.

A strong political party can generate collective responsibility by creating incentive for leaders, followers, and popular supporters to think and act in collective terms. First, by providing party leaders with the capability (e.g., control of institutional patronage, nominations, and so on) to discipline party members, genuine leadership becomes possible. Legislative output is less likely to be a least common denominator—a residue of myriad conflicting proposals—and more likely to consist of a program actually intended to solve a problem or move the nation in a particular direction. Second, the subordination of individual officeholders to the party lessens their ability to separate themselves from party actions. Like it or not, their performance becomes identified with the performance of the collectivity to which they belong. Third, with individual candidate variation greatly reduced, voters have less incentive to support individuals and more incentive to support or oppose the party as a whole. And fourth, the circle closes as party-line voting in the electorate provides party leaders with the incentive to propose policies that will earn the support of a national majority, and party back-benchers with the personal incentive to cooperate with leaders in the attempt to compile a good record for the party as a whole.

In the American context, strong parties have traditionally clarified politics in two ways. First, they allow citizens to assess responsibility easily, at least when the government is unified, which it more often was in earlier eras when party meant more than it does today. Citizens need only evaluate the social, economic, and international conditions they observe and make a simple decision for or against change. They do not need to decide whether the energy, inflation, urban, and defense policies advocated by their congressman would be superior to those advocated by Carter—were any of them to be enacted!

The second way in which strong parties clarify American politics follows from the first. When citizens assess responsibility on the party as a whole, party members have personal incentives to see the party evaluated favorably. They have little to gain from gutting their president's program one day and attacking him for lack of leadership the next, since they share in the president's fate when voters do not differentiate within the party. Put simply, party responsibility provides party members with a personal stake in their collective performance.

Admittedly, party responsibility is a blunt instrument. The objection immediately arises that party responsibility condemns junior Democratic representatives to suffer electorally for an inflation they could do little to affect. An unhappy situation, true, but unless we accept it, Congress as a whole escapes electoral retribution for an inflation they *could* have done something to affect. Responsibility requires acceptance of both conditions. The choice is between a blunt instrument or none at all. . . .

In earlier times, when citizens voted for the party, not the person, parties had incentives to nominate good candidates, because poor ones could have harmful fallout on the ticket as a whole. In particular, the existence of presidential coattails (positive and negative) provided an inducement to avoid the nomination of narrowly based candidates, no matter how committed their supporters. And, once in office, the existence of party voting in the electorate provided party members with the incentive to compile a good *party* record. In particular, the tendency of national midterm electionsto serve as referenda on the performance of the president provided aclear inducement for congressmen to do what they could to see that their president was perceived as a solid performer. By stimulating electoral phenomena such as coattail effects and mid-term referenda, party transformed some degree of personal ambition into concern with collective performance. . . .

The Continuing Decline of Party in the United States

Party Organizations

In the United States, party organization has traditionally meant state and local party organization. The national party generally has been a loose confederacy of subnational units that swings into action for a brief period every four years. This characterization remains true today, despite the somewhat greater influence and augmented functions of the national organizations. Though such things are difficult to measure precisely, there is general agreement that the formal party organizations have undergone a secular decline since their peak at the end of the nineteenth century. The prototype of the old-style organization was the urban machine, a form approximated today only in Chicago. . . .

[Fiorina discusses the reforms of the late nineteenth and early twentieth century discussed in the text.]

In the 1970s two series of reforms further weakened the influence of organized parties in American national politics. The first was a series of legal changes deliberately intended to lessen organized party influence in the presidential nominating process. In the Democratic party, "New Politics" activists captured the national party apparatus and imposed a series of rules changes designed to "open up" the politics of presidential nominations. The Republican party—long more amateur and open than the Democratic party—adopted weaker versions of the Democratic rules changes. In addition, modifications of state electoral laws to conform to the Democratic rules changes (enforced by the federal courts) stimulated Republican rules changes as well. . . .

A second series of 1970s reforms lessened the role of formal party organizations in the conduct of political campaigns. These are financing regulations growing out of the Federal Election Campaign Act of 1971 as amended in 1974 and 1976. In this case the reforms were aimed at cleaning up corruption in the financing of campaigns; their effects on the parties were a by-product, though many individuals accurately predicted its nature. Serious presidential candidates are now publicly financed. Though the law permits the national party to spend two cents per eligible voter on behalf of the nominee, it also obliges the candidate to set up a finance committee separate from the national party. Between this legally mandated separation and fear of violating spending limits or accounting regulations, for example, the law has the effect of encouraging the candidate to keep his party at arm's length. . . .

The ultimate results of such reforms are easy to predict. A lesser party role in the nominating and financing of candidates encourages candidates to organize and conduct independent campaigns, which further weakens the role of parties. . . . [I]f parties do not grant nominations, fund their choices, and work for them, why should those choices feel any commitment to their party?

Party in the Electorate

In the citizenry at large, party takes the form of a psychological attachment. The typical American traditionally has been likely to identify with one or the other of the two major parties. Such identifications are transmitted across generations to some degree, and within the individual they tend to be fairly stable. But there is mounting evidence that the basis of identification lies in the individual's experiences (direct and vicarious, through family and social groups) with the parties in the past. Our current party system, of course, is based on the dislocations of the Depression period and the New Deal attempts to alleviate them. Though only a small proportion of those who experienced the Depression directly are active voters today, the general outlines of citizen party identifications much resemble those established at that time.

Again, there is reason to believe that the extent of citizen attachments to parties has undergone a long-term decline from a nineteenth-century high. And again, the New Deal appears to have been a period during which the decline was arrested, even temporarily reversed. But again, the decline of party has reasserted itself in the 1970s. . . .

As the 1960s wore on, the heretofore stable distribution of citizen party identifications began to change in the general direction of weakened attachments to the parties. Between 1960 and 1976, independents, broadly defined, increased from less than a quarter to more than a third of the voting-age population. Strong identifiers declined from slightly more than a third to about a quarter of the population. . . .

Indisputably, party in the electorate has declined in recent years. Why? To some extent the electoral decline results from the organizational decline. Few party organizations any longer have the tangible incentives to turn out the faithful and assure their loyalty. Candidates run independent campaigns and deemphasize their partisan ties whenever they see any short-term electoral gain in doing so. If party is increasingly less important in the nomination and election of candidates, it is not surprising that such diminished importance is reflected in the attitudes and behavior of the voter.

Certain long-term sociological and technological trends also appear to work against party in the electorate. The population is younger, and younger citizens traditionally are less attached to the parties than their elders. The population is more highly educated; fewer voters need some means of simplifying the choices they face in the political arena, and party, of course, has been the principal means of simplification. And the media revolution has vastly expanded the amount of information easily available to the citizenry. Candidates would have little incentive to operate campaigns independent of the parties if there were no means to apprise the citizenry of their independence. The media provide the means.

Finally, our present party system is an old one. For increasing numbers of citizens, party attachments based on the Great Depression seem lacking in relevance to the problems of the late twentieth century. Beginning with the racial issue in the 1960s, proceeding to the social issue of the 1970s, and to the energy, environment, and inflation issues of today, the parties have been rent by internal dissension. Sometimes they failed to take stands, at other times they took the wrong ones from the standpoint of the rank and file, and at most times they have failed to solve the new problems in any genuine sense. Since 1965 the parties have done little or nothing to earn the loyalties of modern Americans.

Party in Government

If the organizational capabilities of the parties have weakened, and their psychological ties to the voters have loosened, one would expect predictable consequences for the party in government. In particular, one would expect to see an increasing degree of split party control within and across the levels of American government. The evidence on this point is overwhelming. . . .

The increased fragmentation of the party in government makes it more difficult for government officeholders to work together than in times past (not that it has ever been terribly easy). Voters meanwhile have a more difficult time attributing responsibility for government performance, and this only further fragments party control. The result is lessened collective responsibility in the system.

What has taken up the slack left by the weakening of the traditional [party] determinants of congressional voting? It appears that a variety of personal and local influences now play a major role in citizen evaluations of their representatives. Along with the expansion of the federal presence in American life, the traditional role of the congressman as an all-purpose ombudsman has greatly expanded. Tens of millions of citizens now are directly affected by federal decisions. Myriad programs provide opportunities to profit from government largesse, and myriad regulations impose costs and/or constraints on citizen activities. And, whether seeking to gain profit or avoid costs, citizens seek the aid of their congressmen. When a court imposes a desegregation plan on an urban school board, the congressional offices immediately are contacted for aid in safeguarding existing sources of funding and in determining eligibility for new ones. When a major employer announces plans to quit an area, the congressional offices immediately are contacted to explore possibilities for using federal programs to persuade the employer to reconsider. Contractors appreciate a good congressional word with DOD procurement officers. Local artistic groups cannot survive without NEA funding. And, of course, there are the major individual programs such as social security and veterans' benefits that create a steady demand for congressional information and aid services. Such activities are nonpartisan, nonideological, and, most important, noncontroversial. Moreover, the contribution of the congressman in the realm of district service appears considerably greater than the impact of his or her single vote on major national issues. Constituents respond rationally to this modern state of affairs by weighing nonprogrammatic constituency service heavily when casting their congressional votes. And this emphasis on the part of constituents provides the means for incumbents to solidify their hold on the office. Even if elected by a narrow margin, diligent service activities enable a congressman to neutralize or even convert a portion of those who would otherwise oppose him on policy or ideological grounds. Emphasis on local, nonpartisan factors in congressional voting enables the modern congressman to withstand national swings, whereas yesteryear's uninsulated congressmen were more dependent on preventing the occurrence of the swings. . . .

[The result is the insulation of the modern congressional member from national forces altogether.]

The withering away of the party organizations and the weakening of party in the electorate have begun to show up as disarray in the party in government. As the electoral fates of congressmen and the president have diverged, their incentives to cooperate have diverged as well. Congressmen have little personal incentive to bear any risk in their president's behalf, since they no longer expect to gain much from his successes or suffer much from his failures. Only those who personally agree with the president's program and/or those who find that program well suited for their particular district support the president. And there are not enough of these to construct the coalitions necessary for action on the major issues now facing the country. By holding only the president responsible for national conditions, the electorate enables officialdom as a whole to escape responsibility. This situation lies at the root of many of the problems that now plague American public life.

Some Consequences of the Decline of Collective Responsibility

The weakening of party has contributed directly to the severity of several of the important problems the nation faces. For some of these, such as the government's inability to deal with inflation and energy, the connections are obvious. But for other problems, such as the growing importance of single-issue politics and the growing alienation of the American citizenry, the connections are more subtle.

Immobilism

As the electoral interdependence of the party in government declines, its ability to act also declines. If responsibility can be shifted to another level or to another officeholder, there is less incentive to stick one's neck out in an attempt to solve a given problem. Leadership becomes more difficult, the ever-present bias toward the short-term solution becomes more pronounced, and the possibility of solving any given problem lessens.

. . . [P]olitical inability to take actions that entail short-run costs ordinarily will result in much higher costs in the long run—we cannot continually depend on the technological fix. So the present American immobilism cannot be dismissed lightly. The sad thing is that the American people appear to understand the depth of our present problems and, at least in principle, appear prepared to sacrifice in furtherance of the long-run good. But they will not have an opportunity to choose between two or more such long-term plans. Although both parties promise tough, equitable policies, in the present state of our politics, neither can deliver.

Single-Issue Politics

In recent years both political analysts and politicians have decried the increased importance of single-issue groups in American politics. Some in fact would claim that the present immobilism in our politics owes more to the rise of single-issue groups than to the decline of party. A little thought, however, should reveal that the two trends are connected. Is single-issue politics a recent phenomenon? The contention is doubtful; such groups have always been active participants in American politics. The gun lobby already was a classic example at the time of President Kennedy's assassination. And however impressive the antiabortionists appear today, remember the temperance movement, which succeeded in getting its constitutional amendment. American history contains numerous forerunners of today's groups, from anti-Masons to abolitionists to the Klan—singularity of purpose is by no means a modern phenomenon. Why, then, do we hear all the contemporary hoopla about single-issue groups? Probably because politicians fear them now more than before and thus allow them to play a larger role in our politics. Why should this be so? Simply because the parties are too weak to protect their members and thus to contain single-issue politics.

In earlier times single-issue groups were under greater pressures to reach accommodations with the parties. After all, the parties nominated candidates, financed candidates, worked for candidates, and, perhaps most important, party voting protected candidates. When a contemporary single-issue group threatens to "get" an officeholder, the threat must be taken seriously. . . .

Not only did the party organization have greater ability to resist single-issue pressures at the electoral level, but the party in government had greater ability to control the agenda, and thereby contain single-issue pressures at the policy-making level. Today we seem condemned to go through an annual agony over federal abortion funding. There is little doubt that politicians on both sides would prefer to reach some reasonable compromise at the committee level and settle the issue. But in today's decentralized Congress there is no way to put the lid on. In contrast, historians tell us that in the late nineteenth century a large portion of the Republican constituency was far less interested in the tariff and other questions of national economic development than in whether German immigrants should be permitted to teach their native language in their local schools, and whether Catholics and "liturgical Protestants" should be permitted to consume alcohol. Interestingly, however, the national agenda of the period is devoid of such issues. And when they do show up on the state level, the exceptions prove the rule; they produce party splits and striking defeats for the party that allowed them to surface.

In sum, a strong party that is held accountable for the government of a nation-state has both the ability and the incentive to contain particularistic pressures. It controls nominations, elections, and the agenda, and it collectively realizes that small minorities are small minorities no matter how intense they are. But as the parties decline they lose control over nominations and campaigns, they lose the loyalty of the voters, and they lose control of the agenda. Party officeholders cease to be held collectively accountable for party performance, but they become individually exposed to the political pressure of myriad interest groups. The decline of party permits interest groups to wield greater influence, their success encourages the formation of still more interest groups, politics becomes increasingly fragmented, and collective responsibility becomes still more elusive.

Popular Alienation from Government

For at least a decade political analysts have pondered the significance of survey data indicative of a steady increase in the alienation of the American public from the political process . . . The American public is in a nasty mood, a cynical, distrusting, and resentful mood. The question is, Why?

If the same national problems not only persist but worsen while ever-greater amounts of revenue are directed at them, why shouldn't the typical citizen conclude that most of the money must be wasted by incompetent officials? If narrowly based interest groups increasingly affect our politics, why shouldn't citizens increasingly conclude that the interests run the government? For fifteen years the citizenry has listened to a steady stream of promises but has seen very little in the way of follow-through. An increasing proportion of the electorate does not believe that elections make a difference, a fact that largely explains the much-discussed post-1960 decline in voting turnout.

Continued public disillusionment with the political process poses several real dangers. For one thing, disillusionment begets further disillusionment. Leadership becomes more difficult if citizens do not trust their leaders and will not give them the benefit of a doubt. Policy failure becomes more likely if citizens expect the policy to fail. Waste increases and government competence decreases as citizen disrespect for politics encourages a lesser breed of person to make careers in government. And "government by a few big interests" becomes more than a cliché if citizens increasingly decide the cliché is true and cease participating for that reason.

Finally, there is the real danger that continued disappointment with particular government officials ultimately metamorphoses into disillusionment with government per se. Increasing numbers of citizens believe that government is not simply overextended but perhaps incapable of any further bettering of the world. Yes, government is overextended, inefficiency is pervasive, and ineffectiveness is all too common. But government is one of the few instruments of collective action we have, and even those committed to selective pruning of government programs cannot blithely allow the concept of an activist government to fall into disrepute.

Of late, however, some political commentators have begun to wonder whether contemporary thought places sufficient emphasis on government *for* the people. In stressing participation have we lost sight of *accountability?* Surely, we should be as concerned with what government produces as with how many participate. What good is participation if the citizenry is unable to determine who merits their support?

Participation and responsibility are not logically incompatible, but there is a degree of tension between the two, and the quest for either may be carried to extremes. Participation maximizers find themselves involved with quotas and virtual representation schemes, while responsibility maximizers can find themselves with a closed shop under boss rule. Moreover, both qualities can weaken the democracy they supposedly underpin. Unfettered participation produces Hyde Amendments and immobilism. Responsible parties can use agenda power to thwart democratic decision—for more than a century the Democratic party used what control it had to suppress the racial issue. Neither participation nor responsibility should be pursued at the expense of all other values, but that is what has happened with participation over the course of the past two decades, and we now reap the consequences in our politics.

In 1970 journalist David Broder wrote:

. . . what we have is a society in which discontent, disbelief, cynicism and political inertia characterize the public mood; a country whose economy suffers from severe dislocations, whose currency is endangered, where unemployment and inflation coexist, where increasing numbers of people and even giant enterprises live on the public dole; a country whose two races continue to withdraw from each other in growing physical and social isolation; a country whose major public institutions command steadily less allegiance from its citizens; whose education, transportation, law enforcement, health and sanitation systems fall far short of filling their functions; a country whose largest city is close to being ungovernable and uninhabitable; and a country still far from reconciling its international responsibilities with its unmet domestic needs. We are in trouble.

The depressing thing is that no rays of light shine through the dark clouds. The trends that underlie the decline of parties continue unabated, and the kinds of structural reforms that might override those trends are too sweeping and/or outlandish to stand any chance of adoption. Through a complex mixture of accident and intention we have constructed for ourselves a system that articulates interests superbly but aggregates them poorly. We hold our politicians individually accountable for the proposals they advocate, but less so for the adoption of those proposals, and not at all for overseeing the implementation of those proposals and the evaluation of their results. In contemporary America officials do not govern, they merely posture.

CHAPTER 11

Groups and Interests

THE CHARACTER OF INTEREST GROUPS

See text p. 287

The guarantee of a right to associate with others in the pursuit of political objectives was a key point in the American political structure from its outset, and was in marked contrast to the structure of political systems in Europe at the time, which often suppressed political associations that posed threats to the stability of the existing regime. This phenomenon of political association was noted by Alexis de Tocqueville, who observed that the right to associate provided an important check on democratic regimes, where the tyranny of the majority always threatened to swallow up the interests of the minority. In reading the remainder of this chapter and thinking about the realities of political representation in the United States, you should consider whether you agree with Tocqueville's endorsement of political associations as a means of checking the despotic tendencies of democratic government.

Alexis de Tocqueville
"Political Association in the United States"*

BETTER USE HAS BEEN MADE OF association and this powerful instrument of action has been applied to more varied aims in America than anywhere else in the world. . . .

The inhabitant of the United States learns from birth that he must rely on himself to combat the ills and trials of life; he is restless and defiant in his outlook toward the authority of society and appeals to its power only when he cannot do without it. The beginnings of this attitude first appear at school, where the childen, even in their games, submit to rules settled by themselves and punish offenses which they have defined themselves. The same attitude turns up again in all the affairs of social life. If some obstacle blocks the public road halting the circulation of traffic, the neighbors at once form a deliberative body; this improvised assembly produces an executive authority which remedies the trouble before anyone has thought of the possibility of some previously constituted authority beyond that of those

---

*Alexis de Tocqueville, "Political Associations in the United States," in *Democracy in America*, ed. J.P. Mayer and Max Lerner, tr. G. Lawrence. English translation copyright © 1965 by Harper & Row, Publishers, Inc. Reprinted by permission of Harper-Collins Publishers.

concerned. Where enjoyment is concerned, people associate to make festivities grander and more orderly. Finally, associations are formed to combat exclusively moral troubles: intemperance is fought in common. Public security, trade and industry, and morals and religion all provide the aims for associations in the United States. There is no end which the human will despairs of attaining by the free action of the collective power of individuals. . . .

The right of association being recognized, citizens can use it in different ways. An association simply consists in the public and formal support of specific doctrines by a certain number of individuals who have undertaken to cooperate in a stated way in order to make these doctrines prevail. Thus the right of association can almost be identified with freedom to write, but already associations are more powerful than the press. When some view is represented by an association, it must take clearer and more precise shape. It counts its supporters and involves them in its cause; these supporters get to know one another, and numbers increase zeal. An association unites the energies of divergent minds and vigorously directs them toward a clearly indicated goal.

Freedom of assembly marks the second stage in the use made of the right of association. When a political association is allowed to form centers of action at certain important places in the country, its activity becomes greater and its influence more widespread. There men meet, active measures are planned, and opinions are expressed with that strength and warmth which the written word can never attain.

But the final stage is the use of association in the sphere of politics. The supporters of an agreed view may meet in electoral colleges and appoint mandatories to represent them in a central assembly. That is, properly speaking, the application of the representative system to one party. . . .

In our own day freedom of association has become a necessary guarantee against the tyranny of the majority. In the United States, once a party has become predominant, all public power passes into its hands; its close supporters occupy all offices and have control of all organized forces. The most distinguished men of the opposite party, unable to cross the barrier keeping them from power, must be able to establish themselves outside it; the minority must use the whole of its moral authority to oppose the physical power oppressing it. Thus the one danger has to be balanced against a more formidable one.

The omnipotence of the majority seems to me such a danger to the American republics that the dangerous expedient used to curb it is actually something good.

Here I would repeat something which I have put in other words when speaking of municipal freedom: no countries need associations more—to prevent either despotism of parties or the arbitrary rule of a prince—than those with a democratic social state. In aristocratic nations secondary bodies form natural associations which hold abuses of power in check. In countries where such associations do not exist, if private people did not artificially and temporarily create something like them, I see no other dike to hold back tyranny of whatever sort, and a great nation might with impunity be oppressed by some tiny faction or by a single man. . . .

In America the citizens who form the minority associate in the first place to show their numbers and to lessen the moral authority of the majority, and secondly, by stimulating competition, to discover the arguments most likely to make an impression on the majority, for they always hope to draw the majority over to their side and then to exercise power in its name.

Political associations in the United States are therefore peaceful in their objects and legal in the means used; and when they say that they only wish to prevail legally, in general they are telling the truth. . . .

The Americans . . . have provided a form of government within their associations, but it is, if I may put it so, a civil government. There is a place for individual independence there; as in society, all the members are advancing at the same time toward the same goal, but they are not obliged to follow exactly the same path. There has been no sacrifice of will or of reason, but rather will and reason are applied to bring success to a common enterprise.

STRATEGIES: THE QUEST FOR POLITICAL POWER

See text p. 296

While interest groups usually tend to create political issues themselves, occasionally the process is somewhat reversed. Interest groups emerged on all sides of the abortion issue following the Supreme Court's decision in Roe v. Wade, *declaring that a woman's right to privacy protected her authority to make a decision about abortion. The issue is complex, and lobbyists for all sides have worked to determine which approaches will garner the greatest public support, as the following article on the "abortion wars" demonstrates.*

Carol Matlack
"Abortion Wars"*

Kate Michelman vividly remembers watching the scene from behind a one-way mirror. It was early 1989, and the president of the National Abortion Rights Action League (NARAL) was observing a focus group convened in Tampa, Florida, by pollster R. Harrison Hickman to discuss an abortion case soon to be decided by the Supreme Court.

As the discussion spun on, a middle-aged woman pushed back from the table. "She put her hands on her hips and looked at Harrison and said, 'You know, the real question is, who decides?' " Michelman recalled. "I looked at the person next to me and said, 'That's it.' "

Within weeks, the words "Who decides?" were emblazoned on bumper

---

*Carol Matlack, "Abortion Wars," *National Journal* (March 16, 1991). Reprinted with permission.

stickers, banners and television spots across the country. The slogan, coupled with NARAL's longtime Statue of Liberty logo, "mainstreamed the issue," Michelman said. "It made being anti-choice anti-American."

NARAL was by no means alone in using the 1989 *Webster* v. *Reproductive Services* ruling as a springboard for launching big-bucks abortion-lobbying campaigns. Activists on both sides of the issue are now spending millions of dollars on efforts to mold public opinion and win elections and legislative battles. Increasingly, the combatants are turning to political consultants, pollsters and media experts to frame their messages.

And NARAL, testing the limits of federal campaign finance laws, has begun pouring money directly from its treasury into congressional campaigns.

Anti-abortion groups initially criticized NARAL for using slick professionals, saying they preferred to rely on in-house and volunteer help. But it wasn't long before they, too, were taking polls and convening focus groups.

Anti-abortion groups were forced to respond because the opposition "did a great job . . . deciding how they were going to frame the *Webster* case," said Nancy Myers, the National Right to Life Committee communications director.

The committee hired the polling firm the Wirthlin Group, and asked V. Lance Tarrance, a Texas pollster, to convene focus groups to test the committee's own slogan, "Abortion stops a beating heart."

"Our research showed that more people are persuaded against abortion by the statement 'Abortion stops a beating heart' than by their statement 'Who decides?' " David O'Steen, the committee's executive director, said. The "beating heart" message now appears in virtually all the committee's literature and on television spots that it regularly airs around the country. . . .

Bulging Budgets

The boom in spending has been most dramatic at NARAL, the self-described political arm of the abortion-rights movement. The league's budget, which only three years ago was half that of the National Right to Life Committee, has tripled since *Webster* and now exceeds the committee's. . . .

NARAL wasn't a newcomer to high-powered lobbying techniques. It used focus groups, for example, to hone its message during the 1987 fight against the Supreme Court nomination of Robert H. Bork. But the surge in revenues after Webster enabled NARAL to broadcast its message as never before. . . .

Donations to the Planned Parenthood Federation of America Inc. have risen sharply as well. And the federation, originally a charity concerned mostly with family planning, recently added a lobbying and political arm— testimony to its transformation into a leading voice in the abortion-rights movement. . . .

Anti-abortion organizations are growing, too. Revenues at the National

Right to Life Committee have risen 35 per cent since 1988. The committee runs a massive direct-mail program, and its officials estimate they spent $1 million last year on anti-abortion advertising. . . .

Exchanging Fire

Opponents in the abortion debate differ stylistically as well as substantively. Anti-abortion groups seem eager to cultivate a poor-cousin image. The National Right to Life Committee operates out of a cramped warren of rooms in a down-at-the-heels building that somehow escaped the downtown Washington redevelopment binge. NARAL used to occupy similarly dingy quarters but moved in 1985 to more upscale digs.

Anti-abortion activists reserve their sharpest criticism for Planned Parenthood. With an annual budget of about $300 million, the New York-based federation and its affiliates dwarf the other players in the arena (NARAL's 1990 revenues were about $12.8 million, and the National Right to Life Committee's were about $11.1 million). . . .

[Planned Parenthood] has a massive direct-mail operation—a recent mailing showed a photograph of televangelist Jimmy Swaggart under the heading "Listen to the anti-choice leaders—then help us stop them before it's too late!" And in 1989, Planned Parenthood ran hard-hitting advertisements attacking the anti-abortion voting records of several House Members. . . .

Planned Parenthood has financed most of these activists with tax-deductible contributions. Unlike most other abortion-rights advocacy groups, the federation operates as an educational and charitable organization under federal tax laws, which in theory bar it from engaging in partisan politics or in extensive lobbying.

Questions about its tax status have been surprisingly muted—perhaps because other abortion groups, including the Right to Life Committeeand NARAL, operate educational and charitable affiliates that also advertise. . . .

Rival Strategies

If the anti-abortion and abortion-rights forces are now using some of the same sophisticated weaponry, their battle plans are markedly different.

For most of the 1970s and 1980s, the abortion-rights movement focused most of its lobbying and political activity on Congress, where efforts were under way to restrict federal financing of abortions and adopt a proposed anti-abortion constitutional amendment.

Abortion-rights advocates concede that not paying enough attention to state government during this period put them at a disadvantage when *Webster* tossed the issue back to the states. "The antis have done a very effective job, since 1973, of packing the state legislatures," James Wagoner, NARAL's political director, said. . . .

Electoral Standoff

The November 1990 elections were the first big opportunity for abortion groups to flex their post-*Webster* political muscle, and both sides tried hard. . . .

While both sides brought home some trophies, neither side could claim a knockout blow.

NARAL won four of eight congressional and gubernatorial races that it had targeted; the best that Right to Life could say in a postelection analysis was that anti-abortion candidates "pretty much held their own." . . .

The state legislative scenario since *Webster* has been mixed as well. Michigan, Pennsylvania, South Carolina, Utah and Guam have enacted curbs on abortion, and restrictive laws are expected to pass in some other states. But most legislatures and governors have blocked such efforts. . . .

Still, both sides are gearing up for even heavier investments in the 1992 elections. . . .

The question now is momentum. Contributions to NARAL have leveled off in recent months, and while officials at the National Right to Life Committee say they've seen no similar trend, attendance at the annual right-to-life march declined sharply this year. Committee officials attributed the dropoff at the Jan. 23 event to the Persian Gulf War. . . .

Abortion-rights advocates, though they speak in cataclysmic terms about the prospect of another adverse Supreme Court ruling, admit that such a ruling might be the only way to marshal enough support to pass federal abortion-rights legislation. . . .

See text p. 297

Gaining access to the levers of power in Washington is no easy task, even for someone familiar with Washington politics. The difficulty is multiplied for those who are not only unfamiliar with Washington, but with the American political system itself. In the following article, Washington reporter Rochelle Stanfield discusses those lobbyists who perform on behalf of Third World countries. Whether the lobbyists actually affect U.S. foreign policy seems to be an open question. Nonetheless, the countries who take advantage of lobbying services do so because they perceive their own limited experience in Washington politics as a handicap. These countries rely on lobbyists to provide them with access to policy makers.

Rochelle L. Stanfield
"Lobbyists for the Lowly"*

Official designation as registered foreign agents is one thing they have in common. Another is the clients they represent: small, poor Third World countries. And to varying degrees, they're all in this business for the money.

But there, most similarities end.

Lobbyists for the world's least-developed countries include conservative Republicans, left-wing Democrats and everything in between. They range from wealthy, big-name firms with wood-paneled offices and oriental carpets to shoestring outfits operating out of cluttered apartments. They include law partnerships, lobbying firms and public relations consultants. And their styles vary from bombastic to low-key, hardball to hightone.

But in their own ways, they all aggressively hustle for a distinct, and surprisingly lucrative, slice of the Washington lobbying business. All registered foreign agents must file public reports with the Justice Department listing their clients, what they do for them and how much they charge.

For most of these lobbyists, the rewards are handsome. Black, Manafort, Stone & Kelly, the conservative lobbying firm based in Alexandria, Virginia, has million-dollar-a-year contracts with African clients such as Kenya and Zaire. Neill & Co., serious-talking government relations consultants, and van Kloberg & Associates Ltd., flamboyant public relations advisers, receive annual retainers of $300,000–$500,000. The lowest annual fee—obtained by solo lobbyist Bruce P. Cameron, who boasts about its meagerness—is $100,000.

Neither the lobbyists nor their clients have much difficulty justifying such princely sums for acting on behalf of countries with average per capita incomes of less than $500 a year.

"It's a lot of hard work, and we earn every penny we make," a lobbyist said. "It is the practice here," an African diplomat said. "Everybody must do it."

Not every poor country does do it, however. In some cases, the reason is a lack of money. Ephraim Namukombo, communications officer at the Zambian Embassy, bemoaned that "we seem not to be financially sound to hire some of these services," saying, "The government really would like to use such services" when his nation's economic situation improves.

Botswana, one of the few functioning multiparty democracies in Africa, has never used a Washington lobbying firm, either. "We don't have any controversies at home," A. Thabo Yalala, commercial attache at Botswana's Embassy, said. "We don't have any particular legislation we want to push. We don't have anything we have to be apologetic about, so we will not have one." Botswana is looking for help in promoting U.S. investment in the country, but it will probably hire a New York City firm, Yalala said.

---

*Rochelle L. Stanfield, "Lobbyists for the Lowly," *National Journal* (August 4, 1990). Reprinted with permission.

In the majority view, however, hiring a lobbyist is the only way for a Third World country to get more-favorable treatment from the U.S. government. Because these countries are poor and small—some have populations of only a few million—their embassy staffs are very small. The embassy staffs' ability to get help for their home countries is limited.

And official Washington is very large and extremely complicated. Its multipolar decision-making system is bewildering—especially to those experienced in dealing with a parliamentary system in which the word of the president or foreign minister is final.

In Washington, "each organization within the executive is a small world in which different points of view may prevail, and in the Congress, it is even worse," Ambassador Valeriano Ferrao of Mozambique said in an interview. "It is not so easy to work in this labyrinth." Ferrao, a savvy politician considered by the foreign policy community to be one of the most effective African envoys, has an embassy staff of three, plus two drivers. The World Bank lists Mozambique as the poorest country in the world, with an average annual per capita income of $100. Ferrao, who arrived in Washington in 1983—and was "very naive," he said—took four years to hire a lobbyist. He picked Cameron.

"If I had a staff of 50 people," Ferrao said, "I am not sure I would be able to target all those places that we should, because not only do you need to know the places, you must have the contacts there, and know how to work it."

For some Third World countries with authoritarian governments, whose leaders have unsavory reputations and are said to be responsible for a long list of human rights violations—Somalia or Zaire, for example—the logic of hiring a Washington lobbyist is clearer. The central government is often quite flush with money, and the president-for-life doesn't have to justify the expense to a parliament.

"In some instances, [the governments] believe they can jump over the hurdle of problems at home and get something from the United States despite their image and their policies—if they hire the right people," said Donald F. McHenry, a professor at the Georgetown University School of Foreign Service. McHenry, who was ambassador to the United Nations during the Carter Administration and is considered an astute observer of the Third World, said, "It's unfortunate, but in some instances, they can."

"However, in most instances, these countries get taken," McHenry continued. "They pay very large sums of money, and they get very little in return."

McHenry and many of his colleagues in the academic and think-tank community contend that in the absence of lobbyists, the distribution of U.S. foreign aid probably would be much the same. Congressional aides agree. "We make our judgments here not based on lobbyists," a House Appropriations Committee staff member said.

Others point to incremental, but important, changes wrought by clever lobbyists who know the intricacies of the appropriations process in Congress or the policy development process in the State Department.

Knowing the top guy is also considered important. Black, Manafort, Stone & Kelly served as advisers in 1988 to George Bush and his campaign manager, James A. Baker III, now Secretary of State. Many attribute to this connection the Bush Administration's decision to continue military support to the UNITA rebels in Angola, who are clients of Black, Manafort.

Whatever the lobbyists could achieve for these poor Third World countries in the past, the end of the Cold War and the sweeping changes in big-power relations may reduce the lobbyists' ability to keep the foreign aid pipeline open. The Administration is rethinking its support of UNITA, for example, and U.S. aid has been reduced to several African nations that traditionally received large allocations because of their anti-Communist stand or their perceived geostrategic importance.

"I think the whole background of Communism versus democracy is dead," said C. Paine Lucas, executive director of Africare, a Washington nonprofit organization devoted to Africa's development. "What lobbyists and PR firms have got to focus on," Lucas said, "is finding opportunities for the private sector to invest in a country, not whether or not the president of a certain country made an anti-U.S. statement. That has nothing to do with the real world."

Hired Guns

Most of the business of representing the Third World in Washington is concentrated among about a dozen government relations, public relations and law firms. A handful of other law firms perform such tasks as drawing up leases or real estate contracts for these countries.

Within the lobbying community, the competition is keen. "It's an enormously cutthroat business," Edward J. van Kloberg III, president of van Kloberg & Associates Ltd., acknowledged. "Washington is a very small circle. Competition and dirty games are much more evident here in seeking country clients."

Lobbyists eagerly regaled a reporter (though not for attribution) with tales of their competitors' ineffectiveness. Most of them also told stories about how their competitors take every opportunity to undermine their relationships with clients. Most of the lobbyists, for example, referred to an unflattering profile of van Kloberg in the July 5 *Washington Post;* van Kloberg provided his own stack of unfavorable clippings about competitors such as Black, Manafort.

This all-out competition may present Third World countries with a buyers' market. Indeed, diplomats say that they are beseiged by companies seeking their business. Some lobbyists acknowledged that that is the case. "Anybody who tells you the countries come to you is blowing smoke," Dennis M. Neill, president of Neill & Co., said. "It doesn't work that way."

But the scramble for Third World business doesn't seem to have driven rates down.

Even though money is the ultimate attraction for just about every lobbyist for a Third World country, most of the lobbyists also have other reasons—personal, ideological or political.

Black, Manafort "has generally represented countries that have strategic importance to U.S. foreign policy," partner Paul J. Manafort Jr. said.

Most of the principals of Neill & Co. started out in government. Neill was assistant Agency for International Development (AID) administrator for legislative affairs in the Ford Administration, for example.

"We started with the fundamental attitude that we wanted to do the same thing in private business that we did in government," Neill said. "That put us into the Third World business to begin with. We started out there, and we've been comfortable there."

For David Fenton, president of Fenton Communications, the reason is ideological. He came out of the anti-Vietnam war movement in the 1960s and uses his public relations firm to promote what he terms progressive causes. "I have been very fortunate that I've been able to maintain a business that somehow holds on to and reflects the values that I learned during that era," he said. "We don't work for people we don't like. We will not work for just anybody who comes in the door." Fenton has contracts with the governments of Angola and Jamaica and handled public relations for the Washington visit of South African black leader Nelson Mandela.

Van Kloberg cultivates the hard cases. His clients include Samuel K. Doe, the beseiged president of Liberia, and President Mobutu Sese Seko of Zaire, whose foreign aid has been restricted because of human rights violations. He also has more-prosperous, though still controversial, clients, such as Iraq.

He says he does it to enable these countries to tell their side of the story and to help them become more democratic. Van Kloberg insists on the propriety of his business. In "Consulting Is a Public Service," an op-ed piece in the *Journal of Commerce* last Nov. 22, [1989], he wrote: "In the American tradition, every person—every nation—is entitled to representation, including those who have been condemned for various offenses. . . . Lawyers represent both guilty and innocent clients. Why should a different standard be applied to public relations and government affairs counsels?"

Neill & Co. is someplace in between. It won't take countries whose foreign policy is antagonistic to the United States. Until now, that has meant Communist governments, but in the post-Cold War period, the company's perspective might change. It has not represented opposition groups, such as UNITA. And, Neill said, the company won't take clients "where the representation of the client is going to be ineffective, where we are called upon to represent a client for a purpose that can't be achieved."

Justice Department records show a $500,000 Neill & Co. contract with Liberia, but not to lobby for the government. Rather, the company agreed to analyze the U.S. government's attitude toward Liberia and spell out what American officials thought Liberia had to do to find favor with them.

Neill & Co. also has a long-standing contract with Kenya, a major foreign aid recipient and an old ally of the United States but a government that has recently been in the news for human rights violations.

"I don't think Kenya thinks they're buying an image," George A. Dalley, a Neill principal, said. "What they're hoping for, through their hiring of firms, is access to decision makers to tell their story, because they believe they have a story to tell. The story in the case of Kenya is that multipartyism as a prescription is perhaps correct in the long run but in the short term presents real problems because of the continuing lingering tribal hostilities within the country. People have to understand the circumstances and the dangers inherent in them before they quickly condemn."

Capital Contacts

Access is an important asset for firms in obtaining clients, but so is expertise. "Ten or 15 years ago, you were hired simply because of who you knew," Manafort said. "Today, it is much broader than that. You have to have expertise in international finance, aid, food programs."

Many of the lobbyists used to work on congressional committees and can offer expertise in slipping favorable wording into legislation. Robert B. Washington Jr., a black lawyer and former congressional aide, has entree to the Congressional Black Caucus, an important voice in legislation affecting Africa.

Black, Manafort's access to the White House is almost legendary. In January 1989, the firm drafted a letter that was sent by Bush to UNITA leader Jonas Savimbi. The letter promised continued U.S. covert aid to the rebels.

"Let's face it: They have a handle on foreign policy that's unbelievable," a rival lobbyist said of Black, Manafort. "How much value do you put on a presidential letter like the one to Savimbi? Is it worth a million dollars? Of course it is!"

Manafort said, "It's [access to] the Congress that's more important."

That's somewhat surprising, because the company's connections don't open a lot of doors on Capitol Hill. Many Members and aides are contemptuous of the firm.

"They never come around here," an aide to a conservative Republican Senator said. "We don't see them," a House Appropriations staff member agreed. And an aide on another committee said, "The only time we ever get a call from them is when one of their countries is in trouble, and then we don't listen."

Some of Black, Manafort's African clients have suffered aid reductions: Congress has blocked assistance to Somalia for three years, and this year, the House cut military aid to Zaire and permitted humanitarian aid only if it is channeled through private voluntary organizations, not Zaire's government.

Neill & Co., on the other hand, is known for its dogged working of congressional committees. Neill knows the process from his days as AID's congressional liaison. Dalley worked for Rep. Charles B. Rangel, D-N.Y., a Ways and Means subcommittee chairman. Congressional aides credit the company with working not only to increase aid to their clients but to enhance aid to all of sub-Sahara Africa.

M. Graeme Bannerman, who represents Bangladesh—the world's fifth-poorest country, according to the World Bank—and several more-prosperous countries in the Middle East, is another habitue of Capitol Hill hearing rooms and offices. When Sen. Richard G. Lugar, R-Ind., chaired the Foreign Relations Committee from 1985–86, Bannerman served as staff director. A low-key operator who doesn't like to be quoted, Bannerman is well regarded on Capitol Hill and among academics and think-tank specialists because he is a serious Arabist.

Of a very different nature is Cameron, a former human rights activist who is also a devotee of congressional operations, particularly the appropriations process, and a super-specialist in access. A Democrat who worked for the Nicaraguan contras in Washington, he knows how to reach conservative Democrats and moderate Republicans. Ferrao, who had support among liberal Democrats and figured that conservative Republicans were a lost cause, recognized the need to get the support of middle-of-the-road Members, and signed up Cameron for that job.

Mozambique, a Soviet client state for years since gaining independence from Portugal, had no diplomatic relations with the United States until Ferrao opened the embassy in 1983. The country got its first $5 million in U.S. foreign assistance in 1984, but the aid didn't really begin to flow until 1987—coincidentally, the year Cameron was hired. This year, it will receive $105 million.

"When the Mozambiquans hired me, I brought what they needed at that time, which was the swing votes on foreign policy issues," Cameron said. "Mozambique needed to get enough of those votes to defeat the conservative opposition."

Cameron's other area of expertise, the subtleties of appropriations legislation, also came in handy. "I can write legislation like that!" he said, snapping his fingers. "So that it cripples the aid or so that it has the same elements as crippling legislation but doesn't cripple it." One Sunday morning in 1987, he recalled, he drafted language that he was able to slip into that year's foreign aid appropriations bill, making it easier for Mozambique to obtain assistance.

But Cameron acknowledged that a combination of factors has helped Mozambique's cause in Congress, including the Mozambique government's steps toward democratization and its willingness to engage in peace talks with the rebel RENAMO guerrillas to end 14 years of civil war. "I add some legislative expertise and contacts with moderate Democrats," he said. "But what you've had is a whole bunch of other things coming together for Mozambique."

No Real Difference?

Critics outside the lobbying game are skeptical that lobbyists make any real difference in American foreign policy toward the least-developed countries. Most U.S. policies toward Africa and the foreign aid that implemented them grew out of historical relationships (Liberia was founded by American blacks), strategic objectives (Somalia was a staging area for the Persian Gulf) or Cold War exigencies (UNITA's Savimbi was viewed as an anti-Communist freedom fighter). "Perhaps the American policy with regard to Angola would be the same with or without Black, Manafort and Stone, given the history of American actions in Angola and the fact we have this hangup about Cubans," McHenry said. (Cuban soldiers supported the Angolan government against UNITA but were withdrawn as part of a 1988 regional peace pact.) "But I think there would be more debate."

In any case, the Angola policy might be changing. The State Department, which is reviewing the policy, sent a team of diplomats to meet with Angolan government officials to discuss food shipments and peace talks being brokered by Portugal. The House Select Intelligence Committee voted to postpone consideration of whether to continue, in fiscal 1991, the $50 million in covert military aid funneled to Savimbi. However, Manafort predicted that "they are not going to pull the plug on assistance to UNITA."

Others suggest that the waning of the Cold War and the warming of U.S.-Soviet relations have more to do with such changes than anything the lobbyists do.

The evidence suggests, however, that Angola's lobbyists had a hand in delaying approval of the aid to UNITA. Attorney Washington, who represents the Angolan government, made a lengthy presentation to the House Intelligence Committee on the new democratic, market-oriented, peace-making steps of President Jose Eduardo dos Santos. On the day the committee was considering the question, Washington took Angolan Ambassador to the United Nations Manuel Pedro Pacavira (Angola has no ambassador in Washington) around Capitol Hill to talk about cooperating on getting international food shipments to Angola.

As analysts such as McHenry explain it, historical, geostrategic or Cold War rationalizations for U.S. aid to Africa for years outweighed questions of human rights, democratization and economic restructuring.

That is no longer likely to be the case. Congress has already cut aid to Liberia, Somalia and the Sudan. It is in the process of reducing it to Zaire, and aid to Kenya is likely to undergo severe questioning, although most analysts predict that it will go through this year.

"We're now looking internally at these countries rather than at the utility of strategic friends and enemies, and that's going to make them a much harder sell," said Pauline H. Baker, an Africa expert at the Washington-based Carnegie Endowment for International Peace. "Maybe these countries will need lobbyists all the more—the more their stock goes down, the more apple-polishing they're going to need."

See text p. 304

During the 1970s, campaign spending reforms were enacted that limited the amount of money individuals could contribute to candidates for office. In the face of these limitations, however, spending by organized interest groups—called political ac-

tion committees or PACs—grew exponentially. Concentrated spending efforts by PACs have been enormously successful for the interest groups involved, primarily by insuring that incumbents will remain in office: a candidate who solicits funds from a PAC must, in turn, at least give thoughtful consideration to the issues raised by that interest group.

In recent years, campaign financing reform has been a major issue on the political agenda, as widespread abuse of power has been perceived. The issue of reform, however, is a thorny one: it is difficult for incumbents to vote for changes to the system when their political survival depends upon the continuation of the present structure.

Lauren Chambliss
"Big PAC Attack"*

Consider these startling statistics: In the 1990–96 election cycle, during which all 435 House seats will be contested three times and the 100 Senate seats once, more than $350 million will be raised for each biennial House campaign and $600 million for the Senate, based on 1990's experience. That's a staggering $1.5 billion-plus for the full six-year period.

These days, reelection doesn't come cheaply. In the 1990 contest, Senators spent $1.87 per potential voter, up from $1.41 just two years before.

But as spending goes up, voter satisfaction is plunging. Opinion polls show that the vast majority of Americans believes politicians are more concerned with serving special interests, such as those represented by political action committees (PACs), than their constituents.

Now politicians are scrambling for ways to revive public interest and trust in Congress before they have to roll out their wares in front of skeptical voters in 1992. The Senate will soon bring to the floor a bill sponsored by the Democratic leadership. And Republicans in the House and Senate are crafting their own agenda, with backing from the White House.

But for all the talk, most of the "reforms" amount to blatant attempts by one side to further enrich its own reelection coffers at the expense of the other. "Both parties are playing a partisan charade," scoffs Larry Sabato, a professor of political science at the University of Virginia. "They are trying to pose as reformers without having to really address the issue."

Public concern about the influence of special interests, particularly PACs, is understandable. PAC's frustrate the democratic process, primarily because they perpetuate incumbents at the expense of challengers. In the 1990 election, for example, PACs directed $87.4 million to House incumbents, while providing just $7.6 million for challengers. Incoming freshmen actually can count on getting as much, if not more, in the year after they are elected than they received while trying to get to Capitol Hill in the first place. According to the Campaign Research Center, a nonprofit agency, freshmen politicians pulled in 27% of their PAC contributions for 1990 in the month after election day.

Freshman Representative James Moran (D-Va.) wasn't in office two

*Lauren Chambliss, "Big PAC Attack," *Financial World* (April 16, 1991). Reprinted with permission.

weeks before his staff began soliciting PAC contributions from banking groups. During a nasty campaign, Moran took frequent shots at Republican opponent Stan Parris's ties to "special interests." Moran is now sitting on the banking committee where he draws on the very PAC funds he criticized Parris for accepting. Moran insists his votes won't be swayed by the contributions.

He is probably right. Academic surveys that have tried to make a link between votes and political contributions generally have come to naught. But no one disputes that PAC money helps keep incumbents in office and buys access. "We expect to get in to see Congressman X or Senator Y to make our views on legislation known," says a PAC administrator for a major U.S. chemical corporation who asked to remain anonymous. "Any PAC that says they aren't buying access is lying."

The public disgust at the situation is reflected in the growing number of powerful consumer lobbies—including the American Association of Retired Persons and Ralph Nader's Common Cause—that call for reform. Says Ellen Miller, director of the Washington, D.C.-based Center for Responsive Politics: "In a country which calls itself a democracy, clear and fair elections with politicians not bought by special interests ought to be a priority."

Ironically, Democrats created PACs to counter Republicans, who were more adept at garnering large quantities of money from individual sources. Now PACs give across party lines even as contributions by individuals, particularly Republicans, continue to grow. Individual contributions are supposedly limited to $1,000, but a truck-size loophole in the law permits "bundling" of these $1,000 contributions. This was used by S&L owner Charles Keating to raise huge sums for favored politicians, according to the Senate Ethics Committee.

Even corporate PAC managers voice disgust at the system. Privately, some business PAC managers admit they would be just as happy to see the system abolished. A few companies even are getting out of the PAC business. Exxon, for example, won't contribute to an industry PAC, although it does have one for employees.

"We can't have affinity groups deciding who will get elected to Congress," says Bill Pearle, chairman of Carlyle Capital, a Long Island, N.Y.-based merchant bank that doesn't support PACs. "If some challenger is going to spend $50,000, he shouldn't be up against an incumbent with a war chest of $5 million."

Last year, both the House and Senate considered campaign finance reform bills, but they died for lack of interest. Legislation of some sort stands a better chance of passage now, because lawmakers are feeling the heat from a disgruntled public. The so-called Keating Five scandal has embarrassed Congress, where politicians know their own finances couldn't stand up to similar scrutiny.

"I have a fear I'm going to get a contribution from someone who is today an esteemed pillar of the community and next month he turns out to be an ax murderer," Joseph Biden (D-Del.) recently told the Senate Rules

Committee. "The devil has turned around on us, and for our own sake we have to deal with it."

But here's the sticking point: The party chiefs have not even agreed on what's wrong with the system—let alone how to fix it. And both sides have come up with reforms that are baldly self-serving.

The Democrats think cost is the problem; they want to put a ceiling on campaign spending—clearly targeted at rich GOP givers—and have taxpayers foot part of the bill. The Republicans, on the other hand, aren't worried about cost, they are more concerned with supply: Where is the money coming from and how is it being spent?

The Democratic initiative that is soon to be debated on the Senate floor permits candidates to dip into the public purse to the tune of about $130 million if they agree to limit campaign spending to between $1 million and $5.5 million in each state, depending on the population. Candidates who keep within the limits would have access to subsidized television time, mass mailings and other taxpayer-financed freebies. The subsidies would partially make up for lost PAC money; the bill eliminates most PAC contributions.

But the Democrats have not answered the pivotal question: How to raise the $130 million. Would it be raised through taxes—hardly a winning proposal; or would it come from a check-off system where taxpayers can contribute a dollar or more by checking a box on their tax forms—a scheme that bombed in the recent past.

Republicans, generally better at filling campaign coffers than Democrats, don't like the idea of spending limits and aren't thrilled about public subsidies, either. "It takes some gall to tell the American public that we don't have enough money for education, for nutrition or for the homeless, but we do have enough for one new entitlement program, and it is us," says Senator Bob Packwood (R-Ore.).

The Republicans, including President Bush, would like to eliminate PAC contributions. According to the Campaign Research Center, eight of the top twelve PAC givers since 1990 were affiliated with union groups, traditionally Democratic. Republicans also want to limit out-of-state contributions to candidates, an obvious ploy aimed at Democratic forays to Hollywood to raise campaign funds from liberal-minded entertainers.

The GOP wants to give more power to the political parties to support challenger candidates, including matching grants for grass-roots campaigns. But the record on party spending shows that handing the purse strings to the national parties isn't a cure for incumbentitis. A study by the Campaign Research Center shows that in the House, the parties gave more to incumbents than challengers, $1.2 million versus $950,000.

One of the biggest costs of campaigning, of course, is television, and Senate Republicans want broadcasters to provide up to five hours of time to candidates.

But while Republicans don't hesitate to demand that broadcasters provide air time, they refuse to consider spending caps or content restraints. That means there is nothing to stop incumbent politicians from simply adding the TV time to their already regal campaign budgets.

According to Curtis Gans, director of the Committee for the Study of the American Electorate, about 90% of campaign budgets already go for advertising and related expenses. "Nothing, or next to nothing is spent on any activity that involves the citizenry," Gans recently told the Senate Rules Committee. "It is no wonder that we have developed the political equivalent of the Silent Spring in American politics."

What can be done? Probably the answer would be public financing—that is, taxpayers' money—to pay for all campaigns, from primary to general elections. That would put an end to the money-grubbing by politicians and special interests. The problem, of course, is practical. As Packwood notes, with domestic programs wanting, it is hard to convince the American public to pay for elections.

Nevertheless, backed by consumer groups, such as Nader's Common Cause, some Democrats are advocating public financing as a way to solve the endless money chase. Senators Biden, John Kerry (D-Mass.) and Bill Bradley (D-N.J.) want the public to pay for 90% of all general elections. President Bush would veto any such measure if, by some miracle, it was approved.

Unfortunately, partial financing, such as the Democrats have proposed, doesn't go far enough. It simply adds taxpayer dollars to the campaign pot without changing the basic nature of the brew.

A quick and tidy way to get rid of the PAC problem is to simply make it unethical under congressional rules for politicians to accept PAC money from organizations whose business falls under their committee's jurisdiction. PACs could still function, but they would not appear to be paying off politicians in exchange for crafting legislation.

It is important to level the playing field so that challengers have at least a fighting chance. Providing candidates with free television time and mailings will cost taxpayers money but in the interest of true competition, the few millions spent would be worth it.

Disclosure is another area that needs serious attention. While PACs are subject to rigid filing requirements, individual givers are not. A new law should make it easier to track the flow of special-interest dollars from private sources. Also, there should be restrictions on so-called "soft money," whereby givers route campaign contributions through state and local party associations.

Whether Congress has the will to seriously—and honestly—move toward reform depends on a continued show of outrage from the public.

CHAPTER 12

Introduction to Public Policy

THE WELFARE STATE AS FISCAL AND SOCIAL POLICY

See text p. 320

Few institutions are more fundamental to our understanding of American life than that of private property. The American economic system is built upon the assumption that property will be privately owned—in the pure capitalist vision, private entrepreneurs produce goods as demand requires, and the market will regulate itself as though guided by an invisible hand. As the text notes, however, private property ownership is not a natural phenomenon. Private property would be of little value without public policies to protect it—policies that enforce contracts or prohibit theft.

Home ownership has always been linked to our understanding of private property, beginning with the Jeffersonian ideal of a nation of self-sufficient farmers. As the text notes, many federal policies have encouraged home ownership on the assumption that an individual who has property interests at stake will be a model citizen and will respect the law.

Today, the vision of home ownership is fading for a large percentage of Americans. The following article suggests that the reason is that federal housing policy is "out of whack": Too many federal dollars are spent subsidizing home ownership for people who do not need the subsidy. And yet, the prospect for change is not a bright one; altering the system will adversely affect those who have the money and resources to defend the present system.

Carol F. Steinbach
"Housing the 'Haves' "*

Paula and Perry Nesmith aren't the kind of people who usually make the news. Nor are Rose Konda and her husband, Mike Rodenbaugh. But they and other middle-class couples like them are all over the newspapers these days because of something they have in common: They can't afford to buy a house.

Twenty years ago, families just like theirs had a pretty good shot at owning a home before their children finished elementary school. Today, some will eventually achieve the goal of homeownership, but for many others it seems a distant prospect—if a prospect at all.

---

*Carol F. Steinbach, "Housing the 'Haves'," *National Journal* (June 29, 1991). Reprinted with permission.

The Nesmiths, with a combined annual income of more than $40,000, hope to be able to save enough money to buy a house in six years, when Perry will turn 40. But with home prices in Washington, D.C., averaging $132,000, and with student loans and car loans to pay off, they're not sure they'll make that goal.

Konda, 27, a legal secretary who moved from Montana to Springfield, Va., two years ago, is not much better off. Although she and Rodenbaugh bring home $60,000 a year between them, they can't afford the down payment on a new home. As renters, Konda noted, "we don't get any tax break; we feel like we're throwing our money away. We work and work and have nothing to show for it."

A growing number of housing experts think they know why the Nesmiths and Konda and Rosenbaugh are having such a hard time realizing the American Dream. The reason, they say, is that the federal government's housing policies are out of whack. . . .

No Help in Sight

Among Washington policy makers, promoting homeownership for their middle-class constituents has long been a staple ingredient in the recipe for political success. Not surprisingly, President Bush put his full weight behind an omnibus housing bill, which Congress passed in November. Appealingly titled the 1990 National Affordable Housing Act, the measure included a provision creating a National Homeowners Trust, a fund intended to assist first-time homebuyers in raising down payments and to bring their mortgage rates down to 6 per cent.

But the trust, which was authorized to receive $250 million in its first year, has yet to get off the ground. Congress, itself strapped for cash, apparently has decided it can't afford to finance the trust this year. The House voted no funds for it in its fiscal 1992 appropriations bill, and the Senate is expected to follow suit.

[To] critics of the government's housing policies, the fate, thus far, of the National Homeowners Trust is a paradigm of what's wrong with federal housing policy. So much is being provided in subsidies to people who already own homes—including very wealthy householders—that there's not enough left in the public coffers to help people who don't or to assist millions of low-income renters and people with no shelter at all.

Homeowners tax deductions—which permit homeowners to write off from their federal tax bill the interest they pay on home mortgages, property taxes and capital gains realized when selling a house—will cost the federal treasury an estimated $70 billion in lost revenues in 1992. That total is almost twice as much as the government will spend on programs for would-be homebuyers, the homeless, low-income and elderly renters and public housing tenants combined. A third of the benefit from mortgage interest and property tax deductions, a congressional study indicates, goes to households with taxable earnings above $100,000, and 12 per cent goes to families with earnings above $200,000. Critics of the current system of subsidies have proposed capping homeowner deductions for wealthier households and using the recaptured resources to help aspiring homeowners and the poor.

But homeowner subsidies aren't the only problem with Washington policies that affect housing, the critics say. The federal government also backs trillions of dollars worth of real estate lending through credit mechanisms ranging from insurance on deposits in banks and thrifts to guarantees on the mortgages insured by the FHA, the government's prime vehicle for assisting middle-income buyers. The wallop such credit policies pack is enormous, dwarfing the impact of the outlays Congress appropriates for housing assistance in any given year.

During the 1980s, the government's regulation of credit got sloppy, and speculative lending spun out of control. The high costs incurred by taxpayers because of the much-celebrated failures in the thrift and banking industries aren't the only consequence. The system of credit guarantees also helped fuel massive over-building of office buildings and high-priced housing, while homes that middle-class families could afford became scarce in many parts of the country. At the FHA, poor management contributed to massive losses in FHA reserve funds and threatened to bring the FHA to the brink of insolvency.

Cushing N. Dolbeare, a longtime advocate of housing policy reforms, observed of the current situation: "Our housing system is so badly out of whack that if we repealed everything and started with a clean slate, [and] then wrote down what we had now, not only would it never pass Congress, no Member of Congress would even dare to introduce it. It's that bad."

But reforming housing policies to make them friendlier to aspiring homebuyers won't be easy. Credit policies are complicated and not well understood by most lawmakers. And homeowner deductions, a stalwart of federal tax policy since the Civil War, enjoy widespread public support. Trying to put caps on the deductions would force Congress to go toe-to-toe with powerful lobbies—homebuilders, real estate brokers and mortgage bankers—that adamantly oppose any tampering with the write-offs and argue that housing will become more plentiful once the economy rights itself.

Few in Congress are eager to launch an assault against the deductions, especially while the real estate industry is in its worst slump since World War II. Even so, advocates of housing reforms believe their cause will gain momentum as the reality of flagging homeownership sinks in. New Jersey Assemblyman David C. Schwartz states the issue bluntly: "The housing system that worked well for Ozzie and Harriet isn't able to help their grandchildren." . . .

Alms for the Rich

There would be plenty of money to help aspiring homebuyers—as well as the renters and the homeless below them on the income ladder—if Congress would apply the brakes to the housing subsidies that now flow to upper-income families, advocates of housing policy reform contend.

Homeowners tax deductions are available to anyone who owns a home. The price tag for such federal largesse is high. The Bush Administration's 1992 budget projects that the major deductions in that category will cost the federal treasury more than $70 billion in revenues next year.

The deductions were initially intended to help middle-income home-owners; and they still do. More than 30 million households, the vast bulk of them middle class, claimed such tax breaks in 1990. But a disproportionate share of the total benefit goes to a relatively small number of upper-class households. That's because the bigger the mortgage and the higher the property taxes, the larger the deduction claimed.

Critics say the tax breaks drive up the over-all housing costs because buyers take the deductions into account when deciding how much they can afford to spend on a house. They also argue that the writeoffs assist many families who don't need help. "Wealthy families can take the money they save from their homeowner deductions, put it into a higher-yield investment and get even richer," said Dolbeare, who has been lobbying Congress to put caps on the deductions for nearly two decades. . . . To find out who benefits most from federal housing subsidies, Dolbeare added up the cost of the homeowner tax deductions, together with federal outlays in several other housing assistance programs, including those serving the poor. According to her calculations, families earning above $53,000, the top income quintile, received 58 per cent of the combined benefits, while the poorest families got 15 per cent. Households living just above dire poverty, earning $12,-000–$23,000, received the least amount of federal subsidies.

Russell T. Davis, assistant to the FHA commissioner from 1989–90, has compiled a similar analysis incorporating many more housing-related federal programs. Using the Administration's 1992 budget estimates, Davis added up the forgone tax revenues, the estimated cost of selected credit supports and the projected direct outlays for more than 30 federal housing programs ranging from homeowner write-offs to public housing operating expenses. The total came to more than $113 billion, of which nearly $78 billion, or 69 per cent, will go next year to people who already own homes.

Davis, a partner in an investment group, found that the 30 million homeowner households that claim tax deductions will receive twice as much federal support as the nation's 33 million renter households, many of them made up of low-income families. "Poor people have to go through the appropriations process and fight for their scraps," he said, "but upper-class people get their benefits bequeathed to them." . . . Reforms that could have significant impact on aspiring middle-class buyers—and everyone else below them on the housing ladder—will require lawmakers to take a broad look at a federal policy system that appears to be badly in disarray. It also will require them to take on some formidable sacred cows. No one familiar with Congress expects that to happen fast.

In the meantime, it looks like Paula and Perry Nesmith, Rose Konda and Mike Rodenbaugh will just have to wait to see whether the American Dream of homeownership will ever come true for them.

See text p. 320

Given this nation's commitment to a free market economy, it is not surprising that we have never had a fully articulated "industrial policy." Yet, as this chapter has emphasized, the failure to specify an industrial policy has not meant that the market has gone unregulated. Indeed, the problem is precisely that the free market as such does not exist: even in a capitalist economy, certain policies—like those supporting the institution of private property—are essential prerequisites.

More importantly, we have discovered that many factors argue against the establishment of a truly "free" market. In some cases, government has stepped in to regulate the economy to mitigate the harsher consequences of capitalism when the human costs have proven too great to bear; in other cases, we have simply been dissatisfied with the speed at which the market "corrects" itself, such as when we decide that we do not have time to wait until the market itself forces companies to clean up the environment. But the basic commitment to a free market economy has led to a piecemeal approach, and the result is a confusing and often inefficient array of regulatory policies.

The following article, written for Financial World *magazine, provides an interesting look into the paradoxes of market regulation in a capitalist economy. The author suggests that "Washington's adversarial stance toward business is unique among [Western] industrialized countries. . . . [M]any of our most formidable foreign competitors enjoy something approaching a commercial alliance with their governments." The author is clearly concerned about the level of governmental regulation, but a close look at the arguments reveals the extent to which the author considers governmental regulation a necessity: "[G]overnment regulation should enhance competition, not suppress it."*

Financial World
"Government vs. Business: The Endless Struggle"*

When President Jimmy Carter signed the Airline Deregulation Act in October 1978, it was hailed as a turning point in business-government relations—the reversal of a century-long trend toward greater government intervention in the affairs of private enterprise.

Today, that euphoria seems premature. True, in a number of industries, the heavy hand of bureaucratic control has indeed been lifted. But the

*"Government vs. Business: The Endless Struggle," *Financial World* (June 25, 1991). Reprinted with permission.

results are, in many cases, highly controversial. What's more, a series of new rules—designed to clean up the environment, enhance public safety, protect workers, accommodate the handicapped and increase job opportunities for minorities—have been imposed that now affect more companies than ever before. And proposals to make new social demands on business are put forward almost daily.

Washington's adversarial stance toward business is unique among the industrialized countries in the non-Communist world. In no other nation are companies subjected to so many bureaucratic restraints by their own government. Indeed, many of our most formidable foreign competitors enjoy something approaching a commercial alliance with their governments.

That fact, in the context of today's intense global competition, has prompted many business leaders, economists and politicians to call for a revolutionary change in the relationship between business and government in the U.S. Some would even like to establish a formal industrial policy in this country, with Uncle Sam selecting which industries and new technologies to subsidize. . . .

Regulation began in the form of state commissions to supervise public utilities. It was clear to most people that these [utilities] were "natural monopolies"—businesses in which investment costs and economies of scale were so great that encouraging competition and duplication of facilities would be wasteful and do little to improve service. To keep such companies from gouging customers, regulation would take the place of competition.

The railroads were another obvious target. Railroads were the first really large companies in the U.S., with widely scattered operations. And because they were often the economic lifeblood of the communities they served, they represented a unique concentration of power.

By the mid-1800s, a number of states had established railroad commissions, but it quickly became apparent that companies doing business in many states could only be regulated effectively by a national agency. So, in 1887, the Interstate Commerce Commission was formed. It became the model for many federal regulatory agencies that followed. The ICC's early experience also foreshadowed the problems that have plagued most regulators since; notably the time-consuming, case-by-case determination of rates to balance the diametrically opposed interests of producers and consumers. The task proved incredibly difficult.

In 1898, the Supreme Court ruled that a railroad was entitled to a "reasonable" return on "the fair value of the property being used for the convenience of the public." That seemed sensible enough, but according to McCraw it simply opened a bottomless can of worms [because no one could decide what amounted to a fair rate of return]. . . .

As some early experts also recognized, establishing a fixed rate of return on investment (however defined) made little economic sense. Among other things, they pointed out, it destroyed any incentive to improve efficiency. In fact, regulators over the years have often used their influence over pricing to preserve competition by restricting it: They have kept weak firms in business by forbidding stronger rivals to take advantage of their efficiency and ability to cut prices.

As the ICC was getting under way, Congress also laid down the fundamental law against monopoly. The Sherman Antitrust Act of 1890 made illegal "every contact, combination of the form of trust or otherwise, or conspiracy, in restraint of trade or commerce." . . . By 1904, the law had prevented a big railroad merger, and a few years later, it was used to break up Standard Oil, American Tobacco and the Sugar Trust. In 1914, Congress toughened the rules further by passing the Clayton Act (which forbade corporations that were not holding companies to acquire the stock of other firms or to engage in price discrimination) and by establishing the Federal Trade Commission to enforce the law.

At this point, however, the early trust-busting fervor was waning. During World War I, business cooperation proved so useful in expanding production that people began to see that larger organizations could have value. What's more, according to William A. Lovett, professor of law and history at Tulane University, "prosperity and economic growth with a significant spread of new industries—automobiles, gasoline stations, airplanes, radios, movies, records and plastics—continued through World War I into the 1920s. A proliferation of new appliances and improved technology changed everyday life. In these circumstances, with a shift to more conservative faith in free enterprise, there was less populist alarm about the dangers of bigger business."

In that atmosphere, the courts drew distinctions between "good trusts" and "bad trusts." In particular, the Supreme Court held that "mere size" or the "existence of unexerted power" did not constitute violations of the law. Some actions that had been considered anticompetitive were also deemed legal—for example, granting big discounts to large distributors of manufactured products.

With the Great Depression, though, came a violent new shift in the public's attitude toward business. Not only were its leaders bitterly criticized, but there was a widespread conviction that the system itself was fatally flawed. With Roosevelt's New Deal came a proliferation of new regulatory agencies.

The Securities and Exchange Commission brought Wall Street under control. The Federal Communications Commission took over management of the airwaves. The National Labor Relations Board issued rules governing companies' treatment of their workers. The Civil Aeronautics Board took jurisdiction over the nation's airlines. In addition, existing regulators were given new powers and wider authority.

The idea, to which most New Dealers subscribed, was that because the free market was not functioning properly, government should take a hand. Expert public servants, they believed, would be more likely than business executives to make decisions that would bring the greatest benefits to society.

The late Thirties turned out to be the high-water mark of regulation. World War II rehabilitated business's reputation, and postwar prosperity boosted it even higher. There was little public interest in riding herd on the companies that were providing Americans with such a cornucopia of material blessings.

At the same time, many experts had begun to call for reform of the regulatory agencies, which had become somnolent bureaucracies, peopled by second-raters. Their performance showed it. By 1960, the Federal Power Commission had a 13-year back log of undecided cases and, according to a report written for President-elect John F. Kennedy, "with the contemplated 6,500 cases that would be filed during that 13-year period, it could not become current until 2043 A.D., even if its staff were tripled."

Critics also charged that the agencies had largely become captives of the very industries they were supposed to supervise. In particular, says McCraw, the CAB and FCC "appeared to be following policies that equated the public interest with the desires of the most powerful elements in the airline and communications industries."

When Kennedy took office, he raised the caliber of regulators significantly and tried to launch a program of reform. But Congress rejected some of his most important recommendations, and his attention quickly turned to more pressing issues: foreign affairs, civil rights, tax policy. The issue of reforming the regulatory process was largely set aside.

Meanwhile, a new generation of trustbusters in the Justice Department strove to enlarge the definition of illegal conduct. This was a logical outcome of the landmark 1945 decision of Judge Learned Hand in the Alcoa case. "Great industrial concentrations," he wrote, "are inherently undesirable regardless of their economic consequences."

In the years that followed, Lovett observes, "A tough line was laid down on larger horizontal and vertical mergers. Big companies with hefty market shares were not allowed to make mergers within their own industries or markets nor to buy up their leading competitors or suppliers. The only significant exception was the 'failing company' doctrine, under which firms in serious financial trouble with doubtful prospects of survival could be acquired."

As the economy slowed in the 1970s, a new attitude toward business was gaining adherents. In their view, economics was replacing ideology as the rationale for regulation and antitrust—with greater concern for efficiency and less worry about equity. When the "Chicago school" of economists called for more freedom of action for business during this period, they found increasing favor.

The shift toward deregulation took place, ironically, during a Democratic Administration. The Civil Aeronautics Board, formed in 1938, was one of the youngest regulatory commissions, but it shared most of the bad habits and counter-productive policies of its older models. While the CAB had stabilized what had become a chaotic business, it had essentially cartelized the industry. "The overall effect of board policies," says McCraw, "tended to freeze the industry more or less in its configuration. In fact, over the entire history of CAB, no trunk-line carrier had been permitted to join the 16 that existed in 1938." . . . Most of the CAB's flaws were glaringly obvious when Alfred E. Kahn came to Washington in 1977 after a career as a professor of economics at Cornell University and as the reformist chairman of the New York Public Service Commission. In fact, a remarkable coalition of groups from across the political and ideological spectrum had formed to urge a change in the rules that would at least permit lower fares.

Kahn set to work to revitalize the CAB—with the ultimate aim of eliminating it. In spite of the almost unanimous opposition of the airlines, he managed to decontrol fares, permit new firms to enter the industry and allow airlines to fly where they wished. Perhaps more important, he was a tireless advocate of deregulation, citing the fare cuts that permitted millions of new passengers to fly and responding to complaints about deteriorating service (which he acknowledged as the chief cost of expanding business).

In October 1978, persuaded that the airlines no longer needed government control, Congress passed the Airline Deregulation Act—calling for the disappearance of the CAB in 1985.

The CAB decision opened the floodgates of deregulation. Many rules governing the railroads, truckers, telecommunications firms and financial institutions were relaxed or jettisoned over the next few years. The rush to deregulate got an enormous boost from President Ronald Reagan and the aggressive free marketers who accompanied him to Washington. The new Administration also held a more permissive view of antitrust than any since Herbert Hoover's. It issued guidelines that virtually ended government challenges of mergers, and the 1980s saw an explosive increase in such combinations.

Many Americans, though, worried that the pendulum had swung too far. Deregulation had some unexpected and occasionally grave results: failing airlines and S&Ls, or higher prices for some telephone services. Benign neglect of antitrust facilitated a wave of takeovers that piled up corporate debt (sometimes resulting in defaults and bankruptcies) and cost thousands of workers their jobs.

Since President Bush's inauguration, there has been no official policy reversal, but enthusiasm for more mergers or further deregulation (in banking, for example) has clearly been dampened. In a few cases, calls for reregulation are being heard. And there is strong political support for laws that sometimes specify in rigid detail what companies must do to avoid polluting the air and water or to assure the rights of their workers. The costs of these mandates—often tougher than the rules laid down by the old regulatory agencies—are literally incalculable. And that has added force to a new debate over the proper relationship of business and government.

In today's global market domestic antitrust policy has inevitably become entangled with the issues of international competitiveness. As Professor Lovett puts it: "To some degree, the U.S. will have to match, respond in kind, or achieve more effective responses to foreign industrial policies."

That means that our antitrust and regulatory policies may have to be tempered lest they cripple U.S. companies in global markets. And they may have to set new goals such as encouraging research and development of new technology, enabling American companies to work together in ways that are now considered illegal, perhaps even directing resources to industries held to be vital to our national interests.

A small library of books has been published in recent years offering a plethora of prescriptions to cure what one of them labeled The American Disease. Most of them call for massive doses of government intervention. Another stage in the endless search for the proper balance between business freedom and government control may well be getting under way. What is crucial, warns Kahn, is that government intervention should enhance competition, rather than suppress it.

IMPERFECTIONS IN THE SOCIETY: CHANGING THE RULES OF INEQUALITY

See text p. 328

The American welfare state, as the text notes, found its beginnings in the 1930s, as citizens demanded relief from the consequences of the Great Depression. Since that time, welfare programs have expanded, albeit rather haphazardly, in response to specific problems.

Today, one of the most widely discussed problems in the public arena concerns the delivery of health care: costs have spiraled while fewer and fewer people have had the resources to obtain services. As the problem reaches crisis proportions, demands for public intervention have become acute.

In the following article, political journalist Barbara Ehrenreich argues that the institution of a national health insurance system is long overdue. She asserts that while the majority of Americans favor some form of national health insurance, the health insurance industry has successfully derailed serious efforts at reform. Her plea for change is aimed at the shortcomings of the capitalist market system: "If private enterprise won't do the job, then let private enterprise get out of the way."

Barbara Ehrenreich
"Our Health-Care Disgrace"*

National health insurance is an idea whose time has come . . . and gone . . . and come again, sounding a little more querulous with each return, like any good intention that has been put off much too long. It was once, way back in the 1930s, a brisk, young, up-and-coming idea. By the late '60s, when Richard Nixon first declared a health-care "crisis," it was already beginning to sound a little middle-aged and weary. Today, with the health-care situation moving rapidly beyond crisis to near catastrophe, the age-old and obvious solution has the tone of a desperate whine: Why can't we have

*Barbara Ehrenreich, "Our Health-Care Disgrace," *Time Magazine* (December 10, 1990). Copyright 1990 The Time Inc. Magazine Company. Reprinted by permission.

national health insurance—like just about everybody else in the civilized world, please?

Health-care costs have nearly doubled since 1980, to become the leading cause of personal and small-business bankruptcy. Collectively we spend $600 billion a year on medical care, or 11% of the GNP—a higher percentage than any other nation devotes to health. But the U.S. health system may be one of the few instances of social pathology that truly deserve to be compared to cancer. It grows uncontrollably—in terms of dollars—but seems to become more dysfunctional with every metastatic leap.

For a thumbnail index of failure, consider the number of people left out in the cold. Despite per capita medical expenditures that dwarf those of socialized systems, 37 million Americans have no health insurance at all. For the uninsured and the underinsured—who amount to 28% of the population—a diagnostic work-up can mean a missed car payment; a child's sore throat, an empty dinner table.

Even among those fortunate enough to be insured, the leading side effect of illness is often financial doom. Consider the elderly, whose federally sponsored insurance program, Medicare, inspires so much drooling and sharpening of knives at budget time. Even with Medicare, older Americans are forced to spend more than 15% of their income for medical care annually. And since nursing-home care is virtually uncovered, the elderly are pushed to degrading extremes—like divorcing a beloved spouse—in order to qualify for help through a long-term debilitating illness. Or, as more than one public figure has suggested, they can shuffle off prematurely to their reward.

We can't go on like this. Our infant-mortality rate is higher than Singapore's; our life expectancy is lower than Cubans'. As many as 50% of inner-city infants and toddlers go unimmunized. In the face of AIDS, our first major epidemic since polio, we are nearly helpless. Our city hospitals are overflowing with victims of tuberculosis, poverty, AIDS, old age and exposure. Our rural areas don't have this problem; they have fewer and fewer hospitals or, increasingly, less medical personnel of any kind.

But everyone knows that the system is broken beyond repair. According to the New England Journal of Medicine, 3 out of 4 Americans favor a government-financed national health-care program. The AFL-CIO is campaigning vigorously for national health care, and Big Business, terrified by the skyrocketing cost of employee health benefits, seems ready to go along. Even in the medical profession—the ancient redoubt of free-enterprise traditionalists—a majority now favor national health insurance.

So what stands in the way? There's still the American Medical Association, of course, which has yet to catch up to its physician constituency. But the interest group that arguably has the most to lose is the health-insurance industry, which spends more than $1 million a year to forestall any thoroughgoing government action. And why not? The insurance industry already enjoys a richly rewarding, gruesomely parasitic relationship to the public health domain. In broad schematic outline, it goes like this:

For decades the private insurers have fanned the crisis by blithely reimbursing the fees of greedy practitioners and expansionary hospitals. Then, as costs rise, the private insurers seek to shed the poorest and the sickest customers, who get priced out or summarily dropped. For some companies, a serious and costly illness is a good enough reason to cancel a policy. Others refuse to insure anybody who might be gay and hence, actuarially speaking, might get AIDS.

So over the years, government has moved in to pick up the rejects: first the elderly, then the extremely poor. Since the rejects are of course the most expensive to insure, government is soon faced with a budget nightmare. Draconian cost-control measures follow. But because government can only attempt to control the costs of its own programs, the providers of care simply shift their costs onto the bills of privately insured patients. Faced with ever rising costs, the private insurers become more determined to shed the poorest and the sickest . . . and so the cycle goes.

The technical term for this kind of arrangement is lemon socialism: the private sector gets the profitable share of the market, and the public sector gets what's left. The problem with this particular lemon is that it tends to sour us on the possibility of real reform. Even those who crave a national program covering everyone are wont to throw up their hands in despair: Nothing works! It's so complex! Maybe in 100 years!

It's time to cut the life-support system leading to the hungry maw of the insurance industry. The insurance companies can't have it both ways: they can't refuse to insure the poor, the old and the sick while simultaneously campaigning to prevent a government program to cover everyone alike. The very meaning of insurance is risk sharing—the well throwing in their lot with the sick, the young with the old, the affluent with the down-and-out. If private enterprise won't do the job, then let private enterprise get out of the way.

With the largest-ever consensus behind it, national health care's time is surely here at last. Otherwise, let us bow our heads together and recite the old Episcopal prayer: "We have left undone those things which we ought to have done . . . and there is no health in us."

See text p. 328

As the text makes clear, an adequate public policy response to the problem of poverty is difficult not just because the problem itself is immensely complex but because Americans are unsure of how they characterize their obligations to one another in this highly individualistic society. As Jason DeParle reports in the following article, no quick fix to the poverty problem is in sight. While no policy maker has indicated an unwillingness to address the problem, the suggested solutions themselves often conflict, and reflect widely disparate understandings of the nature of the poverty problem itself and the nature of the state's obligations to respond to it.

Jason DeParle with Peter Applebome
"Ideas to Help Poor Abound, But a Consensus Is Wanting"*

Wanted: An American anti-poverty policy. Strategy must offer reasonable prospect for ending cycles of dependency and despair that disfigure urban America. Long hours and serious commitment needed. Costs may be high. Costs of doing nothing may be higher.

The want ad for an American social policy might go on to list other requirements: a passionate leader to articulate it, taxpayers willing to pay for it, special interests that sacrifice for it, skilled administrators to apply it.

While some have argued that the nation has run out of ideas, a wealth of research in the late 1980s has produced many new proposals for helping the disadvantaged.

"There's been increased attention and vigorous debate among a range of specialists and some policy makers about new approaches," said Robert Greenstein, director of the Center on Budget and Policy Priorities, a Washington research and advocacy group. "But I think the public is only dimly aware of a fair amount of the policy debate."

Ideas on ghetto poverty tend to cluster in four schools of thought. One emphasizes an expanded network of traditional government social services. Another stresses economic policies to create more good jobs that would offer a way out of poverty. A third stresses welfare reform. The fourth calls for "empowering" poor people with programs that let them make choices in areas like housing and education.

Some of the strategies are complementary: expanded social programs and welfare reform might work hand in hand, for instance, and some experts call for both. But other proposals are in conflict. Some emphasize building up inner-city areas, while others talk about helping people escape them. Some suggest universal programs in which all Americans can participate, while others say efforts should be aimed at the neediest.

The last Congress acted on some of these ideas when it expanded tax credits that provide cash supplements for the working poor, and financing for Medicaid and Head Start, despite tight budgets. And Housing Secretary Jack F. Kemp, the Administration's chief antipoverty strategist, has sent President Bush a list of possible initiatives and urged him to use [his] State of the Union Message to propose "audacious solutions" to inner-city poverty. But Administration officials say that after much bickering among aides President Bush has chosen a less ambitious domestic line. . . .

A Social Approach: Old Programs Provide Models

To many liberals, the bitterest element of today's domestic policy environment is the widespread perception that government programs for the poor do not work, an attitude they say was stoked by the anti-government attitudes of the Reagan Administration.

Liberal academics like Lisbeth B. Schorr of Harvard University or advocates like Marian Wright Edelman of the Children's Defense Fund argue that there is ample evidence that government spending, if properly targeted, on schools, housing, health care and job training can be invaluable in breaking the cycle of poverty.

"It's a lie that nothing works," said Ms. Edelman, "and I think more and more people are realizing that. The fact is we made dramatic progress in the 1960s in eradicating hunger and improving the health status of children, and then we just stopped trying."

When arguing the effectiveness of government programs, advocates cite one more than any other: Head Start. A study of the best-known program applying Head Start principles, the Perry Preschool in Ypsilanti, Michigan, tracked students for 16 years after they finished the program, and concluded that each dollar spent saved $6 in subsequent expense for things like remedial education, criminal justice and social services. . . .

Skeptics Raise Questions

Many other experts have pointed to the work of Dr. James Comer, a New Haven educator, in arguing that the sustained efforts of educators and social workers can make a difference in the lives of the poor. His School Development Program has raised the academic performance of poor children by using teachers and social workers to get parents involved in the schools.

But skeptics abound. Some say that the successes, including Head Start, have been oversold and that few programs have worked for the most imperiled group: young, noncollege-bound males. Others say the underlying social ills of slums and larger economic forces working against the urban poor mean that government programs can produce only isolated successes at best. And some successes, skeptics argue, are built from the efforts of especially talented administrators. They may therefore be impossible to replicate on a large scale.

Cost is also often an issue in these times of tight budgets, with estimates for a broad array of antipoverty programs ranging from $10 billion to $25 billion. But Ms. Schorr argues that the problem is will, not wallet.

"I don't know why it is 'possible' to find $500 billion to bail out the savings and loan industry and the money it takes to fight Saddam Hussein," she said, "but it's not 'possible' to find the money it takes to meet this equally grave threat."

An Economic Approach: Job Opportunity Is Seen as the Key

While liberal intervention programs focus on raising the mental and emotional capital of the poor, a different set of policies focuses more directly on their economic prospects.

One of the most influential thinkers on urban poverty over the past decade has been William Julius Wilson, the University of Chicago professor and author of "The Truly Disadvantaged," published by the University of Chicago Press. He argues that poverty and its associated problems ultimately arise from economic forces that are beyond the control of poor people.

Slums deteriorated, he argues, primarily because well-paying industrial jobs died out or companies fled the central cities. Any serious solution must take aim at the roots of inner-city problems through economic policies that promote full and profitable employment.

"I really believe that if you increase educational opportunity and employment opportunity, a lot of the social problems would disappear," Mr. Wilson said. "If all of a sudden people see they have some chance of moving out of their situation, then their behavior changes."

Those who agree with Professor Wilson's analysis call for a broad array of economic approaches, including policies to promote full employment, programs to train and relocate all displaced or new workers and the creation of government jobs.

In addition, most call for other policies to insure that working people are able to support their families. These include the use of tax benefits to supplement the earnings of the working poor, national health insurance, and a stricter enforcement of child-support awards, with the Government making the payment when it fails to collect.

Programs Available to All

Professor Wilson says the main provisions of his plan—like the job training and relocation programs, the health insurance and the child support guarantees—would be available to all Americans, not just the poor.

Supporters of such universal programs argue that they would bring more political support, and less social stigma, than programs exclusively for the poor. The call for universal programs also reflects the belief that the problems of the poor are not so much a separate phenomenon as they are a concentrated example of the larger national social and economic difficulties.

Other analysts who are skeptical of such a macroeconomic approach note that creation of a full-employment economy has eluded policy makers for most of the century. Some say racism is so much a part of the inner-city problem that a strong economy would not always benefit the black poor.

Others note that many immigrants continue to succeed in the American economy as it is. The main inner-city problem, they argue, is not economics but social ills like the underground drug economy and welfare dependency that leave many inner-city poor people incapable of capitalizing on the opportunities that already exist.

"The behavior of the long-term poor is a real mystery," said Professor Mead, the New York University welfare expert. "It's not clear why they don't do what most immigrants do—work hard and get ahead." . . .

An "Empowering" Approach: Making Success a Matter of Choice

When Mr. Kemp, the Housing Secretary, is asked to summarize his plans for what he calls "a new war on poverty," he sometimes resorts to a single word: "empowerment."

What is it?

Philosophically, it is the argument that poor people have been robbed of the choices available to others by their reliance on monopolistic government bureaucracies, particularly in the areas of welfare, housing and schools. "Empower" them with choices, the argument goes, and they will thrive.

In its particulars, empowerment most often boils down to policies that encourage the poor to run their own housing projects or own their own homes and that allow parents to choose which schools their children will attend. If forced to compete for students, the empowerment argument goes, schools will improve.

In addition, Mr. Kemp has called for tax policies, most notably capital gains cuts and the creation of "enterprise zones," which he says will provide the incentives to attract businesses and new job opportunities to the inner cities.

Mr. Kemp often attacks the current welfare system, but he has been unspecific in proposing an alternative. Of programs that require work in exchange for welfare benefits he said, "Workfare is a form of a stick; I think we need, dramatically, more carrots."

In his own nod toward empowerment, President Bush [in 1990] appointed Mr. Kemp to head an Administration task force charged with finding other applications for the principle.

A list of options from across the Government, submitted to the President by Mr. Kemp late last fall, ranged from the bold to the bland. At one end was a proposal to "empower" families by raising the personal income tax exemption to $3,300 from $2,050, at a cost of $50 billion a year in lost revenue. At the other was a vague call to "enhance victims' rights."

Mr. Kemp rejects Professor Wilson's contention that the problems originate in the general economy. The problem, he argues, is that Government policies on housing, education and welfare have created what he terms socialist economies in the inner city that have eliminated incentives for personal effort.

Critics argue that Mr. Kemp has substituted windy optimism for a clear appraisal of the depths of inner city need. Exhortations about the joys of entrepreneurship and home ownership, they say, will do little for people who have never worked or whose skills can land them only minimum-wage jobs.

"It's Pollyannish," said Isabel Sawhill of the Urban Institute, a Washington research center. "I think it's too optimistic about the ability of the poor to suddenly transform themselves into middle-class citizens."

Some argue the best solution is not to build up slums but to get their residents out. One conspicuous success story is the Gautreaux program in Chicago, which, under a 1976 court order, has relocated more than 4,150 families from public housing into subsidized apartments in neighborhoods throughout the Chicago area.

Studies show that those relocated have far better chances of working and avoiding antisocial acts. Only budget constraints and a shortage of available apartments keep the program from being larger.

Ed Marciniak, an urban affairs professor at Loyola University in Chicago, says that Mr. Kemp "is in dream world when he talks of tenant ownership."

"What people in poverty need are neighborhoods, communities," Mr. Marciniak added, "and it's difficult to have a neighborhood in a public housing project. What you need to do is build ladders out."

But such complaints fall on deaf ears, and Mr. Kemp responds evangelically. "Entrepreneurial capitalism and empowerment can work," he said. "Let's unleash the greatest wealth our nation has: the pent-up talents and potential of our people."

CHAPTER 14

Foreign Policy

THE SETTING: A WORLD OF NATION-STATES

See text p. 335

Since 1988, the global order has changed dramatically. The Cold War has ended, and Americans must not only seek new answers to the questions that have dominated foreign policy concerns for decades, but must rethink the questions asked altogether. Changes in the world military and economic situation have raised questions about the very utility of nation-states themselves; problems have tended to be either entirely internal, as states like the Soviet Union struggle with pressures from republics within their borders claiming independence, or they require regional resolution transcending national boundaries. In the following article from the New York Times, *commentator Thomas Friedman looks at how internal disruptions in a number of nation-states have affected our understanding of the traditional world order and how those changes can be expected to affect American foreign policy interests overall.*

Thomas L. Friedman
"Today's Threat to Peace Is the Guy Down the Street"*

Soon after word reached Washington that Rajiv Gandhi had been assassinated in India, President Bush remarked: "I just don't know what the world is coming to." That was a startling comment, coming from a man who only weeks earlier was proclaiming the birth of a new world order in the wake of the Gulf War. In a way, though, there was no contradiction. The world is coming to a new order, but it is not the one that President Bush envisaged— or one that he will have much ability to shape.

The main principle President Bush invoked to justify his opposition to Iraq's invasion of Kuwait was that unless international boundaries between sovereign nation states are respected, the alternative is chaos. But the sort of threat posed by Saddam Hussein—one nation state simply devouring its neighbor—is increasingly obsolete in world politics today.

Instead, what are becoming increasingly common are challenges to the sovereignty and sanctity of nation states from within—from ethnic, tribal and religious groups dissatisfied with the shape or the content of their nations and ready to use any sort of violence to bring about change.

So it is not the Gulf War, but events that have taken place since that really characterize the dominant trend and challenge in the post-cold war world—the Kurdish drive to split off from Iraq, the assassination of Mr. Gandhi by opponents amid ethnic strife in India, the takeover of Ethiopia by secessionist rebels from Eritrea and others seeking to replace Ethiopia's traditional tribal elite. Indeed, it is the same from Yugoslavia to Quebec and from the Soviet Union to South Africa: the predominant threat to stability is conflict within nations and not between them.

"The Gulf War is the wave of the past," remarked Michael Mandelbaum, director of East-West studies at the Council on Foreign Relations. "India, Ethiopia, Yugoslavia and the breakup of the Soviet Union are the wave of the future.

"Most nation states arose as a result of the breakup of great empires following World War I and World War II," he said. "But the third great cataclysm of this century, the end of the cold war, is shaping up to be a story not so much about the unmaking of empires and the birth of nation states, but the unmaking of nation states that were born earlier in the century."

It is not surprising that the end of the cold war has been accompanied by the fragmentation of some nation states. The cold war not only held together by force such artificial nation states as Yugoslavia; it also enabled regimes in many weak states, such as Ethiopia and Iraq, to strengthen and sustain themselves far longer than they might have otherwise. They accomplished this by getting economic help and diplomatic backing from superpowers eager to bid for their support in the grand contest between East and West.

But those days are over, and life promises to be much more complicated not only for many weak nation states but for the superpowers as well. Generally speaking, the sorts of threats to international stability that the United States is likely to face now—those coming from within states that are imploding—will not easily be treated by classic great-power diplomacy. Nor will these threats offer the moral clarity that was available when there was a clear-cut villain or an "Evil Empire" challenging America. They also may not be responsive to brute force.

The NATO allies more or less acknowledged the changed environment [in May of 1991] when they announced that they were revamping their forces from a massive dam designed to resist a Soviet invasion across Europe, to smaller mobile units better able to put out brush fires ignited by small states or tensions between European ethnic and regional groups.

Standard international relations texts—including all the classic balance-of-power theories from Clausewitz to Kissinger—will have to be revised somewhat, to teach statesmen how to improvise for these new challenges. For example, when the United States wanted to get a new Security Council resolution that would dispatch a United Nations police force to protect Kurds wanting to return home, and to replace the American troops, the Soviets and Chinese balked. They said they were afraid that if the United

Nations could intervene to protect the Kurds in Iraq, it might later be asked to do the same for the Baltic peoples or those of Tibet. In the end, a murky compromise was cobbled together.

"What I am struck by," said Stanley Hoffmann, a professor of government at Harvard, "is the fact that the world order, or whatever there is of it, is still very much based on state sovereignty, and that is quite inadequate, and indeed dangerous when you consider that many of the most destabilizing troubles are likely to come from within states—either because of ethnic strife or terrifying repressive measures that governments, like South Africa or the Soviet Union, might take that invite external intervention."

Mr. Hoffmann added: "There is very little in our repertoire of ideas that helps us to cope with such internal disorders. Each time statesmen have opened this Pandora's box of what goes on inside states, they have closed it in horror."

Washington also has less influence in these internal conflicts because in most cases they are going to be decided by small arms, an assassin's bullet or backwoods deals between peoples with whom America has little contact or understanding. If the Soviet republic of Georgia declares its independence tomorrow, with whom will Washington deal?

Moreover, the United States is not only less capable of intervening, but less interested in doing so. In the post-cold war world, when America no longer feels impelled to compete with the Soviet Union for every corner of the globe, it is far less urgent to many people who rules in Ethiopia, or whether it is one country or three.

But in another sense the United States has also acquired new leverage to influence some of these internal contests. This is because America's triumph in the cold war was not a territorial victory but a victory for a set of political and economic principles: democracy and the free market.

Many third-world countries that, in the first flush of independence, rejected capitalism for socialism, have now concluded that the free market is the wave of the future—a future for which America is both the gatekeeper and the model.

It is precisely this economic leverage that the United States has over the Soviet President, Mikhail S. Gorbachev—whether to grant him everything from food credits to access to international lending agencies—that enables Washington to press him to open his society more, to give more freedom to the republics and different ethnic groups and to loosen the reins of central economic control.

Call it diplomacy by the Federalist Papers. It is being used in Ethiopia too, where the once-Marxist rebels have gone from preaching Communism to pragmatism. The Assistant Secretary of State for African Affairs, Herman J. Cohen, who has been helping to mediate in the Ethiopian civil war, bluntly told Ethiopia's new leaders: "No democracy, no cooperation."

But such diplomacy by moral and economic suasion has its limits, as anti-American protests in [a number of countries in 1991] demonstrated. There is no more violent cocktail than ethnic and tribal hatreds combined with uneven economic growth. In an era when there is far more economic advice than resources to implement it, and far more ethnic passions than traditions of pluralism to contain them, there are going to be far more new world disorders than new world orders.

THE VALUES IN AMERICAN FOREIGN POLICY

See text p. 337

No one who has watched the progress of international affairs over the last several months can deny the need for rethinking American foreign policy. But understanding the need for change is the easy step: the hard question is thinking about what direction change ought to take us. Since the end of World War II, American foreign policy has been decidedly internationalist; as the world order has changed, however, and as domestic problems have mounted, that foreign policy stance has come under attack from all sides. In an article written for The Atlantic *in July 1991, for example, foreign policy analyst Alan Tonelson argued for an "interest-based" foreign policy, under which Americans would abandon their impulses to remake the world in its own image and act strategically and pragmatically to enhance its own security and prosperity above all else—reflecting a return to the unilateralist posture that characterized United States' foreign policy before the Second World War, as discussed in the text.*

In the following article, political observer Peter McGrath discusses the crisis in values affecting the development of American foreign policy today. As he notes, it is difficult to decide upon the appropriate role the United States should play in the international arena (see discussion in text at p. 783) without first articulating the principles that guide it.

Peter McGrath
"The Lonely Superpower"*

We have passed this way before. In 1945, with Europe a guttering ruin, the British Empire a hollow shell and the Soviet Union still reeling from the loss of 27 million people during World War II, the United States was the world's sole superpower. It had a monopoly on atomic weapons. Its economy was thriving on a wartime industrial regimen. America faced a choice: inward or outward? Would it take up Britain's former global role? Or would it retreat into the isolationism that followed World War I? The debate was brief. By 1947, resurgent Soviet power plunged the United States into the four-decade conflict that historian Hajo Holborn called "international civil war" between the rival Western ideologies of Marxism and liberal capitalism. The expansion of American responsibilities took place in an atmosphere of crisis, with Republican leaders urging President Harry Truman to "scare hell out of the American people" if he wanted them to support American inter-

---

vention in Europe. He succeeded. As a result, the American people never had the chance to make an unhurried decision about their degree of involvement around the world. The end of the cold war has restored that opportunity.

George Bush wants to continue the internationalist policies of the last 45 years. In his speech on nuclear-arms reduction [in September 1991], he, too, sounded the sole-superpower theme: "America must lead again—as it always has, as only it can." But isolationism is a strain deeply embedded in the American psyche. Even before George Washington warned against foreign entanglements, Americans thought of the Old World their ancestors left as a decadent zone best left alone. That instinct remained strong well into the 20th century: it is worth recalling that less than four months before Pearl Harbor, with Europe already overrun and Japan in control of East Asia, a bill to extend compulsory military service to 18 months passed the House of Representatives by a single vote. Following the demise of the Soviet threat, isolationism is making a comeback. Patrick Buchanan, the conservative scold and former Reagan speechwriter, speaks for the Republican Party's old Fortress America wing. "All that buncombe about what history 'placed on our shoulders' sucked the Brits into two wars," he said in the *Washington Post*. "If America does not wish to end her days in the same nursing home as Britannia, she had best can this Beltway geo-babble about 'unipolarity' and 'our responsibility to lead'." Suitably modified, such views have even percolated to the heart of the foreign-policy establishment. Last spring William Hyland, the editor of *Foreign Affairs* quarterly, wrote in the *New York Times* of the "need to start selectively disengaging abroad to save resources" for domestic problems. "What is desperately required," he said, "is a psychological turn inward."

This change in mood makes internationalists uneasy. "Americans are endlessly resourceful in trying to escape [global] responsibilities," the columnist Charles Krauthammer wrote in *The New Republic* in July. But the world is at least as dangerous as it was at the height of the cold war, he argued; the spread of weapons of mass destruction makes it possible for "relatively small, peripheral and backward states" to emerge as security threats. The United States should be prepared to assert "American interests and values" anywhere in the world, unilaterally if necessary. "Our best hope for safety," said Krauthammer, "is in American strength and will: the strength to recognize the unipolar world and the will to lead it." Bush agrees, though with polite bows in the direction of collective action under United Nations auspices.

Global balance: But what does it mean to be a superpower today? The term itself is a product of the cold war: it described the way the two adversarial nuclear-weapons states related to each other. The superpowers were not simply old-fashioned "great powers" with ICBMs. They were not interested in the politics of shifting alliances, of playing countries against each other to achieve some global balance. Each superpower claimed to be a model for the rest of the world, and sought worldwide dominance in the ideological sphere. Each had a military capacity that controlled the fate of humankind. Each brought to the conflict what Zbigniew Brzezinski calls "an unprecedented degree of intellectual self-righteousness." All this gave both countries a sense of mission transcending mere national interests. It was precisely this rivalry that defined the United States and the Soviet Union as superpowers. Without it, the category "superpower" is drained of meaning. It is a dialectical concept: either there are two superpowers, or there is none.

America's loss of mission explains why the president has such difficulty arousing public enthusiasm for his "quest for a new world order." When he tries to articulate it, as he did last April in a speech at Maxwell Air Force Base, he talks generally in terms of conflict resolution and "solidarity against aggression." He seems to regard instability anywhere in the world as a danger requiring American attention. References to "freedom" and "democratic ideals"—justifications for U.S. intervention since the time of Woodrow Wilson—appear almost to be afterthoughts. As Krauthammer tartly observed, "For Bush, the new world order is principally about order." Order is a worthy goal. But as the linchpin of a policy of global reach, it is hardly inspiring. Worse, it furnishes no criteria for distinguishing great dangers from small ones. In a world where American commitments chronically outrun the ability to pay for them there must be, as Alan Tonelson of the Washington-based Economic Strategy Institute wrote in *The Atlantic* last July, "a strategic basis for selectivity."

"Selectivity" is in fact the new foreign-policy buzzword. Amid a general recognition that the United States' economic problems have left it relatively weaker than it was at midcentury, there is a growing emphasis on cold-blooded views of the national interest. Exactly which contingencies merit preparation? Where, and at what price? The cold-war policy of containing communism dictated an ability to project power worldwide. The result by 1990 was a fleet of 14 aircraft-carrier battle groups costing $53.5 billion for that year alone. It meant a forward deployment of troops and equipment to Central Europe that by itself consumed 29 percent of all U.S. military spending, according to the study "Decisions for Defense," published [in September 1991] by William W. Kaufmann and John D. Steinbruner of the Brookings Institution. This is an obsolete forces structure. The Bush administration plans to complete a 25 percent reduction in it by 1995. What policy will shape the new structure?

Accepted maxims: Historically, Americans have not shown much skill in defining the national interest—in part because they find interest-driven policies too cynical. But there are a few commonly accepted maxims. First is that as an industrial country, the United States must maintain access to sources of raw material. Oil is the most obvious example. But America is also dependent on imports for many other critical substances, such as graphite, bauxite and diamonds. Second, as a maritime, trading nation, the United States must insist on freedom of the seas. Third, there is a direct interest in the health of overseas markets for U.S. exports—this was the consideration underlying postwar aid to Europe under the Marshall Plan. At a minimum, then, America has an interest in the stability and security of such suppliers of raw materials as South Africa; of countries like Egypt that sit astride the choke points of vital sea lanes, and of nations that are or that could grow into important trading partners, such as Venezuela and eventually some of the Soviet republics.

This is still a broad canvas. It implies a different mix of armed forces, one with less emphasis on mass power projection and more emphasis on sea and air mobility and on America's technological edge. But as Clausewitz pointed out, military force is what is left when a nation's political goals can't be achieved by nonviolent means. It is a confession of failure. This implies a diplomacy of global range, too. In the case of overseas markets, for example, a farsighted policy would probably call for extensive technical assistance to the resource-rich but technologically backward Russian Republic. It would anticipate the eventual change in power arrangements in South Africa and make sure that the next generation of black leaders is not unfriendly to the United States. Washington should also put high priority on minimizing the greatest single threat to stability in the post-cold-war world: proliferation of nuclear and other unconventional weapons among the regional powers. India has already detonated a nuclear device; Israel and South Africa almost certainly have them, too. Pakistan is close to a nuclear capability, and Iraq and North Korea have been working on it. The example of Iraq reveals how the current nonproliferation regime can be circumvented. It also suggests that all the nations of the developed world have a collective interest in choking off the flow of nuclear technology and materials. If, for example, either India or Pakistan used nuclear weapons in a future confrontation, it is not hard to imagine the conflict spreading beyond the subcontinent.

It has become fashionable to debunk the principle of collective action. Krauthammer, for example, regards it as mere protective coloration for U.S. unilateralism—nice to have but not in the end necessary. But some things, such as nuclear nonproliferation, can be done no other way. Others, like producing the levels of economic help necessary for stability in third World countries important to the industrial West, are beyond American resources alone. Some problems are unresponsive to the only real power the United States can wield unilaterally; the continuation of the Gulf War by other means shows the inherent limits on the value of military force.

Modest tools: But this does not mean the United States has to respond to every crisis around the world. If civil unrest in Zaire cuts off the world's cobalt supply, as happened in 1978, the manufacturers of airplane turbine blades will be able to find substitute materials, as they did then. If Vietnam reprises its 1978 aggression against Cambodia, there is no compelling U.S. interest at stake. Even where there does appear to be a concrete interest, say in the event of hostilities between Syria and Iraq, it is important to recognize, as Alan Tonelson says, the modesty of the "policy tools actually at a government's command—weapons, money and suasion." Some crises are beyond American influence. Intervention in others might exact an unacceptably high cost in either blood or treasure.

It follows that America needs a coherent view of the world cast mainly in terms of cost and risk. Such a policy won't be easy to develop. It is alien to the American temper, which tends to lurch between isolationism and idealism. Those two policies have already been tried and found wanting. Americans will never accept the first half of Lord Palmerston's aphorism, that a nation has no eternal friends: an immigrant nation's sentimental ties to countries of origin are too strong. But they may come to see the wisdom of the second half: there are such things as eternal interests.

THE INSTRUMENTS OF AMERICAN FOREIGN POLICY

See text p. 343

If there is any organization with the capacity to affect the development of a new world order, that organization would surely appear to be the United Nations. And yet, despite some clear successes, as the text notes, the United Nations has not proved to be particularly effective to date in forging a new international system.

The following article by Rochelle Stanfield was written shortly after Iraq's invasion of Kuwait in 1990, with an eye to events unfolding in the Middle East at that time. Nonetheless, Stanfield's discussion of the role of the United Nations remains timely. Like the United States itself, the ability of the United Nations to foster cooperation among different states depends upon reassessing its own role in a new and markedly different global order.

Rochelle Stanfield
"Worldly Visions"*

"A new partnership of nations has begun," President Bush said in a speech to Congress on Sept. 11 [1990]. "The crisis in the Persian Gulf, as grave as it is, also offers a rare opportunity to move toward a historic period of cooperation."

"The United Nations can help bring about a new day," the President told the U.N. General Assembly on Oct. 2, elaborating on his vision of a new partnership of nations "based on consultation, cooperation and collective action, especially through international and regional organizations . . . united by principle and the rule of law and supported by an equitable sharing of both cost and commitment."

Other world leaders echo these sentiments. Soviet Foreign Minister Eduard A. Shevardnadze told the U.N. General Assembly on Sept. 25: "Partnership is replacing rivalry. It is becoming the basis for relations between many countries that used to regard each other as adversaries and rivals."

Almost everyone agrees that the old world order dominated by U.S.-Soviet Cold War competition is dead and that some form of multilateralism will figure prominently in whatever replaces it.

---

*Rochelle Stanfield, "Worldly Visions," *National Journal* (October 27, 1990). Reprinted with permission.

The commission vision stops there.

"I think the talk of a new world order is premature," Andrew J. Pierre, a European specialist at the Carnegie Endowment for International Peace in Washington, said. "We're groping toward it, but we're doing it solely in the context of the Persian Gulf. It could collapse very quickly if we don't get a beneficial result."

Skeptics . . . don't expect the United Nations to serve as global policeman or fixer of regional conflicts, especially disputes not instigated by East-West competition. Indeed, they question the relevance of the United Nations, as currently structured, to the emerging realities of international relations.

Oil makes [the Gulf] crisis different from all other regional disputes. "It is not a test case because of this one feature," Robert E. Hunter, director of European studies at the Center for Strategic and International Studies (CSIS) in Washington, insisted. "There is no spot on the earth other than the Persian Gulf about which so many countries care so much."

Some analysts conclude, therefore, that even though many nations are willing to cooperate in the Gulf crisis, they won't work together elsewhere. Other analysts take a contrary view, saying that if nations can collaborate when their self-interest is so keen, they will be more likely to collaborate on issues that aren't so vital.

Many specialists don't view the world's response to the Gulf crisis as a foundation for a new order because, they say, they don't see a lot of partnership there. The United States has obtained U.N. agreement on the political and economic aspects—economic sanctions against Iraq, for example—but has run the military show unilaterally, seeking help from other nations only after the fact.

"I think the Americanization of the collective security arrangement was clear from the start," said Richard J. Barnet, co-director of the Institute for Policy Studies, a left-of-center think tank in Washington. "That was confirmed in a very important sentence in the President's speech to Congress in which he said, 'Within three days . . . I decided to check that [Iraqi] aggression.' That was an 'I' that was totally personal."

Fundamental questions about fashioning a new world order include whether the United States would be willing to relinquish military control to a multinational body, whether the United Nations or some other agency would be capable of accepting it and whether nations—even close allies such as NATO members—can resolve differences over how military forces would be directed.

Enthusiasm for the United Nations is at an all-time high. Declarations abound about how U.S.-Soviet cooperation finally allows the U.N. charter to operate as it was written 45 years ago. Still, skeptics question whether the organization can police regional conflicts.

"What we're going to see in the post-Cold War period is a distinct lessening of concern on the part of the United States and the West about instability outside Europe," said Michael E. Mandelbaum, professor of foreign policy at the Johns Hopkins School of Advanced International Studies in Washington and director of the Council on Foreign Relations' East-West studies program. "The [Gulf crisis] therefore is an exception."

There isn't much the United Nations can do to solve many intractable conflicts in the Third World, anyway. "My own view is that the Third World is going to be a less safe place in the '90s and beyond for the simple reason that all the causes of conflicts within countries, and wars between countries, still exist and, if anything, have been exacerbated," said John W. Sewell, president of the Overseas Development Council, a Washington think tank that specializes in Third World economic development.

Even if the world wanted the United Nations to take charge, its structure may be outmoded. "The United Nations really was designed by the people who fought and won the last war [World War II] and therefore has this big gap that leaves out the Germans and Japanese and the European Community," said Gregory F. Treverton, senior fellow for Europe at the New York City-based Council on Foreign Relations. . . .

Gulf Partners

It's no coincidence that political and economic cooperation in the Gulf far exceeds military collaboration. Fundamental differences in approach to security remain between the United States and its closest allies in NATO. Differences between the United States and Japan are far greater.

"Even the word 'security' we conceive of in military terms," said Robert Gerald Livingston, director of the American Institute for Contemporary German Studies at Johns Hopkins in Washington. "The Germans have always conceived of security in a much broader, multifaceted framework. There's an economic dimension, political dimension, diplomatic dimension, and only then is there a military dimension."

Members of Congress, reflecting their constituents' anger, expressed irritation that the Europeans didn't send significant numbers of troops to stand beside Americans in the desert.

Specialists in European affairs weren't surprised. They considered the responses of the British, French, Germans, Italians, Dutch and others as natural reactions of countries that now view fighting as a last resort.

Paolo Liebl, associate director of the Defense Industries Project at Georgetown University, put it this way: "The United States jumped in and said, 'Well, come in, everybody—what are you waiting for?' And the Europeans, who are waiting for this thing to go away, said, 'We cannot condone aggression, but this matter should be settled diplomatically and not escalated to an armed attack.' "

There were also differences between those countries. "The British have supported the United States with determination, the French with hesitation and the Germans with trepidation," Pierre of the Carnegie Endowment quipped. Indeed, British Prime Minister Margaret Thatcher used the Gulf crisis to try to regain the special U.S.-British relationship, which paled as U.S.-German ties became stronger. French President Francois Mitterrand took the opportunity to reassert France's independence within the cooperative framework. Germany (and Japan) resorted to their constitutional prohibitions against engaging in military action away from home. . . .

"I suspect there will always be a point where somebody's got to take the lead, and we will always be in the forefront of taking the lead on freedom," David E. Bonior, D-Mich., the deputy House majority whip, said. "I think that's a hallmark of American foreign policy. I think people look to us to continue to do that."

But the U.S. government can no longer afford to underwrite American preeminence. What many observers consider amazing about the Gulf crisis is that the Europeans, several Arab nations and the Japanese agreed—even if reluctantly—to pay for an operation staged by the Americans. Only the threat to the world's oil resources makes that possible, they say. . . .

Updating the United Nations

If Desert Shield, the Persian Gulf operation, were turned over to the United Nations—as the Soviet Union, a few Western European officials and some American analysts have recommended—it would dramatically change the nature of the exercise.

"The U.N. is not an organization that uses force," Toby T. Gati, senior vice president for research of the New York City-based United Nations Association of the United States of America, explained. "It's a peacekeeping organization—unarmed soldiers and blue helmets. In Iraq it's not going to be unarmed soldiers and blue helmuts. It's going to be bulletproof vests and bazookas." . . .

The United Nations—in theory, at least—controlled Western forces in the Korean war. But that experience is not now cited as an appropriate precedent. The Security Council was able to sanction military action only because the Soviet Union, North Korea's patron, was boycotting the council. When the Soviets returned to the council, they created a deadlock. The United States turned to the General Assembly, which passed a resolution giving itself power to authorize the mission and turned the 16-nation exercise over to the United States.

That resolution now is considered to have had dubious legal standing. More important, a U.N. delegation of authority to the United States would now lack political credibility. Treverton of the Council on Foreign Relations, recounting his discussions with Europeans about the possibility of turning the Gulf crisis over to the United Nations, said that they referred derogatorily to "another blue-hat operation like Korea, where the hats were blue but the soldiers underneath were American."

The U.N. Security Council has carried out numerous peacekeeping missions—and won the 1988 Nobel peace prize in the process—but is not specifically authorized to do so in the U.N. charter. The charter spells out the authorization to raise a standing U.N. army, but its provisions have never been implemented. . . .

Some analysts question the relevance of the United Nations, which has focused primarily on politics and peacekeeping over its 45-year history, in a world in which power is likely to be based on economic strength.

"It may well be that there will now be a much more concerted multilateral approach in those issues in which Japan and Germany will play a more prominent role, but they won't be through the United Nations," Mandelbaum of Hopkins said. "It may be through the International Monetary Fund or the OECD [Organization for Economic Cooperation and Development] or through ad hoc [economic] bodies." . . .

Regional Security

Even before the old world order collapsed and died, the United Nations grew more active in regional conflict mediation: in Afghanistan, Cambodia, Namibia and Nicaragua, among other places. In light of these successes—and the unparalleled cooperation in the Gulf—Bush, Shevardnadze and others envision a major regional role for the United Nations in the new world order.

Skeptics aren't so sure.

The United Nations has worked most effectively in places, such as the Gulf, where everyone has an economic interest in the outcome, as well as in regional conflicts instigated or exacerbated by cold war competition. In Afghanistan and Nicaragua, for example, after the United States and the Soviet Union decided to step back, they invited the United Nations to step in: to mediate in Afghanistan or supervise elections in Nicaragua.

The Cambodian civil war is older and more complex. Three of the five permanent Security Council members have been patrons of three of the factions—the Soviet Union of the Vietnamese-backed government, the United States of the non-Communist coalition, and China of the Khmer Rouge. The involvement of these nations increases the United Nations' leverage. The Cambodian factions have agreed in principle to a plan worked out by the so-called Perm Five.

When the major powers have no vested interest in regional disputes and when these disputes arise from traditional, religious or ethnic conflicts, the United Nations is less likely to be effective—or even to be called in.

Analysts envision several possible approaches as the new world order unfolds. Charles William Maynes, editor of *Foreign Policy* magazine, described "a mutual strategic disengagement, where the major powers decide that they're not going to allow disruptions—in Liberia, for example—to have a negative impact on the central relationships in the world system." Liberia has been writhing in civil war for more than year without the United Nations or the United States lifting a finger.

In conflicts such as this, a regional organization, a dominant regional power or a major power with ties to the dispute may intervene. In Liberia, an African multilateral peace force has intervened. Sewell of the Overseas Development Council sees this as a very hopeful sign of the new world order.

"I think it's remarkable," he said. "It's unheard of for Africans to intervene in one of their brother society's internal conflicts.

In Southeast Asia, India has taken on the role of regional peacekeeper, moving into conflicts in the Maldive Islands and Sri Lanka. "India has become the dominant hegemon in that area, and we are not going to challenge it," Maynes said.

Most recently, France and Belgium, former Central African colonial powers, sent troops to Rwanda to defend the Hutu-dominated government from an attack by a refugee army of Tutsi tribesmen.

Something has to replace the old world order, which is gone. "But it may be a chaotic, fragmented order," Maynes said.

"It will be a system, but it might be a very disorderly system." . . .

CHAPTER 14

The State of the Union

CONCLUDING THOUGHTS

See text p. 364

Once again, Alexis de Tocqueville's insightful analyses of the American democratic system are worthy of consideration. The problem of balancing freedom and order has been at the center of this book: it is the central problem of the American political system. Democracy is not a panacea; as de Tocqueville notes, the tyranny of a democratic system may lie in the extent to which it anesthetizes its citizens to the realities of how power over them is exercised.

Alexis de Tocqueville
"What Sort of Despotism Democratic Nations Have to Fear"*

I noticed during my stay in the United States that a democratic state of society similar to that found there could lay itself peculiarly open to the establishment of a despotism. . . .

In past ages there had never been a sovereign so absolute and so powerful that he could by himself alone, without the aid of secondary powers, undertake to administer every part of a great empire. No one had ever tried to subject all his people indiscriminately to the details of a uniform code, nor personally to prompt and lead every single one of his subjects. It had never occurred to the mind of man to embark on such an undertaking, and had it done so, inadequate education, imperfect administrative machinery, and above all the natural obstacles raised by unequal conditions would soon have put a stop to so grandiose a design. . . . But if a despotism should be established among the democratic nations of our day, it would probably have a different character. It would be more widespread and milder; it would degrade men rather than torment them.

Doubtless, in such an age of education and equality as our own, rulers could more easily bring all public powers into their own hands alone, and

---

*Alexis de Tocqueville, "What Sort of Despotism Democratic Nations Have to Fear," in *Democracy in America*, ed. J.P. Mayer and Max Lerner, tr. George Lawrence. English translation copyright © 1965 by Harper & Row, Publishers, Inc. Reprinted by permission of HarperCollins Publishers.

they could impinge deeper and more habitually into the sphere of private interests than was ever possible in antiquity. But that same equality which makes despotism easy tempers it. We have seen how, as men become more alike and more nearly equal, public mores become more humane and gentle. When there is no citizen with great power or wealth, tyranny in some degree lacks both target and stage. When all fortunes are middling, passions are naturally restrained, imagination limited, and pleasures simple. Such universal moderation tempers the sovereign's own spirit and keeps within certain limits the disorderly urges of desire. . . .

Democratic governments might become violent and cruel at times of great excitement and danger, but such crises will be rare and brief.

Taking into consideration the trivial nature of men's passions now, the softness of their mores, the extent of their education, the purity of their religion, their steady habits of patient work, and the restraint which they all show in the indulgence of both their vices and their virtues, I do not expect their leaders to be tyrants, but rather schoolmasters.

Thus I think that the type of oppression which threatens democracies is different from anything there has ever been in the world before. . . .

I am trying to imagine under what novel features despotism may appear in the world. In the first place, I see an innumerable multitude of men, alike and equal, constantly circling around in pursuit of the petty and banal pleasures with which they glut their souls. Each one of them, withdrawn into himself, is almost unaware of the fate of the rest. Mankind, for him, consists in his children and his personal friends. As for the rest of his fellow citizens, they are near enough, but he does not notice them. He touches them but feels nothing. He exists in and for himself, and though he still may have a family, one can at least say that he has not got a fatherland.

Over this kind of men stands an immense, protective power which is alone responsible for securing their enjoyment and watching over their fate. That power is absolute, thoughtful of detail, orderly, provident, and gentle. It would resemble parental authority if, fatherlike, it tried to prepare its charges for a man's life, but on the contrary, it only tries to keep them in perpetual childhood. It likes to see the citizens enjoy themselves, provided that they think of nothing but enjoyment. It gladly works for their happiness but wants to be sole agent and judge of it. It provides for their security, foresees and supplies their necessities, facilitates their pleasures, manages their principal concerns, directs their industry, makes rules for their testaments, and divides their inheritances. Why should it not entirely relieve them from the trouble of thinking and all the cares of living?

Thus it daily makes the exercise of free choice less useful and rarer, restricts the activity of free will within a narrower compass, and little by little robs each citizen of the proper use of his own faculties. Equality has prepared men for all this, predisposing them to endure it and often even regard it as beneficial.

Having thus taken each citizen in turn in its powerful grasp and shaped him to its will, government then extends its embrace to include the whole of society. It covers the whole of social life with a network of petty, complicated rules that are both minute and uniform, through which even men of the greatest originality and the most vigorous temperament cannot force their heads above the crowd. It does not break men's will, but softens, bends, and guides it; it seldom enjoins, but often inhibits, action; it does not destroy anything, but prevents much being born; it is not at all tyrannical, but it hinders, restrains, enervates, stifles, and stultifies so much that in the end each nation is no more than a flock of timid and hardworking animals with the government as its shepherd.

I have always thought that this brand of orderly, gentle, peaceful slavery which I have just described could be combined, more easily than is generally supposed, with some of the external forms of freedom, and that there is a possibility of its getting itself established even under the shadow of the sovereignty of the people.

Our contemporaries are ever a prey to two conflicting passions: they feel the need of guidance, and they long to stay free. Unable to wipe out these two contradictory instincts, they try to satisfy them both together. Their imagination conceives a government which is unitary, protective, and all-powerful, but elected by the people. Centralization is combined with the sovereignty of the people. That gives them a chance to relax. They console themselves for being under schoolmasters by thinking that they have chosen them themselves. Each individual lets them put the collar on, for he sees that it is not a person, or a class of persons, but society itself which holds the end of the chain.

Under this system the citizens quit their state of dependence just long enough to choose their masters and then fall back into it.

A great many people nowadays very easily fall in with this brand of compromise between administrative despotism and the sovereignty of the people. They think they have done enough to guarantee personal freedom when it is to the government of the state that they have handed it over. That is not good enough for me. I am much less interested in the question who my master is than in the fact of obedience. . . . Subjection in petty affairs, is manifest daily and touches all citizens indiscriminately. It never drives men to despair, but continually thwarts them and leads them to give up using their free will. It slowly stifles their spirits and enervates their souls, whereas obedience demanded only occasionally in matters of great moment brings servitude into play only from time to time, and its weight falls only on certain people. It does little good to summon those very citizens who have been made so dependent on the central power to choose the representatives of that power from time to time. However important, this brief and occasional exercise of free will will not prevent them from gradually losing the faculty of thinking, feeling, and acting for themselves, so that they will slowly fall below the level of humanity.

I must add that they will soon become incapable of using the one great privilege left to them. Those democratic peoples which have introduced freedom into the sphere of politics, while allowing despotism to grow in the administrative sphere, have been led into the strangest paradoxes. For the conduct of small affairs, where plain common sense is enough, they hold that the citizens are not up to the job. But they give these citizens immense prerogatives where the government of the whole state is concerned. They are turned alternatively into the playthings of the sovereign and into his masters, being either greater than kings or less than men. When they have tried all the different systems of election without finding one to suit them, they look surprised and go on seeking for another, as if the ills they see did not belong much more to the constitution of the country itself than to that of the electoral body.

It really is difficult to imagine how people who have entirely given up managing their own affairs could make a wise choice of those who are to do that for them. One should never expect a liberal, energetic, and wise government to originate in the votes of a people of servants.

The Study Guide

CHAPTER 1

Freedom and Power: An Introduction to the Problem

CHAPTER OUTLINE

I. Government and Control
  A. The essential foundations of government have historically included a means of coercion and a means of collecting revenue.
    1. A means of coercion gives government the power to order people around, to get people to obey its edicts, and to punish them if they do not.
    2. Governments must have a means of collecting revenue from citizens in order to support their institutions and programs.
  B. Forms of government vary in their institutional structure, size, modes of operation, and in terms of how they govern.
  C. A nation's politics influence its government, and at the same time, the character and actions of a government also influence a nation's politics.

II. From Coercion to Consent
  A. The relationship between rulers and the ruled was transformed by a shift in emphasis from limits on government power to increasing citizen participation and influence through politics.
    1. The bourgeoisie was the key force behind the imposition of limits on government power because they wanted to protect and defend their own interests.
    2. Internal conflict and external threat forced rulers to give ordinary citizens a greater voice in public affairs.
    3. The main external threat to a government's power is the existence of other nation-states.
  B. Once citizens perceived that government could operate in response to their demands, they became increasingly willing to support the expansion of government.

III. Freedom and Power: The Problem
  A. Expansion of governmental powers inevitably reduces popular influence over policy making.
  B. As government has grown in size and power, the need for citizen cooperation had diminished.
  C. Americans believe it is possible to have both individual freedom and the benefits of strong government, while at the same time maintaining control over government.

STUDY QUESTIONS

1. Describe how the American national government has changed over the last fifty years or so. Focus upon its growth, relation to state governments, and what most Americans perceive its role to be.

2. How do rulers strengthen and perpetuate their control over a territory and its habitants? What roles do institutions play in government?

3. What means of coercion and revenue collection does the American government employ? How are you, as a citizen, coerced? How do taxes maintain both political integration and governmental functions?

4. What is an oligarchy? What social groups compose it?

5. How does the United States permit a relatively large segment of the populace to have some influence over the government's actions? What defines and limits the government's powers in theory? What term describes the above kind of government? And about how many governments of this type exist among the world's approximately 200 nations?

6. Define an authoritarian nation. Compare it to constitutional democracies. What political and social institutions provide limits on such a government?

7. How do political scientists use the word "coercion"?

8. What type of government did the bourgeoisie favor to protect its interests and curb royal power?

9. Why did the bourgeoisie favor limitations on the power of government? How were its reforms revolutionary?

10. How can elections be seen as both an institution of representation and of coercion?

11. What lessons did the French Revolution provide for rulers and citizens?

12. Describe why democratic institutions changed citizens' views of government.

13. One way to compare governments is to note if they have a written constitution and a democratic form of government. What do such characteristics reveal and conceal? What other nations besides the United States might fit into this category?

14. One might argue that coercion is something in which all governments engage. Provide a definition and examples. How might you distinguish coercion from oppression, tyranny, influence, or manipulation? Provide examples and support your arguments.

15. Why did the bourgeoisie favor restraints on the power of government? Why was this considered radical at the time?

16. How much influence do elections in the United States provide citizens? How might you measure influence?

17. Why is popular support so important with respect to foreign and domestic policy? Under what conditions, perhaps, is it not so important?

18. Note the relationship between the power of rulers and citizens in representative governments. How might you assess the power of each?
19. What fears of government do people have? How has representative government (and its institutions) changed these perceptions?
20. What is the relationship between freedom and power in America? Include a definition of both freedom and power.

KEY TERMS

The following are key terms. Define or identify each. Where appropriate, include examples and illustrations. Note such items as the originator of the term, his or her major work and argument, and/or the people a given policy or document affected.

Coercion	Conscription
Representation	Power

ANNOTATED BIBLIOGRAPHY

Bendix, Reinhard, *Nation-Building and Citizenship* (New York: Wiley, 1964). In this comprehensive survey of authority relationships within various national societies since the Middle Ages, Bendix highlights the determinants of social and political change.

Dahl, Robert A., *Democracy and Its Critics* (New Haven, CT: Yale University Press, 1989). Dahl conducts a dialogue of reason in his discussion of the major ideas and arguments in the field of democratic theory broadly defined. The overarching historical thrust of his analysis is the progression of three major transformations of democarcy.

Hartz, Louis, *The Liberal Tradition in America* (New York: Harcourt, Brace, 1955). One of the most influential theorists of the consensus school of American politics, Hartz contends that the absence of a feudal past explains why no mass-based Socialist trade unions or political parties ever developed in the United States and why liberalism has always been America's dominant ideology.

Huntington, Samuel P., *American Politics: The Promise of Disharmony* (Cambridge, MA: Harvard University Press, 1981). This book examines the role that political ideas and moral causes have played in American politics, and argues that the gap between America's ideals and reality has engendered political disharmony.

Moore, Barrington, *Social Origins of Dictatorship and Democracy* (Boston: Beacon Press, 1966). Moore provides a comparative analysis of the political roles of the landed upper classes and peasantry in six countries during each country's transformation from an agrarian society to a modern industrial one. His aim is to determine which historical conditions contribute to the emergence of parliamentary democracies or totalitarian states.

de Tocqueville, Alexis, *Democracy in America* (New York: Random House, 1945). Tocqueville came to the United States in 1831 intending to investigate the country's prisons and instead wrote what is probably the most insightful and prescient survey of American institutions and culture ever composed by a foreign observer. His discussion of the tensions inherent in American democracy has made this work a classic in political philosophy as well.

Wolin, Sheldon S., *The Presence of the Past: Essays on the State and the Constitution* (Baltimore: Johns Hopkins University Press, 1989). Wolin's work is intended as a contribution to the renewed democratic discourse that must confront the meaning of the state and of its cohabitation with corporate power. His theme is that meaningful politics is public discourse over how power is to be used.

CHAPTER 2

Constructing a Government: The Founding and the Constitution

CHAPTER OUTLINE

I. The First Founding: Interests and Conflicts
   A. Beginning in the 1750s, British tax and trade policies started to split the colonial elite according to interests, and set into motion a chain of events that culminated in the American Revolution.
   B. The Declaration of Independence was an attempt to identify and articulate a history and set of principles that might help to forge national unity.
   C. The Articles of Confederation, the United States' first written constitution adopted in November 1777, was primarily concerned with limiting the powers of the central government.
II. The Second Founding: From Compromise to Constitution
   A. International weakness and domestic economic concerns led to the Annapolis Convention in the fall of 1786, which was the first step toward the second founding.
   B. Fifty-five delegates from every state except Rhode Island attended the Constitutional Convention in Philadelphia in May 1787, where they committed themselves to a second founding.
      1. The framers of the Constitution married interest and principle as they sought to create a new government capable of promoting commerce and protecting property from radical state legislatures.
      2. The Great Compromise created the United States' bicameral legislature based on two different principles of representation.
      3. The Three-fifths Compromise addressed the question of slavery by apportioning the seats in the House of Representatives according to a "population" in which five slaves would count as three persons.
III. The Constitution
   A. The Congress was designed to contribute to governmental power, promote popular consent for the new government, and limit the popular political currents that many of the framers saw as a radical threat to the economic and social order.
   B. The framers of the Constitution hoped to create an executive branch that would make the federal government capable of

timely and decisive action in response to public issues and problems.

C. The establishment of the Supreme Court reflected the framers' preoccupation with nationalizing governmental power and checking radical democratic impulses, while guarding against potential interference with liberty and property from the new national government itself.

D. The framers addressed national unity and power by establishing several comity clauses in the Constitution intended to promote unobstructed national and international movement of persons and goods.

E. The Constitution requires a two-thirds vote in Congress and adoption by three-fourths of the states in order for it to be amended.

F. The Constitution also provides rules for its ratification.

G. In order to guard against possible misuse and abuse of national governmental power, the framers incorporated separation of powers, the principle of federalism, and a bill of rights into the Constitution.

1. The separation of powers is based on the political principle that power must be used to balance power.

2. Federalism is a system of two sovereigns—the states and the nation—where each serves as a limitation on the power of the other.

3. Although originally intended to be a part of the Constitution itself, the Bill of Rights was adopted as the first ten amendments in 1791 to further limit the power of government.

IV. The Fight for Ratification

V. Reflections on the Founding

STUDY QUESTIONS

1. Heroism and divine providence founded the United States. Do you agree?

2. Discuss the political conflict of planters, merchants, and royalists against farmers, shopkeepers, and laborers. What were each group's resources and methods to achieve its respective goals?

3. How did Britain divide the above groups? What British policies changed and intensified the above conflict? What were Britain's interests?

4. What economic problems faced Britain in the 1760s? What policy did Britain employ to solve its troubles?

5. Discuss the Stamp Act of 1765. Why did Britain impose the act? Whom did it affect most? How did it influence the merchants and planters?

6. Who was the leader of the radical shopkeepers, artisans, and laborers? What course of action did he favor?

7. What was the important effect of the Boston Tea Party? What myths regarding this event should be dispelled and why?

8. What political events precipitated the First Continental Congress? What interests were represented? What measures were pursued by this group?

9. What was the Declaration of Independence? Who wrote it? What values were implicit and explicit in it? Whose interests did it represent? Support your answer to the last question with an argument.

10. Describe the Articles of Confederation. What did they say about the relationship between the national, state, and local governments? Why did they fail?

11. What functions did the Articles of Confederation outline for the national government?

12. Compare the relationship between the United Nations and its member states with that between the U.S. Congress and the individual states.

13. What is the "Second Founding"? Why is this term an appropriate description?

14. What was the Annapolis Convention? How did it differ from the Philadelphia Convention of 1787?

15. What contributions did Alexander Hamilton make to the founding of the United States?

16. What was Shays's Rebellion? What social groups were in conflict? How was the conflict put to rest?

17. Why did Shays's Rebellion help bring about a new Constitution?

18. How and why did the framers of the Constitution avoid the issue of slavery? Why didn't they abolish this institution?

19. What was James Madison's greatest contribution to the founding of the United States?

20. What was Randolph's motion?

21. Why is the Connecticut Compromise called the Great Compromise?

22. What was the "Three-fifths Compromise"? What is its political significance?

23. Define the following key terms: bicameralism, checks and balances, indirect election, and federalism. How are they related?

24. What does Article I of the Constitution establish?

25. Which branch of the national government was designed to be the most democratic and responsive to the people? Note the role of the other branches, and specify to what degree they are or are not responsive.

26. What did the framers mean by "excessive democracy"? What were their concerns? How did they design the national government to avoid "excessive democracy"?

27. What does the doctrine of expressed power do? In your opinion, how has it been used or abused? Support your answer with examples.

28. What did *McCulloch* v. *Maryland* establish?

29. What constitutional provisions prevent states from interfering with commerce?

30. What powers does Article II of the Constitution grant the president?

31. What powers does Article III of the Constitution grant the Supreme Court?

32. What is judicial review?

33. What are the provisions in Article IV of the Constitution that promote a national market for commerce?

34. In the Constitution, what is the relationship between the national, state, and local governments?

35. To what does the "supremacy clause" in Article VI of the Constitution refer?

36. During the First Congress, the national government assumed all revolutionary-period state debts. Why was this significant?

37. How did the Constitution differ from the Articles of Confederation?

38. How many amendments to the Constitution have been adopted since 1791?

39. Discuss how the Bill of Rights, federalism, and separation of powers are limitations on the national government. What are they designed to limit? Why are limitations on the national government so important?

40. Provide examples of checks and balances.

41. Define "separation of powers."

42. Define "federalism."

43. How does the Constitution establish property, commerce, and a strong national government? Why are these important? How do they compare to the ideals of the Declaration of Independence?

44. Discuss the political role of taxes. How did Britain's policies influence American merchants?

45. In broad terms, compare and contrast the Declaration of Independence and the Constitution. Each is an example of what?

46. What clause in the Constitution permitted the national government to levy taxes? Why was the issue of taxation so important?

KEY TERMS

The following are key terms. Define or identify each. Where appropriate, include examples and illustrations. Note such items as the originator of the term, his or her major work and argument, and/or the people a given policy or document affected.

Shay's Rebellion
First Continental Congress
Stamp Act of 1765
McCulloch v. *Maryland* (1819)
Annapolis Convention
Samuel Adams
James Madison
Senate
Judicial Review
Boston Tea Party
Bill of Rights
Article II
Bicameralism

Articles of Confederation
Virginia Plan
Doctrine of Expressed Power
Barron v. *Baltimore* (1833)
Alexander Hamilton
Presidency
House of Representatives
Federalism
Three-fifths Compromise
Supremacy Clause
Article I
Article III
Connecticut Compromise
   or Great Compromise

ANNOTATED BIBLIOGRAPHY

Bailyn, Bernard, *Ideological Origins of the American Revolution* (Cambridge, MA: Harvard University Press, 1967). In response to political realist and determinist explanations for the causes of the American Revolution, Bailyn resurrects and refines the idealist interpretation, which emphasizes the primary role of ideas and values in sparking the outbreak of the war against Britain.

Hamilton, Alexander; James Madison; and John Jay, *The Federalist*, ed. Isaac Kramnick (New York: Viking Press, 1987). This collection of essays in support of ratification of the Constitution remains the essential starting point for understanding the origins of American government. The introduction of this edition offers a particularly insightful review of the debate between Federalists and Anti-Federalists.

Reid, John Phillip, *The Concept of Liberty in the Age of the American Revolution* (Chicago: University of Chicago Press, 1988). The author's focus is on the legal interpretations of liberty. Reid's book is a logical outgrowth of works by Rossiter, Bailyn, and Wood in that it directs attention to the need for a more profound understanding of the language that expresses the ideology of liberty.

Wills, Gary, *Explaining America* (New York: Doubleday, 1981). This probing study of *The Federalist Papers* analyzes the intellectual influences that shaped the ideas of Hamilton, Madison, and Jay.

Wood, Gordon S., *The Creation of the American Republic* (New York: W. W. Norton, 1969). This detailed work traces the development of political thought in colonial America and its influence upon the Constitution. Wood is mainly interested in delineating the determinative role of ideas amidst the relevant social and political structures of the period.

CHAPTER 3

The Constitutional Framework: Federalism and the Separation of Powers

CHAPTER OUTLINE

I. Introduction: Contract as the American Approach to Legitimacy
  A. Federalism is the principle that recognizes and affirms the coexistence of two separate and independent sovereigns, the national government and the state governments.
  B. The separation of powers seeks to limit the power of the national government by dividing it against itself—giving the legislative, executive, and judicial branches separate functions.
  C. The principle of individual rights seeks to limit government by granting to each individual an identity in opposition to government itself.
II. The First Principle: The Federal Framework
  A. Under the traditional system of dual federalism, which lasted from 1789 until 1937, most of the functions of the rather weak national government were aimed at assisting commerce, while the policies and functions of state governments directly coerced citizens.
  B. Until the Supreme Court reversed its position in 1937, the principle of federalism operated as a restraint on the federal government's ability to use the concept of interstate commerce to regulate the economy directly.
  C. After 1937, the national government began to expand, but in a way which did not effect the distribution of power between the two dual sovereign systems of government.
    1. The notion of local governments was created by state governments as a bureaucratic convenience and is not mandated by the federal Constitution.
    2. The national government began to exert more influence on state and local governments through the use of grants-in-aid.
      a. Categoric grants are those that must be used for a specific problem or to benefit a particular group.
      b. The modern principle of cooperative federalism reflects the strategic use of grants to encourage states and localities to pursue nationally defined goals.
      c. Revenue sharing is a scheme that allocates national revenues to states according to a population and income

formula, rather than as an attempt to intervene in states' affairs.

III. The Second Principle: The Separation of Powers
   A. Checks and Balances are the principle by which separate institutions of government share power with each other.
   B. The Constitution provides for legislative supremacy within the system of separated powers.
IV. Changing the Framework: Constitutional Amendment
   A. Between 1789 and 1979, 9100 constitutional amendments were proposed, but only 26 were eventually ratified because much more than majority support is required for constitutional change.
   B. The Equal Rights Amendment is one of the few proposals that achieved the necessary two-thirds vote in Congress and then failed to obtain the support of thirty-eight states.
   C. A successful constitutional amendment is one that is concerned with the structure or composition of the government itself.

STUDY QUESTIONS

1. What is the relationship between interests and principles in political life?
2. What is "legitimacy"?
3. The American Constitution's legitimacy is based on contract. Explain this.
4. Relate the following: federalism, separation of powers, and individual rights. Describe how federalism, separation of powers, and a written constitution limit the power of the national government.
5. Define the principle of federalism.
6. How does the Tenth Amendment reaffirm the principle of federalism?
7. What fundamental principle of American government tries to ensure that no single individual or branch of government can accumulate too much political power?
8. Discuss the separation of powers as it relates to legislative, executive, and judicial functions.
9. Federalism deals with the relationships between state and national governments, between the various state governments, and it concerns itself with the economic power of the central authority. Discuss these relationships and note why they are of major concern to political leaders.
10. To what does "dual sovereignty" refer?
11. What is the traditional system of government as defined by the authors?

12. Why did the traditional system of weak national government prevail for over a century?
13. Describe the roles of state and national banking legislation. How do they differ?
14. How is private property affected by state and national laws?
15. What is dealt with at the state level of government? Compare the types of regulation that come from state and national governments.
16. What role did state governments play in the traditional system?
17. If you were asked to assess the formal intentions of the founders concerning the relation between state and national governing, how would you respond? How does this relate to the traditional system?
18. Discuss the ways in which federalism helps maintain political stability.
19. Why was *McCulloch* v. *Maryland* (1819) important? In answering, note the relationship between state and national laws.
20. Describe why *Gibbons* v. *Ogden* (1824) was important. What did it establish about interstate commerce? Relate it to the regulatory power of the national government, transportation, and the production of goods.
21. What Supreme Court case marked the end of the Court's restrictions on the national government's efforts to reach local conditions?
22. Discuss the political role of local governments. Note why they originally developed and their status within the U.S. Constitution.
23. Local laws existed to apply state laws to local conditions. Provide examples.
24. What enabled cities and some counties to adopt local charters?
25. What are appropriations of national government revenues to state or local governments that must be used in accordance with conditions set by Congress?
26. What originated in nineteenth-century cash and land grants to states, reduced the disparity between rich and poor states, and limited change in state administrative patterns?
27. With respect to grants-in-aid, discuss the relationship between Congress and local governments. How often were grants-in-aid distributed to local governments and under what conditions? When did grants-in-aid begin to be used more frequently?
28. Compare grants-in-aid to block grants.
29. According to Madison, how and why were the branches of government to be separated?
30. Relate checks and balances to the principle of separation of powers and to the workings of the different branches of government.
31. Provide examples of checks and balances.
32. Within the system of separated powers, the framers anticipated legislative supremacy. Why?
33. What was the power relationship between Congress and the presidency in the nineteenth century?

34. How did national conventions to nominate presidential candidates change the power relationship between Congress and presidents?
35. Describe the legislative power of Congress, and relate it to the power of the president. Why did the separation of powers between the president and Congress work in the negative sense during the nineteenth century?
36. Discuss the Supreme Court's propensity to review the constitutionality of state laws. Why is this an important issue for study?
37. What is statutory interpretation?
38. Is the Constitution difficult to amend? What types of amendments have been passed? What does each type reveal about the U.S. government and its structure?
39. Describe the methods of amending the Constitution. How many amendments have been added to the Constitution since the Bill of Rights?
40. Discuss the Bill of Rights. Note when it was adopted and how it related to each of the three branches of government.
41. What was the only amendment that addressed a specific social issue and was later repealed?
42. What do all the existing amendments to the Constitution concern? What does this reveal about constitutions in general?
43. By whom and how was the Equal Rights Amendment defeated?
44. What is a good constitution?
45. Why has the American Constitution endured for so many years?

KEY TERMS

The following are key terms. Define or identify each. Where appropriate, include examples and illustrations. Note such items as the originator of the term, his or her major work and argument, and/or the people a given policy or document affected.

Traditional System
Federalism
Duel Sovereignty
Grant-in-Aid
Commercial Republic
Substantive Social Problems
Gibbons v. *Ogden* (1824)
Judicial Review
Structure of Federal Government

Founding
Sovereignty
Separation of Powers
State Government
McCulloch v. *Maryland* (1819)
Presidency
Congress
New Deal

ANNOTATED BIBLIOGRAPHY

Anton, Thomas, *American Federalism and Public Policy: How the System Works* (Philadelphia: Temple University Press, 1989). Anton's major focus is on actions taken by public officials as they craft and implement public policy. Based on a general scrutiny of the federal system, he offers only very guarded optimism for the future of government policy.

Bowman, Ann O'M, and Richard Kearney, *The Resurgence of the States* (Englewood Cliffs, NJ: Prentice-Hall, 1986). This book challenges the view that state governments have become minor actors in the American political system by presenting thoroughly documented evidence of state innovation in various policy areas and increased citizen participation in state politics.

Elazar, Daniel J., *The American Constitutional Tradition* (Lincoln, NE: University of Nebraska Press, 1988). Elazar's volume is a collection of essays about federalism. Through an exploration of several different themes, most importantly federalism as covenant, the author addresses the dangers of an excessive individualism in the United States today.

Peterson, Paul; Barry Rabe; and Kenneth K. Wong, *When Federalism Works* (Washington, DC: The Brookings Institution, 1986). The authors begin with an overview of federalism in the United States today and then consider whether various programs for education, health care, and housing are directed toward groups in need. The book stresses the part of policy professionals in predicting the success of such programs while criticizing the intrusive activities of politicians.

Wright, Deil S., *Understanding Intergovernmental Relations*, 2nd ed. (Monterey, CA: Brooks/cole Publishing Co., 1982). This comprehensive treatise examines the dynamics of federalism, emphasizing its practice and problems.

The Constitution and the Individual: The Bill of Rights, Civil Liberties, and Civil Rights

CHAPTER OUTLINE

I. Introduction
  A. Substantive limits are restraints on what the government shall and shall not have power to do, while procedural limits deal with how the government is supposed to act.
  B. Civil Rights are obligations imposed on government to take affirmative action to protect citizens from the illegal actions of other private citizens and government agencies.
II. Civil Liberties: Nationalizing the Bill of Rights
  A. Americans enjoy dual citizenship because each is a citizen of the national government as well as a citizen of one of the states.
  B. Although the Fourteenth Amendment is now accepted as nationalizing the Bill of Rights, the Supreme Court did not adopt this view until more than one hundred years after its ratification.
  C. The Second Constitutional Revolution began with the *Brown* decision in 1954, at which time the Supreme Court started actively incorporating the Bill of Rights into the Fourteenth Amendment.
  D. Chief Justice Earl Warren precipitated the Second Constitutional Revolution and charted the Supreme Court's subsequent direction, which was continued by his replacement, Warren Burger, until 1988, when William Rehnquist became Chief Justice.
    1. The Burger Court gave opinions of the Warren Court more conservatively interpretations, especially in the areas of police freedom and defendants' rights.
    2. The Burger Court expanded the Second Constitutional Revolution to women by establishing a right to privacy, and rendering unconstitutional all state laws making abortion a crime.
III. Civil Rights
  A. From 1896 until the end of World War II, the Supreme Court held that the Fourteenth Amendment's equal protection clause was not violated by racial distinction as long as the facilities were equal.
  B. After World War II, the Supreme Court began to undermine the

separate but equal doctrine, eventually declaring it unconstitutional in *Brown* v. *Board of Education of Topeka, Kansas.*
C. The *Brown* decision marked only the beginning of a difficult battle for equal protection in education, employment, housing, voting, and other areas of social and economic activity.
   1. The first phase of school desegregation was met with such massive resistance in the South that, ten years after *Brown*, less than one percent of black children were attending schools with whites.
   2. In 1971, the Supreme Court held that state-imposed desegregation could be brought about by busing children across school districts.
   3. Title VII of the Civil Rights Act of 1964 outlawed job discrimination by all private and public employers, including governmental agencies, that employed more than fifteen workers.
D. Prior to any discernable positive effect of equality opinions and laws, the politics of rights spread to increasing numbers of groups in society and expanded its goal to include the notion of affirmative action.

STUDY QUESTIONS

1. What are civil rights?
2. What are civil liberties?
3. Compare the original conception of the Bill of Rights with how we now perceive it.
4. Why is *Barron* v. *Baltimore* (1833) an important Supreme Court case? What political issue did it settle? Refer to the Fifth Amendment and dual citizenship.
5. Relate dual citizenship to the consequences of the Civil War.
6. Discuss the Fourteenth Amendment with relation to newly freed blacks.
7. Why is the "nationalization" of the Bill of Rights important?
8. Describe the importance of the Bill of Rights and what the authors refer to as the Second Constitutional Revolution. When did the Second Constitutional Revolution begin?
9. Explain how the Fourteenth Amendment affected the guarantee of civil liberties and the protection of civil rights.
10. What was the only change in civil liberties in the sixty years following the adoption of the Fourteenth Amendment?
11. To what does "strict construction" refer?
12. What did the Burger Court contribute to the Second Constitutional

Revolution? Discuss the Burger Court's rulings on the following issues: right to privacy and procedural rights of criminal defendants.

13. Discuss the implications of *Roe* v. *Wade* (1973) with respect to abortion, the right to privacy, and the Constitution. Have there been any changes to that decision? If so, what are they based on?

14. What term describes the action whereby unreasonable criteria are used to exclude certain people from the effects of the law?

15. Why was *Brown* v. *Board of Education of Topeka* (1954) important? Compare *Brown* to *Plessy* v. *Ferguson* and state policy regarding discrimination in law. How did *Brown* affect the national government's power to intervene in local governments, schools, and the workplace?

16. Which president brought the issue of discrimination to the attention of the national public? Note how the President's Committee on Civil Rights attempted to use the government to end segregation and discrimination.

17. What is a "restrictive covenant"?

18. How did *Brown* v. *Board of Education of Topeka* (1954) intensify the conflict between the states and the national government? Provide examples of state laws that circumvented federal rules, and discuss President Eisenhower's reasons for sending federal troops to Little Rock in 1957.

19. How effective was *Brown* v. *Board of Education of Topeka* (1954) in eliminating segregation in the South? Why did it take so long? What actions were taken when it was clear that the courts alone couldn't solve the problem of segregation?

20. Discuss the impact of the Rehnquist Court on civil liberties and civil rights.

21. What constitutional phrase came to be interpreted broadly, giving Congress the power to end discrimination in the workplace?

22. What other groups, besides blacks, have successfully claimed the right not to be discriminated against?

23. Define and describe the "politics of rights."

24. Which case introduced what is commonly referred to as "reverse discrimination"? What was that case about?

25. What do both opponents and supporters of affirmative action argue with respect to the relationship between the individual and the group?

26. How did the Rehnquist Court change the way job discrimination cases will be decided in the future?

27. Discuss the relationship between the Constitution and individuals' political rights. How does the Constitution help ensure an individual's rights?

28. Describe the increase or decrease in scope and definition of civil rights during the Warren era of the Supreme Court.

29. What case was the Supreme Court's first step towards an active role in affirming civil rights?

30. Discuss the stability of the interpretations of the Constitution and note how this is fundamental to individuals' political rights.

KEY TERMS

The following are key terms. Define or identify each. Where appropriate, include examples and illustrations. Note such items as the originator of the term, his or her major work and argument, and/or the people a given policy or document affected.

Dual Citizenship

William Rehnquist

Civil Liberties

De jure

First Amendment

Fourteenth Amendment (1868)

Barron v. *Baltimore* (1833)

Plessy v. *Ferguson* (1896)

First Constitutional Revolution

Nationalization of the Bill of Rights

Brown v. *Board of Education of Topeka* (1954)

Strict Construction

Separate but Equal

Earl Warren

Civil Rights

De facto

Warren Burger

Roe v. *Wade* (1973)

Second Constitutional Revolution

Federalism

Regents of the University of California v. *Bakke* (1978)

ANNOTATED BIBLIOGRAPHY

Brigham, John, *Civil Liberties and American Democracy* (Wasington, DC: Congressional Quarterly Press, 1984). In discussing freedom of expression, press, speech, due process, and property rights, Brigham explores the inherent tension between democracy and the Supreme Court's protection of individual rights.

Hentoff, Nat, *The First Freedom: The Tumultuous History of Free Speech in America* (New York: Delacorte, 1980). Hentoff provides a fascinating account of the evolution of freedom of speech from the trial of colonial printer John Peter Zenger to the Nazi marches in Skokie, Illinois.

Lewis, Anthony, *Gideon's Trumpet* (New York: Vintage, 1964). This book follows the story of a Florida indigent, Clarence Gideon, as he fought from behind prison bars for the right to be defended by an attorney. Lewis's account of the case also offers an illuminating description of how the Supreme Court operates.

Rabkin, Jeremy, *Judicial Compulsions: How Public Law Distorts Public Policy* (New York: Basic Books, 1989). Rabkin argues for a return to the traditional, limited role of the courts in federal policymaking where responsibility for policymaking is held by politically accountable policymakers.

Silberman, Charles, *Criminal Violence, Criminal Justice* (New York: Random House, 1978). This comprehensive work illustrates how recent attempts to reform the criminal justice system have turned out to be counter-productive. Special attention is devoted to the rights of the accused and juvenile offenders.

CHAPTER 5

Congress: The First Branch

CHAPTER OUTLINE

I. Making Law
   A. The Framers of the Constitution provided for a bicameral legislature, a legislature body consisting of 2 chambers.
   B. The House of Representatives and Senate play different roles in the legislative process and represent somewhat different forces in American political life.
II. Political Parties: Congress's Oldest Hierarchy
   A. Parties play an important role in the House of Representatives where the elected leader of the majority party becomes Speaker of the House.
   B. Although either the vice-president of the United States or a president pro tempore is the ceremonial presiding officer of the Senate, it is the majority and minority leaders together that actually control the calendar.
   C. Party discipline, or influence by party leaders over the behavior of their party members, is still an important factor in congressional voting despite the decline of strict party voting.
      1. Modern party leaders have regularly relied upon a set of resources to help secure the support of party members.
         a. Committee assignments are one important long-term resource that leaders use to create a bond of obligation.
         b. The Speaker of the House and majority leader of the Senate control access to the floors because they possess the power of recognition.
         c. The whip system, which is primarily a communications network, is essential to creating and maintaining party unity in both houses of Congress.
         d. Logrolling, an agreement between two or more members of Congress who have nothing in common except the need for support, is another party resource that creates obligations between members.
         e. The influence of the presidency is probably the most important of all the resources that maintain party discipline in Congress.

III. The Committee System: The Core of Congress
   A. The committee system provides Congress with a second
   organizational structure that is more a division of labor than the
   party-based hierarchy of power.
   B. Power struggles over committee chairs have become more
   apparent since the 1971 rule changes, which loosened constraints
   upon advancement formerly imposed by the congressional
   seniority system.
IV. The Staff System: Staffers and Agencies
   A. Individual senators and representatives have personal staff that
   serve them specifically by dealing with constituency requests and,
   increasingly, with the details of legislative and administrative
   oversight.
   B. Congress also employs permanent committee staffers who are
   responsible for organizing and administering the committees'
   work.
   C. Congress has also established four staff agencies designed to
   provide the legislative branch with resources and expertise—the
   Congressional Research Service, the General Accounting Office,
   the Office of Technology Assessment, and the Congressional
   Budget Office.
V. Informal Organization: The Caucuses
VI. Rules of Lawmaking: How a Bill Becomes a Law
   A. Committee deliberation, which typically includes subcommittee
   referral and expert testimony, is necessary before floor action on
   any bill.
   B. After a bill is reported out of both a "subject matter" committee
   and the Rules Committee (in the House), it is placed on one of
   the House or Senate calendars.
   C. Debate in the House is controlled by a bill's sponsor, its leading
   opponent, and the Rules Committee, while Senate debate is
   unlimited and controlled less by the leadership.
   D. Bills on the floor of the House or the Senate are subject to both
   debate and amendment.
   E. Conferences are often required to reconcile House and Senate
   versions of bills that began with similar provisions, but emerged
   with little resemblance to each other.
   F. After a bill is adopted by the House and Senate, it goes to the
   president, who may choose to sign the bill into law or veto it and
   risk legislative override.
   G. The rules of congressional procedures influence the fate of every
   bill and help to determine the distribution of power in Congress.
VII. Beyond Legislation: Additional Congressional Powers
   A. The making of statutes is the only means given to Congress by
   the Constitution to use the enumerated powers of the national
   government.
   B. Because it is difficult to draft and pass statutes clear in wording

and intent, Congress has increasingly relied on legislative oversight of administrators.

C. The Senate also has the additional power of granting advice and consent to the president regarding treaties and appointments.

D. Congressional debate is often important as a record of legislative intent that can have great influence over administrative conduct.

E. The modern Congress functions by direct committee government, which is the practice of delegating certain powers from the whole Congress to one of its committees.

F. The legislative veto is an important source of power because it allows Congress to legislate in a roundabout way by enacting statutes that require congressional approval of presidential actions.

G. Pork barrel legislation, private bills, and intervention with federal administrative agencies are examples of the most effective forms of direct patronage for constituents available to members of Congress.

VIII. Congress and the Future: The Fall and Rise of Congressional Power

A. During the first century of American government, Congress was more powerful than the Executive branch.

B. The New Deal marked the beginning of a change in the balance of power as the executive branch became the more accessible, hospitable and dominant branch of American government.

C. Recently, the balance of power between Congress and the executive branch has oscillated in reaction to domestic and international events.

STUDY QUESTIONS

1. What was the United State's central policy-making institution until the twentieth century?

2. How do the House and Senate differ in regard to their constituencies, their length of terms, their members' relations to locally entrenched interests, and their electoral politics and procedures?

3. Whom were the Senate and House designed to represent respectively in society?

4. What does the Constitution say about Congress' reliance on party organization and committees?

5. Why are committee assignments the most important decisions political parties make in Congress?

6. Describe the following positions in the House of Representatives: Speaker, the majority leader, the chief whip, and chair of the majority caucus.
7. How are leaders in the House of Representatives selected?
8. What does the House Steering and Policy Committee do?
9. What does the president pro tempore of the Senate do?
10. What is the most important role in the Senate? Why?
11. Compare the House and Senate with respect to debates and amendments. Why has the Senate traditionally allowed more floor debate and amendments to bills than the House of Representatives?
12. Why is party membership a poor predictor of how congressmen and congresswomen will vote?
13. Discuss committee assignments, access to the floor, and logrolling as examples of leadership resources. How are they in fact resources?
14. Why is access to the floor the most important resource available to leaders on a daily basis?
15. What congressional system provides a communications network for party leaders, polls members to see how they'll vote on specific bills, and puts pressure on party members when leaders expect a close vote?
16. What is the agreement whereby two or more members of Congress agree to trade votes on different bills?
17. How does the president affect party discipline in Congress?
18. How did the parties in the House begin to reassert themselves during the 1970s?
19. In what ways are committee members responsible to the president, committee chairs, party leaders, and the electorate?
20. How many standing committees are in the House and Senate combined?
21. Describe standing committees. Note their status, rules governing membership and staff, and jurisdictions.
22. What does the House Rules Committee do?
23. How are bills assigned to committees?
24. How have most standing committees developed their jurisdictions?
25. How are committee assignments determined?
26. What determines who chairs a committee?
27. How many staff people do members of the House and Senate employ?
28. What do the staff agencies attached to Congress do for the representatives and senators?
29. Why is the seniority system in Congress so important?
30. Why did Congress begin to impose stricter rules on access to the floor, on debate, and on attendance?
31. What is a cloture rule?
32. When does a bill receive floor action?
33. How do party caucuses form and what do they do?
34. What must happen before a bill becomes a law?

35. What are the president's legislative resources?
36. Compare and contrast a presidential veto and the refusal of a president to sign a bill.
37. To what does legislative liaison refer?
38. On what does the president's success in pushing his legislative agenda through Congress depend?
39. Discuss how the congressional investigation of the Iran-Contra affair demonstrates how Congress can use its investigating power to prevent the president from pursuing a legislative agenda.
40. What has added to Congress' loss of real power?
41. What is "legiscide"?
42. Congress' resurgence in the 1960s and 1970s can be traced to the rise of new groups and forces in American society that have used Congress as an institutional base. Give examples of some new groups and forces.
43. What does the War Powers Act of 1973 do? Did Ronald Reagan violate this act when he ordered the attacks on Grenada and Libya? Why or why not?
44. Note how the following represent congressional efforts to regain power in the 1970s: the writing of specific statutes that allowed very little discretion, the investigation of Watergate, and the Budget and Impoundment Act of 1974.
45. In recent years, Congress has gained more power relative to the executive branch. Why?

KEY TERMS

The following are key terms. Define or identify each. Where appropriate, include examples and illustrations. Note such items as the originator of the term, his or her major work and argument, and/or the people a given policy or document affected.

Investigation	Committee
Private Bill	Hearings
Constituency Service	Advice and Consent
Legislative Veto	Oversight
Committee Government	Political Party
Rules Committee	Johnson Rule
Speaker	President Pro Tempore
Vice-President	Party Whip
Veto	House of Representatives
Senate	Legislative Calendar
Cloture Rule	Party Regularity

Party Discipline

Logrolling

Patronage

Legislative Liaison

Standing Committees

Filibuster

Party Caucus

Seniority

Floor Access

Ad Hoc Committees

Steering and Policy Committee

ANNOTATED BIBLIOGRAPHY

Dodd, Lawrence, and Bruce J. Oppenheimer, eds., *Congress Reconsidered* (Washington, DC: Congressional Quarterly Press, 1988). This collection of essays assesses reforms of the 1970s which transformed the structure of congressional power and enabled Congress to reassert itself as a decisive actor in national politics. A key theme underlying the entire book concerns the capacity of Congress to play its constitutional part as the most democratic branch of government.

Fenno, Richard, *Homestyle: House Members in Their Districts* (Boston: Little, Brown, 1978). The focus of this work is upon the relationship between members of the House of Representatives and their constituents. By accompanying various representatives into their home districts, Fenno was able to compile unique data illuminating how representative democracies really function.

Fiorina, Morris, *Congress: Keystone of the Washington Establishment* (New Haven, CT: Yale University Press, 1977). The author asks why congressmen tend to be re-elected when the public image of Congress as an institution remains so poor. The key, Fiorina argues, is that the legislative activities of most representatives are consciously designed to boost their re-election possibilities.

Fisher, Louis, *The Politics of Shared Power: Congress and the Executive* (Washington, DC: Congressional Quarterly Press, 1981). Fisher demonstrates how legislative-executive relations have evolved within the context of separation of powers theory. The book is especially provocative when it delves into areas where the two branches often overlap, such as the legislative powers of the president, congressional control over bureaucratic activity, and the operations of independent regulatory commissions.

Longley, Lawrence D., and Walter J. Oleszek, *Bicameral Politics: Conference Committees in Congress* (New Haven, CT: Yale University Press, 1989). The authors present a comprehensive synthesis of research and commentary as they explore the question of "What goes on?" in congressional conference committees.

Mayhew, David R., *Congress: The Electoral Connection* (New Haven, CT: Yale University Press, 1974). Mayhew's concise book explores how members of Congress try to obtain re-election and how this preoccupation in turn influences individual effectiveness and institutional accountability.

Oleszek, Walter J., *Congressional Procedures and the Policy Process* (Washington, DC: Congressional Quarterly Press, 1983). The author demonstrates how congressional rules and procedures affect the course and content of legislation. An excellent, updated version of how a bill becomes a law.

Ornstein, Norman, *Interest Groups, Lobbying and Policymaking* (Washington, DC: Congressional Quarterly Press, 1978). A short but lively work utilizing three case studies to illustrate the increasing fragmentation of interests within the United States, the effectiveness of grass-roots participation, and the trend away from lobbying efforts directed solely at senior congressmen.

Ripley, Randall B., *Congress: Process and Policy*, 4th ed. (New York: W. W. Norton, 1988). This penetrating analysis examines the key internal forces at work in Congress—party leaders, committees, state delegations, staffs—as well as external forces that influence the lawmaking process, such as interest groups, constituents, the president, and the bureaucracy. Ripley's treatment of the congressional role in public policy making may be the most comprehensive available.

Smith, Steven S., *Call to Order: Floor Politics in the House and Senate* (Washington, DC: The Brookings Institution, 1989). Smith's institutional focus reveals a House and a Senate in which committee autonomy has frayed over the past two decades. As he conducts a detailed bicameral comparison, Smith examines the determinants of activism, pays close attention to the import of formal rules in the House, and analyzes the limited role of conference committees' ex post veto powers.

Sundquist, James L., *The Decline and Resurgence of Congress* (Washington, DC: The Brookings Institution, 1981). This historical appraisal of congressional-executive relations demonstrates how Congress delegated most of its authority to the president during much of this century, but then began to reassert its power in the early 1970s.

CHAPTER 6

The President and the Executive Branch

CHAPTER OUTLINE

I. The Constitutional Basis of the Presidency
  A. The president as head of state is defined by three constitutional provisions, which are the source of some of the most important powers on which the president can draw.
    1. The position of commander in chief makes the president the highest military authority in the United States, giving him control of the entire military establishment.
    2. The presidential power to grant reprieves, pardons, and amnesties involves the power of life and death over all individuals who may be a threat to the security of the United States.
    3. The power to receive ambassadors and other public ministers allows the president almost unconditional authority to determine whether a new ruling group can indeed commit their country to treaties and other agreements.
  B. The constitutional basis of the domestic presidency consists of the executive power, military sources of domestic presidential power, and the president's legislative power.
    1. The executive power requires that the president make sure all laws are executed faithfully, and that he appoint, remove, and supervise all executive officers, as well as appoint federal judges.
    2. Congress delegated by statute to the president as commander in chief the obligation to protect every state against invasion and domestic violence.
    3. The president's legislative power consists of the obligation to make recommendations for Congress' consideration and the ability to veto legislation.
II. The Rise of Presidential Government
  A. American government was dominated by Congress between 1800 and 1933, at which time the executive office played the secondary role anticipated by the Constitution.
  B. During the New Deal, Congress shifted the balance in favor of the executive office by delegating vast discretionary power to the president for the implementation of policy.
    1. Many New Deal programs expanded the traditional role of

national government by allowing it to intervene in economic life in ways that had been previously reserved to the states.

    2. Presidential power was enhanced by the New Deal's placement of new agencies and programs in the executive branch directly under presidential authority.

III. Presidential Government

  A. Presidents have at their disposal a variety of formal resources—such as the power to fill high-level political positions—that directly effect their ability to govern.

    1. Presidents have increasingly preferred the White House staff to the cabinet as their means of managing the gigantic executive branch.

    2. The White House staff, which is composed mainly of analysts and advisers, has grown from an informal group of fewer than a dozen people to a new presidential bureaucracy.

    3. The Executive Office of the President, often called the institutional presidency, is larger than the White House staff, and is comprised of the president's permanent management agencies.

    4. The vice-presidency is most valuable as a political resource for the president during elections.

  B. The president also has informal resources through which the powers of the executive office can be exercised.

    1. Initiative is an important resource because it allows the president to act decisively and formulate proposals for strategic policies.

    2. Although on the decline, the president's party is still significant as a means of achieving legislative success.

    3. Interest groups and coalitions are also a dependable resource for presidential government.

    4. Over the past half century, the American executive branch has so successfully harnessed mass popularity as a political resource that a plebiscitary presidency has developed.

IV. Bureaucracy in a Democracy

  A. The rise of presidential government means that our system depends upon the president as chief executive to establish and maintain a connection between policy goals and administration.

    1. Each expansion of the national government in the twentieth century has been accompanied by a parallel expansion of presidential management authority.

    2. The White House staff exercises some management control because its members have been given specialized jurisdictions over one or more departments.

  B. Although its legislative powers make Congress constitutionally essential to responsible bureaucracy, it has shifted its efforts from precise legislative drafting to oversight as it delegates more power to the president.

STUDY QUESTIONS

1. Explain how Article II of the Constitution establishes the presidency.
2. Discuss what the president's delegated powers are.
3. Describe what the president can do as the head of state. Note specifically his responsibilities for the nation's military, diplomatic, and judicial functions.
4. Compare and contrast executive agreements and treaties.
5. Discuss the War Powers Act of 1973. What social and political forces brought it into being? How does it change the institutional power relationship between the presidency and Congress?
6. Provide examples of recent presidential disregard for the War Powers Act.
7. Compare the president's roles as head of government and head of state.
8. Discuss the powers at the president's disposal to quell domestic unrest. Provide examples from American history.
9. To what does the power to impound refer?
10. Define the presidential veto. Provide examples.
11. What are the president's formal powers? How important is consent from the popular base to employ these powers?
12. What powers did the framers give to the Congress and the presidency? To which institution did they give more power?
13. Discuss the 1791 *Report on Manufactures*. Whose interests did it serve?
14. Discuss the status and power of the presidency in the nineteenth century with respect to the following: the power relationship between national and local governments, the national government's efforts to expand commerce, and the separation of the president from major national political and social forces.
15. Why did the presidency become stronger during the final years of the 1800s? What social movements took place? How did the advances in mass communications and the adoption of primary elections also play a part?
16. Note the significance of Franklin Roosevelt's "First Hundred Days" in office in 1933. What were the major New Deal programs enacted?
17. Discuss the New Deal. Focus upon the rapid and extensive growth in the size of the national government, the new functions taken on by the national government, and the coercive and regulatory relationship with both business and citizens.
18. What was the Supreme Court's initial reaction to the New Deal policies? What were the Court's justifications for its actions?
19. The New Deal can be seen as a turning point in American history. How did the balance of power between Congress and the presidency change at that time? Why?
20. What do the authors suggest is the equivalent of Roosevelt's first term in office?
21. Why did acts of delegation of power by Congress shift the American

national structure from a Congress-centered government to a president-centered government? Give some examples.

22. Most presidential appointees to the cabinet come from the president's circle of friends. What are the advantages and disadvantages of this process? Discuss why presidents have difficulty using their cabinets effectively.

23. Compare and contrast the American cabinet and parliamentary cabinets.

24. Explain the significance of the growth of the White House staff since 1937. How large is it? What benefits or problems do you see as a result?

25. Compare and contrast Bush and Reagan's White House staff.

26. What is the Executive Office of the President? Whom does it serve? What are its defined tasks? How does it compare to the White House staff?

27. What is the significance of the Gramm-Rudman-Hollings Act?

28. Discuss the role of the vice-president in both fact and theory. How much power does he have? What has been the historical role vice-presidents have played? Provide examples where necessary to illustrate your points. Don't forget to include a brief analysis of the role of the vice-president during elections.

29. To what does "legislative clearance" refer?

30. How can a president use his party as a political resource? What disadvantages might he face as a result?

31. Discuss the importance of interest groups as a possible presidential resource.

32. Explain the noticeable public opinion pattern affecting all presidents since Kennedy. Why has there been a gradual loss of popularity?

33. How was Ronald Reagan, once called the "teflon president," an exception?

34. Discuss the influence of international events on presidential popularity. Note how extended events lower his popularity, while short incidents boost it. Why do you think this is so?

35. Compare and contrast changes in patterns of public support for the president during the Carter and Reagan presidencies.

36. In what ways does George Bush reflect the peculiar nature of the presidency?

37. In what way is presidential behavior affected by public opinion?

38. What term can be used to describe the process whereby Congress handed over to the executive branch a big part of its constitutionally granted power? What powers were handed over? And what effects has this action had on the institutional relationship between the presidency and Congress?

39. How has Congress challenged the presidency's power over the last twenty-five years?

40. Define bureaucracy. What is the core principle of bureaucracy?

41. Why did President Reagan make significant cuts in the activity and

budget of regulatory agencies. What impact did this have on federal regulation in general?

42. Why is the framework of bureaucracy best to explain domestic agencies?

43. Why did the American national government begin to regulate economic and social affairs in the late 1800s? What events and social forces changed the role of government in U.S. politics?

44. Describe independent regulatory agencies. Why did Congress establish them? When were they created? And were they ever ruled unconstitutional?

45. How have regulated companies sometimes been able to turn regulatory programs to their advantage? What problems can (or did) result?

46. Why did regulatory agencies come under considerable public criticism during the 1970s? What are the social benefits of regulation? What are the costs?

47. Ronald Reagan extended and strengthened the power of the presidency to oversee proposed federal regulations. What effect has this had on the amount of regulation itself? Why?

48. What is the OMB?

49. To what does fiscal policy refer? What is the major agency of fiscal policy?

50. What is the function of the Federal Reserve System? Discuss how it regulates the supply of money in the economy, oversees the credit rating and lending activities of banks, and distributes money from areas of surplus to areas of demand.

51. Why is the power of the modern presidency primarily the power to commit?

52. Why was the Budget and Accounting Act of 1921 an important executive branch innovation?

53. How did President Reagan use centralization to accomplish decentralization.

54. Why has the White House staff increasingly performed the function of managing the federal bureaucracy for the president?

55. What is "congressional oversight"?

56. Describe the legislative veto.

57. What problems does congressional oversight cause?

58. If Congress were to make clear instead of vague delegations of power, this would improve the national government's political control over the federal bureaucracy itself. Why?

KEY TERMS

The following are key terms. Define or identify each. Where appropriate, include examples and illustrations. Note such items as the originator of the term, his or her major work and argument, and/or the people a given policy or document affected.

Fiscal Agency

Chief Justice

Bureaucracy

Regulation

Revenue Agency

Oversight

Article II

Executive Agreement

Cabinet

Domestic Policy

Congress

Hundred Days

Public Opinion

Diplomacy

Presidency

New Deal

Executive Office of the President

Bureaucratic Politics

Delegated Powers

Presidential Power

Deregulation

Welfare Agency

Regulatory Management

White House Staff

Article IV

Impoundment

In re Neagle (1890)

War Powers Act of 1973

Franklin Roosevelt

Legislative Veto

Legiscide

Fair Deal

International Incidents

ANNOTATED BIBLIOGRAPHY

Bryner, Gary C., *Bureaucratic Discretion* (New York: Pergamon Press, 1987). Four case studies of federal agencies form the center of this detailed look at bureaucratic regulation. Bryner argues that elaborate efforts over the past two decades to limit bureaucratic discretion have not only failed to do so, but have undermined the effectiveness of regulatory programs.

Heclo, Hugh, *A Government of Strangers* (Washington, DC: The Brookings Institution, 1977). "Executive politics" refers to the relationship between political appointees and high-level bureaucrats within administrative agencies. In exploring the realm of executive politics, Heclo's study ranges from consideration of daily organizational problems to issues of democratic theory.

Lowi, Theodore J., *The Personal President: Power Invested, Promise Unfulfilled* (Ithaca, NY: Cornell University Press, 1985). Lowi begins with an historical overview that follows the evolution of the presidency from a position of relative weakness in the nineteenth

century to one in which the president is now held solely accountable
for the performance of government. The book goes on to evaluate
the implications of what are inevitably dashed expectations.

Neustadt, Richard E., *Presidential Power and the Modern Presidents: The
Politics of Leadership from Roosevelt to Reagan,* rev. ed. (New York:
Free Press, 1990). Neustadt's look at the American President focuses
not on the office, but on the individual as one among many in a set
of institutions. Employing a series of case studies, he shows how
presidents actually use the resources of their office to exercise
power.

Pfiffner, James P., and Gordon R. Hoxie, eds., *The Presidency in Transition*
(New York: Center for the Study of the Presidency, 1989). The work
of distinguished contributors assesses the American presidency, its
organization and staffing, its relationship with Congress, the
processes of decision making, and the nation's priorities in both
foreign and domestic policies over the next four years and beyond.

Wilson, James Q., *Bureaucracy: What Government Agencies Do and Why They
Do It,* (New York: Basic Books, 1989). The essence of Wilson's book
is a description of the essential features of bureaucratic life in the
government agencies of the United States. He explores the impact
associated with different layers of employees in public bureaucracies.

CHAPTER 7

The Federal Courts: Least Dangerous Branch or Imperial Judiciary?

CHAPTER OUTLINE

I. The Judicial Process
  A. Most cases in the United States arise under common and civil law, two types of law that overlap.
    1. Common law has no statutory basis and is derived by judges from the application of previous case decisions to present cases.
    2. In the area of criminal law, either a state government or the federal government is the plaintiff and alleges that someone has committed a crime.
    3. Public law involves questions of whether the government has the constitutional or statutory authority to take action.
    4. An equity case is a court proceeding where the applicable law is either too rigid or too limited to provide a just as well as a legal remedy.
  B. Courts of original jurisdiction are the courts that are responsible for discovering the facts in a controversy and creating the record upon which a judgment is based.
    1. The jury is essential to the American concept of justice. Its role is to bring community values to bear in a trial, help weigh evidence, and decide who is culpable and to what degree.
    2. Although the adversary process has flaws, it does presume innocence in criminal cases and help preserve the equality of the contending parties in criminal as well as civil cases.
II. Federal Jurisdiction
  A. The federal district courts, of which there are 89, are trial courts of general jurisdiction and their cases are, in form, indistinguishable from cases in the state trial courts.
  B. The eleven United States Courts of Appeals review and render decisions in approximately ten percent of all lower court and agency cases.
  C. The Supreme Court is the highest court in the country, and it has the power and the obligation to review any lower court decision involving a substantial issue of public law, state legislation, and acts of Congress.
III. Judicial Review
  A. The Supreme Court's power to review acts of Congress, although

accepted as natural and rarely challenged, is not specifically granted by the Constitution.

B. The Supreme Court's power to review state action or legislation derives from the Constitution's supremacy clause, although it is neither granted specifically by the Constitution nor inherent in the federal system.

C. In an effort to insure that it hears only disputes involving high-level policy, the Supreme Court's appellate jurisdiction is strictly limited.

   1. The writ of *habeas corpus* is a fundamental safeguard of individual rights because it enables an accused to challenge arbitrary detention and force an open trial before a judge.

   2. A lower court decision may reach the Supreme Court on a writ of appeal if it involves an issue the Court believes is too important to return to a lower court for rehearing.

   3. Most cases reach the Supreme Court through the writ of *certiorari,* which is granted whenever four of the nine justices agree to review a case.

D. Many areas of civil and criminal law have been constructed through judicial review, and some are ultimately codified into legislative enactments.

IV. Influences on Supreme Court Decisions

A. The first influence is the individual members of the Supreme Court, their attitudes, and their relationships with each other.

   1. The assignment to write the majority opinion in an important constitutional case is an opportunity for the chosen justice to exercise great influence on the Court.

   2. The most dependable way an individual justice can exercise a direct and clear influence on the Court is to write a dissenting opinion.

B. The solicitor general has great influence over the work of the Supreme Court because he has the greatest control over the flow of cases.

C. The litigation that breaks out with virtually every social change produces a pattern of cases that eventually is recognized by the state and federal appellate courts.

V. Judicial Power and Politics

A. There have been two judicial revolutions since the Second World War, which have brought about substantive changes in judicial policy, as well as changes in judicial procedures that fundamentally expanded the power of the national judiciary.

STUDY QUESTIONS

1. What courts try the most cases each year?
2. What is the plaintiff?
3. What is common law?
4. What is civil law?
5. What is the doctrine of *stare decisis?*
6. Compare and contrast civil and common law.
7. What is the difference between criminal and common law?
8. Who is usually the plaintiff in criminal cases?
9. To what does public law refer?
10. Who is usually the defendant in a case involving public law?
11. What are appellate courts?
12. What is equity? When do courts rely on it? In what sense is it an escape from the laws?
13. What are injunctions? Provide examples.
14. What does "standing to sue" mean?
15. Discuss the following rules governing access to the Supreme Court: controversy, standing, and mootness.
16. What powers does a judge have over a jury?
17. Explain the adversary process. What are its virtues, problems, and advantages?
18. What did the case of *Gideon* v. *Wainwright* (1963) contribute to the judicial process?
19. What is the significance of *Miranda* v. *Arizona* (1966)?
20. What are appellate courts? Why are they important for lawmaking?
21. How does a court's refusal to take a case, in a sense, create law?
22. Certain courts have original jurisdiction over specific classes of cases. Provide examples of such courts and classes.
23. Discuss the Judiciary Act of 1789. What did it entail?
24. What is judicial review? What are its social and political implications? Provide examples.
25. With remedial legislation, Congress and state legislatures can reverse Supreme Court decisions. Explain this process.
26. Why has controversy arisen regarding judicial review of acts of Congress?
27. How did *Marbury* v. *Madison* (1803) influence the relationship between Congress and the Supreme Court?
28. Discuss the supremacy clause of Article VI of the Constitution. What right did it give the Supreme Court?
29. Define the following writs: appeal, *certiorari,* and *habeas corpus.* By which can one reach the Supreme Court?
30. What is judge-made law? How does it favor the status quo?
31. How do the attitudes of the justices, the activities of the solicitor general, and the pattern of cases affect the Supreme Court's impact on society?
32. Discuss the role of the Burger Court with respect to the issue of discrimination against women.

33. President Reagan filled one-third of the appointments to federal courts. What impact will this have?
34. What is the importance of a justice's dissenting opinion?
35. What strategy to bring cases before the courts have the NAACP and the ACLU employed in recent years?
36. What are *amicus curiae* briefs? Who determines who will file such briefs?
37. From what did the imperial judiciary result?
38. What is the role of the FBI in the Justice Department?
39. Provide examples of how social, economic, and political changes create new patterns of cases, and why interest groups try to use patterns as a strategy for getting their cases through the appeals process.
40. What institutional constraints are placed on federal courts? Explain rules of standing, limits of relief courts can provide, and the powers of the president and Congress to change the courts' size, composition, and jurisdiction.
41. Describe the policy changes initiated by the federal courts in the following areas: school desegregation, abortion, legislative apportionment, voting rights, criminal procedure, and free speech.
42. Relate how the Supreme Court expanded its power by liberalizing the concept of standing, widening the scope of relief, and using "structural remedies" to retain jurisdiction over cases after a decision. Give examples to support your analysis.
43. What is a class action?
44. What is the significance of the 1990 Supreme Court decision in the *Missouri* v. *Jenkins* case?

KEY TERMS

The following are key terms. Define or identify each. Where appropriate, include examples and illustrations. Note such items as the originator of the term, his or her major work and argument, and/or the people a given policy or document affected.

Federal Courts	Appellate Courts
State Courts	Civil Law
Public Law	Judicial Review
Amicus Curiae Brief	Adversary Process
Remedial Legislation	Mootness
Standing	Equity
Injunction	Judiciary Act of 1789
Gideon v. *Wainwright* (1963)	Common Law

Marbury v. *Madison* (1803)
Stare Decisis
Solicitor General
Pattern of Cases

Chief Justice
Writ of *Certiorari*
Writ of *Habeas Corpus*

ANNOTATED BIBLIOGRAPHY

Bickel, Alexander, *The Least Dangerous Branch* (Indianapolis: Bobbs-Merrill, 1962). This landmark work continues to set the terms of debate on the vexing issue of judicial review.

Blasi, Vincent, ed., *The Burger Court: The Counter-Revolution That Wasn't* (New Haven, CT: Yale University Press, 1983). This volume of essays by law professors and a prominent federal judge reviews decisions of the Burger Court in nine policy areas, including free speech, criminal procedure, poverty, the family, antitrust, and race and sex discrimination. The authors show how what was presumed to be a very conservative Supreme Court has not dramatically altered the doctrines of the liberal Warren Court.

Davis, Sue, *Justice Rehnquist and the Constitution* (Princeton, NJ: Princeton University Press, 1989). This is a study of the philosophy and values that shape Rehnquist's judicial decision making.

Neely, Richard, *How Courts Govern America* (New Haven, CT: Yale University Press, 1981). This informative book by a sitting judge contends that in a nuts-and-bolts sense judicial activism often works. A compelling response to recent advocates of judicial restraint.

CHAPTER **8**

Public Opinion and the Media

CHAPTER OUTLINE

I. The Marketplace of Ideas
   A. The idea market originated in nineteenth-century Europe as a national forum in which the views of all strata of society would be exchanged.
      1. During the nineteenth century, most Western nations attempted to impose linguistic unification on their citizens.
      2. Western governments tried to expand popular literacy during the nineteenth and twentieth centuries.
      3. Governments also began building roads, railways and telegraph lines to develop networks of communication.
      4. The final component necessary for the marketplace of ideas was legal protection for the free expression of ideas.
   B. Today's American idea market continually exposes individuals to concepts and information that originate outside of their own region, class, or ethnic community.
      1. Most Americans share a common set of political beliefs, such as equality of opportunity, individual freedom, and democracy.
      2. But Americans do differ widely with one another on a variety of issues.
      3. Many Americans describe themselves as either liberal or conservative in political orientation.
II. Shaping Public Opinion
   A. Nationalism, property ownership, education, and political participation are methods used by the government to enlist public support.
      1. Nationalism, the belief that people who occupy the same territory have something important in common, helps weave the social fabric together with a minimum of coercion.
      2. Property ownership is a conservative force in society that discourages disorder and revolution.
      3. Education spreads and changes cultural values, including attitudes towards one's personal qualities as well as general political ideologies.
      4. Cooperation through participation is an instrument of

governance because it encourages people to give their consent to being governed.

    B. Governments and private groups attempt to muster support by using public relations to shape opinion.

        1. Every American administration since the nation's founding has made some effort to influence public sentiment.

        2. Public opinion is also manipulated by private groups of middle- and upper-middle-class citizens who invest time and money in promoting their political ideas.

III. The Media

    A. The media were critically important factors in the shaping of public opinion concerning the civil rights movement, the Vietnam War, and the Watergate affair.

    B. The power of the media stems from several sources, all of which contribute to its great influence in setting the political agenda, shaping electoral outcomes, and interpreting events and political results.

    C. The political power of the news media has greatly increased in recent years through the growing prominence of investigative reporting.

IV. Measuring Public Opinion

    A. The social science of interpreting mass opinion from mass behavior and mass attributes is essential to both business and public affairs.

    B. In order to construct public opinion from surveys, the polling sample must be large, and the views of those in the sample must accurately and proportionately reflect the views of the whole.

    C. The inability of polls to discover public opinion and avoid unintentional distortions of political knowledge allows a certain level of ignorance to function as a restraint on the use of political power.

STUDY QUESTIONS

1. To what does the "marketplace of ideas" refer?
2. Political life in the nineteenth century was different from political life today in terms of the following: amount of contact between regional groups, the diversity of public opinion, and religious and cultural distinctions. Describe what changes took place.
3. Explain how universal education, national communications, and laws protecting freedom of the press facilitate the marketplace of ideas.
4. Why do governments impose a single national language on their citizens?

5. Why is the marketplace of ideas biased toward the middle or upper middle class?

6. Americans believe in equality of opportunity and not equality of outcome. Explain this statement. What are its implications?

7. Economic interests and social characteristics generally shape individuals' opinions. Provide examples and exceptions.

8. To what does the "gender gap" refer?

9. Explain how the views of groups change as their interests and experiences change over time.

10. What do you expect to find when you compare the attitudes of students of the early 1970s to those of the early 1980s?

11. Why do people referred to as "conservatives" want to protect private enterprise and the free market?

12. The term "liberal" has changed. What did it mean historically and to what does it refer today?

13. What is common to a nineteenth century liberal and a twentieth century conservative?

14. What are the conservatives' view on the following: private enterprise, religion, military power, and regulation of the economy?

15. According to the authors, what is the basis underlying contemporary liberal views?

16. According to the authors, what is the basis underlying contemporary conservative views?

17. How did the government shape public opinion during the First World War? Why was Eugene Debs arrested?

18. How was the extension of suffrage to eighteen-year-olds a method of control during the 1960s?

19. What is "cooptation"? How do political leaders coopt individuals or groups that are challenging authority?

20. Explain how the "right to life" and "nuclear freeze" movements show how political ideas can be the result of orchestrated campaigns.

21. How has modern technology limited political leaders' direct knowledge of public opinion?

22. What methods do American politicians employ to understand voters?

23. What mass behavior do politicians study to predict the public's response to various issues?

24. What did the Mississippi state legislature do following the passage in Congress of the 1965 Voting Rights Act?

25. Why is the media so influential? What are the sources of media power?

26. Discuss the role of the media in the following major events of the last twenty years: the Vietnam War, civil rights movement, and Watergate.

27. Why does an issue lose its chance of producing a meaningful policy if it has lost its media appeal?

28. Why can scientifically chosen samples be misleading?

29. On what does a poll's precision depend?

30. How successful have polling organizations been in predicting the outcomes of national and local elections?
31. What are some of the problems with polls in general?
32. Why do politicians often have to choose between a politics of no issues and a politics of too many trivial issues? What are the ramifications of this dilemma for elected officials?
33. Explain why government policy might not accord with public opinion on a given issue.
34. Explain why the Democrats did relatively well in Congress at the same time that they failed to capture the presidency from 1980 to the present.

KEY TERMS

The following are key terms. Define or identify each. Where appropriate, include examples and illustrations. Note such items as the originator of the term, his or her major work and argument, and/or the people a given policy or document affected.

Gender Gap
Cooptation
Liberalism
Random Distribution
Journalists
Press Conference
Public Interest Groups

Marketplace of Ideas
Conservatism
Public Opinion
Survey Research
Nationalization
Political Protest

ANNOTATED BIBLIOGRAPHY

Erikson, Robert S.; Norman Luttbeg; and Kent Tedin, *American Public Opinion: Its Origins, Content and Impact* (New York: Wiley, 1980). The central theme is how public opinion is related to the political decisions and nondecisions that affect government. While finding that opinion and policy are "in agreement more often than not," the authors warn against complacency about the current state of American democracy.

Ginsberg, Benjamin, *The Captive Public: How Mass Opinion Promotes State Power* (New York: Basic Books, 1986). This book challenges a basic tenet of democratic theory: that the institution of public opinion is good because it enables a citizenry to control its government.

Instead, Ginsberg asserts that the state uses public opinion to domesticate mass belief and enhance its own power over the citizenry.

Graber, Doris, *Mass Media and American Politics* 3rd ed. (Washington, DC: Congressional Quarterly Press, 1989). Graber provides an overview of the relationship between media and politics in all aspects of campaigns and elections.

Lipset, Seymour Martin, and William Schneider, *The Confidence Gap: Business, Labor and Government in the Public Mind* (New York: The Free Press, 1983). Based on data from public opinion polls conducted over the previous four decades, the authors document a growing gap perceived by Americans between the promise and performance of major social and political institutions.

Margolis, Michael, and Gary A. Mauser, eds., *Manipulating Public Opinion: Essays on Public Opinion as a Dependent Variable* (Pacific Grove, CA: Brooks/Cole, 1989). The editors offer an alternative to the argument that the development of polling has led much of public opinion research to assume that mass opinion drives policy. This collection of essays demonstrates that surveys can be better viewed as showing how successfully elites gain popular acceptance of their preferred positions.

CHAPTER 9

Elections

CHAPTER OUTLINE

I. Political Participation
   A. Elections play an important role in society because they establish an institutional channel of political activity, expand citizen involvement, and prescribe conditions for acceptable participation in political life.
   B. The American legal and political environment is overwhelmingly weighted in favor of electoral participation.
      1. The legal facilitation and ease of voting is a function of law and public policy, the costs of which are paid mainly by the state.
      2. Civic education is the method through which Americans are taught to equate citizenship with electoral participation.
      3. The party system has been the principal agent responsible for giving citizens the incentive to vote.
II. Regulating the Electoral Process
   A. Manipulation of the electoral composition is perhaps the oldest and most obvious device used to control electoral participation and its consequences.
   B. Contemporary governments prefer to translate voters' choices into electoral outcomes—allowing everyone to vote and then manipulating the electoral outcome.
      1. Different electoral systems use different criteria to determine the winners.
         a. In a majority system, a candidate must receive a majority of all votes cast in the relevant district.
         b. In a plurality system, candidates for office need only receive the most votes in a given election regardless of the actual percentage of votes this represents.
         c. Proportional representation awards legislative seats to competing political parties roughly in proportion to the actual percentage of the popular votes each received.
      2. Rather than seeking to manipulate the criteria for victory, American politicians have usually sought to influence electoral outcomes by gerrymandering, manipulating the organization of electoral districts.
   C. The United States government attempts to insulate its

decision-making process from electoral intervention through the use of various procedural requirements.

III. How Voters Decide

    A. The bases of electoral choice are partisan loyalty, issue and policy concerns, and candidate characteristics.

        1. Partisan loyalty predisposes voters in favor of their party's candidates and against those of the opposing party.

        2. The impact of issues and policy preferences on electoral choice is diminished if competing candidates do not differ substantially or do not focus their campaigns on policy matters.

        3. Candidates' attributes and personality characteristics always influence voters' decisions.

    B. The salience of these three bases of electoral choice vary from contest to contest and from voter to voter.

IV. Electoral Realignments

    A. The United States has experienced five realigning eras, which occurred when the established political elite weakened sufficiently to permit the creation of new coalitions of forces capable of capturing and holding the reins of government.

    B. The recent importance of realignments in American politics has led many analysts to ask whether we might be experiencing a realignment at the present time that will lead to a new Republican era.

        1. The New Deal coalition dominated American government and politics until it was disrupted by conflicts over race relations, the Vietnam War, and the government's fiscal and regulatory policies.

        2. The Reconstituted Right became the dominant force in American electoral politics during the 1980s, and the Reagan administration's policies may have begun to institutionalize this new coalition.

    C. The congressional electoral arena has belonged to the Democrats for the last twenty years, despite a Republican-dominated presidency during that same time.

V. The 1988 Presidential Election

    A. The Democrats lost the 1988 election because Michael Dukakis was unable to escape charges that he was committed to constituencies and causes that could be served only at the expense of middle America.

    B. The Republican triumph in 1988 was due mostly to George Bush's ability to maintain the unity of the Reagan coalition by attacking Dukakis's liberalism.

VI. The Consequences of Consent

STUDY QUESTIONS

1. What are the two key principles underlying the electoral process?
2. Why is the granting of participation to ordinary citizens a risk for rulers and the citizens themselves?
3. How do elections affect the status of citizens?
4. Voting is socialized and institutionalized; rioting is not. What does it mean to be socialized and institutionalized? And what are the political implications?
5. How did the introduction of elections limit mass political involvement?
6. Why is voting the dominant form of political participation in America but not in some other places in the world?
7. How does the law, civic education, and the party system channel political participation into voting?
8. Discuss the management of the electoral procedures.
9. Why does civic education in the United States generally exclude studies of nonelectoral participation like lawsuits, direct action, organizing, and sit-ins?
10. How do political parties mobilize voters?
11. Discuss the competition in the 1790s between the Jeffersonians and the Federalists. Relate this to the origins of the American national electorate.
12. How did the formation of parties diffuse unrest and opposition to the government?
13. Why has the government taken over voter registration drives, public funding of electoral campaigns, and primary elections from parties?
14. Explain how governments can change the composition of the electorate and thus manipulate outcomes.
15. How does the American government regulate the electorate's composition?
16. Why are levels of voting participation in twentieth-century American elections lower than in those of other Western democracies?
17. Why were American voting levels much higher in the nineteenth century than they are now?
18. How did laws requiring personal registration affect voter turnout? When were they passed?
19. Define a plurality electoral system.
20. Define proportional representation. Whom does proportional representation generally benefit?
21. Define gerrymandering.
22. What steps did the framers take to protect the government from mass electoral influence?
23. What is the impact of staggered terms on the Senate as an institution?
24. What is the Australian ballot?
25. Describe split-ticket voting.

26. Why do registration requirements make the electorate better educated, richer, and whiter than the citizenry as a whole?
27. If the electorate in the United States were expanded, would it be more liberal or more conservative?
28. Describe the effects of partisan loyalty, issue and policy concerns, and candidate characteristics on voters' decisions at the polls. Provide some recent examples.
29. How do partisan ties affect local elections?
30. Is partisan loyalty weaker today than during the 1940s and 1950s? Why is partisanship hard to change? When is it most influential today?
31. What is a critical electoral realignment?
32. When were the critical realignments in American politics?
33. Discuss the realignment associated with the election of Franklin Roosevelt. What groups were involved? How was a coalition formed?
34. Why did the New Deal coalition fall apart in the 1960s?
35. Discuss the current American political coalitions. From where has the Reconstituted Right drawn most of its constituency? What ethnic, geographic, and economic groups comprise it?
36. What strategies did Ronald Reagan use during the 1980 election to win support from the Reconstituted Right?
37. What is proportional representation? When is it used in the United States?

KEY TERMS

The following are key terms. Define or identify each. Where appropriate, include examples and illustrations. Note such items as the originator of the term, his or her major work and argument, and/or the people a given policy or document affected.

Partisan Competition	Partisan Identification
Poll Tax	Staggered Terms
Proportional Representation	Indirect Election
Australian Ballot	Party Ballot
Split-Ticket Voting	Plurality System
Personal Registration	Civic Education
Majority System	Progressives
Jeffersonians	Jacksonians
Democrats	Whigs
New Deal Coalition	Critical Realignment
Reconstituted Right	Voter Turnout
Gerrymandering	Republicans

ANNOTATED BIBLIOGRAPHY

Burnham, Walter D., *The Current Crisis in American Politics* (New York: Oxford University Press, 1982). Burnham attributes "the spectacular decline of electoral participation after 1900" to the tension between democracy and ascendant capitalism. The resulting crisis of mass nonparticipation and overwhelming distrust of political institutions, particularly among the working class, is not likely to be redressed within the present constitutional framework.

Ginsberg, Benjamin, and Martin Shefter, *Politics by Other Means: Institutional Conflict and the Declining Significance of Elections in America* (New York: Basic Books, 1990). The authors argue that the significance of elections in American politics is declining—a development that has led to the emergence of a "post-electoral" political order in which most elections are decided before the polls open.

Piven, Frances Fox, and Richard A. Cloward, *Why Americans Don't Vote* (New York: Pantheon, 1988). This study looks at institutional arrangements responsible for widespread nonvoting by lower-class and working-class people in the United States, and then considers the implications of eliminating obstacles to voting.

Reed, Adolph, *The Jesse Jackson Phenomenon* (New Haven, CT: Yale University Press, 1987). The author evaluates Jesse Jackson's 1984 presidential campaign and concludes that charismatic, "protest-style" leaders such as Jackson may no longer be capable of developing a policy agenda adequate to an increasingly diverse and complex black community.

Reichley, A. James, ed., *Elections American Style* (Washington, DC: The Brookings Institution, 1987). The aim of this collection of essays by political scientists specializing in the electoral system is to examine core problems associated with American elections and to prescribe possible remedies.

CHAPTER **10**

Political Parties

CHAPTER OUTLINE

I. The Two-Party System in America
   A. Historically, parties originate through either internal or external mobilization by those seeking to win governmental power.
      1. The Democratic party originated through a process of internal organization as the Jeffersonian party splintered into four factions in 1824, and Andrew Jackson emerged as the leader of one of the groups.
      2. The Republican party grew through a process of external mobilization; antislavery groups mobilized to form a new party to oppose the 1854 Kansas-Nebraska Act.
   B. Despite the existence of some real philosophical differences between the Democratic and Republican parties, there is considerable overlap between them because each seeks to represent a wide range of interests.
II. Functions of the Parties
   A. Although parties perform a wide variety of functions, they are mainly involved in providing the candidates for office, getting out the vote, and facilitating mass electoral choice.
      1. The caucus, an informal meeting among local party leaders, was the method of candidate nomination used in the eighteenth and early nineteenth centuries.
      2. A nominating convention is a formalized version of the caucus bound by rules that govern participation and procedures.
      3. In primary elections, party members select the party's nominees directly rather than selecting convention delegates who then select the nominees.
      4. State laws extend the right of independent candidacy to individuals who do not wish to be nominated by political parties or who are unable to secure a party nomination.
      5. Although they deplete party resources and interfere with campaign strategy, contested nominations contribute to healthier politics by exposing parties to different interests.
      6. Nominating conventions and primaries yield a good deal of free publicity for parties and candidates.
   B. Parties have the essential electoral role of motivating citizens to

vote, and providing them with information for choosing among candidates and policies.

   C. The ultimate test of the party system is its relationship to and influence on the institutions of national government.

      1. The party system is crucial to Congress because it governs the choice of House speaker as well as committee assignments in both chambers.

      2. The two-party system is crucial to the presidential election because it keeps the presidency independent of Congress by keeping Congress out of the selection process.

   D. Parties facilitate mass electoral choices by increasing the electorate's capacity to recognize its options and encouraging electoral competition by groups lacking substantial economic or institutional resources.

III. Weakening of Party Organization

   A. The erosion of the parties' organizational strength allowed high-tech communications techniques to replace manpower.

      1. Polling provides the information that candidates and their staffs use to craft campaign strategies.

      2. The use of broadcast media permits the delivery of a candidate's message to a target audience, and encourages communication with voters en masse and impersonally.

      3. Phone banks allow campaign workers to make personal contact with hundreds of thousands of voters.

      4. Direct mail serves both as a vehicle for communicating with voters and as a mechanism for raising funds.

      5. Professional public relations consultants typically direct the modern campaign.

   B. The displacement of organizational methods by the new political technology is a shift from labor-intensive to capital-intensive competitive electoral practices.

   C. The contemporary political parties are essentially coalitions that lack the direct organizational ties to rank and file voters that formerly had permitted parties to shape all aspects of politics and government in the United States.

STUDY QUESTIONS

1. During his farewell address, George Washington spoke of "the baneful effects of the spirit of party." To what did he refer?
2. What were the Alien and Sedition Acts of 1798? Why were they introduced by the ruling party?
3. What were these acts primarily designed to accomplish?

4. Discuss party organizations, focusing upon levels of organization, committee elections, and national committee roles.

5. Describe party nominations. Why did conventions for presidential candidates begin? How were candidates originally selected?

6. Define "King Caucus."

7. Define "open and closed primaries."

8. Explain why it is difficult for an independent candidate to get on the ballot.

9. Discuss the ways in which primary elections make it easier or more difficult for new interests to be heard.

10. What is a referendum?

11. Describe the makeup of the Democratic party. When was it formed? Who founded it? What was its stance on the Constitution, states' rights, federal spending, and slavery? When was it dominant? When did it split and decline?

12. How did Franklin Roosevelt make the Democratic party strong?

13. Why did southern whites stop supporting the Democrats?

14. Describe the makeup of the Republican party. When was it formed? What were its views on homesteading, internal improvements, transcontinental railroads, and protective tariffs? When and for how long did it dominate national politics?

15. Explain how the differences between Democratic and Republican positions increased during the Reagan administration.

16. Explain the electoral college system.

17. Why is it rare for more than two candidates to get many votes in the general election?

18. How does the two-party system keep the presidency independent of Congress?

19. Why do single-member districts hurt third parties?

20. Discuss the Progressives of the late nineteenth century. Why were they the most important third party in the last hundred years?

21. Explain why the role of party organizations in electoral politics has declined in recent years.

22. What do Eugene Debs, Theodore Roosevelt, George Wallace, and John Anderson have in common?

23. Provide examples of influential third parties in the United States.

24. Why have third parties been less than successful in American politics?

25. What were the goals of the Progressives in the late nineteenth century as to political parties, corruption, and the role of elites in social and economic affairs?

26. What are the Australian ballot and the direct primary? What was the result of these Progressive reforms?

27. Discuss the function of polling, direct mail, TV, and phone banks as new forms of political technology.

28. What is the advantage of spot ads in political campaigns?

29. Explain why the post–WW II shift in the organizational methods of

American political campaigns can be characterized as a move from labor-intensive to capital-intensive methods.

30. Discuss campaign spending. How has total campaign spending in the United States increased in recent years? Why did the Supreme Court declare unconstitutional some attempts to impose limits on campaign contributions?

31. Why have American political parties declined in significance? In what ways are they still major political institutions?

32. Does success in contemporary American politics depend on money?

KEY TERMS

The following are key terms. Define or identify each. Where appropriate, include examples and illustrations. Note such items as the originator of the term, his or her major work and argument, and/or the people a given policy or document affected.

King Caucus	Labor-intensive Politics
Capital-intensive Politics	Alien and Sedition Acts
Popular Vote	Machine Politics
Precinct	Closed Primary
Open Primary	Public Opinion Polling
Political Action Committee	Single-member District
Referendum	Republican Party
Australian Ballot	Socialist Party
Democratic Party	Progressives
Electoral College	George Wallace's American Independent Party

ANNOTATED BIBLIOGRAPHY

Broder, David, *The Party's Over* (New York: Harper & Row, 1971). In accounting for declining popular confidence in America's two-party system, Broder considers the lack of clear party leadership, the effect of powerful interest groups, and an excess of consensus politics.

Chambers, William N., and Walter D. Burnham, *The American Party Systems: Stages of Political Development* (New York: Oxford University Press, 1975). Leading political scientists and historians consider the origins, characteristics, and functions of American political parties. Among the more specific issues addressed are: How has America's socioeconomic system shaped the major parties? What factors account for the moderate, nonideological bent of our political culture? What conditions have supported the emergence of bipartisan politics in the United States?

Herrnson, Paul S., *Party Campaigning in the 1980s* (Cambridge, MA: Harvard University Press, 1988). The author's thesis is that the political parties are not dying. Rather, they have become important as intermediaries between PACs and candidates.

Hofstadter, Richard, *The Idea of a Party System: The Rise of Legitimate Opposition in the United States, 1780–1840* (Berkeley and Los Angeles: University of California Press, 1970). This intellectual history examines how American leaders during the early years of the nation gradually set aside their philosophical rejection of political parties and embraced a party system. Hofstadter shows how parties came to be seen as essential to a vital democracy.

Kayden, Xandra, and Eddie Mahe, Jr., *The Party Goes On: The Persistence of the Two-Party System in the United States* (New York: Basic Books, 1985). Contrary to the plethora of recent studies reporting the demise of political parties, this book contends that party organizations are experiencing a renaissance. The authors are particularly convincing when they illustrate how each major party utilizes sophisticated campaign and fund-raising techniques to reach voters.

Polsby, Nelson W., *Consequences of Party Reform* (New York: Oxford University Press, 1983). Polsby argues that the electoral reforms instituted by Democratic party activists after 1968 have hastened the decline of parties and led directly to the ruinous state of American politics today.

Sabato, Larry J., *The Party's Just Begun: Shaping Political Parties for America's Future* (Glenview, IL: Scott, Foresman, 1988). Sabato points out the resurgence of political parties rather than their decline, and presents a variety of reform suggestions that range from institutional advertising to the discouragement of nonpartisan elections and third parties.

CHAPTER 11

Groups and Interests

CHAPTER OUTLINE

I. Character of Interest Groups
   A. There are an enormous number of diverse interest groups in the United States.
   B. Most interest groups share key organizational components, such as developing mechanisms for member recruitment, constructing financial and decision-making apparatus, and establishing agencies that actually carry out group goals.
   C. Interest-group politics in the United States tends to have a very pronounced upper-class bias because of the characteristics of its members.

II. The Proliferation of Groups
   A. The modern expansion of governmental economic and social programs has contributed extensively to the enormous increase in the number of groups seeking to influence the American political process.
   B. The second factor accounting for the explosion of interest-group activity in recent years was the emergence of a new set of forces in American politics that has been named the New Politics movement.

III. Strategies: The Quest for Political Power
   A. Going public is a strategy that attempts to mobilize the widest and most favorable climate of opinion.
   B. Lobbying is an effort by outsiders to exert influence on Congress or government agencies by providing them with information about issues, giving them support, and even threatening them with retaliation.
   C. Gaining access is actual involvement and influence in the decision-making process.
   D. Interest groups often turn to litigation when they lack access or feel they have insufficient influence over the formulation and implementation of public policy.
   E. Many groups use a partisan strategy in electoral politics to avoid giving up access to one party by embracing the other.

STUDY QUESTIONS

1. James Madison's theory of interest groups continues to be extremely influential. What were its points concerning the multitude of interest groups, competition among these groups, and the government's task of regulating different interests?

2. Some might argue that the presence of a large number of groups indicates that every significant interest in America is represented. What arguments can you make against this claim?

3. All interest groups have key organizational components: mechanisms for recruitment and retention of members, a financial structure, and a leadership and decision-making structure. Provide examples of how these components work and why they are important. Include both successful and unsuccessful cases.

4. Levels of income, amount of education, and type of employment serve as indicators of interest group membership. Explain how each signifies if someone is likely to belong to an interest group.

5. Why is it more difficult for the poor to organize on a large scale than the rich? Why are political parties better at organizing the poor than interest groups? Why has the power of interest groups increased?

6. Define the New Politics movement.

7. Explain how the Vietnam War and racial inequality sparked the growth of liberal reform movements. Include a discussion on the growth of environmental and consumer-oriented regulation by the federal government.

8. What effects have liberal reform movements had on U.S. foreign or defense policy?

9. Explain why liberal reform movements established public interest groups as an important political tactic.

10. What does it mean for a group to "go public"? Provide cases of political groups going public.

11. Define lobbying. What branch is its main focus? About how many people lobby in Washington? Describe the typical lobbyist. Provide examples of lobbying.

12. Define the term "gaining access."

13. An important pattern of access in American politics at the national level includes a person in the executive branch, a legislative committee, and a well-organized interest group. Explain the dynamics of this pattern and show why it can be successful.

14. President Eisenhower spoke of the military-industrial complex. Relate his warnings to the access pattern between the defense industry and the U.S. military.

15. Discuss how public interest groups might be better defined, in general, as self-interest groups. What problems might such groups cause? Provide examples.

16. Describe the relationship between education, income, and membership in an interest group.

17. How has Congress changed the rules governing campaign contributions since Watergate? What opportunities exist for special interests legally to influence elections?
18. How have campaign reform laws affected Political Action Committees?
19. Bribery is considered an important topic in American politics. Why is it a strategy of last resort, evidence of weakness, and most influential with regard to narrow political issues?
20. Describe the relationship between the United Auto Workers (UAW) and the Democrats.
21. Describe the following scandals: Watergate, Iran-Contra, Koreagate, and Abscam.
22. Define and provide examples of the following strategies: lobbying, gaining access, litigation, going public, and electoral politics.
23. Explain how seeing politics as a contest of interest groups overlooks the inability of the poor, the uneducated, and the unorganized to participate.
24. What does "public interest" mean? How can public interests be distinguished from private interests?
25. What political strategy do political action committees (PACs) use? Why has the role of PACs become more important in recent years?
26. What does the American Association of Retired Persons (AARP) suggest about interest group politics?
27. What political technique was used very effectively by the NAACP to influence civil rights policy during the 1950s?
28. What public officials are bound by the "Ethics in Government" Act? Does this act apply to all branches of government?
29. What are "iron triangles?" What role do they play in the policy-making process?
30. How did the political strategy of the Southern Christian Leadership Conference (SCLC) differ from the strategy pursued by the NAACP?
31. What political strategies have been employed by members of the pro-life movement during the 1980s?
32. Has the number of interest groups in the United States increased or diminished over the past two decades? What factors explain this growth or decline?
33. Why has the National Rifle Association (NRA) been highly effective in blocking attempts to enact gun control measures in recent years?

KEY TERMS

The following are key terms. Define or identify each. Where appropriate, include examples and illustrations. Note such items as the originator of the term, his or her major work and argument, and/or the people a given policy or document affected.

Electoral Spending	Direct Democracy
Political Machine	Special Interest Group
Going Partisan	Injunction
Litigation	Bribery
Going Public	Lobbying
Pluralism	Political Action Committee
Gaining Access	Populism
Campaign Funds Committee	Public Interest Group
Reconstituted Right	New Politics Movement
Liberals	

ANNOTATED BIBLIOGRAPHY

Cigler, Alan J., and Burdett A. Loomis, *Interest Group Politics* (Washington, DC: Congressional Quarterly Press, 1983). This volume surveys many of the most influential interest groups of the past decade, including the pro-life organizations, the Christian right, the agriculture lobby, and the women's lobby.

Lowi, Theodore J., *The End of Liberalism* (New York: W. W. Norton, 1979). The crisis of public authority developed when government responded to the demands of all major organized interests, assumed responsibility for programs sought by those interests, and then delegated responsibility to administrative agencies. As interest groups tightened their grip upon national policy making, the liberal state spun out of control and demoralized democratic government.

Sabato, Larry J., *PAC Power: Inside the World of Political Action Committees* (New York: W. W. Norton, 1984). Sabato shows how the "web of politics" that enshrouds PACs extends beyond campaign finance to political education programs and voter registration drives. The author argues that reform efforts should be geared toward minimizing the least desirable aspects of PAC activity while encouraging their many positive attributes.

Schlozman, Kay Lehman, and John T. Tierney, *Organized Interests and American Democracy* (New York: Harper & Row, 1986). The culmination of five years of research and extensive interviews with 175 organized interests, this book supplies a detailed look at what interest groups have been doing throughout the 1980s.

Stockman, David, *The Triumph of Politics* (New York: Harper & Row, 1986). The former director of the Office of Management and Budget provides a startling description of political life inside the

Reagan administration. More significant, however, is Stockman's account of how interest group politics dashed Reagan's "radical" promise to cut dramatically the size of the federal government.

Vogel, David, *Fluctuating Fortunes: The Political Power of Business in America* (New York: Basic Books, 1989). This book is a history of the significant changes in the relationship between business and government in the United States that have taken place since 1960.

CHAPTER 12

Introduction to Public Policy

CHAPTER OUTLINE

I. Techniques of Control
   A. Promotional techniques, which promote private activity through unconditional benefits, are the carrots of public policy.
      1. Subsidies are government grants of cash or other valuable commodities, such as land.
      2. Contracting allows government agencies to use their power to encourage certain desirable goals or behavior, and as a means of helping to build up whole sectors of the economy.
      3. A license is a privilege granted by a government to do something that is otherwise illegal.
   B. Regulatory Techniques come in several forms, but share the common trait of direct government control of conduct.
      1. Police regulations come closest to the traditional exercise of "police power," and generally consist of both civil and criminal penalties to discourage conduct considered immoral.
      2. Administrative regulation is a technique that allows administrative agencies to control conduct that is considered bad mainly in its consequences.
      3. The primary purpose of regulatory taxation in many instances is not to raise revenue but to discourage or eliminate an activity altogether by making it too expensive for most people.
      4. Expropriation, the seizing of private property for a public use, is a widely used technique of control in the United States, especially in land-use regulation.
   C. Redistributive techniques usually take one of two forms, but their common purpose is to control people by manipulating the entire economy rather than by regulating people directly.
      1. Fiscal techniques of control arise out of taxing and spending powers.
      2. Monetary techniques also seek to influence conduct by manipulating the entire economy through the supply or availability of money.
      3. The government's spending power may be the most important fiscal technique since it can be used for policy goals beyond the goods and services bought and the individual conduct regulated.

II. Substantive Uses of the Policies
   A. The architects of the original Social Security System in the 1930s were well aware that a large welfare system could be both good fiscal policy and social strategy by attempting to alleviate poverty as well as redistributing wealth.
      1. Contributory programs, which are financed by taxation, are what msot people have in mind when they refer to social security or social insurance.
      2. The two most important noncontributory or public assistance programs are the Supplemental Security Income for the aged, blind, and disabled, and Aid to Families with Dependent Children.
   B. Public policies must intervene by changing the rules of inequality in order to counteract the effect of bias and prejudice in society.
      1. The most important piece of legislation passed by Congress was the Civil Rights Act of 1964.
      2. Most affirmative action comes not from new legislation, but from more vigorous and positive interpretations of existing legislation arising out of feelings on the part of many that postive actions are necessary to overcome the long years of discrimination.

STUDY QUESTIONS

1. Define public policy. What is its first priority? And what forms can it take?
2. What is a sanction?
3. Why are all public policies coercive?
4. Discuss the importance of the following regarding public policy: a stated technique of control, specific standards, and clear jurisdiction.
5. Explain how subsidies as techniques of control have played a fundamental role in the American government's influence over the economy.
6. How do subsidies change individuals' behavior?
7. Describe the Reagan administration's policy concerning subsidies.
8. "Contracting" is an important power of the American national government. Relate how it affects the economy, and provide an example.
9. Define "privatization."
10. What is a license?
11. Government regulation uses both police and administrative powers to control and influence behavior toward appropriate channels. Provide examples.
12. Define "administrative regulation."
13. Regulatory agencies have broad jurisdiction, often write the rules

they enforce, and employ court orders as a means of control. Explain how and why this is politically significant and provide examples.

14. Discuss the politics of distributive policies. Why are federal land grants the best examples? Why are they too individualized and disaggregated to be called pluralism? Are they coercive?

15. Define and give examples of "regulatory policy."

16. What is redistributive policy? How does it differ from distributive policy?

17. Explain how taxation can be used as a regulatory technique of control.

18. Discuss the government's power of expropriation. Is it a regulatory power?

19. Define the following governmental techniques to regulate people: fiscal and monetary policy.

20. Why is the government's most important redistributive or macroeconomic technique of control its spending power?

21. What is the Federal Trade Commission? What is the rationale for its activities?

22. What is the power of "eminent domain"? Are there any limits on this power?

23. Are changes in income tax rates examples of the use of fiscal or monetary techniques?

24. Describe the strengths and weaknesses of taxation as a regulatory technique of control.

25. Discuss the difference between a governmental ideal based upon equality of outcomes and one based upon equality of opportunity.

26. What are some reasons for inequality of outcomes? What popular justifications, depending upon one's point of view, are given for claiming that the socioeconomic situation is not that bad?

27. Define welfare and civil rights policies. Explain how the first deals with what is to be done about the poor, while the latter determines who shall be poor.

28. How have Americans often distinguished between the "deserving" and the "undeserving" poor?

29. Explain the social, economic, and political significance of the Social Security Act of 1935.

30. Define contributory and noncontributory welfare programs.

31. Discuss the following: Medicare and Medicaid, "in-kind" payments, "means tested," and "indexing."

32. Discuss Lyndon Johnson's War on Poverty. Whom did it help? How were the local neighborhoods involved? How much more did it cost the federal government?

33. Explain how the following influenced the "fiscal crisis" of the 1970s: public assistance programs of the 1960s; the ratio of current workers to retired persons; and the oil industry.

34. How does the welfare system act as an "automatic stabilizer" against the dynamics of the business cycle?

35. Discuss the good points and the criticisms of the American welfare state.
36. Explain how the most important cause of inequality is previous inequality. Relate how education and health policies are the most significant policies in breaking the cycle of poverty and dependency in America.
37. Discuss educational policy. At what level has it traditionally been made? Why was the universal compulsory education policy the most important public policy concerning it?
38. What proof do the authors give for their claim that housing programs have been a success despite much abuse and corruption?
39. Does equality of opportunity guarantee equality of results?
40. Do the poorest 20 percent of American families now receive a larger or smaller share of total U.S. family income than at the beginning of the twentieth century?
41. What was the impact of the Great Depression on the government's role in providing help for the poor in the U.S.?
42. Describe the federal Aid to Families with Dependent Children (AFDC) Program.
43. What is the Supplemental Security Income (SSI) Program?
44. Did the Reagan administration have a significant impact upon levels of welfare spending in the U.S.?
45. Does the American welfare system encourage the poor to participate in politics?
46. How poor are children in the United States compared to children in other advanced industrial states? Why?
47. What is the function of the Consumer Products Safety Commission?
48. Define Ricardo's "iron law of wages."
49. What Supreme Court case opened the modern era of civil rights?
50. What was the most important piece of civil rights legislation enacted by Congress?
51. Define affirmative action. What are examples of programs designed to promote affirmative action?
52. Describe federal job training programs. Were these eliminated during the Reagan era?
53. What programs are most important for breaking the "cycle of poverty"?
54. How can capitalist poverty be seen as objective and neutral? Is this an accurate characterization?
55. Explain how registration requirements can limit voter turnout. Against whom do they discriminate?
56. Discuss the 1964 Voting Rights Act. How did it affect voter registration in the South among blacks?

KEY TERMS

The following are key terms. Define or identify each. Where appropriate, include examples and illustrations. Note such items as the originator of the term, his or her major work and argument, and/or the people a given policy or document affected.

Spending Power
Constituent Policy
Fiscal Technique
Technique of Control
Redistributive Policy
Subsidy
Privatization
Regulation
Social Regulation
Bureaucracy
Administrative Regulation
Logrolling
Civil Rights Policies
Affirmative Action
Fiscal Crisis of the 1970s
Equality of Outcomes
Social Security Act of 1935
Indexing
Grant-in-Aid
CETA
Medicare
Consumer Product Safety
    Commission

Common Good
Redistricting
Monetary Technique
Macroeconomic Technique
Sanction
Contracting Power
License
Promotional Policy
Deterrence
Expropriation
Federal Income Tax
Private Property
Welfare Policies
War on Poverty
Great Depression
Equality of Opportunity
Education and Health Policies
Iron Law of Wages
In-kind Benefits
Medicaid
Contributory Welfare Programs
Noncontributory Welfare
    Programs

ANNOTATED BIBLIOGRAPHY

Bullock, Charles, III, and Charles M. Lamb, *Implementation of Civil Rights Policy* (Monterey, CA: Brooks/Cole, 1984). A survey of federal civil rights policies implemented during the past twenty-five years indicates that government activism is more likely to succeed when policy goals are clearly enunciated, precise compliance standards are established, and agencies and courts are genuinely committed to enforcing the law. This volume demonstrates why the Voting Rights Act of 1965 may be considered a model regulatory act while other civil rights policies have yielded disappointing results.

Chubb, John, and Paul Peterson, eds., *Can the Government Govern?* (Washington, DC: 1989). The authors of this volume conclude that without fundamental change in the structure of government, public policy cannot serve the public. A recurring theme is that the most important battles in Washington are over decision-making structures, bureaucratic arrangements, procedures, and criteria, rather than substance.

Derthick, Martha, and Paul J. Quirk, *The Politics of Deregulation* (Washington, DC: The Brookings Institution, 1985). This book challenges the conventional view that federal regulatory agencies are captured by the regulated industries. The authors scrutinize three industries—telecommunications, trucking, and airlines—to show how the policy of deregulation worked against narrow, but potent, interests and in favor of the general public.

Greider, William, *Secrets of the Temple: How the Federal Reserve Runs the Country* (New York: Simon and Schuster, 1987). In examining the policies of the Federal Reserve Board under Paul Volker, this book charges that the Fed deliberately thrust the United States into a long recession that unnecessarily punished millions of poor and working-class people. Greider questions the wisdom of allowing unelected officials. largely sheltered from the public limelight, to make such momentous decisions about the nation's monetary policy.

Gutman, Amy, *Democratic Education (Princeton, NJ: Princeton University Press, 1987). Gutman's survey of contemporary policy issues on education is grounded on the premise that citizen participation in public affairs is the critical element of a democratic society.*

Piven, Frances Fox, and Richard A. Cloward, *Regulating the Poor* (New York: Pantheon, 1971). The authors combine historical and sociological evidence to show how welfare programs are operated according to a cyclical pattern: expanded during periods of disorder and retracted during periods of social stability. A provocative study of the political purposes underlying social welfare policies.

Rubin, Irene S., *The Politics of Public Budgeting: Getting and Spending, Borrowing and Balancing* (Chatham, NJ: Chatha House, 1989). Rubin presents a panoramic view of the fiscal politics, from city hall to statehouse to Capitol Hill.

Weir, Margaret, Ann Orloff, and Theda Skocpol, *The Politics of Social Policy in the United States (Princeton, NJ: Princeton University Press, 1988). This book explores the fundamental patterns of American social politics in an historical perspective.*

CHAPTER 13

Foreign Policy

CHAPTER OUTLINE

I. The Setting: A World of Nation-States
   A. Sovereignty may be defined as respect by other nations for the claim by a government that it has conquered its territory and is the sole authority over its population.
   B. Sovereignty is a continuum which has new, small, and relatively weak nation-states at one end, superpowers at the other end, and somewhat wealthy and strong nation-states not always able to pursue their own foreign policy in between.

II. The Values in American Foreign Policy
   A. The intermingling of domestic and foreign policy institutions and unilateralism are the two identifiable legacies of our traditional system of maintaining sovereignty.
      1. Intermingling of domestic and foreign policy institutions was originally possible because it was the major European powers that policed the world.
      2. Traditionally, unilateralism, the desire to go-it-alone, was the American posture toward the world.
   B. Although the traditional era of American foreign policy came to an end with World War I, there was no discernible change in approach to such policy until thirty years later after World War II.

III. The Instruments of Modern American Foreign Policy
   A. Diplomacy is the representation of a government to other foreign governments, and it is the foreign policy instrument to which all other instruments must be subordinated.
   B. The United Nations is an instrument whose usefulness to American foreign policy can too easily be underestimated.
   C. The international monetary structure, which consists of the World Bank and the International Monetary Fund, was created to avoid the economic devastation that followed World War I.
   D. Economic aid has been important as an instrument of American foreign policy, but it was put together as a balance between traditional values and the modern needs of a great, imperial power.
   E. After World War II, the United States recognized the importance of collective security, and subsequently entered into multilateral

collective security treaties and other bilateral treaties.

F. World War II broke the American cycle of demobilization-remobilization, and led to a new policy of preparedness based on a strategy of military deterrence.

IV. Roles Nations Play

    A. Although presidents have some freedom in choosing a role for our nation to play, they are limited by the choices of their predecessors, as well as by the way the presidency is constructed and its relationship with the public.

        1. The Napoleonic role is one that is war-like and interventionist.

        2. The Holy Alliance role makes use of every kind of political weapon available in order to keep existing governments in power.

        3. The balance-of-power role plays the major powers against each other so that no great power or combination of great and lesser powers can impose conditions on the others.

        4. The economic expansionist or capitalist role focuses on the question of whether a country has anything to buy or sell, and whether its entrepreneurs, corporations, and government agencies will honor their contracts.

    B. Although our nation played the Napoleonic role during the post-war era and then switched to the Holy Alliance role, the United States is now beginning to adopt all four roles, playing whichever one is appropriate to the specific region of the world and circumstances.

    C. The bureaucratization of international relations may be an attractive alternative to diplomacy, which is necessarily inconsistent and unpredictable.

STUDY QUESTIONS

1. Why, according to Alexis de Tocqueville, does foreign policy give democracies problems?

2. Why did President Washington warn the United States against "permanent alliances"?

3. Define the Monroe Doctrine. When was it formulated? What did it say about European powers? What role did domestic politics play?

4. Explain how U.S. domestic political conflicts are "dumped" on the outside world. Provide an example.

5. What changes occurred after World War I regarding the following: the power of the great empires; the United States vis à vis other countries; and the growth of the federal government?

6. World War II caused the United States to take on a more active role and develop a professional diplomatic corps. Explain this.

7. Discuss the relationship between the president and the State Department regarding foreign policy decisions.
8. In what way can the U.N. serve as an instrument of U.S. foreign policy?
9. What is the International Monetary Fund?
10. Discuss the Marshall Plan. Whose policy was it? What did it aim to do? Was it successful?
11. Define the following: OAS, NATO, SEATO, ANZUS, and the Warsaw Pact.
12. What is a mutual security treaty? Why do most Americans continue to favor such treaties?
13. What does it mean, when one says, that "the United States prefers to exercise power-without-diplomacy"?
14. What is a satellite state?
15. What are the chief characteristics of a client state?
16. What is national sovereignty? What is its significance?
17. What are the major underlying factors that influence American foreign policy?
18. What is the meaning of "unilateralism" in foreign policy?
19. Describe the role of the foreign service in American foreign policy.
20. How does President Bush's record in nominating ambassadors compare to that of Reagan?
21. Define collective security. What are examples of the use of this strategy?
22. What factors undermined the international economic structure established by the U.S. after World War II?
23. Describe deterrence theory.
24. What is the significance of the concept of "overkill"?
25. Describe and assess the "balance-of-power" role.
26. Describe and assess the "Holy Alliance" role.
27. Describe and assess the "economic expansionist" role.
28. Describe and assess the "Napoleonic" role.
29. Which role did the United States assume during most of the years after World War II?
30. What role did the United States play in the Gulf War?
31. What was the Bretton Woods agreement? What was its significance?
32. What is the World Bank? What role does it play?

KEY TERMS

The following are key terms. Define or identify each. Where appropriate, include examples and illustrations. Note such items as the originator of the term, his or her major work and argument, and/or the people a given policy or document affected.

Deterrence	Unilateralism
Diplomacy	Bretton Woods
Sovereignty	World Bank
Client state	United Nations
World War I	World War II
Economic Expansionist Role	Napoleonic Role
Balance-of-Power Role	Holy Alliance Role
Bureaucratic Community Role	International Monetary Fund
George Washington	Marshall Plan

ANNOTATED BIBLIOGRAPHY

Bundy, McGeorge, *Danger & Survival: Choices About the Bomb in the First Fifty Years* (New York: Random House, 1989). Bundy writes from the perspective of historian, participant, and commentator about crisis and debate concerning nuclear choices made by governments during the first fifty years of man-made nuclear fission.

Crabb, Cecil V., and Kevin V. Mulcahy, *Presidents and Foreign Policymaking: From FDR to Reagan* (Baton Rouge, LA: Louisiana State University Press, 1986). This book explores the increasing fragmentation of authority within the executive branch on foreign policy matters and the resultant confusion on vital issues. The authors emphasize the diminishing role played by the State Department in the policy process.

Franck, Thomas M., and Edward Weisband, *Foreign Policy by Congress* (New York: Oxford University Press, 1979). Franck reviews how Congress reacted to Nixon's imperial presidency by enacting measures such as the War Powers Act aimed at democratizing foreign policy making. A thoughtful volume documenting Congress' arrival as a key actor in the formation and implementation of American foreign policy.

Gilpin, Robert, *The Political Economy of International Relations* (Princeton, NJ: Princeton University Press, 1987). A comprehensive treatise on international political economy, Gilpin covers subjects ranging from foreign investment to international finance to North-South trade relations. The book is theoretically rich as well, providing liberal, nationalist, and Marxist perspectives on many issues.

Hilsman, Roger, *The Politics of Policymaking in Defense and Foreign Affairs* (Englewood Cliffs, NJ: Prentice-Hall, 1987). Hilsman applies various theories of foreign policy making to seven case studies ranging from the Cuban Missile Crisis to Soviet arms shipments to El Salvador. The book is an effective summary of the power centers influencing U.S. foreign policy decisions.

LaFeber, Walter, *The American Age: U.S. Foreign Policy at Home and Abroad since 1750* (New York: W.W. Norton, 1989). This book is a narrative history of America's place in the world and how we got there. LaFeber, through the use of biographical sketches and profiles of revolutions and revolutionaries, traces the rise of America to superpower status in 1945 and its subsequent decline beginning in the mid 1950s.

Yarmolinsky, Adam, and Gregory D. Foster, *Paradoxes of Power: The Military Establishment in the Eighties* (Bloomington, IN: Indiana University Press, 1983). This overview of U.S. military policies contrasts what Americans expect of the defense establishment and what the system delivers.

CHAPTER **14**

The State of the Union

CHAPTER OUTLINE

I. Freedom or Power?
  A. At the end of the twentieth century, the triumph of democracy, including the collapse of the Soviet Union and democratic reforms in Eastern Europe, have again made America a beacon for the world. But while others look to America as an example of freedom and power, we must examine ourselves.
  B. Americans were profoundly distrustful of government during the first century of our nation's history.
  C. Americans began to agitate for a larger national government toward the end of the nineteenth century, especially one that could regulate a growing economy.
  D. The democratic theory of state power, which supplanted the liberal theory of weak and limited government, resolves the contradiction between freedom and government by strengthening democratic controls.
  E. For most Americans, the expansion of democratic control of government led to the growth of popular belief in the mutual existence of freedom and power.
II. The Limits of Control: Democracy as a Consequence of Freedom
III. Freedom or Power? Government Power and the Erosion of Freedom

STUDY QUESTIONS

1. In what ways is America's government today similar to and different from the government established by the framers? Would they approve of today's government?
2. What is the basic contradiction between freedom and power? Can it be overcome?
3. Why has the American government expanded in scope and power? Will it continue to grow or has its growth stopped?
4. How are freedom and democracy linked to one another?
5. What end did de Tocqueville foresee for American democracy? Why?

ANNOTATED BIBLIOGRAPHY

Locke, John, *The Second Treatise of Government* (Indianapolis, IN: Bobbs-Merrill, 1972). Probably the most important political philosopher in the minds of the founding fathers, Locke's influence extends beyond the Declaration of Independence and the Constitution. He also laid the theoretical foundation of liberalism, a political philosophy that has dominated American politics and culture since the colonial period.

Mill, John Stuart, *On Liberty* (New York: W. W. Norton, 1975). Although a forceful advocate of universal suffrage, Mill also expressed reservations over the threats to individual liberties posed by mass democracy. Mill's thinking continues to influence proponents of judicial review who see contemporary courts as providing essential safeguards against the occasional overzealousness of legislatures.

Schumpeter, Joseph A., *Capitalism, Socialism and Democracy* (New York: Harper & Row, 1950). This work has set the terms of debate for generations of political scientists seeking to explore the relationship between capitalism and democracy.